Wild Flowers

OF NORTH AMERICA

Eastern woodland in spring, with White Trilliums (*Trillium alba*), Virginia Bluebells (*Mertensia virginica*), and False Rue Anemones (*Isopyrum biternatum*).

Wild Flowers

OF NORTH AMERICA

Pamela Forey

JG PRESS

Published in the USA 1998 by JG Press
Distributed by World Publications, Inc.

The JG Press imprint is a trademark of
JG Press, Inc.
455 Somerset Avenue
North Dighton, MA 02764

ISBN 1-57215-261-3

Editor: Trish Burgess
Designer: Ann Doolan
Editorial Director: Pippa Rubinstein

Printed in China

CONTENTS

Introduction

A world without plants would be a world without life, for it is plants that trap the sun's energy and make it available to animals. There are over 20,000 flowering plants in North America, a reflection of its many different habitats. They grow in mountains and deserts, prairies and tundra, woods and barrens, lakes and rivers, swamps and coastal beaches. These are natural habitats in the main, but plants also grow in the manmade habitats of cities and wasteland, on roadsides, and along railroads. They come in an apparently infinite variety of shapes, their forms linked to the places in which they live. Huge trees grow on the foggy Pacific coast, mat-forming and cushion-forming plants in the mountains and tundra, water-storing cactuses in the deserts, filmy water plants in ponds and streams, leafy, spring-flowering plants in the eastern woodlands.

Plants adapt to these habitats from one main form. They have roots which enable them to absorb water from the soil and which anchor them in the ground. The stem forms the body of the plant, linking roots and leaves, and carrying water and nutrients to all parts. The leaves trap the sunlight in the process of photosynthesis and provide the plants with energy and food to grow. Flowering plants bear flowers, which produce the female ovules and the male pollen. Pollination results in the formation of seeds, which develop within the fruits and then disperse, spreading the plants to new areas of suitable habitat.

Desert plants may have deep and spreading roots to tap water sources deep in the ground, stems which store water, and spines or hairs and small thick leaves to reduce water loss. Plants which grow in prairies or woods do not need such extreme adaptations to survive in their much less harsh environments. However, many plants of deciduous woods have their main growing and flowering season in the spring before the light is dimmed in the heavy shade of summer; many of them die down in midsummer, surviving until the following spring by thick underground roots or bulbs which store food. Alpine plants frequently hug the ground to withstand the drying winds of summer, and to gain protection from snow cover in winter. Water plants often lack roots and hairs, and many have dissected leaves; they absorb water directly through their stems and leaves, and hairs would hinder this process.

The flowering plants have not arrived at this diversity overnight. Their history goes back more than 110 million years to a time when they began to replace Gymnosperms as the dominant plants on Earth. Since then they have evolved into many different families. Some families have been highly successful, with thousands of species in many different parts of the world and in many different habitats; others have remained small and confined to specific areas. Present-day families share similar features or may show patterns that reflect their evolutionary history. For instance, some families have a high proportion of members that are poisonous, often because they all contain the same kinds of poisonous alkaloids or other chemicals. Presumably the presence of the poisons prevented animals from eating the plants, so their toxicity this became a survival characteristic—a feature that was positively useful in the competition for survival that goes on all the time among the plants and animals of our planet. Other families have a high proportion of edible members, some families have mainly white or yellow flowers, others blue ones. Some families are found primarily in deserts or water, others form bulbs or have bristly hairs. Some patterns may be of interest to people because the families are economically important, while others are not. Some families have bright, showy flowers, but others have dull ones. This often reflects a difference in pollination mechanisms, the bright, showy flowers designed to attract insects, while the dull ones rely on wind to spread their pollen.

It is this variety of patterns and differences that makes plants fascinating. What may seem interesting about one plant may seem dull in another; but the second one may have some other aspect of its biology that catches the attention. This book is intended as a celebration of the flowering plants of North America. They are arranged in their families so that the patterns can be perceived clearly, and related families have also been kept together. Trees and shrubs have, on the whole, been left out, and grasses, sedges, and rushes have also been omitted from the book for reasons of space.

Some plants are common, others are rare or becoming scarcer. The habitats of many native plants and animals are being changed to suit the people who live there, not maintained to meet the needs of the plants and animals. It is becoming clear that this process cannot continue indefinitely if we wish to maintain the ancient diversity of our planet on which its health seems to depend. Preservation of habitats and of individual species is becoming an urgent priority, one to which all who value our heritage and who would wish to preserve our future need to give their support.

Key to the Flower Families

Wild flowers can be enjoyed in many ways—in the open on summer vacations, in the winter by browsing through guides like this one. This book can be used to identify plants in the field with the help of the Key to the Flower Families. It is also a source of fascinating information. There are far too many species in North America for all to be included in a book of this size, but plants from all parts of the U.S. and Canada, and from the vast majority of wild flower families, are represented.

To identify a plant using this key, you are provided with a series of alternatives, the object being to lead you to one of the flower families. The number at the end of each paragraph refers you to the next paragraph you should read in your search. It is a bit like following a maze with many endings. Once you reach a family name, turn to the relevant page(s) and check there to find your plant.

A floral key can look daunting, especially if the language is unfamiliar. But finding a wild flower and tracking it down through a key is an extremely satisfying experience. All the terms which might be strange are explained in the glossary at the back of the book.

1 Plants without chlorophyll **2**
Green plants **3**

2 Flowers regular. **Indian Pipe fam**. p. 124, **Morning Glory fam**. (dodders) p. 150.
Flowers bilaterally symmetrical. **Broomrape fam**. p. 176, **Orchid fam**. p. 242.

3 Epiphytic plants growing on trees, with scaly stems and tiny leaves. **Pineapple fam**. (Spanish Moss) p. 240.
Herbaceous plants growing on the ground, not as above. **4**

4 Leaves modified into pitchers for catching insects. **Pitcher-plant fam**. p. 49.
Leaves normal, not modified into such pitchers. **5**

5 Plants that have their flower parts in threes, and their leaves have parallel veins. Their name comes from the fact that their seeds contain only one seed leaf or cotyledon. **Monocotyledons 6**
Plants that have their flower parts in fours, fives, or have numerous flower parts, and that have veins forming a branched network, not parallel veins, in their leaves. Their name comes from the fact that their seeds contain two seed leaves or cotyledons. **Dicotyledons 14**

Monocotyledons

6 Flowers with three similar sepals, two similar petals (sometimes all five are alike), and a central, hanging lip. **Orchid fam**. p. 242.
Flowers not as above. **7**

7 Climbing plants with heart-shaped leaves and spikes of tiny, greenish flowers in the leaf axils. **Yam fam**. p. 234.
Plants not as above. **8**

8 Desert plants, usually shrubs, with fleshy or fibrous leaves and fleshy flowers. **Agave fam**. p. 221.
Plants not as above. **9**

9 Aquatic plants with green flowers in globular clusters, male and female separate, female flowers in the basal clusters. **Bur-reed fam**. p. 239.
Plants not as above. **10**

10 Mostly aquatic or marsh plants. Flowers lack petals or sepals and are crowded into dense heads on the tops of erect stalks. **Pipewort fam**. p. 238.
Plants not as above. **11**

11 Flowers borne in a tight, cylindrical spike. **Arum fam**. p. 240, **Cattail fam**. p. 239.
Flowers yellow, borne in a cone-like spike of woody bracts. **Yellow-eyed Grass fam**. p. 236.
Flowers not borne in a tight, cylindrical spike or spike of woody bracts. **12**

12 Aquatic or marsh plants, with many carpels in the center of each flower, and fruits formed of many achenes. **Water Plantain fam**. p. 220.
Aquatic or herbaceous plants, with flowers not as above. Fruits capsules or fleshy. **13**

13 Ovary superior. **Lily fam**. p.222, **Spiderwort fam**. p. 235, **Pickerelweed fam**. p. 233.
Ovary inferior. **Iris fam**. p. 236, **Amaryllis fam**. p. 233.

Dicotyledons

14 Aquatic plants with erect stems, whorls of linear leaves, and tiny petal-less and sepal-less flowers in the leaf axils. Flowers contain only one stamen, or one stamen and one carpel. **Mare's-tail fam**. p. 114.

Plants not as above. **15**

15 Flowers with five free sepals, two large inner ones modified into colored wings, and five petals, the lowermost one boat-shaped and fringed. **Milkwort fam**. p. 94.

Flowers not as above. **16**

16 Petals free from each other, not united into a tube; or petals absent. **17**

Petals united into a tube, at least at the base. **43**

17 Flowers regular. **18**

Flowers bilaterally symmetrical. **42**

18 Center of flower often has corona of several rows of filaments, and 3–5 styles, often on a stalk. **Passion Flower fam**. p. 106.

Flowers not as above. **19**

19 Aquatic plants with submerged stems, or stems prostrate on mud, with dissected leaves and tiny flowers in the leaf axils. The flowers have 4–8 stamens. Fruits split into four sections. **Water-milfoil fam**. p. 114.

Plants not as above. **20**

20 Flowers small, with tiny calyx and five petals, borne in umbels or heads. **Carrot fam**. p. 116, **Ginseng fam**. p. 115.

Flowers not borne in such umbels or heads. **21**

21 Sepals and petals both absent. **22**

Petals and sepals both present, or petals present, or sepals present. **23**

22 Flowers hermaphrodite, borne in spikes. Stamens 6–8. **Lizard's Tail fam**. p. 51.

Flowers hermaphrodite, or male and female flowers on separate plants. Stamens many. **Buttercup fam**. p. 37.

Flowers minute; male and female flowers separate but on same plant, and consisting of one stamen and one carpel. **Spurge fam**. p. 96.

23 Petals absent. Sepals may be green and sepal-like, or may be colored and resemble petals. In either event, only one whorl of perianth segments is present. **24**

Petals and sepals present. Petals four or five. **28**

Petals and sepals present. Petals more than five, and may be numerous. **40**

Petals and sepals present and similar in two whorls of three. **Crowberry fam**. p. 129.

24 Leaves with distinctive sheathing stipules at the base. **Smartweed fam**. p. 14.

Leaves without sheathing stipules. **25**

25 Flowers green and tiny, borne in spikes or dangling in leaf axils. Male and female flowers often separate. **26**

Flowers are not green and tiny. **27**

26 Stipules present. **Nettle fam**. p. 12, **Spurge fam**. p. 96.

Stipules absent. **Goosefoot fam**. p. 22, **Amaranth fam**. p. 21.

27 Stamens numerous; fruit of many achenes or several pods. **Buttercup fam**. p. 37.

Stamens 4–8, fruit a capsule. **Saxifrage fam**. p. 64.

Stamens five; fruit a dry or juicy drupe. **Sandalwood fam**. p. 13.

Stamens 5–30; fruit a berry. **Pokeweed fam**. p. 23.

28 Flowers with four petals. **29**

Flowers with five petals. **30**

29 Flowers with numerous stamens. **Poppy fam**. p. 53, **Caper fam**. p. 56.

Flowers with six stamens. **Mustard fam**. p. 57.

Flowers with four or eight stamens. **Evening Primrose fam**. p. 109, **Meadow Beauty fam**. p. 107, **Spurge fam**. (*Croton* spp.) p. 96.

Flowers with 8–10 stamens. **Stonecrop fam**. p. 63.

30 Male and female flowers separate, stamens 1–5 and united, fruit a fleshy berry. **Gourd fam**. p. 104.

Male and female flowers separate. Stamens free, five to many, fruit a capsule with one seed in each cell. **Spurge fam**. p. 96.

Flowers hermaphrodite, not as above. **31**

31 Stamens numerous. **32**

Stamens 10 or less. **35**

32 Ovary inferior, stamens free or in bundles opposite petals. **Stickleaf fam**. p. 105.

Ovary superior. **33**

33 Stamens joined at the base to form a tube, fruit a capsule or formed of many segments, often in a ring. **Mallow fam**. p. 98.

Stamens free or united into bundles. **34**

34 Fruit formed of many separate achenes, or a cluster of pods. **Buttercup fam**. p. 37.

Fruit a capsule. **St John's-wort fam**. p. 52, **Poppy fam**. p. 53, **Rockrose fam**. p. 106, **Purslane fam**. p. 24.

35 Ovary inferior. **Evening Primrose fam**. p. 109.

Ovary superior. **36**

36 Fruits in sections, each section containing a single seed and with a long "beak" formed from the style. **Geranium fam**. p. 92.

Fruits are follicles, legumes, or capsules, and not as above. **37**

37 Fruits are follicles. **Stonecrop fam**. p. 240.

Fruits are legumes. **Pea fam**. (Caesalpinia subfam.) p. 76.

Fruits are capsules. **38**

38 Leaves clover-like, with three jointed leaflets which often close downward at night. **Wood Sorrel fam**. p. 90.

Leaves not as above. **39**

39 Leaves alternate or in a basal rosette. **Saxifrage fam**. p. 64, **Flax fam**. p.91, **Purslane fam**. p. 24, **Wintergreen fam**. p. 125.

Leaves opposite or in distinct whorls. **Pink fam**. p. 26, **Loosestrife fam**. p. 108, **Purslane fam**. p. 24.

40 Succulent, spiny, desert plants, without leaves. **Cactus fam**. p. 32.

Floating aquatic plants. **Water Lily fam**. p. 47.

Not as either above. **41**

41 Stamens numerous. **Buttercup fam**. p. 37, **Poppy fam**. p. 53, **Carpet-weed fam**. p. 24.

Stamens 4–8. **Barberry fam**. p. 46, **Loosestrife fam**. p. 108, **Purslane fam**. p. 24.

42 Flower with five petals: one large one at the back, one at each side, and one forming a keel. Fruit is a pod. **Pea fam**. p. 76.

Flower with five petals: one large upper one, and two on each side fused together. One of the sepals is spurred. Fruit an explosive capsule. **Touch-me-not fam**. p. 94.

Flower with four petals, outer two spurred, joined at tips, inner two often joined. Brittle plants with watery juice. **Fumitory fam**. p. 55.

Flowers with five petals, the lowermost spurred. Fruit a capsule. **Violet fam**. p. 102.

Flower hooded or spurred. Fruit a cluster of pods. **Buttercup fam**. p. 37.

43 Flowers in distinctive four-sided heads, one flower on each side and one on the top. **Moschatel fam**. p. 178.

Flowers not as above. **44**

44 Flowers in heads made up of many smaller flowers, each head subtended by an involucre of bracts and resembling a single flower. Fruits are hard, single-seeded achenes. **Sunflower fam**. p. 186.

Flowers in heads of many smaller flowers, each flower subtended by an epicalyx and a bract. Fruits are hard, single-seeded achenes enclosed in epicalyx. **Teasel fam**. p. 182.

Flowers not in heads as above. **45**

45 Flowers without petals, calyx corolla-like (therefore only one perianth whorl present). **46**

Flowers with both sepals and petals. **47**

46 Flowers regular, with tubular, lobed calyx which looks like a corolla. **Four-o'clock fam**. p. 19, **Pokeweed fam**. p.23, **Sandalwood fam**. p. 13.

Flowers bilaterally symmetrical, with three-lobed, corolla-like calyx. **Birthwort fam**. p. 51.

47 Flowers tiny, green, and inconspicuous, in spikes. **Plantain fam**. p. 179.

Flowers not as above. **48**

48 Flowers regular and tubular. **49**

Flowers bilaterally symmetrical, tubular, often two-lipped. **60**

49 Flowers with a crown or corona between the petals and stamens. Anthers of stamens joined together in pairs. **Milkweed fam**. p. 138.

Flowers not as above. **50**

50 Twining or climbing plants. Stems contain milky juice. **Morning Glory fam**. p. 150.

Plants not as above. **51**

51 Inflorescence is a coiled, one-sided cluster which straightens as it ages. Fruit consists of four nutlets. **Forget-me-not fam**. p. 152.

Not as above. **52**

52 Ovary inferior. **53**

Ovary superior. **54**

53 Fruit dry and one-seeded, or a berry. Leaves opposite. **Honeysuckle fam**. p. 180.

Fruit a capsule. Leaves opposite or in whorls. **Bedstraw fam**. p. 141.

Fruit a capsule. Leaves alternate, simple, without stipules. Plants have milky juice. **Bellflower fam.** p. 183.

Fruit a legume. Leaves alternate, twice-pinnate with leafy stipules. **Pea fam.** (Mimosa subfam.) p. 76.

54 Flowers have five fused petals and 10 fertile stamens. **Heath fam.** p. 126, **Stonecrop fam.** p. 63.

Flowers have five fused petals, and five fertile stamens alternating with five sterile ones. **Diapensia fam.** p. 126.

Flowers have five fused petals and four stamens. **Snapdragon fam.** p. 168.

Flowers have as many stamens as petal-lobes, or stamens numerous. **55**

55 Stamens as many as and opposite petal-lobes, or numerous. **Purslane fam.** p. 24, **Leadwort fam.** p. 133, **Primula fam.** p. 130.

Stamens alternating with corolla-lobes. **56**

56 Fruit consists of two pods. **Dogbane fam.** p. 134.

Fruit is a capsule or berry. **57**

57 Aquatic plants with showy flowers and alternate leaves. **Buckbean fam.** p. 135.

Terrestrial plants, or if marsh plants, then leaves opposite. **58**

58 Corolla-lobes 4–12, leaves entire, opposite, and often connected across the stem; ovary with one cell and a single style. **Gentian fam.** p. 136.

Corolla-lobes five, leaves not connected across the stem

if opposite; ovary with more than one cell, or more than one style. **59**

59 Ovary with two cells and a single style. **Nightshade fam.** p. 164, **Snapdragon fam.** p. 168.

Ovary with three cells and a single style. **Phlox fam.** p. 146, **Diapensia fam.** p. 126.

Ovary with one or two cells and two styles. **Waterleaf fam.** p. 142.

60 Insectivorous plants, either with rosettes of leaves with sticky blades, or aquatic plants with bladder-like traps on dissected leaves. **Butterwort fam.** p. 50.

Not as above. **61**

61 At least the terminal branches of the stems are four-angled. **62**

Stems not four-angled. **63**

62 Fruit consists of four nutlets. **Mint fam.** p. 157, **Vervain fam.** p. 156.

Fruit dry and indehiscent, hanging downward on stem, and enclosed in calyx. **Lopseed fam.** p. 180.

63 Ovary inferior. **64**

Ovary superior. **Snapdragon fam.** p. 168, **Acanthus fam.** p. 178.

64 Fruit dry and indehiscent, with single seed. **Valerian fam.** p. 181

Fruit a capsule or berry. **Honeysuckle fam.** p. 180, **Bellflower fam.** p. 183.

NOTE *Page references within the main text following relate to those plants whose illustrations do not fall on the same page as their accompanying text.*

Nettle family

Urticaceae

A family of herbs and small shrubs with about 45 genera and 550 species, found throughout the world, but more common and with all the shrubs in the tropics. Many have stinging hairs. Some are noxious weeds. Others have fibers in their stems which are used for making fishing nets and cord, while some, like several *Pilea* species, are grown as houseplants. The Cow-itch, *Urera baccifera*, which grows in tropical America, is used as a cattle-hedge; its hairs inflict a very painful sting.

Family features The flowers are unisexual, very small, and usually borne in clusters. They lack petals but have four or five calyx lobes, with the same number of stamens opposite the calyx lobes in the male flowers, and a superior ovary in the female flowers. The fruits are achenes or drupes. The leaves are simple, opposite or alternate. Stipules are usually present.

Stinging Nettle, *Urtica dioica*, is one of the most familiar of the nettles, with native and introduced European forms growing in waste places throughout much of North America. It is a perennial plant which can spread to form extensive colonies. Its 3–4ft tall, four-angled stems bear opposite, toothed leaves; both stems and leaves are all covered with stinging hairs, which leave a burning red rash on the skin if the plant is handled incautiously; the rash wears off after an hour or so. In summer tiny, greenish flowers grow in branched clusters in the leaf axils, male and female flowers on separate plants. The **Small Nettle**, *U. urens*, is a similar but smaller annual plant, only growing to 2ft tall, with a single simple or branched stem. It has both male and female flowers on the same plant. This European species grows as a weed in waste places in North America.

The **Wood Nettle**, *Laportea canadensis*, is a native nettle, found in the rich moist woods of the east and midwest, from Nova Scotia to Manitoba, and south to Georgia and Oklahoma. It is a perennial plant, with erect stems up to 4ft tall, and alternate, ovate leaves; these are large and thin with serrated edges and long stalks. Stems and leaves have stinging hairs. The flowers appear in summer in long, greenish clusters, female flowers growing from the axils of the uppermost leaves and terminating the stem, male flowers from the axils of the leaves below.

False Nettle, *Boehmeria cylindrica* (p.13), gets its name from its lack of stinging hairs, although in other respects it looks like a typical nettle. It is a perennial plant, with erect stems up to 3ft tall, opposite, long-stalked leaves with serrated margins, and small spike-like clusters of greenish flowers in the leaf axils in summer. It grows in moist places from Quebec to Minnesota, south to Florida and New Mexico.

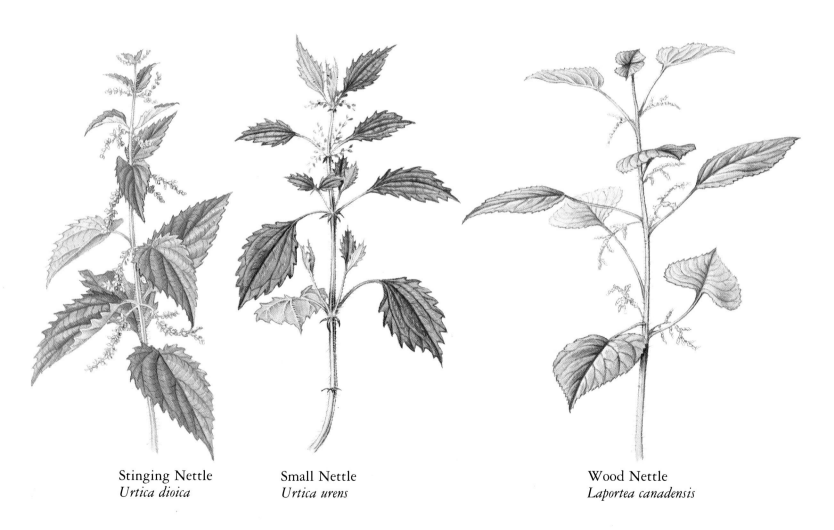

Stinging Nettle
Urtica dioica

Small Nettle
Urtica urens

Wood Nettle
Laportea canadensis

Pellitory, *Parietaria pensylvanica*, is an annual plant, another member of the family without stinging hairs. It forms a clump of branched stems up to 15in tall, clothed with many lance-shaped leaves, and with short clusters of green male and female flowers in the axils of the upper leaves. It grows in dry woods and on roadside banks from Maine to British Columbia, south to Alabama and Texas, and on into Mexico.

Clearweed, *Pilea pumila*, gets its name from its almost transparent, watery-looking stems. It is found in swamps and wet woods, often forming wide-spreading colonies in such places, from Quebec to Minnesota, and south to Florida and Oklahoma. It is an annual plant, with erect stems up to 2ft tall, and opposite, long-stalked, serrated leaves. It does not have stinging hairs. The greenish-white flowers appear in summer, growing in dense clusters in the leaf axils, male and female mixed together in the same clusters. A similar species, *Pilea fontana*, is less transparent.

Sandalwood family

Santalaceae

A mostly tropical family of trees, shrubs and herbs, with about 26 genera and 600 species. Perhaps the most well known are the Sandalwood trees, from the Pacific Islands and Australasia.

Their sweet-scented wood is used for making boxes and gift items, and in the perfume industry.

Family features The flowers are regular, hermaphrodite or unisexual, frequently greenish. The calyx is often fleshy with 3–6 lobes, and petals are absent. There are as many stamens as calyx-lobes inserted opposite the lobes. The ovary is inferior or partly inferior with one cell. The fruit resembles a nut or drupe. The leaves are entire, opposite or alternate, and stipules are absent.

Few species from this family are found in North America. However, **Bastard Toadflax**, *Comandra umbellata*, is widespread, growing in prairies, fields, and thickets from Quebec to British Columbia, and south to Georgia, Arkansas, and Oregon. Although it looks like a normal green plant, it is partially parasitic, its roots connecting with those of trees and shrubs and obtaining nutrients from them. The plant forms colonies of erect stems 6–15in tall, with many narrowly oval leaves growing in opposite pairs. The greenish-white, funnel-shaped flowers are borne in clusters on long stalks growing in the leaf axils; the color comes from the five sepals, for the flowers lack petals. The plants bloom in early summer, and the dry, green berries which follow the flowers can be eaten as a trail nibble. The related Northern Comandra, *C. livida*, grows in bogs and wet coniferous woods in Canada and northeastern areas of the U.S. It has juicy red berries.

False Nettle
Boehmeria cylindrica

Clearweed
Pilea pumila

Bastard Toadflax
Comandra umbellata

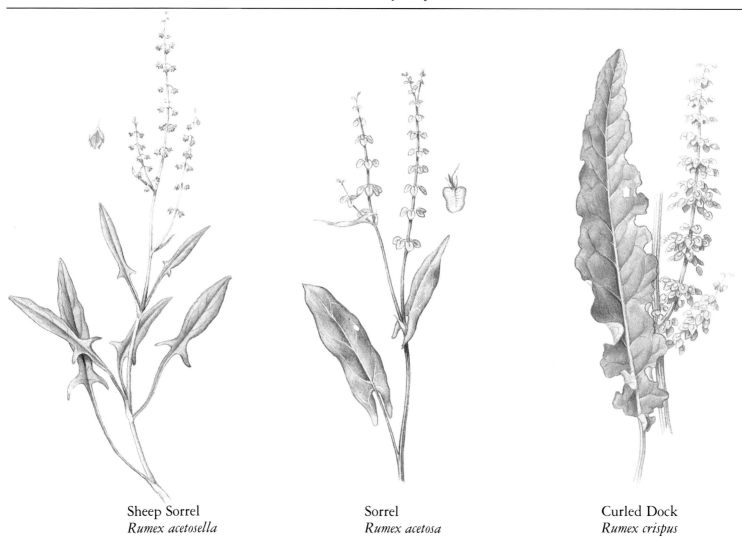

Sheep Sorrel
Rumex acetosella

Sorrel
Rumex acetosa

Curled Dock
Rumex crispus

Smartweed family

Polygonaceae

Also called **Buckwheat family**. Most of the plants in this family are herbs or shrubs; there are about 40 genera and 800 species throughout the world, mainly in temperate regions. Several of the *Polygonum* species are garden plants grown in flower borders and rock gardens. Some species, like Russian-vine, are vigorous climbers. There are several invasive plants and weeds, like docks and Japanese Knotweed, in the family. A few of the species are economically significant food plants, including Buckwheat, *Fagopyrum esculentum*, and Rhubarb, *Rheum rhaponticum*.

Family features The flowers are small and regular, and often borne in conspicuous inflorescences. Each has 3–6 perianth segments which may resemble petals or sepals, 4–9 stamens, and a superior ovary. The perianth segments often persist to enclose the fruits, which are hard, dry, two-sided or three-sided achenes. The leaves are usually alternate and simple, with a distinctive stipule (or ochrea) sheathing the stem at the base of the leaf stalk.

There are many **Docks** and **Sorrels**, *Rumex* species, in North America. Some of the most familiar are European plants which have become weeds in waste places, fields, and yards.

Many of the native species grow in wet places, on shores, and beside streams, in marshes and wet woods.

Sheep Sorrel, *Rumex acetosella*, also called Common Sorrel or Red Sorrel, is a European plant, widely naturalized in acid soils in waste land, fields, and back yards throughout most of North America. It is a perennial plant with a clump of bright green leaves in spring, many of the leaves like spearheads with spreading lobes on the bases. They have long stalks and each has a silvery, sheath-like ochrea where the stalk joins the stem. The leaves are sour and can be eaten in salads, cooked as a potherb, or made into a refreshing drink. In summer the plants form leafy flowering stems up to 1ft tall, with the flowers in whorls. Male and female flowers grow on separate plants. The fruits are three-sided, golden brown nutlets, individually small, but conspicuous in masses.

Sorrel, Green Sorrel or Sour Dock, *Rumex acetosa*, is a larger plant, with flowering stems up to 3ft tall. The spear-shaped leaves are broader, with fringed, silvery ochreae, and the leaves turn red in fall. Like many members of the family, when the plants are in fruit the perianth segments of the female flowers enlarge to become heart-shaped and winged, red-brown in color with conspicuous veins. This European plant grows as a weed in waste places across Canada and in northern areas of the U.S., but it is much less common than Sheep Sorrel. Its sour leaves can be used in salads.

Bitter Dock
Rumex obtusifolius

Sharp Dock
Rumex conglomeratus

Golden Dock
Rumex maritimus

Curled Dock, *Rumex crispus* (p.14), also called Sour Dock, is another European plant found as a weed in waste ground, fields, and on roadsides throughout the U.S. and southern Canada, often in the same places as Stinging Nettles. Its leaves are a traditional remedy for nettle stings, and were at one time more widely used to dress burns and scalds. They grow up to 1ft long, and have curly, "crisped" edges. The flowering stems grow up to 3ft tall, with whorls of greenish flowers followed by three-angled green fruits. Each is strongly veined with three red tubercles, one larger than the others.

Bitter Dock or Broad-leaved Dock, *Rumex obtusifolius*, is another common weed from Europe, growing in moist waste places in many parts of the U.S. and southern Canada. It is similar to Curled Dock, but the edges of its broad leaves are wavy, not curly, and there is only one large red tubercle on each three-angled fruit.

Sharp Dock, *Rumex conglomeratus*, is a much less common weed in the east but is found in many low-lying, moist places in the west, another plant from Europe that has found a new home in North America. It is a more slender plant than many docks, a perennial with an erect stem up to 6ft tall, and large, oblong leaves. The small red flowers grow in widely separated whorls in the axils of the leaves (giving the plant its other name of Whorled Dock), and soon produce fruits, each one with three reddish tubercles.

Golden Dock, *Rumex maritimus*, grows on shores, on the margins of streams and ponds, and in wet, often brackish places along the Atlantic and Pacific coasts of the U.S., and much more rarely across the continent. It grows in Europe and in South America too. It is an annual or biennial, often bushy plant, growing up to 3ft tall, with lance-shaped leaves. The flowers grow in leafy spikes formed of many crowded whorls. The feature of this plant that makes it special is the golden yellow color that it turns when its fruits form.

Mountain Sorrel, *Oxyria digyna* (p. 16), grows in rocky places and mountains around the North Pole, south in mountains in the U.S. to California in the west and New Hampshire in the east. This perennial plant forms a clump of long-stalked leaves with kidney-shaped, rather fleshy blades. In late summer its leafless flowering stems bear terminal clusters of greenish or reddish flowers. The color comes from the perianth segments, which turn bright red and persist around the small winged fruits, so that the fruits are more conspicuous than the flowers. The leaves are sour and rich in Vitamin C, edible in salads or as a potherb.

October-flower, *Polygonella polygama* (p. 16), is a perennial plant like a small, tangled shrub, with branched stems and linear or spoon-shaped leaves; it rarely grows more than 2ft tall. The leaves have cylindrical ochreae which surround the stems. The flowers are borne in late summer on the upper parts of the plant, their color coming from pink, red or white sepals. This is a common plant of sandhills and pine-barrens in the coastal plain, from Virginia to Florida and Texas. Several other species of *Polygonella* are also found in the east, the majority in the south and in dry, sandy places. They are known as jointweeds from the jointed appearance of their stems created by the ochreae; all are somewhat shrubby, branched plants.

The plants known variously as **Smartweeds**, **Knotweeds**, and **Bistorts** belong to the genus *Polygonum*, a large genus with about 170 species throughout the world. Some are grown in gardens, others are weeds. Several are associated with wet places like marshes and swamps; some, like Water Smartweed, *P. natans*, even growing in shallow water. Japanese Knotweed, *P. cuspidatum*, was introduced as a garden plant, but is highly invasive and now grows in wet waste places from Newfoundland to Ontario, and southward. It grows up to 10ft tall and has jointed stems like a bamboo (giving it its other name of Japanese Bamboo) and invasive roots. It is extremely difficult to eradicate once established and can pose a considerable menace to North American native plants.

Some of the *Polygonum* species are acrid (hence the name smartweeds), but **Lady's Thumb** or Redleg, *Polygonum persicaria*, is edible; its young leaves can be used in salads or cooked as a vegetable. This is a smooth, hairless, annual plant, with many branched, reddish stems, characteristically swollen above each node. It has small, lance-shaped leaves, often with a single black blotch on each leaf. The sheathing ochrea at the base of each leaf is fringed. Many pink flowers grow in dense cylindrical spikes terminating the leafless, flowering stems. This plant grows as a weed in moist places, in waste and cultivated ground, and on roadsides throughout much of North America.

Pale Persicaria, *Polygonum lapathifolium*, is a similar species but it has green stems rather than red ones, and nodding spikes of greenish-white, rarely pink flowers. Its ochreae are unfringed. This annual plant forms branched stems up to 5ft tall, and grows in moist places throughout much of the temperate northern hemisphere.

Common Smartweed or Water Pepper, *Polygonum hydropiper* (p. 17), is another annual with lance-shaped leaves, short ochreae, and spikes of greenish flowers. This is a very acrid plant that grows in wet places throughout much of southern Canada, south through the U.S. to Alabama and California; it has invaded North America from Europe.

Knotweed, *Polygonum aviculare* (p. 17), is a ubiquitous weed found throughout the world, only absent from the Arctic and Antarctic regions, growing in lawns, streets, and waste ground, and on beaches and shores. It is a hairless annual plant, often forming more or less prostrate mats, with branched stems up to 6ft long. It has small, linear or

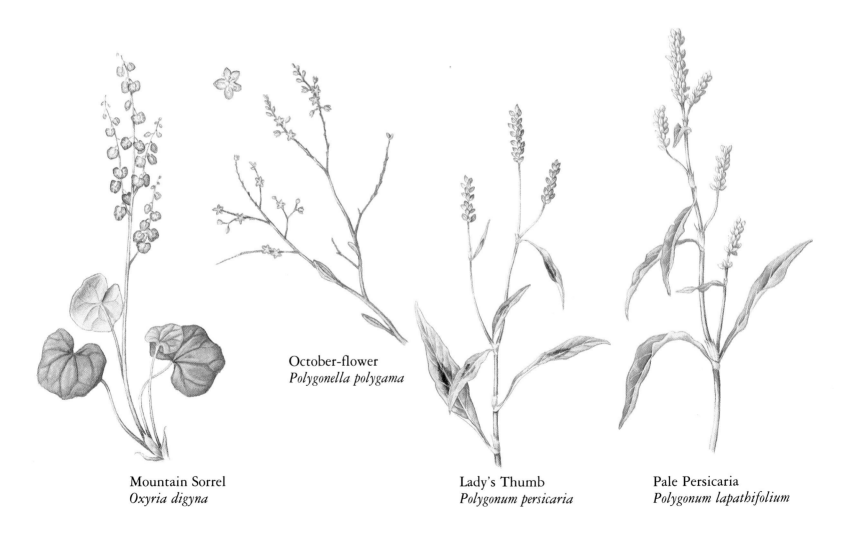

Mountain Sorrel
Oxyria digyna

October-flower
Polygonella polygama

Lady's Thumb
Polygonum persicaria

Pale Persicaria
Polygonum lapathifolium

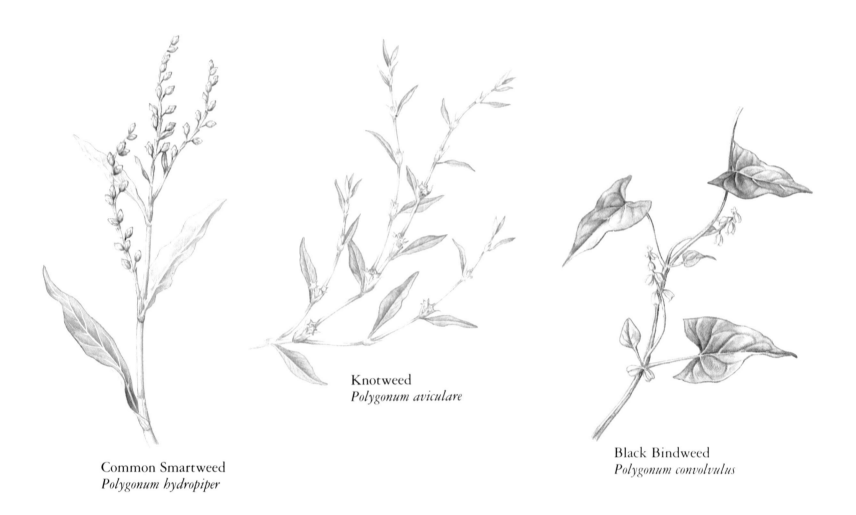

Common Smartweed
Polygonum hydropiper

Knotweed
Polygonum aviculare

Black Bindweed
Polygonum convolvulus

lance-shaped leaves with silvery, jagged ochreae, and clusters of small, pinkish flowers in the leaf axils. The dull brown, three-sided fruits are enclosed in the persistent perianth segments. These "seeds" can remain buried and viable for years, so that the Knotweeds spring up as if by magic on newly disturbed ground.

Black Bindweed, *Polygonum convolvulus*, is a rather different species, a climbing annual plant with thin scrambling stems which reach 6ft in length. It has triangular leaves on long stalks, and small clusters of 3–6 flowers growing on short stalks in the leaf axils. This European plant grows in waste places, beside roads and railroads in much of North America.

False Buckwheat, *Polygonum scandens*, is a similar native species, which grows in moist woods and thickets, in the east and midwest, from Quebec to North Dakota, south to Florida and Texas. Its angled twining stems grow up to 15ft long and bear pointed, heart-shaped leaves. Slender racemes of pinkish flowers grow in the leaf axils. They are followed by glossy black achenes enclosed in persistent calyces which develop broadly winged midribs. The related, true Buckwheat, *Fagopyrum esculentum*, is widely cultivated and often escapes to grow wild.

There are about 150 species of **Wild Buckwheats**, *Eriogonum* species, in North America, growing in a variety of dry habitats, from mountain ridges to deserts and scrub, hills,

plains, and badlands, almost all of them in the west and midwest. Unlike the related Cultivated Buckwheat, they are not edible. They vary in form from tangled, much-branched annuals to low-growing, often mat-forming perennial plants and bushy shrubs.

Sulphur Flower, *Eriogonum umbellatum* (p. 18), is one of the perennials, with woody branches at the base and a clump of leaves at the tip of each branch. The leaves are spoon-shaped with long stalks, green and more or less hairless on the upper surface, white with hairs beneath. Bright yellow flowers grow in compound umbels at the tops of long stalks about 1ft tall. This plant is common on dry slopes, in the foothills and in sagebrush scrub, in the Coast Ranges and Sierra Nevada from California to Oregon.

There are many others with this form, like **Northern Buckwheat**, *Eriogonum compositum* (p. 18), which has tufts of ovate, basal leaves. The leaves are smooth and greenish on the upper surface, and gray-white with woolly hairs beneath. In early summer it bears dense umbels of yellow-white flowers on leafless stalks, often only 6–12in tall. This plant grows on dry, rocky slopes in coniferous forests, in the mountains from Washington to California. Naked Eriogonum, *E. nudum*, has dark green leaves and dense heads of white flowers; and Yellow Eriogonum, *E. flavum*, has linear, gray leaves and dense heads of yellow flowers.

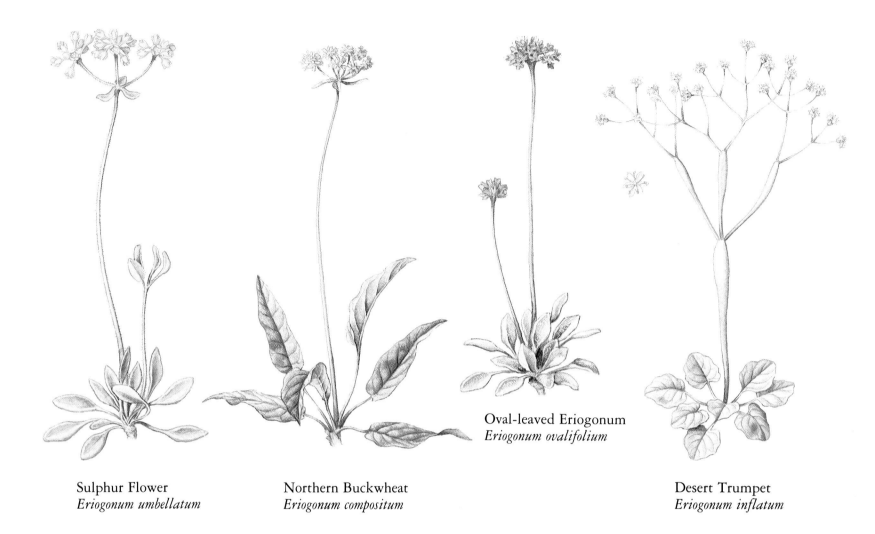

Sulphur Flower
Eriogonum umbellatum

Northern Buckwheat
Eriogonum compositum

Oval-leaved Eriogonum
Eriogonum ovalifolium

Desert Trumpet
Eriogonum inflatum

Oval-leaved Eriogonum, *Eriogonum ovalifolium*, is another perennial, one with tiny, white-woolly tufts or cushions of basal leaves, so that it is sometimes called the Cushion Buckwheat. It bears dense umbels of flowers that start out cream-colored or yellow and turn red or pink as they age. This is a very widespread species, growing from British Columbia to California, and east through the mountains to Alberta and New Mexico, in dry flats and on slopes, among sagebrush, in open woods, and on rocky ledges.

The **Desert Trumpet**, *Eriogonum inflatum*, is another perennial eriogonum, with a basal rosette of long-stalked, oval leaves. But when it flowers in late spring and early summer, it forms spindly inflorescences up to 4ft tall, with tiny, hairy, yellow flowers. These are immediately recognizable, for they are branched in a characteristic way, each junction producing three branches, and the stem is swollen beneath the lowest branches. The dried, swollen stems were used by the Indians as tobacco pipes. Desert Trumpet is a conspicuous plant in both the Mojave and Colorado deserts, growing in scrub, on mesas, and in washes.

Flat-crowned Eriogonum, *Eriogonum deflexum* (p. 19), is an annual species, forming a small basal clump of long-stalked, kidney-shaped, densely woolly leaves, and leafless, widely spreading, branched flowering stems. The many small, whitish flowers are borne in hanging clusters. This plant grows in washes and on nearby slopes, and in scrub, in the Mojave and Colorado deserts, in Nevada and Arizona.

Other annual species include the **Anglestem Eriogonum**, *Eriogonum angulosum* (p. 19), a much branched plant, with angled flower-stems emerging from every leaf axil. The leaves grow in pairs or whorls, and are more or less lance-shaped with crisped edges; its many rose-pink flowers face the sky. This plant can be found in dry grassland and deserts, scrub and open woods, in the foothills of the California mountains and in the Great Basin. Slender Eriogonum, *E. gracile*, has branched, erect stems and whorls of flowers. It grows in scrub and woodland in California. Spurry Eriogonum, *E. spergulinum*, has open spreading branches with white flowers on many threadlike stems; it grows on dry mountain slopes from Washington to California.

Many of the *Chorizanthe* species are called **Spineflowers**, from the whorl of spiky bracts beneath their flowers. In many species the bracts are so large and obvious in comparison to the actual flowers that they may be mistaken for the flowers. There are about 35 species in the U.S., all in the west, and the great majority in California. They are low-growing, often much-branched annual plants, prostrate or with erect stems. Their leaves are entire, often in a basal rosette, and the stems may be leafless. When the stems do have leaves, they are often reduced higher up to bracts, borne in opposite pairs or in whorls. In some species the bracts are fused together around the stems. These plants grow in dry sandy, gravelly or rocky places, in chaparral, open woods and scrub, near the coast, in the foothills, and in the deserts.

Clustered Spineflower, *Chorizanthe membranacea*, is an erect, woolly plant about 18in tall, with a few branches higher up its stem. It has a rosette of linear to lance-shaped leaves, woolly beneath, and a few leaves on the lower stem. Its pink flowers grow in dense clusters in the axils of the upper leaves. There are six hooked flower bracts to each flower, all attached together by a spreading membrane. The woolly calyx is at the center of each whorl of bracts and there are no petals. In other species, the flower bracts may form a cylindrical or tubular structure, they may be toothed, ribbed or hooked; in some the bracts are missing altogether.

Four-o'clock family
Nyctaginaceae

This is a mainly tropical family of herbs, shrubs, and trees with about 30 genera and 300 species, many from tropical America. Some family members are spectacular plants for tropical gardens and greenhouses. Chief among these are the bougain-villeas, climbing shrubs which appear to have brightly colored flowers; in fact, the colors come mostly from bracts beneath the flowers and from the petal-like sepals. Another popular garden plant is Marvel-of-Peru or Four-o'clock Plant, so called because its flowers open at four o'clock. It can be planted in tropical flower borders, in pots, and for summer bedding in cooler climates.

Family features The flowers may be of separate sexes or hermaphrodite, and in some species are surrounded by brightly colored bracts; they are borne in cymes. Each flower has a tubular calyx, often resembling a corolla, and petals are absent. They have one to many stamens and a superior ovary with one cell. The fruits are indehiscent. The leaves are simple, alternate or opposite.

Sand Verbenas are a group of about 18 western species in the genus *Abronia*, several found on the Pacific coast, others in dry, sandy places and scrub in the west. Many are perennial, often sticky-hairy plants with prostrate stems and white or pink flowers. Others are annuals.

The **Desert Sand Verbena**, *Abronia villosa* (p. 20), is an annual, with sprawling stems and opposite, long-stalked, trailing leaves with rounded blades. The plant is covered with long, sticky hairs. Its fragrant flowers are borne in umbels on long stalks growing from the leaf axils; each one has an elongated, tubular, rose-purple calyx with a white center. It grows in open, sandy places and in Creosote Bush scrub, in California, Arizona, and Nevada.

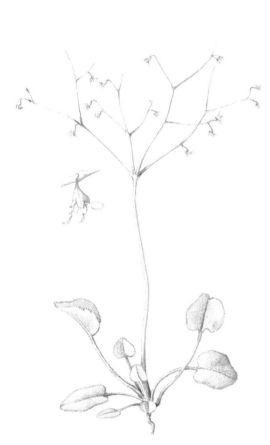

Flat-crowned Eriogonum
Eriogonum deflexum

Anglestem Eriogonum
Eriogonum angulosum

Clustered Spineflower
Chorizanthe membranacea

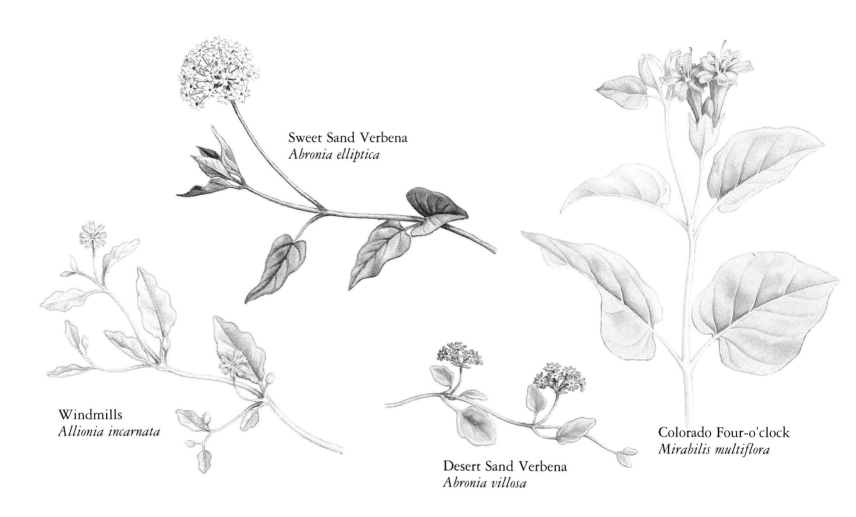

Sweet Sand Verbena
Abronia elliptica

Windmills
Allionia incarnata

Desert Sand Verbena
Abronia villosa

Colorado Four-o'clock
Mirabilis multiflora

The **Sweet Sand Verbena**, *Abronia elliptica*, has trailing, often almost prostrate, stems growing up to 20in long, and opposite, lance-shaped leaves. Its white flowers grow in umbels on long stems in the upper leaf axils. This plant is found in dry, sandy grassland, among pinyon and juniper scrub, from Nevada to Wyoming, and south to northern Arizona and New Mexico.

There are about 20 species of **Four-o'clocks**, *Mirabilis* species, most growing in the warmer parts of western America, but one species spreading into the prairies and the east. Four-o'clocks are perennial plants of dry and stony places, found in deserts and scrub. They have much-branched stems, opposite leaves, and bell-shaped flowers, the bell formed by the white or pink, petal-like sepals. The flowers grow in clusters in five-lobed "cups," often clustered near the ends of the branches and opening in the evening.

The **Colorado Four-o'clock**, *Mirabilis multiflora*, grows in deserts and dry grassland, among pinyon and junipers, in rocky places and on mesas, from southern California to southern Texas, and into Mexico. It is a bushy plant, growing up to 18in tall, with broad, heart-shaped leaves and clusters of striking, deep pink flowers growing in their "cups" in the leaf axils. When they open in the evening, the plant becomes visible from miles away. This is a medicinal plant, used by the Indians to suppress the appetite.

The **Sweet Four-o'clock**, *Mirabilis longiflora* (p. 21), has very different, very striking flowers. They are long, white or pale pink trumpets with purple stamens; they grow in cups in the axils of the upper leaves, opening in the evenings. This bushy plant has stout stems growing up to 5ft tall, with opposite, pointed, heart-shaped leaves. It grows in brushy canyons and around boulder rocks, from Texas to Arizona, and south into Mexico.

Windmills or Trailing Four-o'clock, *Allionia incarnata*, grows on dry, stony slopes and in scrub, from southern California to Utah and Texas, south into Mexico. It is a trailing, glandular-hairy plant, with opposite leaves, often one large and one small in each pair. The flowers grow in the leaf axils and are formed in threes, arranged so as to appear to be one flower. Each flower is itself bilaterally symmetrical but the three together resemble one radially symmetrical flower. They are deep rose-pink in color and open in the morning, remaining open for most of the day.

Angel Trumpets, *Acleisanthes longiflora*, has extraordinarily long flowers, like fragrant trumpets, opening in the afternoon and wilting by the next day. They are white, often tinged with purple. This plant is found in dry, stony places from California to Texas, south into Mexico. It has slender, sprawling, much-branched stems, with wrinkled, arrow-shaped leaves in opposite pairs.

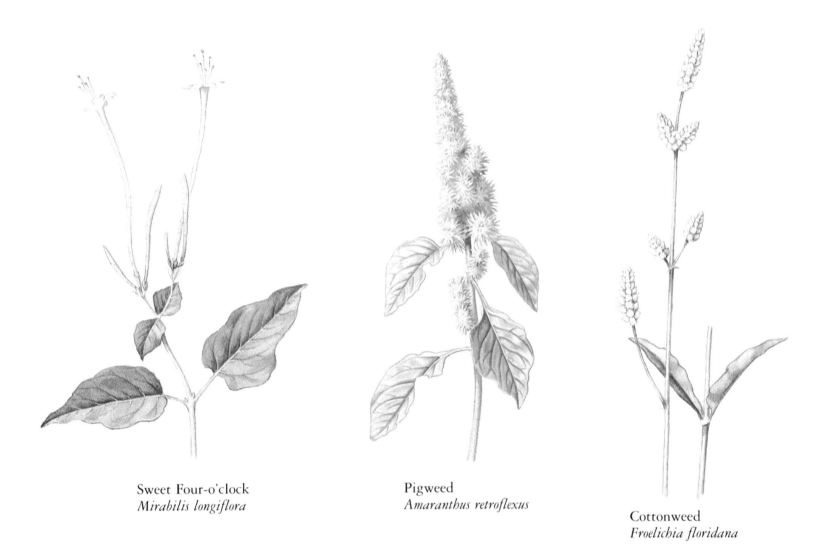

Sweet Four-o'clock
Mirabilis longiflora

Pigweed
Amaranthus retroflexus

Cottonweed
Froelichia floridana

Amaranth family
Amaranthaceae

There are about 65 genera and 850 species in this family, mostly herbs, mainly from the tropical and warm temperate regions of the world. Many are weeds, like the tumbleweeds; others, like Cockscomb and Love-lies-bleeding, are grown as ornamental plants. In South America some members of the family, such as Inca Wheat, *Amaranthus caudatus*, have enjoyed considerable economic significance as food plants.

Family features The flowers are small, inconspicuous, hermaphrodite or unisexual, and regular; they are borne in dense clusters or spikes, often with membranous bracts. Each has 3–5 sepals which may be free or joined at the base. The flowers lack petals. There are as many stamens as sepals, borne opposite the sepals. The ovary is superior with one cell. The fruits are dry and membranous, and they open by a lid or do not open at all. The leaves are alternate or opposite, simple and entire, without stipules.

The **Amaranths** themselves, genus *Amaranthus*, are a group of about 60 species found throughout the world, except in the cold regions. **Pigweed**, *Amaranthus retroflexus*, also known as Green Amaranth or Redroot, is edible, as are many members of the genus. Its young leaves can be cooked and eaten in salads, and the seeds ground into flour. It is an annual

plant found as a weed in much of the U.S. and southern Canada, in gardens and waste places, naturalized from tropical America. It has a branched stem up to 6ft tall, with many long-stalked, more or less triangular-ovate leaves. In the axils of the upper leaves and in a terminal spike are dense, ovoid clusters of green flowers, male and female separate. The fruits which follow open around the middle to reveal dark seeds.

Many other amaranths are weeds, including **Thorny Amaranth**, *Amaranthus spinosus*, found in fields and farm yards in the east. It has spiny stems, and slender nodding flower spikes grow in the axils of the upper leaves.

Tumbleweed, *Amaranthus albus*, must be one of the best known plants of western movies, its bushy stems drying in fruit and blowing about in the wind in every ghost town on film. It grows not only in the west but also in much of North America, in cultivated land and waste places. Its branched, whitish stems bear ovate or spoon-shaped leaves, and small clusters of greenish flowers in the leaf axils.

Cottonweed, *Froelichia floridana*, is an annual plant found in the dry, sandy soils of open fields, sandhills, and pine barrens from Indiana to Minnesota and South Dakota, south to Texas and New Mexico. This loosely hairy plant has erect stems up to 5ft tall, opposite linear or spoon-shaped leaves, and long, woolly flower spikes terminating the stems. The woolly effect comes from the texture of the tubular calyx.

Goosefoot family

Chenopodiaceae

A family of herbs and shrubs, with about 100 genera and over 1400 species, found throughout the world. Many are succulent and grow in arid or salt-rich areas, many are weeds, like Lamb's Quarters and Orache, but others, like beets and spinach, are important vegetables.

Family features The flowers are small or minute and often green, with 3–5 fused sepals, and usually with the same number of stamens inserted opposite the sepals. The flowers lack petals. The ovary is usually superior. The flowers are borne in leaf axils or with bracts in spikes. They may be hermaphrodite, or male and female flowers may be separate on the same plant. The fruits are tiny nuts. The leaves are simple, alternate, and lack stipules.

The **Goosefoots**, *Chenopodium* species, number both weeds and vegetables among their members. They are annual or perennial plants, many with large, lobed leaves and spikes of reddish or greenish, hermaphrodite flowers, the spikes made up of many dense flower clusters.

One of the most conspicuous, at least in fruit, is the **Strawberry-blite**, *Chenopodium capitatum*, for its ball-like flower clusters become bright red and fleshy in fruit, like small strawberries. This plant grows around the North Pole, and may be found in waste places, along tracks and roadsides, and in woodland clearings, especially after a fire. The young leaves and tips make a good vegetable, and the fruits are edible, although somewhat tasteless.

Lamb's Quarters, *Chenopodium album*, is an annual weed that grows in many parts of the world, including North America. It has branched, often reddish stems up to 3ft tall, and diamond-shaped leaves. The leaves are dark green, variably covered with white, bladder-like hairs, especially on the underside, and the larger ones are often toothed. In late summer the plant produces many dense spikes of tiny, greenish flowers in the axils of the narrow upper leaves. The leaves make a good vegetable, and the seeds can be ground to make flour or used as a cereal.

Oraches, *Atriplex* species, are often difficult to distinguish from goosefoots; however, they have separate male and female flowers on the same plant. **Common Orache**, *Atriplex patula*, is a common annual weed found in waste places and saline soils in many parts of the northern hemisphere. It is rather like Lamb's Quarters, but its leaves are often triangular or arrow-shaped.

Many members of this family grow on the seashore or in salt marshes on the coast. **Slender Glasswort**, *Salicornia europaea* (p. 23), is one of the most common and widespread, growing

Strawberry-blite
Chenopodium capitatum

Lamb's Quarters
Chenopodium album

Common Orache
Atriplex patula

Sea-blite
Suaeda maritima

in salt marshes from Quebec to Florida, and from Alaska to California, as well as on European coasts. It is an annual plant, with erect, much branched, jointed stems, its succulent and somewhat translucent aspect coming from its leaves. These are opposite, joined along their margins, and form the "segments." The plants begin their life dark green, but become flushed with yellow and then pink or red as the season progresses. They are edible, can be eaten raw as a trail nibble in unpolluted areas, or can provide a salty contrast in salads, or can be added to soups.

Sea-blite, *Suaeda maritima* (p. 22), is a small, sprawling annual, often blue-green, plant with branched stems up to 2ft tall and fleshy leaves. Small, button-like flowers grow in clusters in the axils of the upper leaves. It is edible and can be added to soups and casseroles. It grows in salt marshes from Quebec to New Jersey; other species grow in alkaline places and salt marshes on both coasts.

Russian Tumbleweed, *Salsola iberica*, also called Russian Thistle, is common throughout the west in open places and on cultivated land, forming a tumbleweed when its fruits form. It is an annual, with intricately branched stems and linear, fleshy, spine-tipped and acrid leaves. The flowers are solitary in the leaf axils, and each one has two leaf-like, prickly-pointed bracts. When the fruits form, the bracts become hard and the calyx of each flower becomes reddish with conspicuous

veins and membranous wings. This plant is not native to North America, but has been introduced from Eurasia. A variety of this plant, known as Saltwort, grows on sea beaches in Newfoundland and Labrador.

Pokeweed family
Phytolaccaceae

A family of herbs, shrubs, and trees with about 15 genera and 100 species, mainly from tropical South America and southern areas of Africa.

Only one species is found in North America. **Pokeweed**, *Phytolacca americana*, grows in damp, open woods, on roadsides, and along fence rows, from Maine to Michigan, and south to the Gulf of Mexico. It can be a weed, and its leaves and dark purple berries are poisonous. However, the toxins are not present in young shoots as they break through the ground in spring, and these are edible. They can be cooked and eaten as a vegetable. This is a perennial plant up to 10ft tall, with branched, reddish stems and alternate, tapering, ovate leaves up to 1ft long. It has a strong, disagreeable scent. Its flowers are borne in vertical, long-stalked racemes opposite the leaves; each has five greenish-white sepals, and a central ovary formed of a ring of about 10 sections. The flowers lack petals.

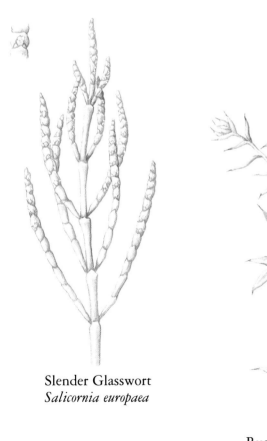

Slender Glasswort
Salicornia europaea

Russian Tumbleweed
Salsola iberica

Pokeweed
Phytolacca americana

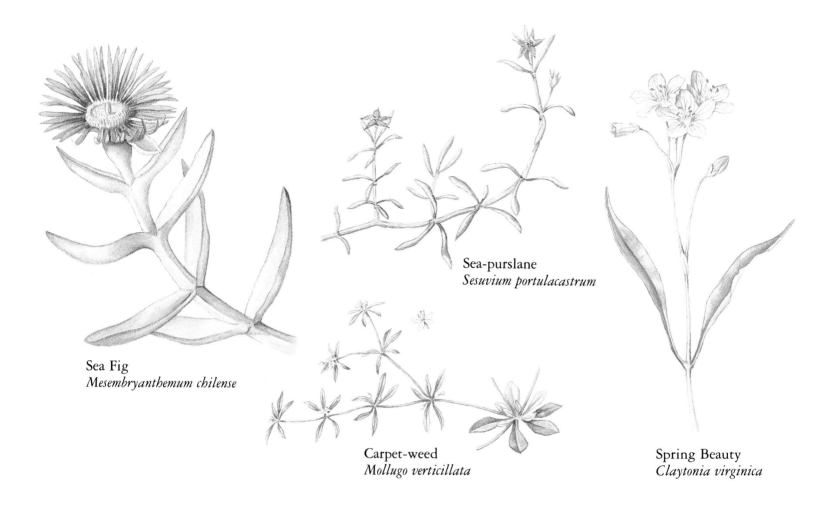

Sea Fig
Mesembryanthemum chilense

Sea-purslane
Sesuvium portulacastrum

Carpet-weed
Mollugo verticillata

Spring Beauty
Claytonia virginica

Carpet-weed family

Aizoaceae

Also called **Ice-plant family**. A mostly tropical family of herbs and shrubs, many from South Africa, with about 130 genera and 1200 species. Some Ice-plants, *Mesembryanthemum* species, are grown in dry, sunny places in gardens.

Family features The flowers are usually regular and hermaphrodite. They have 1–5 sepals, which are frequently fleshy, and sometimes fused into a tube. Often the flowers have numerous petals but in some species the petals are absent. The stamens are also often numerous, either free or united at the base. The ovary may be superior or inferior. The leaves are alternate or opposite. Often these are succulent, fleshy plants.

Ice plants, *Mesembryanthemum* species, are low-growing, succulent plants, the majority from Africa (where several hundred are found), but with a few growing on the west coast of the U.S. **Sea Fig**, *Mesembryanthemum chilense*, grows on sand dunes and bluffs along the Pacific coast of California and Oregon. Its trailing stems form extensive mats with erect, succulent, three-angled leaves; in summer the plant blooms, with large, magenta flowers opening at the tips of the stems. The Common Ice-plant, *M. crystallinum*, also grows in the California dunes; it forms mats of succulent stems and spoon-shaped leaves, all covered with glistening beads full of water. Its flowers have many white or reddish petals.

Sea-purslane, *Sesuvium portulacastrum*, is an east coast species found on dunes, beaches, and salt marshes from North Carolina to Texas. This perennial plant has trailing stems and opposite, fleshy leaves. Its solitary flowers grow in the leaf axils; they lack petals, but have sepals colored pink inside, green outside. A similar annual species, *S. maritimum*, grows on beaches from Texas north to New York.

Carpet-weed, *Mollugo verticillata*, is not succulent or fleshy, but forms a spreading mat of sprawling, branched stems up to 15in across, spreading outward from a central root. It has whorls of narrow or spoon-shaped leaves, and tiny clusters of flowers opposite the leaves. The flowers lack petals but have white-margined sepals, and five of the stamens resemble white petals. This plant is a common weed of moist places, fields, and yards, found throughout much of temperate North America, although it is only native in the south.

Purslane family

Portulacaceae

A family of herbs, with about 19 genera and 350 species in the family, mainly in North and South America. The plants are

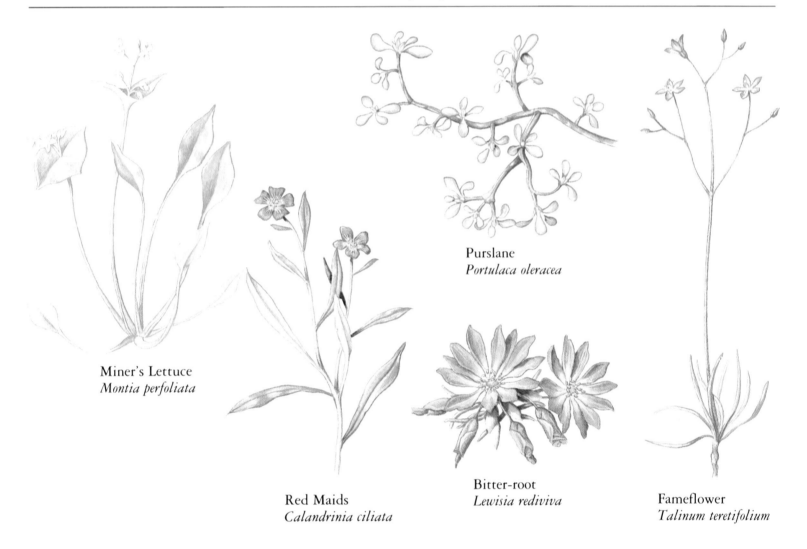

Miner's Lettuce
Montia perfoliata

Purslane
Portulaca oleracea

Red Maids
Calandrinia ciliata

Bitter-root
Lewisia rediviva

Fameflower
Talinum teretifolium

usually smooth in texture and hairless, and many are succulent with fleshy leaves, a feature which enables them to grow in hot, dry places. Some are grown as ornamentals, like the calandrinias and the garden hybrid forms of *Lewisia*, which form spectacular clumps in rock gardens.

Family features The flowers are regular and hermaphrodite, with two free or united sepals and 4–6 petals, free or united at the base, and soon falling. The stamens either number the same as the petals and are opposite them, or are numerous. The ovary is usually superior. The fruits are capsules. The flowers are solitary or borne in clusters, usually opposite the leaves. The leaves are entire, alternate or opposite, with bristly or papery stipules.

Spring Beauty, *Claytonia virginica* (p. 24), is a delicate, sweetly scented, perennial plant which blooms in the spring. It dies down and disappears by midsummer. It is found in damp woods, fields, and clearings from Nova Scotia to Minnesota, and south to Georgia and Texas. The plant has a fleshy underground corm, from which grow several erect stems up to 1ft tall, with a single pair of linear leaves halfway up each one. The top of the stem bears a cluster of white or pink flowers striped with darker pink. These are followed by small capsules enclosed by the two sepals. Several other species of Spring Beauties are found in the Rocky Mountains, as well as Carolina Spring Beauty, *C. caroliniana*, in the east.

Miner's Lettuce, *Montia perfoliata*, was traditionally eaten by gold miners as a salad and source of Vitamin C. It is a variable but quite distinctive plant which grows in damp and shady places from British Columbia to California. It grows up to 1ft tall, forming small, annual clumps of fleshy, spoon-shaped leaves, together with several flowering stems which appear to terminate in broad, bowl-like disks. In the center of each disk is a long-stalked cluster of small, pinkish flowers. In fact, the disk is formed from a pair of leaves which have fused around the flowering stem. The plant flowers in late spring and early summer, and the flowers are followed by small capsules with shining black seeds. Other *Montia* species have similar flowers, but although their leaves are fleshy and opposite, they lack the bowl beneath the flowers.

Purslane, *Portulaca oleracea*, is yet another wild, edible plant, and one of the best. Young leafy tips can be used as a vegetable or in salads. It is a common weed in gardens and on waste ground, on cultivated land, in fields and vacant lots throughout much of the warm temperate areas of the world. It probably came originally from western Asia. It is a prostrate, mat-forming plant, with reddish stems which bear more or less opposite leaves and a final leaf rosette beneath the terminal flowers. The leaves are fleshy and shining, ovate and blunt or spoon-shaped. The flowers are pale yellow, either solitary or in small clusters terminating the stems.

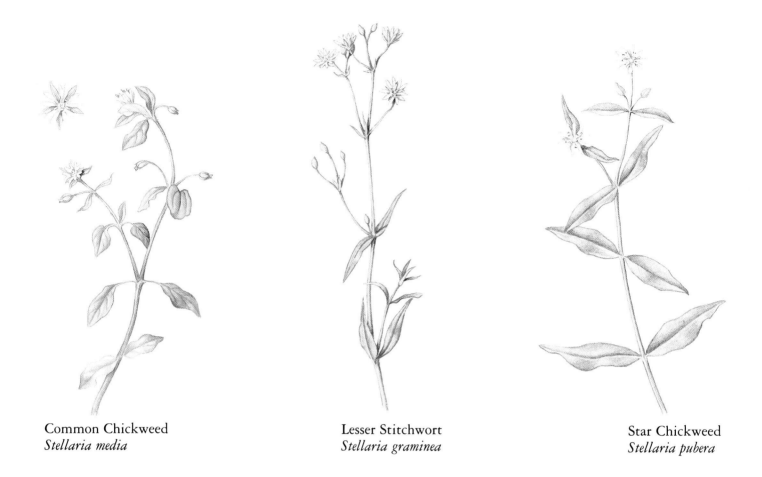

Common Chickweed
Stellaria media

Lesser Stitchwort
Stellaria graminea

Star Chickweed
Stellaria pubera

Fameflower, *Talinum teretifolium* (p. 25), is one of several *Talinum* species found in the east and midwest. They form clumps of succulent leaves and leafless flowering stems up to 1ft tall. Each has several small, pink flowers which open only in full sun, and the petals soon fall; they bloom throughout the summer. Fameflower grows on rocky ground from Pennsylvania south to Georgia and Alabama.

Red Maids, *Calandrinia ciliata* (p. 25), blooms in spring in open, grassy places and cultivated fields where there is water early in the year, from British Columbia to California and New Mexico. It is an annual, succulent plant, with several spreading stems and linear, rather fleshy leaves. The flowers are brilliant, bright rose-red, small and bowl-shaped, and the sepals have hairy margins. The flowers are borne in leafy clusters terminating the stems.

There are about 18 **Lewisias**, *Lewisia* species, found only in western North America. Several are grown in rock gardens, and one species in particular, *Lewisia tweedyi*, from the northern Rockies, has given rise to many brilliant garden hybrids and strains. **Bitter-root**, *L. rediviva* (p. 25), is the state flower of Montana. It grows in foothills, in rocky valleys and slopes in the Rocky Mountains, from British Columbia to Montana, and south to California. The fleshy, strap-shaped leaves push through the soil almost before the snow melts, and wither before the flowers appear. The large, solitary blooms,

up to 2in across and with many petals, are borne on short stems so that they appear to have grown straight out of the ground. The plant has a short, fleshy root, edible when peeled, a staple food used by the Indians. Lewisias are named for Captain Meriwether Lewis, co-leader of the Lewis and Clark expedition, the first to cross the continent from coast to coast.

Pussy-paws, *Calyptridium umbellatum*, forms dense rosettes of narrow, spoon-shaped leaves from which grow prostrate or sprawling stems, only 10in long at most. The stems end in flower clusters that resemble cats' paws, but are actually densely packed, pale pink flowers, each with four papery sepals and four petals. The plants grow in sandy or gravelly places in coniferous woods from Baja California to British Columbia, east to Utah and Montana.

Pink family
Caryophyllaceae

There are about 70 genera and 1750 species of herbs in this family. It is a group with many showy garden species and hybrids. Pinks may be simple rock garden or border plants, not too dissimilar to the original wild plants from which they are derived; or they and their close relatives, the carnations, may be highly bred plants with double flowers, plants grown

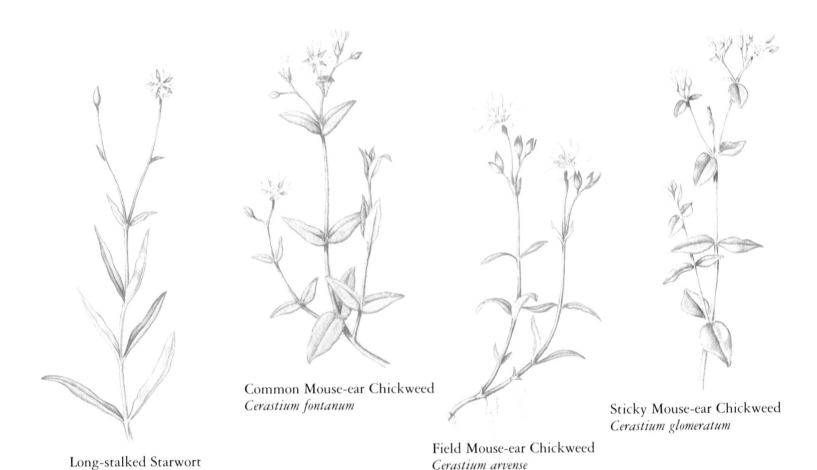

Common Mouse-ear Chickweed
Cerastium fontanum

Sticky Mouse-ear Chickweed
Cerastium glomeratum

Field Mouse-ear Chickweed
Cerastium arvense

Long-stalked Starwort
Stellaria longipes

only in greenhouses and used as cut flowers and buttonholes. Many of the old pinks were scented, the most famous being the Old Clove Pinks, also known as gillyflowers, with a fragrance reminiscent of cloves. Modern pinks and carnations have largely lost this scent, bred out in the quest for yet more double or colorful flowers; some would say the loss is greater than the gain.

Family features The flowers are regular, usually hermaphrodite, with four or five sepals, either free or united into a tube, often with papery margins. There are the same number of petals as sepals, or petals may be absent. Stamens number up to 10, often twice as many as the petals. The ovary is superior. Fruits are dry capsules, usually opening by valves or by teeth at the top. Flowers are solitary or borne in cymes. The leaves are entire, opposite, and often connected by a transverse line; stipules are often absent, but when present are often papery.

Whitlow-worts, *Paronychia* species, are small plants with branched stems and narrow, opposite leaves. Their most conspicuous feature is the large, translucent stipules. The small flowers have white-margined sepals but no petals. Whitlow-worts grow in dry woods, on hills and plains, in the east and across the prairies to the Rockies.

Many of the **Chickweeds** or **Starworts**, *Stellaria* species, are attractive plants with satiny white flowers, often found in damp and shady places. **Common Chickweed**, *Stellaria media*

(p. 26), is a ubiquitous weed of gardens, woods, waste and cultivated land; it is an annual plant which grows throughout the year in favorable climates, and may be found flowering from early spring to late fall. It forms a clump of weak, leafy stems no more than 15in high, with many tiny, white flowers in terminal leafy cymes. Common Chickweed is edible; it is often recommended for salads, but has a fibrous texture and bitter taste and is better boiled briefly and used as a vegetable.

Lesser Stitchwort, *Stellaria graminea* (p. 26), is a European native that now grows on roadsides and other grassy places in eastern and midwestern North America. It is a perennial with a clump of slender stems, linear, grass-like leaves, and flowers in early summer. **Star Chickweed**, *S. pubera* (p. 26), is another perennial, with weakly erect stems, opposite, elliptical leaves, and white flowers in clusters at the tops of the stems. Its petals are so deeply cleft that there appear to be 10 of them, rather than five. This plant grows in woods in the east, from New Jersey to Illinois, south to Florida and Alabama.

Long-stalked Starwort, *Stellaria longipes,* is a circumboreal plant found across Canada and south into New York, Minnesota, and Arizona. It grows in low ground, moist, grassy places and damp woods, in mountain meadows in the southern parts of its range. This delicate plant has weak stems with linear leaves and a few terminal flowers on long stalks; the flowers have deeply cleft petals.

The **Mouse-ear Chickweeds**, *Cerastium* species, can be distinguished from *Stellaria* species because Mouse-ear flowers have three styles, whereas Chickweeds have five. The Mouse-ear Chickweeds are so called because the short, downy hairs on the leaves of some of them resemble the fur on the ears of mice. Several are common weeds of short grassy places, found in lawns, and bare ground.

Common Mouse-ear Chickweed, *Cerastium fontanum* (p. 27), is a cosmopolitan weed, a perennial creeping plant, rooting at the nodes of its sprawling stems. Some of its shoots are non-flowering, and these remain less than 6in tall; the ends of others turn upward to produce flowers, and these may grow as tall as 18in. The stems are sticky-glandular and hairy, and they bear opposite, gray-green, hairy leaves. The flowers grow in terminal, equally branched clusters; each has five hairy sepals, and five cleft, white petals. These are just a little longer than the sepals.

Field Mouse-ear Chickweed, *Cerastium arvense* (p. 27), is a similar plant and another common weed throughout North America. It can be distinguished from Common Mouse-ear Chickweed by its flowers—the petals are twice as long as the sepals, and the plants are often much less hairy, although the species is very variable. **Sticky Mouse-ear Chickweed**, *C. glomeratum* (p. 27), is a common weed of dry, waste places, a small, pale yellow-green plant with long white hairs on the leaves and a sticky texture. The petals are about as long as the sepals in its flowers.

Thyme-leaved Sandwort, *Arenaria serpyllifolia*, is somewhat similar in appearance to Common Chickweed. It is an annual plant, untidy and sprawling in its growth, with many stems and tiny, opposite leaves. However, it is wiry and rough to the touch, not succulent and not edible. Its white flowers have five uncleft petals. This plant is native to Eurasia, but is now widespread as a weed in North America, in dry, sandy or stony places. Several other sandworts are also found in a variety of habitats.

Corn Spurrey, *Spergula arvensis,* is a straggly annual weed of arable and cultivated land, but is also found in waste places in much of North America. It is native to Europe. This plant is easy to spot, for it is distinctive, with slender, green stems and fleshy, linear leaves which are opposite, but so divided that they look as if they are in whorls. It grows up to 15in tall, and in summer bears many terminal clusters of white flowers on thin stems.

Many members of the pink family are small, even insignificant plants, with tiny, often inconspicuous flowers. **Pearlworts**, *Sagina* species, carry this tendency to an extreme. They are tiny, mat-forming plants, with green tangled stems and little, linear leaves, the whole plant no more than a few inches across and 4in tall.

Alpine Pearlwort
Sagina saginoides

Thyme-leaved Sandwort
Arenaria serpyllifolia

Corn Spurrey
Spergula arvensis

Procumbent Pearlwort
Sagina procumbens

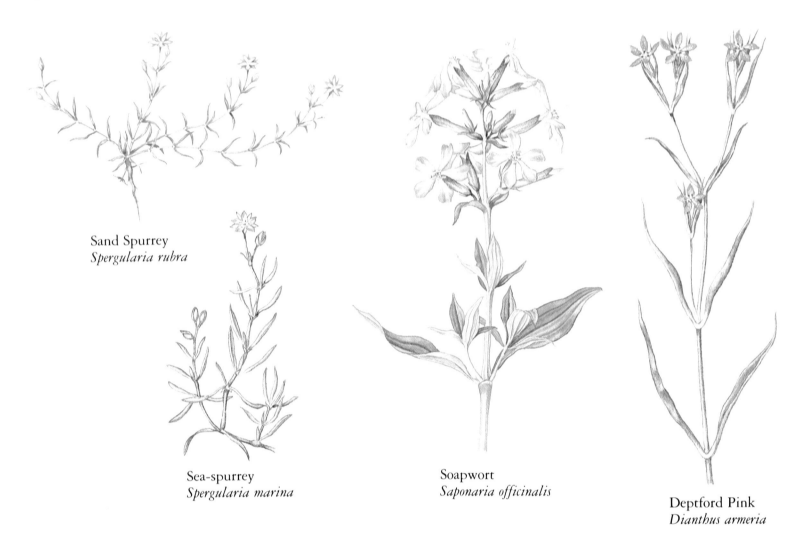

Sand Spurrey
Spergularia rubra

Sea-spurrey
Spergularia marina

Soapwort
Saponaria officinalis

Deptford Pink
Dianthus armeria

Procumbent Pearlwort, *Sagina procumbens* (p. 28), is a perennial weed that grows in damp places, often in lawns and paths in yards. Although small, it seeds profusely, spreading slowly but surely, and can soon cover large areas if left to its own devices. It produces tiny, greenish flowers on long stalks in the leaf axils, each flower with four sepals and often lacking petals. The plant grows throughout much of Europe and North America, south to Delaware in the east and California in the west. **Alpine Pearlwort**, *S. saginoides* (p. 28), is a similar species in appearance, but is confined to the north and to the mountains. It is tempting to speculate on the differences that must be present in two apparently such similar plants, that enable one to spread widely as a weed, while the other is confined to alpine conditions.

Sand Spurrey, *Spergularia rubra*, has branched, often prostrate stems, and linear leaves. It is a small, usually annual plant, but some individuals may survive for more than one year. It bears a few small, pink flowers in clusters at the ends of the stems, the five petals of each flower alternating with the sepals and shorter than them. Sand Spurrey is widespread in southern Canada and much of the U.S., growing in lime-free, sandy or gravelly soils. It has been introduced and naturalized from its native Europe.

Sea-spurrey, *Spergularia marina*, is one of several succulent species growing in brackish marshes and along the shore of both the Atlantic and Pacific coasts, and in alkaline places inland. It is an annual plant which forms prostrate mats of long, fleshy stems with whorls of linear leaves, and terminal clusters of small, pink flowers.

Pinks and carnations are members of the genus *Dianthus*, an Old World group not found in North America, except for a few species which have become naturalized. **Deptford Pink**, *Dianthus armeria*, is established as an attractive weed in dry fields and on roadsides across much of the U.S. and southern Canada. It is a delicate plant with a basal clump of linear leaves, and erect, rigid but slender, flowering stems growing up to 2ft tall in summer. These bear terminal clusters of the typical "pink" flowers; the petals are toothed, bright pink in color, and bearded.

Soapwort, *Saponaria officinalis*, spreads into wide patches, taking over large areas with its deep, invasive roots. Its erect stems, 2–3ft tall, bear dark green, opposite leaves and terminal clusters of delicately scented, pink flowers. An attractive garden form has double blooms. This European plant now grows wild along roadsides and railroads throughout much of temperate North America. It may have been introduced as a garden plant or for the soapy liquid which can be obtained from boiling its stems. In Europe, before the advent of modern soaps, it was widely used for washing wool and woollen cloth.

Some of the **Campions** and **Catchflys**, members of the genera *Silene* and *Lychnis*, are similar to the Chickweeds but many of them are very much showier plants. There are about 300 *Silene* and 15 *Lychnis* species, the majority found in temperate areas of the world. Some are grown in gardens, but most are just attractive wild flowers.

The **Bladder Campion**, *Silene cucubalus*, is a perennial European plant, growing up to 3ft tall and found scattered as a weed on roadsides and in fields in many parts of temperate North America. It forms a clump of erect, branched stems and opposite, pointed, lance-shaped leaves. Terminating the stems in early summer are many branched clusters of distinctive nodding flowers. They have swollen, veined, bladder-like calyces enclosing the lower half of each flower, and the deeply cleft petals seem to emerge from the "bladder" at all sorts of odd angles, so that the flowers often look dishevelled. The capsules which follow are globular, each with six teeth at the top; they are enclosed by the persistent calyces.

Nightflowering Catchfly, *Silene noctiflora*, is an annual plant up to 2ft tall, found as a weed in waste places throughout much of North America. It has soft, downy hairs on its sticky, glandular stems, and scattered hairs on the pointed, lance-shaped leaves. It bears few flowers, and these have deeply cleft, white or pinkish petals which remain rolled inward during the day, spreading outward at night, when their scent attracts moths. The calyx of each flower is somewhat swollen and egg-shaped, sticky and woolly in texture; it remains around the egg-shaped capsule, which often bursts through as it enlarges in seed.

Starry Campion, *Silene stellata*, is a native species which grows in rich woods from Ontario and Michigan, south to Georgia and Texas. It is a finely hairy, perennial plant with clumps of stems up to 2ft tall, flowering in summer. The stems bear lance-shaped leaves, growing in whorls of four halfway up the stem, in opposite pairs near the top. The flowers are conspicuous for their five, deeply fringed petals emerging from bell-shaped calyces; they are borne in loose terminal clusters near the top of the stems. This is a very beautiful wild flower, sometimes grown in wild gardens.

Firepink, *Silene virginica*, is one of several *Silene* species with red or pink flowers. It often forms large patches in open woods and rocky places, from southern Ontario to Minnesota, and south to Georgia and Arkansas. It is a short-lived perennial plant, with leaves in twos or fours and crimson flowers borne in clusters at the tips of weak stems. Each flower has five narrow petals emerging from a long, sticky calyx. **Wild Pink**, *S. caroliniana*, is a tufted perennial that provides bright patches of color in similar habitats in the east, from Ontario to Tennessee; its flowers have rather spoon-shaped, white to dark pink petals.

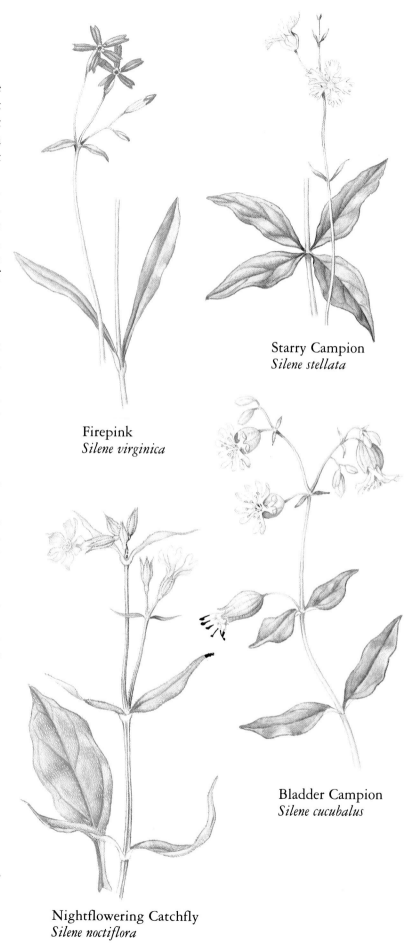

Starry Campion
Silene stellata

Firepink
Silene virginica

Bladder Campion
Silene cucubalus

Nightflowering Catchfly
Silene noctiflora

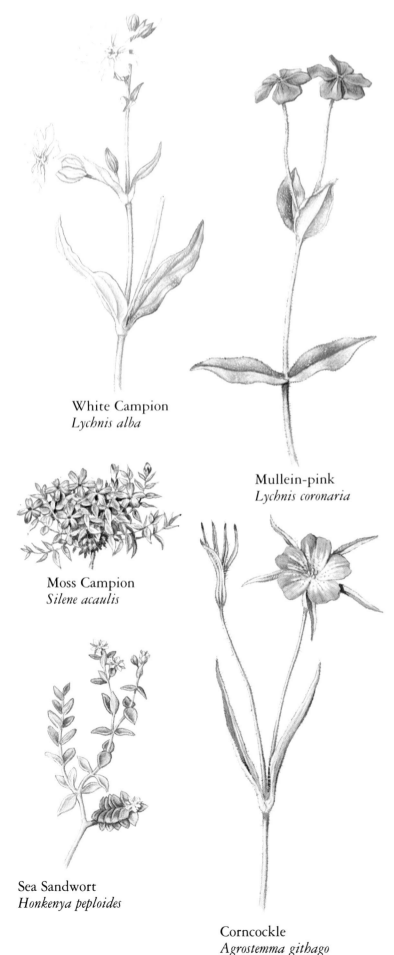

White Campion
Lychnis alba

Moss Campion
Silene acaulis

Mullein-pink
Lychnis coronaria

Sea Sandwort
Honkenya peploides

Corncockle
Agrostemma githago

Moss Campion, *Silene acaulis*, is a different sort of plant, a perennial, tufted, alpine species found on ledges, screes, and mountain tops all around the North Pole, south in North America to the mountains of New Hampshire. It forms dense cushions of short stems with linear leaves, studded with deep rose-pink flowers in late summer. This is a popular plant for rock gardens.

White Campion, *Lychnis alba*, is a European plant, widely established as a weed in fields, on roadsides, and in waste places throughout much of North America. It is a short-lived, softly hairy perennial, with a clump of erect, much branched flowering stems up to 3ft tall. Its lance-shaped leaves grow in opposite pairs. The flowers grow in small clusters terminating the stems, male and female flowers borne on separate plants. They are white, with deeply cleft petals and little flaps in the center of the flower, and they are slightly scented in the evening. A red-flowered counterpart to this species, the Red Campion, *L. dioica*, is established as a weed in the eastern half of the continent.

Several Eurasian species are grown in eastern gardens and they often escape to grow wild. These include **Mullein-pink**, *Lychnis coronaria*, a white-haired perennial plant with erect, 3ft tall stems and conspicuous red flowers with notched petals; Scarlet Lychnis, *L. chalcedonica*, with Y-shaped red petals; and Ragged Robin, *L. flos-cuculi*, with deeply cut, ragged rose-red petals.

Corncockle, *Agrostemma githago*, was once a common cornfield weed in both Europe and North America, but is now considered rare because of the improved techniques of seed screening. When the seeds of this plant were mixed with grain, the resulting contaminated flour was poisoned by toxic glycosides present in the Corncockle seeds. The plant is an attractive one, an annual with erect, 3-ft tall stems, opposite, linear leaves, and large, red flowers in early summer. It is now most often found in waste places.

Sea Sandwort, *Honkenya peploides*, is a coastal species and is a fleshy plant. Succulence is a common phenomenon in coast plants, as in desert plants, and provides a means of storing water. Salt-laden soils are difficult to extract water from, and plants growing in such places may be just as short of water as those growing in deserts. Sea Sandwort is found on beaches and sand-dunes, places which are both arid and salt-laden; few plants grow in such conditions, and those which can are invaluable for stabilizing the sand. The plant forms dense colonies with thick stems which run in and along the sand, frequently buried and then exposed by the shifting grains. Its stems have many fleshy leaves arranged in four overlapping ranks, and it bears small, whitish flowers in the axils of the leaves. Male and female flowers grow on separate plants, female flowers with minute petals.

Cactus family

Cactaceae

An American family of about 150 genera and over 1500 species. Most are tropical and many are adapted to the hot, dry climate of the western deserts; others can be found in the cold climates of Alberta and Patagonia, or in the high mountains of the Andes. Many are small, herbaceous plants, others woody and more shrub-like in their size.

Family features Cactuses are succulent, globular, flattened or columnar perennial plants, mostly leafless, often spiny, many with ribs or nipples, others with jointed stems that break up into sections. They are superbly adapted to desert life, with swollen stems which store water, thick skin and pores which open only at night, no leaves to give off water, wide-reaching roots, and spines which have two roles—to deter the desert animals which might browse on them, and to trap any water given off by the plant. They have surprising flowers, large and exotic, looking as if they belong in a jungle rather than a desert. The flowers are solitary, regular, and hermaphrodite. They have petal-like sepals and several series of petals, the largest at the center, and many stamens. The ovary is inferior with one cell and many seeds. The fruits are berries, often spiny or bristly.

Prickly Pears and **Chollas** belong to the genus *Opuntia*, a large group of cactuses with about 300 species. They have branched, jointed stems forming erect shrubs or spreading mats. The stems of prickly pears are flattened, while those of chollas are cylindrical. In all Opuntias young sections have small, fleshy leaves, but these soon fall off as they grow more mature. The stems are not ribbed but do bear tubercles with two kinds of spines—large, obvious ones, and small, easily detached bristles or glochids, very irritating to the skin.

Plains Prickly Pear, *Opuntia polyacantha*, forms low, spreading mats or mounds of the typical flattened stems, only 6in in height but up to 10ft across, each oval section about 2–4in long. Its tufts of 3-in spines are surrounded by gray, woolly areas of glochids. This cactus has yellow or red flowers in early summer. It grows in plains and prairies from British Columbia to central southern Canada, south to Arizona and Missouri, spreading in overgrazed land.

A few prickly pear species lack large spines, and have only glochids. The **Common Beavertail**, *Opuntia basilaris*, is one of these. It forms clumps of flattened, gray-green pads adorned with patches of glochids, and bearing vivid red-pink flowers in early summer. The clumps grow 1ft tall at most, but may form patches 6ft across. This plant grows in dry, rocky desert areas, on flats and slopes, from Utah to California, and the Sonora Desert.

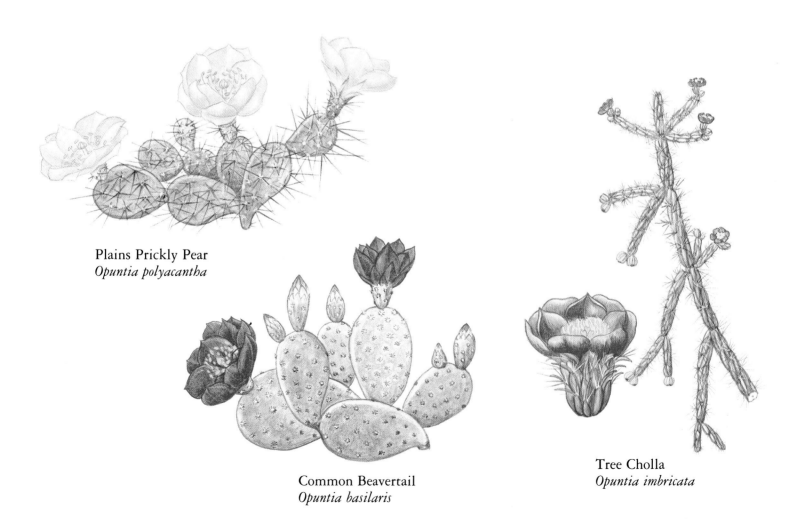

Plains Prickly Pear
Opuntia polyacantha

Common Beavertail
Opuntia basilaris

Tree Cholla
Opuntia imbricata

Some prickly pears (known as tunas in the southwest) have pulpy edible fruits. One such species is the **Indian Fig**, *Opuntia humifusa*, which grows in sandy grasslands from southern Ontario to Minnesota, and south to Georgia and Missouri. The fruits can be used in a variety of ways but must be handled with gloves until their spines are removed with a damp cloth. Then the pulp can be eaten freshly chilled. The spines can also be flamed off, then the pulp can be stewed for dessert or for preserves. Young segments can be roasted.

The **Tree Cholla**, *Opuntia imbricata* (p. 32), grows in plains and foothills, among juniper scrub and in deserts, from Kansas to Texas, and west to the Rocky Mountains. In the east it is the only species of its kind, but other similar species are common further west. This cholla forms a low, spreading, intricately branched shrub with branches that remain as woody skeletons after they have died, so an old plant forms a maze of old dead stems and younger green ones. The stems are cylindrical, with very long joints, and tubercles bearing clusters of 10–30 short, yellowish spines. The dark red or purple flowers appear toward the ends of the branches in the first half of summer.

The **Teddy Bear Cholla** or Jumping Cholla, *Opuntia bigelovii*, is very far from being cuddly, even if its branches do resemble a furry teddy bear from a distance. At close quarters the "fur" turns out to be barbed spines which catch in the flesh and are difficult to remove. It is a tall cactus, with a single, erect, woody stem up to 9ft in height, and much branched in the upper half with many jointed sections. These are densely covered with spines and are easily detached, even if lightly touched, seeming to "jump" away from the stem. In spring it bears yellow or pale greenish flowers, sometimes streaked with lavender. This plant grows in hot, dry places, on fans, and lower slopes, in the deserts from southern California to Arizona, and into Mexico. It is often very common, spreading vegetatively as the sections, which have "jumped" to the ground, root and form new plants.

In the southeastern areas of Arizona the **Saguaro Cactus**, *Carnegiea gigantea*, is difficult to miss. It towers up to 50ft in height, with a thick "trunk" and several side branches originating some way up. It is not called the Giant Cactus without reason. In the first half of summer it produces clusters of creamy-white flowers near the ends of its branches, opening at night and pollinated by bats and moths. This cactus grows on slopes and flats from Arizona into southern California and Mexico. It is the state flower of Arizona, and has been used by the Indians in many ways. Its fleshy fruits are edible, and the reddish pulp can be eaten raw or fermented; its seeds can be used to make butter. The ribs of its stems are woody and have been used in building shelters.

Queen-of-the-Night, *Cereus greggii*, is a weird, twig-like plant with angular stems that look half dead. For most of the

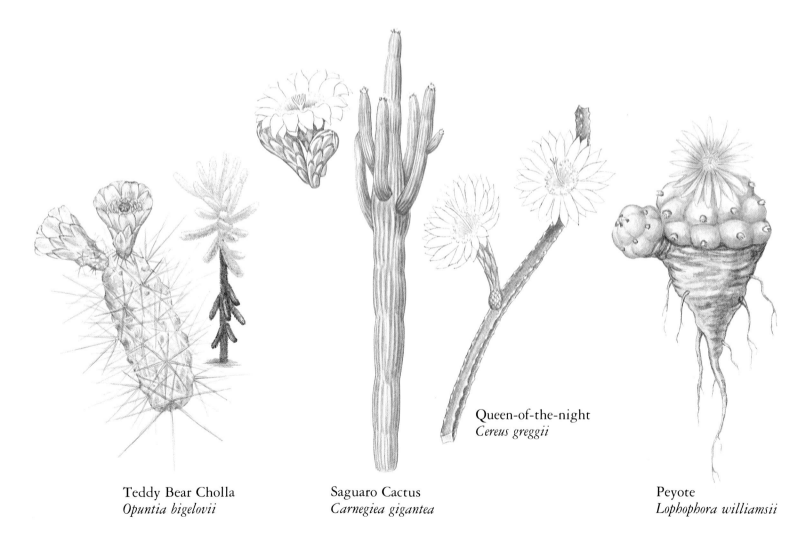

Queen-of-the-night
Cereus greggii

Teddy Bear Cholla
Opuntia bigelovii

Saguaro Cactus
Carnegiea gigantea

Peyote
Lophophora williamsii

Claret Cup Cactus
Echinocereus triglochidiatus

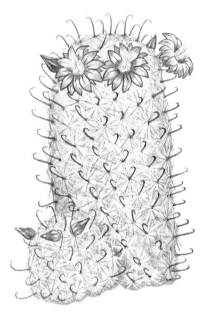

Tangled Fishhook
Mammillaria microcarpa

Plains Nipple Cactus
Coryphantha missouriensis

Green Pitaya
Echinocereus viridiflorus

year the plant is inconspicuous, often growing beneath Creosote Bushes and hidden by them, in desert flats and washes from Arizona to Texas, and into Mexico. However, it has disappeared from many places, dug out to be replanted in desert gardens, for when it flowers, this extraordinary cactus is transformed. The white, many-petalled flowers open just after dark on one or two nights in June, spreading their sweet scent in the air around them.

Peyote, *Lophophora williamsii* (p. 33), is a strange cactus, known since Aztec times for its hallucinogenic properties. The Indians have used it for many years as part of their religious ceremonies. It is now illegal for anyone except certain Indians to eat it, for it contains many alkaloids, among them mescaline which induces hallucinations. It looks like a small, gray, knobby stone (sometimes known as a mescal button) sitting half in the soil, but has a large taproot penetrating deep into the ground. It has no spines, but has tufts of woolly hairs on its ribs and bears pink flowers in summer. The "stones" grow singly or in clumps and at one time were very common, but they are now rare from overcollecting. They grow in limestone areas in the deserts of southern Texas and New Mexico, and along the Rio Grande into Mexico.

The *Echinocereus* cactuses often form low, spreading mounds of globular or cylindrical, strongly ribbed stems, each stem formed from only one joint. Many of them are called hedgehog

cactuses, from the clusters of spines which grow on the ribs. The **Claret Cup Cactus**, *Echinocereus triglochidiatus*, is a very beautiful cactus from this group, growing in dry mountain woods or on rocky slopes and in desert flats, from Utah to California and Texas, and south into Mexico. In early summer it has bright scarlet flowers on the tops of its oblong, ribbed stems followed by fat, red fruits.

Green Pitaya, *Echinocereus viridiflorus*, usually has only a single stem, growing up to 8in tall, with 10–14 ribs, prominent tubercles, and dense spines obscuring the stem. In early summer it bears yellow-green or magenta flowers. It grows in dry grassland, in the plains and deserts, from Wyoming to South Dakota, south to New Mexico and Texas.

There are about 100 *Mammillaria* species found in the southwestern area of the U.S. and in central America. Many of them are **Fishhook Cactuses**. They have globular, single-jointed stems with teatlike tubercles (nipples). On these nipples are clusters of spines, each with a central fishhook-like spine and an outer circle of straight, radial spines. The **Tangled Fishhook**, *Mammillaria microcarpa*, is one of these Fishhook cactuses, with cylindrical stems up to 6in tall, and many small nipples. The fishhook spines point in all directions and the radial spines overlap, giving a tangled appearance to the cactus. In early summer it bears deep pink flowers on the previous season's growth, followed by smooth red fruits. The

Southwestern desert, with Jumping Cholla (*Opuntia bigelovii*) in the foreground.

flowers and fruits are formed in the spaces between the tubercles and are not connected with them. It grows in grassland and woodland, and in dry, gravelly places, from southern California to Texas, and into Mexico.

The *Coryphantha* species form a fairly large group of cactuses similar to the *Mammillaria* species, but their tubercles are grooved and arranged in spiral rows. The flowers of these cactuses are borne near the top of the plant in the axils of the tubercles. One of the most common is the Foxtail Cactus, *Coryphantha vivipara*, which is similar in appearance to a Fishhook cactus. It forms rounded, beehive-like stems up to 2ft tall, with its spirally arranged nipples completely hidden by straight spines. The **Plains Nipple Cactus**, *C. missouriensis* (p. 34), forms globular stems with large nipples arranged in eight spiral rows, and distinct clusters of grayish spines, 10–20 in a cluster. Its flowers are greenish-yellow, often tinged with pink. It grows in plains and hills from Manitoba to Texas and Arizona.

The **Button Cactus**, *Epithelantha micromeris*, is a very small cactus, usually with a single stem only 2–3in high. It has many star-like clusters of spines and white, woolly hairs covering the whole stem, so that it looks like a fuzzy, grayish ball rather than a green plant. At the top of the stem the spines are long and point upward, often almost hiding the small, tubular, pale pink flowers when they appear. Button Cactuses grow on rocky slopes and hills, in deserts and grasslands, from Arizona to Texas.

Simpson's Ball Cactus, *Pediocactus simpsonii*, forms clumps of small, more or less spherical stems, 8in tall at most. Each ball has 8–13 ribs with prominent, spiny nipples on them, 8–10 stout central spines, and 20–23 slender, radial spines in each cluster. It bears yellow-green, white or purple flowers on the nipples near the top of the stem. This cactus grows among sagebrush, pinyon, and juniper, on tablelands, and on the plains from Washington to South Dakota, and south to Arizona and New Mexico.

About 35 **Barrel Cactuses** belong to the genus *Ferocactus*. They are often massive cactuses with globular or cylindrical bodies, thick, prominent, often spiral ribs, and heavy, often hooked, spines. The **Red Barrel Cactus**, *Ferocactus acanthodes*, is globular at first, later columnar in shape, and grows up to 6ft tall, usually unbranched. It has 20–28 ribs, almost hidden by the many spines which are borne in clusters on the ribs. The funnel-shaped flowers grow near the top of the stem; in this species they are yellow. Red Barrel Cactus grows on rocky slopes and canyon walls, on gravel fans and washes, and in deserts from southern California to Arizona. Other species grow in the same area and in other parts of the southwest.

The *Echinocactus* species are also known as Barrel Cactuses. There are about 12 species in this genus, with only four in the

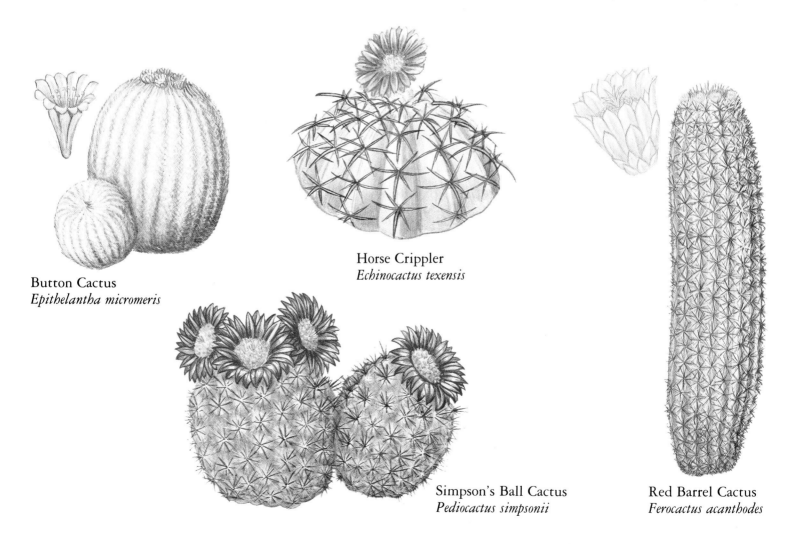

Button Cactus
Epithelantha micromeris

Horse Crippler
Echinocactus texensis

Simpson's Ball Cactus
Pediocactus simpsonii

Red Barrel Cactus
Ferocactus acanthodes

U.S., the others in Mexico. The **Horse Crippler**, *Echinocactus texensis* (p. 36), is a small cactus, often hidden in the long grasses of the plains, where its stout, downward-curving spines are a danger to horses and people alike. It forms a rounded, flattened, heavily ridged mound growing up to 1ft across, and adorned with clusters of strong spines. For much of the year it is inconspicuous, but it becomes easier to see when in bloom or in fruit, for it has striking, bright red flowers, and even brighter red fruits. This plant grows in dry grassland, in plains and hills, in New Mexico and Texas, and into Mexico. Niggerheads, *E. polycephalus*, is a larger plant, forming clumps of barrel-like stems, with dense spines and yellow flowers. It grows in hot, dry places, on rocky slopes, in the Mojave Desert and across to Utah and Arizona.

Buttercup family

Ranunculaceae

Also called **Crowfoot family**. A family of herbs, shrubs, and climbers, with about 50 genera and 1900 species found mostly in the temperate and arctic areas of the northern hemisphere. Some species in this family have given rise to spectacular garden plants, like delphiniums and clematis, or interesting ones, like anemones, hellebores, and aquilegias—plants which are found in almost every garden in some form or another, and with many garden cultivars.

All members of the buttercup family contain acrid alkaloids, and some members are extremely poisonous. Buttercups, anemones, and others are acrid and poisonous when fresh, causing ulceration and inflammation at the least, and possibly diarrhea, kidney damage, and convulsions; poisoning is most common in livestock. When dried in hay, the plants lose their toxicity since the alkaloids break down during drying. Other species, like baneberry and aquilegias, have similarly unpleasant effects, which may include vomiting, kidney damage, delirium, and convulsions. Larkspurs and monkshoods are very much more poisonous, and can cause death by heart failure.

Family features The flowers may be solitary or in terminal inflorescences. They are hermaphrodite and regular, with all the parts free. There are 5–8 sepals in each flower, often overlapping, often falling, sometimes petaloid. There are frequently five petals but they may be absent or numerous; often they are overlapping, often each has a nectary at the base. The stamens are numerous and may be petaloid. The superior ovary is made up of one to many carpels and the fruits are usually either follicles or achenes. The leaves are usually alternate or may grow in a basal clump, and they are often compound or divided. Stipules are usually absent.

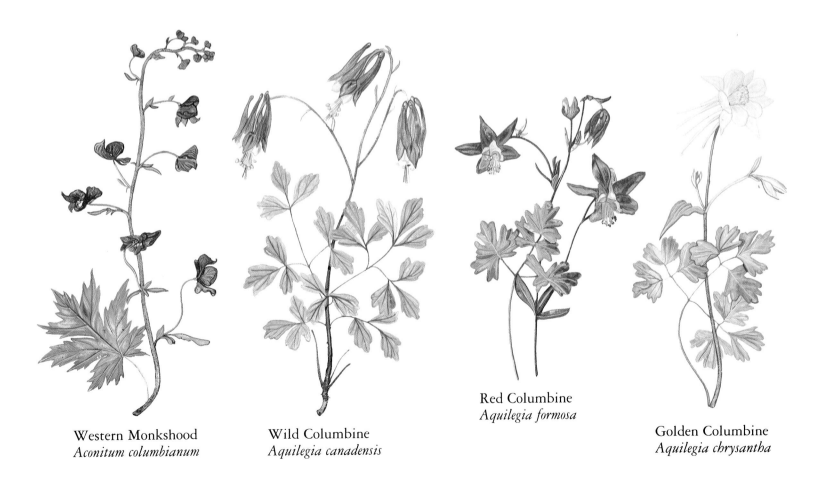

Western Monkshood
Aconitum columbianum

Wild Columbine
Aquilegia canadensis

Red Columbine
Aquilegia formosa

Golden Columbine
Aquilegia chrysantha

Carolina Larkspur
Delphinium carolinianum

Garden Delphinium
Delphinium ajacis

Blue Columbine
Aquilegia coerulea

Plains Delphinium
Delphinium virescens

There are about 15 different **Monkshoods**, *Aconitum* species, in North America, but they are not common. They are distinctive, perennial plants with clumps of large, palmately cleft leaves, and flowering stems of showy blue or white flowers up to 6ft tall, usually in late summer. The flowers have five petal-like sepals, the uppermost forming a helmet-shaped hood and concealing two nectaries, the only remnants of the petals. The flowers are followed by groups of 3–5 pods, each containing many seeds.

Western Monkshood, *Aconitum columbianum* (p. 37), is the most widespread; it grows in mountain woods and meadows from Alaska to California and New Mexico, on both sides of the mountains. The similar *A. uncinatum* is the most widespread eastern species, found in mountain woods from Pennsylvania to Indiana, and south to Georgia. All monkshoods are very poisonous, affecting speech, vision, and coordination, and may cause heart failure.

The **Columbines**, *Aquilegia* species, are a larger, more common and more widespread group than the monkshoods, with over 20 species growing in many parts of North America. They are perennials with clumps of delicate, compound leaves, and erect, flowering stems, usually 2–4ft tall, in summer. Alpine species are much dwarfer. Their flowers are immediately recognizable; the five petal-like sepals have short claws, and the five similar petals have elongated, hollow claws containing

nectar. The flowers are followed by clusters of five pods.

The **Wild Columbine** of the east, *Aquilegia canadensis* (p. 37), has nodding red and yellow flowers; it grows in woods and rocky places from Nova Scotia to Saskatchewan, south to Florida and Texas. **Red Columbine**, *A. formosa* (p. 37), is a similar species from the west, growing in moist places in open woods from Alaska to California, east to Montana and Utah. **Golden Columbine**, *A. chrysantha* (p. 37), is a forest species from the southwest; it has upward-pointing, long-spurred, yellow flowers and waxy, blue-green leaves. **Blue Columbine**, *A. coerulea*, is another Rocky Mountain species and the state flower of Colorado; it has blue sepals and white petals. The Garden Columbine is *A. vulgaris*, a Eurasian species which escapes to grow wild in the cooler parts of North America. Its flowers vary in color from blue to purple or white, and may be double, even in plants growing in the wild.

The **Larkspurs**, *Delphinium* species, are a large group of over 50 species spread throughout North America. Like many other members of the family, they are poisonous, and dangerous to cattle, many of whom die each year from larkspur poisoning. The plants are particularly toxic in the spring, when their lush growth may be attractive to cattle; after flowering they seem to lose their toxicity. Efforts have been made to eradicate them from range lands and forest land where cattle graze.

Larkspurs are annual or perennial plants, with clumps of palmately lobed leaves, and tall stems bearing racemes of showy flowers. The flowers are bilaterally symmetrical, with five unequal sepals, the upper prolonged into a backward-pointing spur, and usually with four petals. The two upper petals have long spurs extending into the calyx spur, and the two lower ones are clawed, bent backward, and often cleft almost into two. Both sepals and petals are colored blue, pink or white, although blue is the most common color. The flowers are followed by clusters of follicles.

Eastern species include **Carolina Larkspur**, *Delphinium carolinianum* (p. 38), a plant of dry woods and prairies, and Spring Larkspur, *D. tricorne*, which grows in rich, moist woods and has blue flowers in spring. **Plains Delphinium**, *D. virescens* (p. 38), is a plant of the central plains and prairies; it has greenish-white flowers. Western species include *D. nelsonii*, with blue flowers, and *D. nudicaule*, with yellow and red flowers, both from the Rocky Mountains, and *D. parryi*, with blue and white flowers, from the Pacific coast. **Garden Delphiniums** come from the European species, *D. ajacis* (p. 38), and numerous varieties have been developed with flowers in shades of pink, blue, and white.

Goldenseal, *Hydrastis canadensis*, once an essential part of Indian herbal medicine and famous in their folk lore, is now a rare and disappearing plant. It has been collected for its medicinal properties, its antiseptic properties, and its ability to stop bleeding. It is used in eyewashes and mouthwashes, as a wash for skin rashes and ringworm, and in a tea to treat stomach disorders and morning sickness. In its fresh state the plant is poisonous, like so many members of this family, and the rhizome must be dried before it can be used.

Goldenseal grows (or grew) only in deep, rich woods, from Vermont to Minnesota, south to Alabama and Arkansas. It is a perennial plant, with a knotted, yellow rhizome (the part used in herb medicine), from which grows a single basal leaf and an erect, hairy stem 6–18in tall, with two lobed leaves, one lower than the other. In spring a solitary flower opens above the leaves; it has three petal-like sepals which soon fall off, leaving numerous stamens and many pistils. Later in summer these develop into a red fruit that resembles a raspberry.

Baneberries, *Actaea* species, are poisonous plants, causing mouth ulcers, cramps, and kidney damage if eaten. By far the most widespread is **Red Baneberry**, *Actaea rubra*, which grows in rich woods from Labrador to Alaska, south to Connecticut and Arizona. This perennial plant has poisonous roots, a few large, pinnate leaves up to 3ft long, and a branched flowering stem. The flowers grow in dense clusters on long stalks in the leaf axils or terminating the stem; the flowers have 3–5 petal-like sepals and 4–10 clawed petals but these soon fall, leaving many white stamens. The flowers are followed by

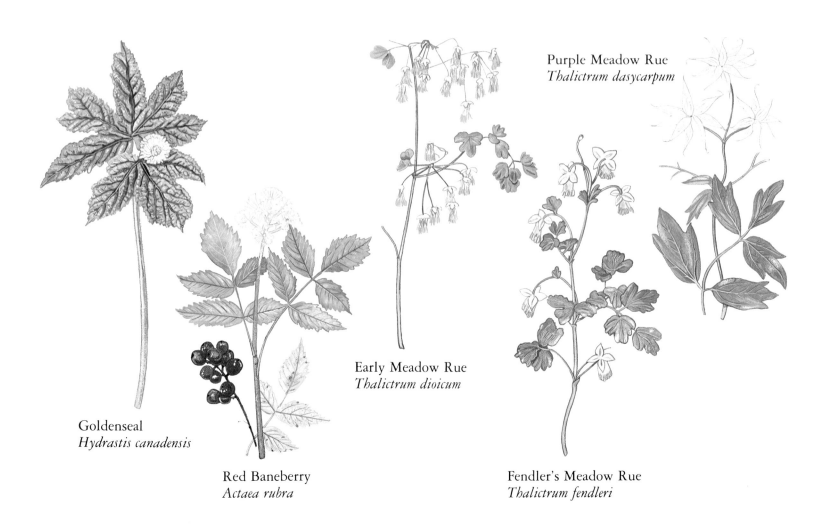

Purple Meadow Rue
Thalictrum dasycarpum

Early Meadow Rue
Thalictrum dioicum

Goldenseal
Hydrastis canadensis

Red Baneberry
Actaea rubra

Fendler's Meadow Rue
Thalictrum fendleri

False Bugbane
Trautvetteria caroliniensis

Marsh Marigold
Caltha palustris

Marsh Marigold
Caltha leptosepala

Goldthread
Coptis groenlandica

poisonous red berries. A similar species, infrequent in eastern woods, is White Baneberry, *A. alba*, which has white berries.

Meadow Rues, *Thalictrum* species, are beautiful both in leaf and in flower, but are inconspicuous plants most often found in wet soils. They grow in woods and meadows, on cliffs and shores, near streams and rivers throughout North America. They are perennials, with clumps of compound leaves divided into many lobed leaflets, very delicate and attractive in appearance. The flowers grow in branched inflorescences on tall stems overtopping the leaves; they have petal-like sepals enclosing the flowers in bud, but these fall as the flowers open, and they lack petals. The color of the flowers comes from the many long, fluffy stamens, which may be yellow, white or purplish.

Many of the species have male and female flowers on separate plants, like **Early Meadow Rue**, *Thalictrum dioicum* (p. 39), an eastern and midwestern species found in moist woods from Quebec to Manitoba, and south to South Carolina and Missouri. **Fendler's Meadow Rue**, *T. fendleri* (p. 39), is a similar western species found near streams and in moist meadows and woods, from California to Texas, north to Oregon and Wyoming. **Purple Meadow Rue**, *T. dasycarpum* (p. 39), comes mostly from the plains and prairie states, growing in swamps and wet woods from Ontario to Alberta and south to Ohio and Arizona.

Black Snakeroot or Bugbane, *Cimifuga racemosa*, is a perennial plant, which forms a large clump of compound leaves in summer woods in the mountains of the east. It bears tall spikes of fluffy white flowers in late summer, their color coming from the stamens, since the sepals soon fall off and the flowers have no petals. This plant is handsome enough to be grown in flower gardens. It has been used in herb medicine for its sedative properties, and for alleviating coughs.

False Bugbane or Tassel Rue, *Trautvetteria caroliniensis*, somewhat resembles Bugbane, but Tassel Rue is very much more descriptive of its appearance. This is a stout perennial plant up to 3ft tall, with large, palmately lobed, toothed leaves, and erect flowering stems. Its flowers soon lose their four or five sepals, leaving nodding bunches of stamens that resemble whitish tassels. This plant grows in moist woods and beside streams, in mountains and prairies in much of the U.S., except the arid southwest, but is not common.

Marsh Marigold, or Cowslip, *Caltha palustris,* resembles some of the buttercups at first glance. It is a hairless, perennial plant only 2ft tall, which forms a clump of long-stalked, dark green leaves with large, heart-shaped blades. Many showy, bright yellow flowers grow on the branched, hollow stems in spring. Each flower may have up to eight petals, 100 stamens, and 5–12 carpels which enlarge into pod-like fruits with many seeds. The plant grows in marshy meadows and wet woods,

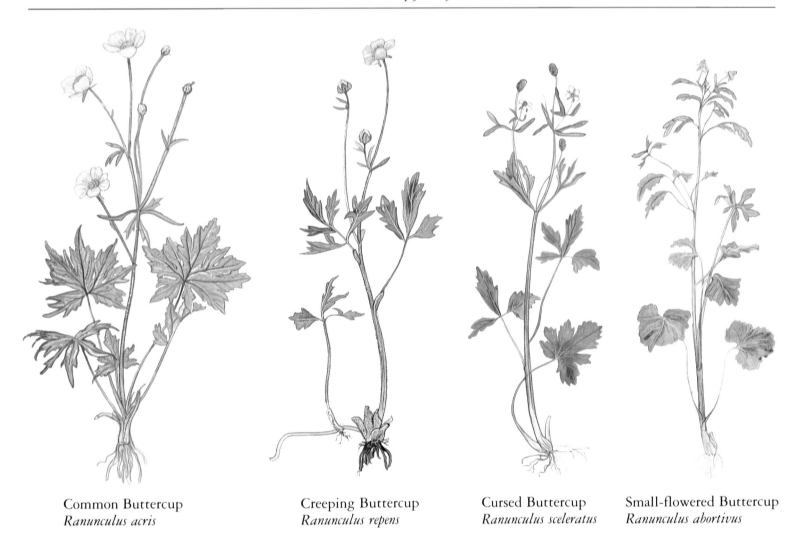

Common Buttercup	Creeping Buttercup	Cursed Buttercup	Small-flowered Buttercup
Ranunculus acris	*Ranunculus repens*	*Ranunculus sceleratus*	*Ranunculus abortivus*

along the edges of streams, and in shallow water across Canada and into the northern U.S., south to North Carolina in the mountains. Unlike most members of this family, Marsh Marigold is considered edible when cooked, although poisonous raw. Its leaves can be cooked as a vegetable and its buds pickled.

A related western species also called **Marsh Marigold**, *Caltha leptosepala* (p. 40), grows in the Rocky Mountains, on the banks of mountain streams and in alpine meadows, from Alaska to Oregon and Colorado. It is similar to *C. palustris* but has white flowers, each bloom adorned with a central tuft of bright yellow stamens in the center.

Goldthread, *Coptis groenlandica* (p. 40), gets its name from its tangled network of yellow roots that look like gold threads in the soil. The plant also has another common name, that of Canker-root. This name came from its use in herb medicine, for its roots were made into a brew that was used as a remedy for sore throats and mouth ulcers. It is a little, perennial plant, only 4–6in tall, with clumps of evergreen, long-stalked leaves, each one with three glossy, toothed leaflets. In early summer solitary white flowers grow on long stalks from the center of the clump; each one has 5–7 petal-like sepals and numerous stamens. This little plant is found in bogs and damp, mossy woods from Greenland to Alaska, south to North Carolina, Indiana, and Idaho.

Buttercups, **Crowfoots**, and **Spearworts**, all belonging to the genus *Ranunculus*, are a group of about 300 species, mostly found in the northern hemisphere outside the tropics. There are about 80 in North America. They grow in a mixture of habitats, from mountain ridges to lowland woods and meadows, but many favor wet places, and some grow in the water of streams and ponds. They have open, yellow or white flowers, usually with five petals, and there is a nectar-secreting pit or depression near the base of each petal. The flowers have numerous stamens and numerous carpels in the center of each flower. These carpels enlarge in fruit to form many single-seeded achenes.

All the *Ranunculus* species are acrid and poisonous to a greater or lesser extent, and are dangerous to cattle and other grazing animals who normally avoid them, repulsed by their burning, acrid taste. It is not uncommon to see a grazed pasture with buttercups in full flower, standing 3ft tall above the short grass. In hay buttercups are harmless, since the drying process destroys the poisonous constituent, protoanemonin, which is unstable and soon breaks down as the plants die.

The **Common Buttercup**, *Ranunculus acris*, is a hairy, perennial plant, with an erect, branched stem up to 3ft tall, compound, palmately cut leaves, and many bright yellow, glossy flowers. It is a European species which has been

Seaside Crowfoot
Ranunculus cymbalaria

Sagebrush Buttercup
Ranunculus glaberrimus

White water-crowfoot
Ranunculus aquatilis

introduced throughout North America to grow on roadsides, in fields and meadows, and other grassy places. **Creeping Buttercup**, *R. repens* (p. 41), is another introduced species found in similar places, and as a weed in lawns. It has rosettes of long-stalked, three-lobed leaves, and sends out runners to form new plants. Its flowers are typical buttercups borne on long stalks in summer.

Cursed Buttercup, *Ranunculus sceleratus* (p. 41), is so called because it is the most acrid and poisonous of all, and because it grows in lush, swampy meadows, beside ditches and streams, and in marshes where the cattle graze in summer when their other grazing lands are dry. Because the Cursed Buttercups are available when other plants are not, cattle are more likely to eat them and be poisoned by them than by other buttercups. Cursed Buttercup is a circumboreal species, found all around the North Pole, south in North America to Virginia, New Mexico, and California. It is an annual plant, with hollow, hairless, branched stems up to 2ft tall, and deeply cut, palmate leaves, the upper ones with quite narrow segments. The plant bears many small, pale yellow flowers in summer, followed by cylindrical heads of many achenes.

Small-flowered Buttercup, *Ranunculus abortivus* (p. 41), is a common, shade-loving species found in moist places in woods, fields, and yards from Labrador to Alaska, and south to Florida, Texas, and Colorado. It is an annual, with a clump of

smooth, rounded or kidney-shaped leaves on long stalks, and several taller leafy stems which bear the flowers. The flowers do not look much like buttercups, for the petals are very small in comparison to the reflexed sepals, but they do have the buttercup gloss. The center of each flower looks like a mound of green carpels surrounded by a ring of stamens. The carpels enlarge in fruit to form a head of achenes. *R. allegheniensis* is a similar species found in mountain woods in the east.

Not all buttercups are common or familiar plants. The **Seaside Crowfoot**, *Ranunculus cymbalaria*, grows in muddy places and wet, marshy meadows, or along the edges of ponds and streams, usually where the water is brackish or alkaline, in much of North America. Because of its specialized habitat requirements, it is often local and confined to small areas, although it may be common in places which suit it. It is a perennial plant which spreads by creeping stems, rooting at the nodes to form new plants. It forms clumps of rounded, heart-shaped or kidney-shaped, lobed leaves, and leafless flowering stems with a few yellow flowers. The fruiting heads of achenes are cylindrical.

A few buttercup species are confined to the west. **Sagebrush Buttercup**, *Ranunculus glaberrimus*, is unusual in growing in drier places than many, in sandy places among sagebrush scrub and open pine woods, from British Columbia to Montana, and south to California. It is a small, hairless,

Spearwort
Ranunculus flammula

Canada Anemone
Anemone canadensis

Thimbleweed
Anemone virginiana

perennial plant with a clump of fleshy, rounded, often lobed leaves. Its stems grow only 6in tall, with terminal flowers, the usual glossy, buttercup yellow fading to white as they age. The flowers are some of the first to appear in spring.

Many of the *Ranunculus* species are aquatic plants, some with yellow flowers, others with white. These species often have two kinds of leaves: floating leaves with normal blades, and submerged leaves with finely dissected leaves. This arrangement is related to the way they absorb oxygen and carbon dioxide, the submerged leaves having an enormous surface area in direct contact with the water, so the dissolved gases simply diffuse in and out. The floating leaves are in contact with the air, and have the stomata, or air-holes, of normal leaves on their upper surface.

White Water-crowfoot, *Ranunculus aquatilis* (p. 42), is one of the most common of these species, growing in slow streams and ponds throughout much of North America. It has finely dissected, submerged leaves on very long, submerged stems, rounded, palmately lobed, floating leaves, and small white flowers projecting above the surface of the water. Rounded heads of achenes follow the flowers and bend downward, back into the water. Yellow Water-crowfoot, *R. flabellaris*, often has only submerged leaves; its yellow flowers are borne on stems which emerge out of the quiet waters where this plant grows. It is found in ponds, slow-moving streams,

and ditches across Canada, and south to New Jersey and Louisiana.

Spearwort, *Ranunculus flammula*, is one of several similar species which grow on muddy ground, on shores, in ditches and swamps. It is found all around the North Pole, south in North America to Pennsylvania, Minnesota, and through the Rocky Mountains to California. It has prostrate stems, rooting at the nodes, and often upturned at the ends to bear linear or lance-shaped leaves and small terminal clusters of glossy, yellow flowers. The overall impression created by the plant is of a straight-leaved buttercup. It is one of the most acrid and poisonous species, and a danger to cattle.

There are about 120 species of **Anemones**, genus *Anemone*, worldwide, mostly in the northern hemisphere. Many are alpine, arctic, and tundra plants. Many species and cultivars are grown in gardens, especially the hybrid Japanese Anemones, which grow in shade and flower in late summer; the De Caen and St Brigid Anemones, cultivars of *A. coronaria*; the small, spring-flowering *A. blanda*; and rock garden plants, like *A. pulsatilla*, the Pasque Flower.

Anemones are poisonous in the same way as buttercups, containing proto-anemonin, and many wild anemone species could be a danger to cattle and other grazing animals when growing in grazing land or meadows. Animals usually avoid them because of their burning acrid taste.

Anemones are usually small, perennial plants, with a clump of palmately divided basal leaves, and flowers borne on separate stems. Each stem has a whorl of three or more leaves, and from this whorl grows one or more flower stalks with one or a few flowers terminating the stalks. The flowers lack petals, although this is not immediately evident as the sepals have taken over the colored role of the petals; they may be white, greenish, blue or red in color. The flowers have numerous stamens, and numerous carpels that enlarge in fruit to form many achenes.

About 20 species of *Anemone* grow in North America. The **Canada Anemone**, *Anemone canadensis* (p. 43), is one of the most widespread and familiar, and is typical of many in its general form. It has long, creeping, underground stems, long-stalked, palmately three-lobed, basal leaves, and erect, flowering stems with white flowers. Unlike other similar species, the leaves on the stem of this anemone are stalkless, an immediately recognizable feature. It grows in damp meadows and prairies, on shores and in woods, from Labrador to Alberta, and south to Maryland and New Mexico. **Thimble-weed**, *A. virginiana* (p. 43), is a similar species which grows in dry, open woods in the east; it has greenish-white flowers and egg-shaped heads of densely woolly achenes. The Wood Anemone, *A. quinquefolia*, is another woodland plant from the east; its spring flowers are white, with red-tinged sepals.

Pasque Flower, *Anemone patens*, is a small plant, never growing more than 15in tall, and a densely hairy one. It produces several solitary, white or blue-purple flowers growing on long stalks from the crown in spring, and then forms a clump of long-stalked, deeply cut leaves. As the flowers die and the fruits ripen, the achenes develop long, feathery tips, so that the plant is as noticeable in fruit as it is beautiful in flower. It grows in dry prairies, grasslands, and barrens from Alaska to Illinois, and south to Washington State and Texas; it is the state flower of South Dakota.

The **Desert Anemone**, *Anemone tuberosa*, is one of several western anemones. It is found growing among rocks and on dry, rocky slopes from California to Utah and New Mexico. It has tuberous roots, a few divided leaves, and flowers in spring. The solitary, terminal blooms vary in color from white to rose-pink or purple.

Rue Anemone, *Anemonella thalictroides*, gets its name from its anemone-like flowers and its leaves like those of a meadow rue. This is a delicate, little, hairless perennial plant, with a cluster of spindle-shaped tubers and slender stems only 4–8in tall. There is a whorl of leaves with lobed leaflets on each stem, and several white or pinkish flowers on long stalks above the leaves. It flowers in springtime in rich woods, from New Hampshire to Minnesota, south to Florida and Arkansas, extending westward to Kansas.

Pasque Flower
Anemone patens

Desert Anemone
Anemone tuberosa

Rue Anemone
Anemonella thalictroides

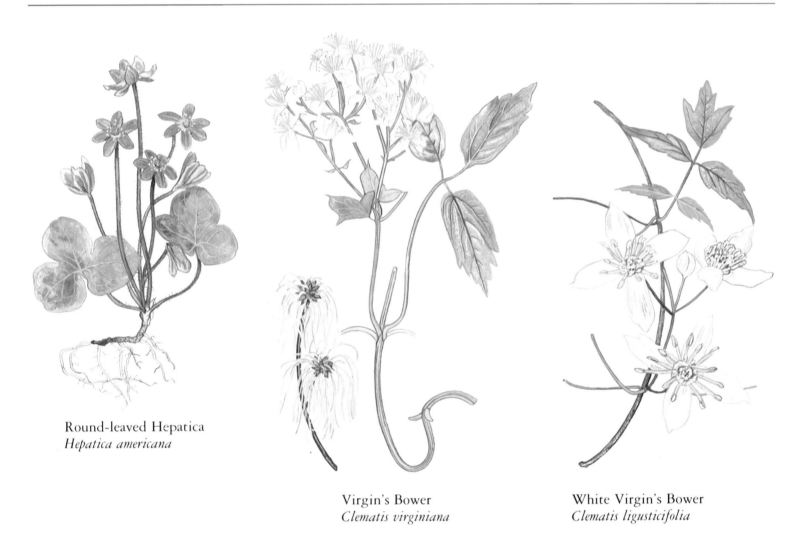

Round-leaved Hepatica
Hepatica americana

Virgin's Bower
Clematis virginiana

White Virgin's Bower
Clematis ligusticifolia

There are two **Hepaticas**, *Hepatica* species, in North America. These are small woodland plants related to the anemones (and placed in the genus *Anemone* by some botanists); they are hairy perennials with clumps of lobed leaves, and several solitary flowers on long stalks in spring. The flowers lack petals and have 5–12 petal-like sepals. The **Round-leaved Hepatica**, *Hepatica americana*, grows in open woods on acid soils from Nova Scotia to Minnesota, and south to Georgia. Its flowers vary in color from white to pink and blue. The lobes of its leaves are rounded, unlike the leaves of the other species, the Sharp-leaved Hepatica, *H. acutiloba*, which has pointed lobes; this otherwise similar species also grows in eastern woods but on calcareous soils.

Hepaticas are sometimes called liverleafs or liverworts because of the supposed resemblance of their leaves to the lobes of the liver. They were at one time used in herb medicine, since by the "Doctrine of Signatures," which supposed that plants resembling parts of the human body could heal those parts, they were thought to be effective in curing liver disorders.

Clematises are unusual among members of the Buttercup family, in that many are woody or herbaceous climbers. They include some of the most popular garden plants, and many hybrids have been developed, often with huge, brilliantly colored flowers. Some wild species in the U.S. are given the name Leatherflower or Vase flower; these are herbaceous or climbing plants found in the woods and prairies of the east and midwest, and they have characteristic small, purplish, nodding, vase-shaped flowers.

Virgin's Bower, *Clematis virginiana*, is a climbing plant up to 10ft tall, common in woods and thickets, on woodland edges, fences and roadsides, in moist places from Nova Scotia to Manitoba, south to Georgia and Louisiana. It has twining stems and compound leaves with twining stalks; each leaf has three ovate, toothed leaflets, and in the axils of many of the leaves grow the clusters of white flowers in summer, male and female flowers on separate plants. Each flower has four white, petal-like sepals and no petals; the male flowers have many stamens and the female flowers several carpels, which enlarge in fruit to form globular heads of achenes, each with a long, plume-like tail. The female plants are especially noticeable in late summer when they may be covered in the plumed fruits.

White Virgin's Bower, *Clematis ligusticifolia*, is a western species, found climbing over trees and bushes in moist places, along gullies and valley bottoms in the mountains from British Columbia to California. It has other names: Traveller's Joy, a name given to many clematises that adorn hedgerows and trailside bushes, and Peppervine, a name that comes from its peppery taste; it was used by Indians and settlers as a remedy for colds and sore throats. In appearance it is similar to the eastern species, but has creamy flowers.

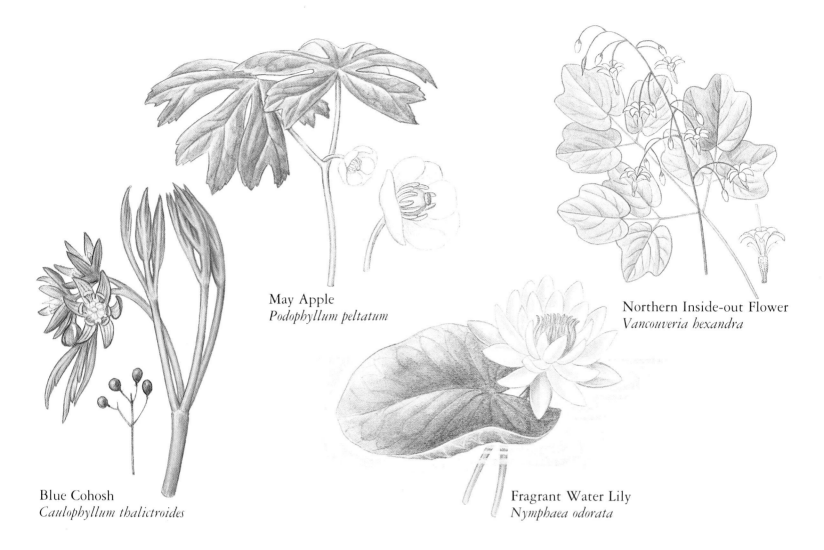

May Apple
Podophyllum peltatum

Northern Inside-out Flower
Vancouveria hexandra

Blue Cohosh
Caulophyllum thalictroides

Fragrant Water Lily
Nymphaea odorata

Barberry family

Berberidaceae

There are about 10 genera and nearly 600 species of herbs and shrubs in this family, mainly confined to the northern hemisphere. Species of *Berberis* and *Mahonia* are grown as garden shrubs. Several members of the family are poisonous; others are edible or have edible parts.

Family features The flowers are solitary or borne in inflorescences. They are regular and hermaphrodite with similar sepals and petals, all free and borne in two or more series. There are six stamens in each flower, borne opposite the petals, and the ovary is superior with one cell. The fruits are berries. The leaves are alternate, simple or compound. Stipules are usually absent.

The **May Apple** or Mandrake, *Podophyllum peltatum*, grows in open woods and on shady roadsides from Quebec to Minnesota, and south to Florida and Texas. It forms carpets of upright leafy stems growing from underground rhizomes. Each stem bears one or two deeply lobed, umbrella-like leaves; those with two leaves also bear a single nodding, waxy white flower in May. The flowers are followed by yellow berries, edible when ripe. The rest of the plant, including seeds, is poisonous, and may be lethal. The plant is also irritant.

Blue Cohosh, *Caulophyllum thalictroides*, grows in moist woods from New Brunswick to Ontario, and south to Alabama. It forms an erect stem, bluish when young, and about 2ft tall when fully grown. Its two leaves are so much divided into segments that they appear to be many more than two. In early summer, in the axil of the upper leaf grows a cluster of rather insignificant yellow-green flowers; each has six petal-like sepals and six hooded, gland-like petals, much smaller than the sepals. The flowers are followed by clusters of deep blue "berries," actually the seeds, which burst the ovary as they enlarge and ripen. The roots and berries of Blue Cohosh are poisonous.

Northern Inside-out Flower, *Vancouveria hexandra*, is one of three similar species that grow in the Pacific states of the U.S., this one in the deep shade of coniferous woods on the western side of the Cascades, from Washington to California. It forms carpets of distinctively shaped leaves, 15in tall at most, growing from underground rhizomes. The leathery leaves are divided into three-lobed leaflets. The clusters of white flowers appear in spring on leafless stalks, growing directly from the rhizomes; each appears to be inside out, with swept-back sepals and petals.

Twinleaf, *Jeffersonia diphylla*, grows in rich woods in the northeast. It has a rosette of bilobed basal leaves, and solitary white flowers in spring.

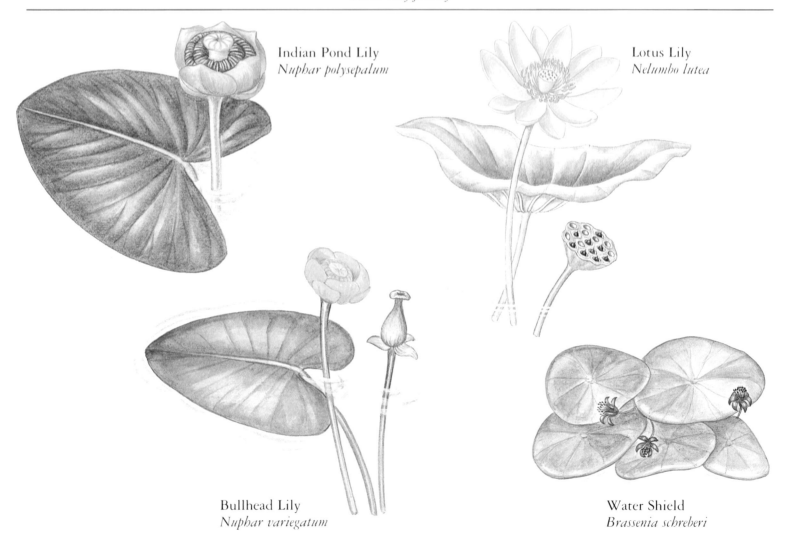

Indian Pond Lily
Nuphar polysepalum

Lotus Lily
Nelumbo lutea

Bullhead Lily
Nuphar variegatum

Water Shield
Brassenia schreberi

Water Lily family

Nymphaeaceae

A small family of aquatic plants with about 6 genera and 70 species found throughout much of the world, with the notable exception of New Zealand. By far the largest genus is *Nymphaea*, from which most garden varieties of water lilies come; they are famous for their beautiful, floating flowers.

Family features These aquatic plants have floating, round or heart-shaped leaves with long stalks attaching them to roots or rhizomes at the bottom of the water. Some species also have thin, translucent, submerged leaves. The flowers float on the water or project into the air on long stalks growing from the rhizomes. Each flower is solitary, often showy, regular, hermaphrodite, with 4–6 free sepals and many petals. In some species the petals become stamen-like near the center of the flower. The flowers have many stamens and eight carpels. The fruits are either spongy capsules or a group of achenes sunk in the receptacle.

The **Fragrant Water Lily**, *Nymphaea odorata* (p. 46), is the most widespread of the American species. It is native from Newfoundland to Manitoba, south to Florida and Texas along the coastal plain, but is planted and naturalized in many other areas. It grows in quiet waters and ponds, its round leaves and flowers floating on the surface. The leaves are often reddish or purple on the underside, while the flowers are fragrant and white, opening in the morning to show many yellow stamens. As the flowers finish, their long stalks coil and pull them back below the surface so that the fleshy capsules ripen under water. When they burst, the seeds rise to the surface and float away.

The **Indian Pond Lily**, *Nuphar polysepalum*, is a western species, which grows in ponds and slow-moving streams from Alaska to California, east to South Dakota and Colorado. It has long-stalked, leathery, heart-shaped floating leaves and thin, delicate submerged leaves. The flowers project above the water on stout stalks. They are bowl-shaped, with 7–9 thick, yellow sepals, and many similar petals and stamens surrounding the broad, disk-like stigma. The egg-shaped fruit ripens above water and the seeds are edible; they can be roasted like popcorn or ground into meal. The roots can also be eaten. Indian Pond Lily is only one of several names given to this plant; others include Yellow Pond Lily and Spatterdock.

The **Bullhead Lily**, *Nuphar variegatum*, is an eastern and midwestern species also known as Yellow Pond Lily. It is similar to the western species, but has only 5–6 sepals. It can be seen floating on ponds across Canada, south to Delaware, Kansas, and Idaho.

The **Lotus Lily** or American Lotus, *Nelumbo lutea* (p. 47), grows in ponds and slow-moving streams from southern

Ontario to Minnesota, south to Florida and Texas. Its leaves and flowers often project above the water surface. The leaves are rounded, up to 2ft across. The pale yellow flowers have numerous similar sepals and petals, many stamens, and a central cone-shaped, flat-topped receptacle with many ovaries sunk into cavities. In fruit this enlarges and the embedded fruits become hard and nut-like. Lotus Lily roots can be eaten like sweet potatoes (if they can be reached!) in fall and spring; new shoots can be used as a potherb and mature seeds can be boiled or roasted.

Water Shield, *Brassenia schreberi* (p. 47), grows in ponds and quiet waters throughout much of the temperate areas of North America, and south into tropical regions. With its creeping rhizomes it spreads through the mud at the bottom of the water, and its small, rounded-elliptical leaves float on the surface; they are usually about 4in across, green above and often purplish beneath. The flowers are small, with 3–4 dull purple sepals and petals.

Sundew family

Droseraceae

This is a family of insectivorous plants, with rosettes of sticky, glandular leaves which act as insect traps. There are 4 genera and about 100 species found throughout the world in acid soils, in sandy and boggy places. Their lifestyle enables them to live in these nitrogen-poor soils, since they obtain extra from the insects they trap and absorb. The flowers are regular, usually with five separate sepals and petals, five stamens, and a single ovary.

The **Round-leaved Sundew**, *Drosera rotundifolia*, is one of eight *Drosera* species in North America. It grows in bogs and swamps, often many plants together in suitable habitats, throughout the temperate regions of the northern hemisphere, in North America south as far as Georgia, Illinois, and California. This small plant forms a flat rosette of long-stalked leaves with circular blades, conspicuous for the red-tipped glands which cover them and which secrete a sticky fluid. Insects, often small flies, get caught on the leaves and die; they are digested by enzymes in the fluid, and absorbed. In summer the plants produce leafless flowering stems about 8in tall, with one-sided clusters of small white or pink flowers.

Great Sundew, *Drosera anglica*, is a circumboreal species, a plant which likes the wettest parts of bogs. It holds its leaves more or less erect, and has long stalks and elongated blades with many glandular hairs. Thread-leaved Sundew, *D. filiformis*, has even longer leaves resembling threads, with blades and stalks merging into each other. It is found along the eastern coast from Massachusetts to Louisiana.

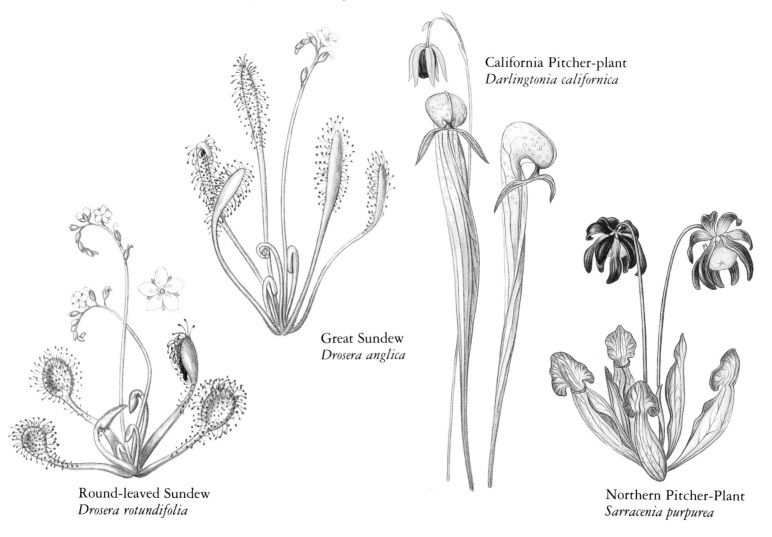

California Pitcher-plant
Darlingtonia californica

Great Sundew
Drosera anglica

Round-leaved Sundew
Drosera rotundifolia

Northern Pitcher-Plant
Sarracenia purpurea

Pitcher-plant family

Sarraceniaceae

A small family of insectivorous plants, with 3 genera and about 17 species found in eastern North America, in California, and in South America. A few are grown in greenhouses by collectors, and some are listed as endangered species. They have been given many names, including Trumpet Plants, Drinking Cups, and Side Saddle Plants.

Family features These are distinctive plants, with a rosette of tubular leaves forming pitchers. The pitchers contain an acid digestive liquid, and are often hooded so that the juice cannot be diluted by rain water. Insects are attracted to the pitchers by their bright colors, crawl under the hoods to try to reach the nectar secreted there, and are trapped by downwardly directed hairs. Eventually they slip down the smooth sides into the liquid which waits below, where they drown. Like sundews, pitcher-plants grow in boggy, nitrogen-poor places, and they obtain additional nitrogen from the insects which they digest and absorb.

The nodding flowers are borne separately on long stalks, either singly or a few together. They are regular and hermaphrodite, with 4–5 free sepals, and either have five free petals or no petals at all. The sepals are large and colored, the petals small and soon falling. The flowers have numerous stamens, and the ovary is superior with 3–5 cells. The fruits are capsules.

The **California Pitcher-plant**, *Darlingtonia californica* (p. 48), has yellow-green pitchers with conspicuous white veins, tubular in shape and gradually enlarged toward the top into a rounded hood with a fishtail-like lobe beneath the hood. The plant is sometimes called Cobra Plant, for it looks like an erect cobra with its hood enlarged, ready to strike. The flowers are borne on long stalks in early summer; they have long, yellow-green sepals and purplish petals. The plants grow in marshes and boggy places, in redwood and other coniferous forests, in coastal Oregon and into California, and in the western Sierra Nevada.

Other North American members of this family belong to the genus *Sarracenia* and are found in the east. **Northern Pitcher-plant**, *Sarracenia purpurea* (p. 48), is the most common and widespread; it has a rosette of sprawling, inflated pitchers, green in color and with a flaring lip, spreading into a hood which does not cover the opening. The single flower is borne on a leafless stalk, rising above the pitchers in summer; it is large and conspicuous, with five maroon petals and an umbrella-shaped style. The plant grows in *Sphagnum* bogs in eastern Canada, south to Florida and Texas, but is rare in the southern part of its range.

Butterwort
Pinguicula vulgaris

Greater Bladderwort
Utricularia vulgaris

Lesser Bladderwort
Utricularia minor

Butterwort family
Lentibulariaceae

A family of insectivorous plants, some growing in bogs or submerged in water, others growing on land or as epiphytes. This is a small family with 4 genera and about 170 species found throughout the world. They are related to the Snapdragon family, but have been included here with the other insectivorous families.

Family features The flowers are solitary or borne in a raceme, and are hermaphrodite and bilaterally symmetrical. The calyx has 2–5 lobes and the corolla is two-lipped, with five lobes and a spur at the back. The flowers have two stamens inserted at the base of the corolla, and a superior ovary with one cell. The fruits are capsules. The leaves form various kinds of traps for insects.

The leaves of **Butterwort**, *Pinguicula vulgaris* (p. 49), are borne in a flat rosette but are less obviously insect traps than those of sundews. The leaf blades are yellowish and fleshy with a soft, slimy texture and rolled-up edges. Insects that land on the leaves are trapped by the slime, and their struggles trigger the leaves into rolling up; the insects are enfolded and digested. The purple flowers are borne on erect, leafless stalks in early summer. Butterworts grow in bogs, wet meadows, and among wet rocks across Canada and Alaska, south in the west to northern California. Other species grow in the east; some have white or violet flowers, others yellow ones.

The **Bladderworts**, *Utricularia* species, are found in wet places or in water where their tiny, elaborate traps catch little water fleas and other aquatic creatures. **Greater Bladderwort**, *Utricularia vulgaris* (p. 49), grows in quiet waters all around the North Pole, south to Florida and California. It forms a network of branching stems with finely dissected leaves, floating just below the surface in summer when the plant is in flower, deeper at other times of year. The leaves bear traps—tiny, translucent bladders with a few hairs at one end which act as a trigger. If a water flea touches the hairs, a trap door opens on the bladder and water rushes in, carrying the luckless crustacean with it. In late summer the bright yellow flowers grow on erect stalks above the water.

Lesser Bladderwort, *Utricularia minor* (p. 49), is a similar but smaller plant, also found around the North Pole, but only south as far as New Jersey and Indiana in the east. Its branching stems are buried in the mud in shallow water. Swollen Bladderwort, *U. inflata*, has a wheel-like arrangement of swollen stems which float on the water; they end in floating, finely divided leaves. This plant is found in ponds on the coastal plain in the east. Other bladderworts are also found in the eastern U.S. and Canada. Some have yellow flowers, others purple ones.

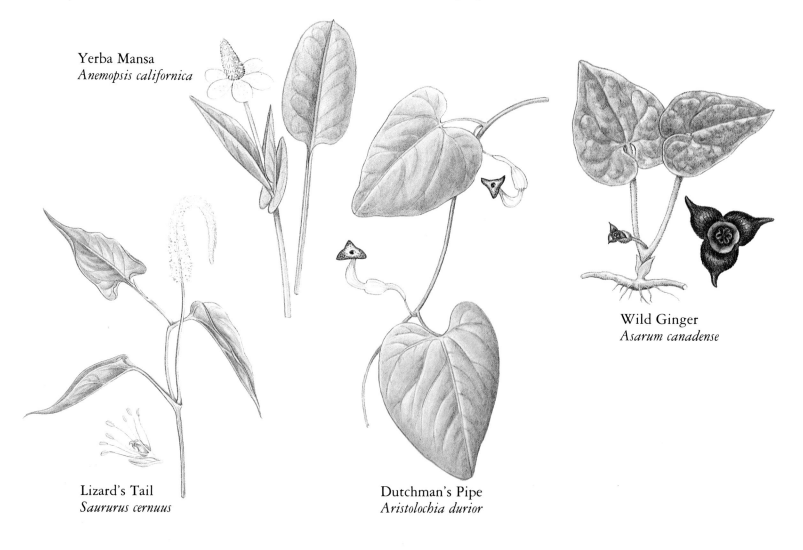

Yerba Mansa
Anemopsis californica

Wild Ginger
Asarum canadense

Lizard's Tail
Saururus cernuus

Dutchman's Pipe
Aristolochia durior

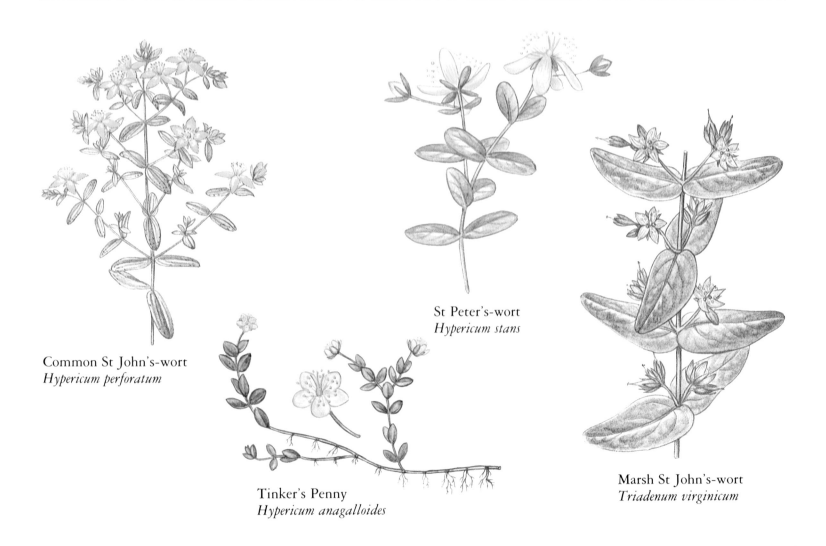

Common St John's-wort
Hypericum perforatum

St Peter's-wort
Hypericum stans

Tinker's Penny
Hypericum anagalloides

Marsh St John's-wort
Triadenum virginicum

Lizard's Tail family

Saururaceae

A very small family of herbs with 5 genera and 7 species, found only in North America and eastern Asia. Some, like *Houttuynia cordata* from Asia, are planted in bog gardens for their interesting flowers and leaves.

Family features The small, regular flowers are often aggregated into spikes or dense clusters with colored bracts; they have no sepals or petals, and either three, six or eight stamens. The fruits are succulent capsules. The leaves are simple and alternate, with stipules.

The **Lizard's Tail**, *Saururus cernuus* (p. 50), is an eastern species, growing in shallow water, swamps, and marshes, and often forming extensive colonies, from Quebec to Minnesota, south to Florida and Texas, but more commonly in the south. Its jointed stems grow up to 5ft high, and bear large, dark, heart-shaped leaves, 3–6in long, and on long stalks. In summer the tiny white flowers form long, fragrant spikes drooping at the tips and resembling lizards' tails.

In the west **Yerba Mansa**, *Anemopsis californica* (p. 50), grows in wet places, usually where soil is saline or alkaline, from Oregon to Mexico, and east into Colorado and Texas, but most commonly in California. It forms patches of large,

elliptical, long-stalked, upright leaves. The flower stalks emerge from among these; each has a few leaves about half way up and a terminal, cone-like spike of tiny flowers above white or red-tinged bracts; the whole spike resembles a single flower at first glance. The thick creeping rhizomes of this plant are aromatic and have been used in Indian and herbal medicine for a variety of purposes.

Birthwort family

Aristolochiaceae

There are about 7 genera and 400 species of twining vines and herbs in this family, found in the tropics and temperate areas of the world. Several of the *Aristolochia* species have traditionally been used in herb medicine.

Family features The flowers grow singly or in clusters in the leaf axils. They are often fetid, usually bilaterally symmetrical, and hermaphrodite. They have a three-lobed, often tubular calyx that is frequently highly colored and like a corolla. Petals are minute or absent. The flowers have six or 12 stamens and usually the ovary is inferior with 4–6 carpels. The fruits are capsules. The leaves are simple and alternate. Stipules are absent.

Dutchman's Pipe, *Aristolochia durior* (p. 50), is a climbing

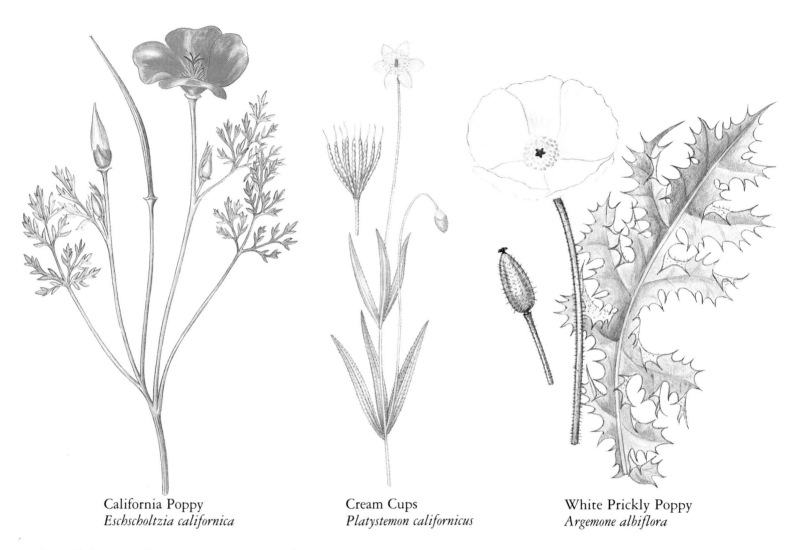

California Poppy
Eschscholtzia californica

Cream Cups
Platystemon californicus

White Prickly Poppy
Argemone albiflora

vine which may twine its way to the tops of tall trees. It has long-stalked, broadly heart-shaped leaves up to 8in long, and unique, pipe-like flowers in the leaf axils. In its native state this plant grows in mountain woods, in moist places, and beside streams from Pennsylvania to Kentucky and Georgia. It is a characteristic plant of the Appalachians. In northeastern areas of the U.S. it is cultivated as a garden plant, often planted around porches. Virginia Snakeroot, *A. serpentaria*, was the species most commonly used in herb medicine; at one time it was supposed to be effective against snakebite and is still used to promote digestion. However, its use is increasingly questioned, since it is suspected of causing mutations.

Wild Ginger, *Asarum canadense* (p. 50), forms spreading patches of leaves, growing from long underground rhizomes. The leaves, 6–10in tall, grow in pairs, with long stalks and broad, heart-shaped blades. At ground level, in the axil between each pair of leaves, a single brownish flower appears in spring. It is cup-shaped with three lobes at the opening. Wild Ginger grows in rich woods from New Brunswick to Ontario, south to North Carolina and Arkansas. The plant has a scent of ginger when bruised, and the roots are even more strongly scented; they can be used as a substitute for true ginger and are used in herb medicine. Wild Ginger is also a useful shade-loving plant for the garden, making an interesting ground cover beneath trees and shrubs.

St John's-wort family

Hypericaceae

There are about 8 genera and 400 species of herbs, shrubs, and trees in this family, found mainly in temperate regions, and in mountainous areas in the tropics. Several shrubby species are used as ornamental plants in gardens.

Family features These plants have showy, yellow or white flowers. Each is hermaphrodite and regular, with five sepals and petals, and numerous stamens, often united into bundles, and appearing to fill the center of the flower in *Hypericum*, by far the largest genus. The ovary is superior, with one, three or five carpels, usually forming a capsule in fruit. The leaves are opposite or in whorls, simple, and often dotted with glands; they lack stipules.

Many St John's-worts, *Hypericum* species, grow in North America. **Common St John's-wort**, *Hypericum perforatum* (p. 51), is a European plant which now grows as a common weed in waste places and on roadsides in much of North America. It is a persistent pasture weed in the west, where it is known as Klamath Weed. This is a perennial with a much branched stem about 2ft tall, and many opposite, linear, stalkless leaves covered by translucent dots (glands), seen when the plant is held up to the light. The flowers are borne in a

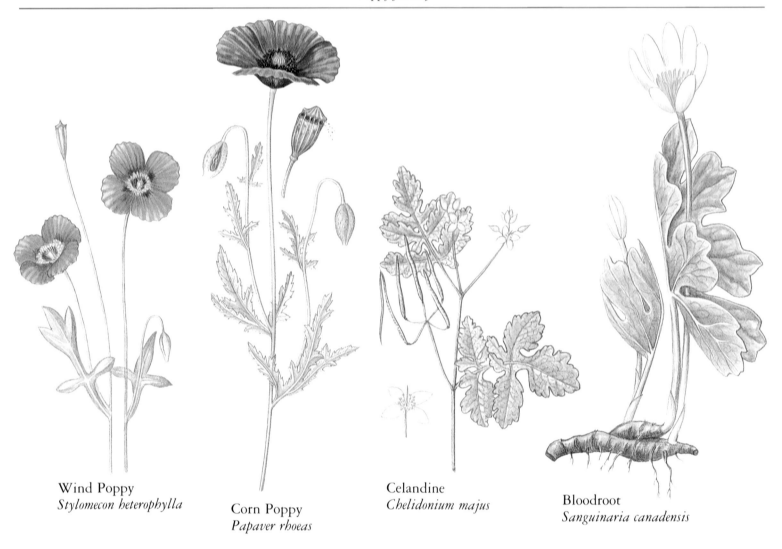

Wind Poppy
Stylomecon heterophylla

Corn Poppy
Papaver rhoeas

Celandine
Chelidonium majus

Bloodroot
Sanguinaria canadensis

compound inflorescence terminating the stems. They are typical of the genus, with yellow petals and many stamens. In this species the petals have black dots around their margins.

Tinker's Penny, *Hypericum anagalloides* (p. 51), is a little, prostrate, mat-forming plant, with stems rooting at the nodes, and tiny, elliptical leaves in opposite pairs. Its stems grow up to 8in long and its golden-yellow or salmon-colored flowers bloom at the ends of short, upright branches. It is found in wet places from California north to British Columbia and Montana.

St Peter's-wort, *Hypericum stans* (p. 51), is one of the shrubby St John's-worts. It forms a small branched shrub, 1–3ft tall, with elliptical leaves and golden-yellow, many-stamened flowers. The flowers are unusual for St John's-worts in having only four petals and four sepals—two larger outer ones and two small, narrow inner ones. This shrub grows in sandy soil and pine barrens from New Jersey to Florida, west to Oklahoma and Texas.

Marsh St John's-wort, *Triadenum virginicum* (p. 51), is one of several perennial swamp and marsh species which grow primarily in the east. They are most commonly found on the coastal plain. It is a perennial plant, with erect stems up to 2ft tall, and opposite, oblong, gland-dotted leaves almost clasping the stems. It has clusters of flesh-colored flowers terminating the stems and growing in the axils of the upper leaves.

Each flower has three groups of three stamens, alternating with three orange glands.

Poppy family

Papaveraceae

There are about 26 genera and 200 species in this family, mostly herbs, found throughout the world, but mainly in the subtropical and temperate regions of the northern hemisphere. Probably the most famous member of the family is the Opium Poppy, *Papaver somniferum*, whose seed-heads are the source of the sap which is crude opium. From this can be derived the painkillers codeine and morphine, or heroin. Poppy seeds are rich in oil which is used in soaps, paints, salad oils, and cattle cake. Opium Poppies are cultivated in many countries, including the U.S., and may be found growing wild, having escaped from cultivation. Many members of the family are grown in gardens.

Family features The flowers are usually solitary. They are regular and hermaphrodite, with 2–3 sepals which soon fall, and either 4–6 or 8–12 often crumpled, separate petals. There are numerous stamens and a superior ovary of two or more united carpels. The fruits are capsules which open by pores or valves, and they contain numerous tiny seeds. The leaves are alternate and often much divided; they lack stipules. The plants contain colored sap.

There are many poppies in western North America. One of the best known is the **California Poppy**, *Eschscholtzia californica* (p. 52), a showy plant often grown in gardens. It grows only 2ft tall, with a clump of smooth, blue-green, dissected leaves, and solitary, orange-yellow flowers borne on long stalks. This is the state flower of California, found from southern California to Oregon and Washington. It is so common in grassy and open places that large areas of these states may be transformed into orange expanses when it is in bloom. The flowers are sensitive to light, opening in sunlight, closing at night, and remaining closed on cloudy days. Several other less showy species of *Eschscholtzia* also grow in dry places in the Pacific states.

Cream Cups, *Platystemon californicus* (p. 52), is found in grassy places from California to Utah and Arizona. It forms a clump of softly hairy, linear leaves, and has several similarly hairy stems, each with a single terminal flower. The flowers vary considerably in color, from white to yellow, to white with yellow spots on the petal bases, and they have numerous stamens in the center.

The **Prickly Poppies**, *Argemone* species, are a group of about 30 tropical and subtropical species. They have divided leaves with prickle-pointed leaflets, and many have prickly stems as well, so that they resemble thistles. Their flowers are white or pale yellow. **White Prickly Poppy**, *Argemone albiflora* (p. 52), is a southern species, growing in dry, sandy places from Virginia to Florida, and west to Missouri and Texas. It is an annual plant, with a branched stem up to 3ft tall, and white flowers borne at the top of the stem in summer. Leaves, stems, and sepals are all prickly, and the capsule is also spiny. The flowers are large and showy, 3in across, and with yellow stamens.

The **Wind Poppy**, *Stylomecon heterophylla* (p. 53), is found only in California, growing in grassy places in the foothills of the Sierra Nevada and Coast Ranges, into Baja California. It is not a common plant, but is a brightly colored one with orange-red petals, purplish at the base. The Fire Poppy, *Papaver californicum*, is a similar plant, with brick-red flowers, but it appears only in the first year after fire has burned through the Californian chaparral in which it grows. Its seeds then remain dormant until the next fire.

One of the most familiar of the *Papaver* species is the **Corn Poppy** or Red Poppy, *Papaver rhoeas* (p. 53), a Eurasian plant grown in gardens; it occasionally escapes to grow wild. It is most familiar as the poppy which grew on Flanders fields after the First World War, and has become the symbol of Remembrance Day. It is a stiffly hairy, annual plant with an erect stem up to 2ft tall, and divided leaves. At the tops of the

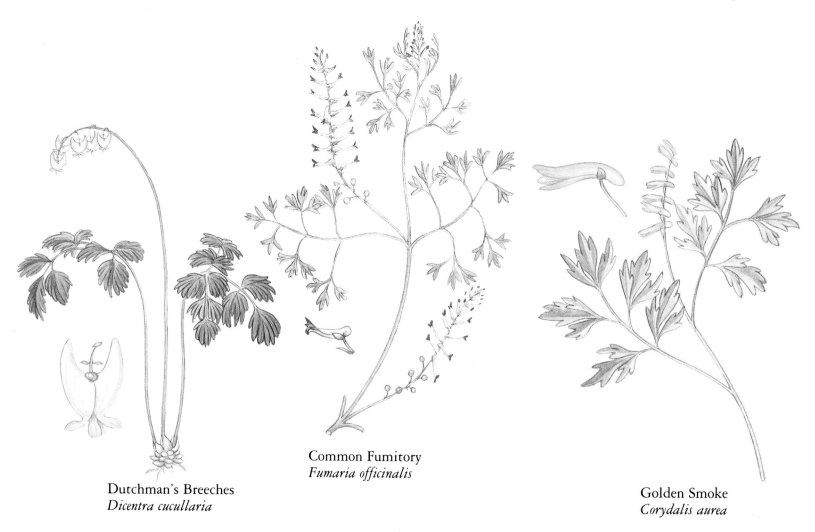

Common Fumitory
Fumaria officinalis

Dutchman's Breeches
Dicentra cucullaria

Golden Smoke
Corydalis aurea

stems are the red, four-petalled, bowl-shaped flowers, opening from nodding buds. The capsules which follow the flowers resemble pepper shakers, with a ring of holes around the rim, beneath the persistent lid of the stigma. The capsule contains many tiny seeds, and as the wind blows the shaker to and fro, the seeds fly out of the holes and are scattered.

Celandine, *Chelidonium majus* (p. 53), is another Eurasian species, a former herbal plant with caustic orange sap which was used to treat warts. It may be found in shady places, usually near towns or on roadsides, in the eastern U.S. and Canada. It is a perennial up to 3ft tall, with almost hairless, slightly blue-green, divided leaves on brittle stems. The small, pale yellow flowers grow in terminal clusters; they are followed by slender capsules which contain black seeds, each with a fleshy white appendage.

Bloodroot, *Sanguinaria canadensis* (p. 53), is a perennial plant with stout rhizomes containing caustic red sap. From these rhizomes grow many round, lobed, blue-green leaves on long stalks about 10in tall. The solitary white flowers appear in spring before the leaves. Bloodroot is found in rich woods from Nova Scotia to Manitoba, south to Florida and Oklahoma. It has been used in herb medicine to treat skin problems like eczema and ringworm but is caustic and probably better reserved for use as a beautiful garden plant, especially in the double form.

Fumitory family
Fumariaceae

This family has about 16 genera and 450 species, all herbs, in the northern temperate regions and North Africa. Several of them, like Bleeding Hearts, Dutchman's Breeches, and the various *Corydalis* species, are good garden plants. They are closely allied to poppies and some botanists include them in the Poppy family.

Family features The flowers are bilaterally symmetrical and hermaphrodite, with two small sepals and four petals. The two inner petals are often joined together over the stigma; the two outer, spurred or pouched petals are separate at the base but joined at their tips. Each flower has six stamens, in two groups of three with joined filaments, opposite the outer petals. The ovary has a single cell which swells in fruit to form a capsule or nutlet. These are smooth, brittle plants with watery juice and alternate divided leaves.

There are nine species of *Dicentra* in North America. **Dutchman's Breeches**, *Dicentra cucullaria* (p. 54), is the most widespread, growing in rich woods from Quebec to Minnesota, and south to Georgia and Kansas. It is a perennial plant with a dense cluster of white, grain-like tubers beneath the ground from which grows a spreading end clump of

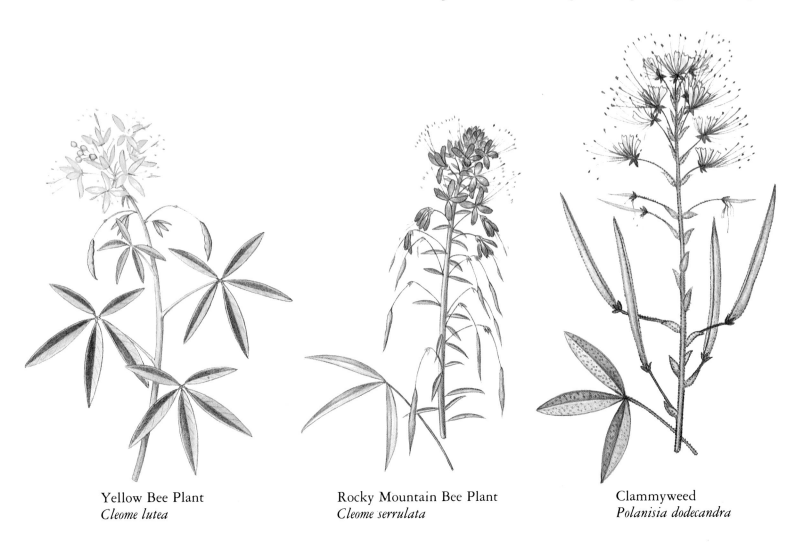

Yellow Bee Plant
Cleome lutea

Rocky Mountain Bee Plant
Cleome serrulata

Clammyweed
Polanisia dodecandra

Shepherd's Purse
Capsella bursa-pastoris

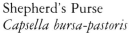

Field Pennycress
Thlaspi arvense

Poor-man's-pepper
Lepidium virginicum

feathery, gray-green basal leaves about 6in tall. Its name describes perfectly the shape of the flowers, which resemble white, pantaloon-like breeches hanging upside-down from the flower stalks. They appear in spring. Squirrel-corn, *D. canadensis*, is a similar species with much shorter "legs" on the "breeches;" it is found in rich woods in the northeastern U.S. and eastern Canada. Two western species, *D. formosa* and *D. eximia*, have pink flowers; they are both grown in gardens.

Common Fumitory, *Fumaria officinalis* (p. 54), is a European plant which is found scattered in waste places throughout much of North America. It is a small, straggling plant with much-divided, whitish blue-green leaves, and curious flowers growing in loose spikes. They are tubular, pink in color, with red-tipped spurs, and appear to be balanced on their stalks.

Climbing Fumitory or Allegheny Vine, *Adlumia fungosa*, is a biennial plant that grows in mountain woods in the east and midwest. In its second year it produces long stems that climb up to 10ft high in the trees, clinging by tendrils on the ends of its leaves. Its handsome, pearly pink flowers hang in drooping clusters from the leaf axils.

Several *Corydalis* species grow in North America; they are attractive plants, some grown in gardens. **Golden Smoke**, *Corydalis aurea* (p. 54), is one of the most widespread, found in open, often disturbed places, from Quebec to Alaska, south to

Texas and California. It is an annual or biennial, branched plant with sprawling stems and pinnate leaves. Its golden-yellow flowers grow in racemes at the ends of the stems; the flowers have the typical family form, with a spurred upper petal. Most other species also have yellow flowers, but Pale Corydalis, *C. sempervirens*, has pink flowers with yellow tips. It grows in woods across Canada, south in mountains in the east to Georgia.

Caper family

Capparidaceae

There are about 30 genera and 650 species in this family, found in the tropical and warm temperate regions of the world. It is mostly a family of trees and shrubs, but in the U.S. the members are usually herbs. A few are grown as ornamental plants in gardens. Capers are the pickled flower buds of *Capparis spinosa*, a thorny Mediterranean shrub.

Family features The flowers are hermaphrodite, and may be regular or irregular, solitary, or borne in terminal racemes. Each flower has four free sepals and petals, many stamens, and a superior ovary with two cells. The fruit is a capsule or berry. The leaves are alternate, simple or palmately compound. Stipules are absent, minute or in the form of thorns.

Fendler's Bladderpod
Lesquerella fendleri

Western Wallflower
Erysimum asperum

Tansy Mustard
Descurainia pinnata

Yellow Bee Plant, *Cleome lutea* (p. 55), is one of several western species. It is a branched annual plant up to 5ft tall, with palmately compound leaves composed of 3–7 oblong leaflets. At the tops of the stems are clusters of yellow flowers, very attractive to bees, dense at first but opening up as time goes on and the slender, arched seed pods form. These plants are found in sandy flats, juniper woodland, and scrub, often near water, from Washington to California, east to Montana and New Mexico.

Rocky Mountain Bee Plant, *Cleome serrulata* (p. 55), has pink flowers; it is found on roadsides, wasteland, and rangeland from the prairies to the Pacific states. All the *Cleome* species have an unpleasant scent, supposedly reminiscent of goats, a fact reflected in the name of the family since the Latin word for goat is *capra*.

Clammyweed, *Polanisia dodecandra* (p. 55), is a western species found in deserts and plains, in washes, and among pinyon and juniper from Oregon to Minnesota, south to California and Texas, and into Mexico. Its name comes from its sticky hairs that make it clammy to the touch. This is an annual plant with an unpleasant scent, a branching stem up to 3ft tall, and palmately divided, compound leaves, each with three lance-shaped leaflets. Its cream or white flowers grow in racemes at the tops of the stems; their most noticeable feature is their long, purple stamens.

Mustard family

Cruciferae

Also known as **Brassicaceae**. There are about 375 genera and 3200 species of herbs in this family, found throughout the world, but mainly in the north temperate regions. This is an important family, with many crop plants, including cabbages and broccoli, kale, turnip, and rutabaga, watercress and mustards. Rape is now grown on a wide scale for the oil extracted from its seeds. Other members of the family, like alyssum, aubrieta, and wallflowers, are grown in spring flower gardens. Some are common weeds, very familiar plants like Shepherd's Purse, found in back yards, waste places, and cultivated land.

Many members of this family contain oils similar to white mustard oil, by far the highest concentrations being in the seeds. Mustard oil is what gives the flavor to mustard, but it is highly irritant and poisonous in large quantities or in its pure form. Mustard poultices were a traditional remedy for rheumatism and chilblains, since they draw blood into the affected area, warming it and improving circulation.

Family features The regular, hermaphrodite flowers of this family are distinctive, with four separate petals in the shape of a cross, alternating with four separate sepals. Each flower has

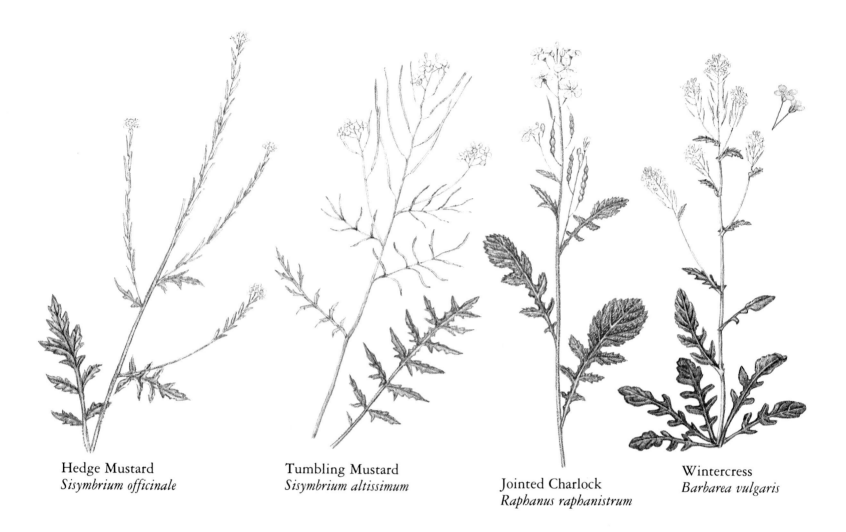

Hedge Mustard
Sisymbrium officinale

Tumbling Mustard
Sisymbrium altissimum

Jointed Charlock
Raphanus raphanistrum

Wintercress
Barbarea vulgaris

six stamens and a superior ovary. Fruits are specialized capsules, called siliquas, with two valves opening from below, exposing a central septum to which many seeds are attached. The flowers grow in racemes. The leaves are arranged alternately and they lack stipules.

Shepherd's Purse, *Capsella bursa-pastoris* (p. 56), is a familiar garden weed found throughout the world. It is a small annual or biennial plant, with a rosette of simple, more or less lobed leaves, and an erect flowering stem up to 15in tall. Plants may be found at any time of year, as long as the ground is not covered in snow, and they flower throughout spring and summer. The flowers are white and very small, and are followed by heart-shaped capsules, like tiny purses. As in all members of the family, the inflorescence starts life as a dense cluster of buds, gradually lengthening as the flowers die and the capsules form.

Field Pennycress, *Thlaspi arvense* (p. 56), is another annual weed from Europe, this one with a fetid scent which has earned it the name of Stinkweed in Canada. It may be found in many waste places in North America and can be a serious pest if allowed to seed so that it becomes abundant. It is a small plant, no more than 2ft tall, and has an erect stem with clasping, lance-shaped leaves. Its lengthening cluster of small white flowers gradually gives way to many flattened, broadly winged fruits, each one notched at the top.

Most of the **Pepper-grasses**, members of the genus *Lepidium*, are weeds, like the widespread **Poor-man's-pepper**, *Lepidium virginicum* (p. 56), which grows on roadsides and in waste places, fields, and gardens across North America. It is a small annual or biennial plant, 2ft tall at most, with a clump of lobed basal leaves and an erect flowering stem. The white flowers are tiny and followed by round, flattened fruits, notched at the top. This plant is edible, with vitamin-rich but rather bitter leaves which can be used sparingly in salads or as a pot-herb. Many other pepper-grasses are similar small plants but some are showier, like Western Pepper-grass, *L. montanum*, which is one of several species found in western deserts and rangeland. Garden Cress is *L. sativum*.

There are about 40 **Bladderpods**, *Lesquerella* species, most of them found in North America, especially in the hills and plains of the Great Plains and the southwest. They are low-growing, annual or perennial, densely hairy plants, with star-shaped hairs, yellow flowers, and inflated pods—the bladderpods. **Fendler's Bladderpod**, *L. fendleri* (p. 57), grows in dry grassland and deserts, especially in limestone areas, from Kansas to Utah, south to Texas and Arizona, and into Mexico. It is a silver-gray perennial plant, with a tuft of erect stems about 1ft tall, simple strap-shaped leaves, and clusters of yellow flowers in spring. The flowers are followed by rounded, inflated pods which resemble peas.

Wallflowers are most familiar as ornamental plants in the flower garden, but they have several wild, showy relatives in the west. The **Western Wallflower** and Plains Wallflower are often considered to belong to one species, *Erysimum asperum* (p. 57), although some people think they belong to separate, closely related species. This is a an extremely variable biennial plant, with a clump of lance-shaped basal leaves in the first year, and an erect, leafy flowering stem in the second, growing up to 3ft tall. This bears a terminal inflorescence of yellow, burnt-orange or brick red flowers, lengthening and developing slender, quadrangular pods held erect or at an oblique angle away from the stem. It grows in dry places, on open hillsides and flats throughout western North America, westward from central Canada and Texas.

Tansy Mustard, *Descurainia pinnata* (p. 57), is a common plant in many dry, open places, open woodland, and waste places across North America. It is an annual plant, forming a basal tuft of divided leaves resembling those of Tansy, hence Tansy Mustard. As the flowering stem develops, the basal leaves wither. The inflorescences are typical cruciferous ones—dense early in the season and elongating as the flowers die and the pods form. The pods are narrowly club-shaped, with two rows of seeds.

Hedge Mustard and Tumbling Mustard are two European species that have become naturalized as weeds in much of North America and southern Canada. They grow in fields among grain, in waste land, and disturbed ground. **Hedge Mustard**, *Sisymbrium officinale* (p. 58), is immediately recognizable for the way the flowering stems jut out from the main branches, almost at right angles; when in fruit, these stems become very elongated, with the long pods overlapping each other and pressed closely against the stems. This is an annual, much branched, roughly bristly plant, growing about 2ft tall, with deeply cut basal leaves, and narrow, toothed stem leaves. The flowers are pale yellow, appearing over a long period during the summer, eventually forming yellow tufts at the tips of long expanses of seed pod.

Tumbling Mustard, *Sisymbrium altissimum* (p. 58), is also an annual plant, growing up to 3ft tall, with many branches. The leaves of its basal rosette are deeply lobed but they die back before flowering, and the stem leaves are deeply divided with linear segments. It has pale yellow flowers in summer, followed by pods carried at an oblique angle to the stems. This plant can be a troublesome weed in western grain fields, along with Loesel's Tumbling Mustard, *S. loeselii*. When their seeds are ripe, the plants die and are then dislodged from the soil by the wind to become tumbleweeds, shedding their seeds as they are blown about.

Jointed Charlock, *Raphanus raphanistrum* (p. 58), is yet another European plant established as a weed of fields, waste

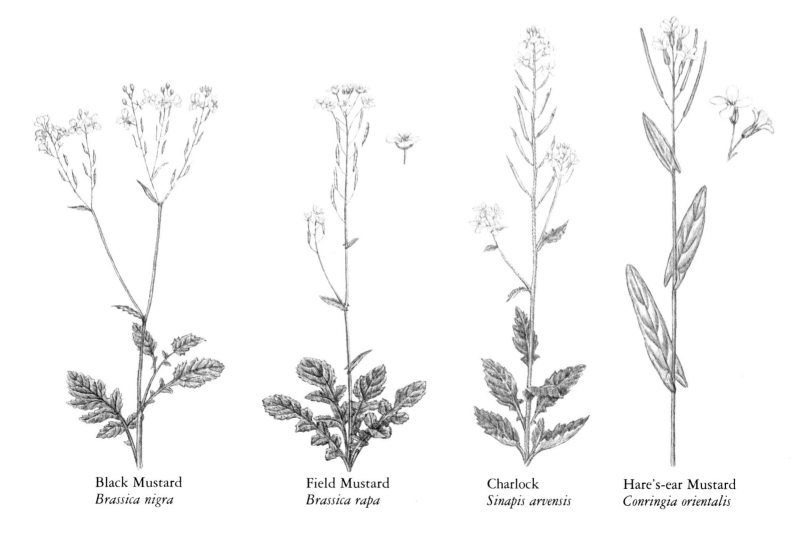

Black Mustard
Brassica nigra

Field Mustard
Brassica rapa

Charlock
Sinapis arvensis

Hare's-ear Mustard
Conringia orientalis

places, and roadsides in North America. It is an annual plant, with rough hairy stems and lobed leaves, and yellowish, mauve-veined flowers, becoming whiter with age. Its fruits are distinctive, long cylindrical pods on ascending stalks, becoming ribbed and constricted between each seed as they dry out; eventually the pods break up, each seed being dispersed still inside its section of pod.

Wintercress, *Barbarea vulgaris* (p. 58), is another invader from Europe, growing in damp places, on roadsides and fields, and in wet meadows. It may be a weed, but it is a potentially useful one, since its late winter rosettes of leaves, rich in Vitamin C and with a taste like watercress, are an excellent addition to salads. The leaves may also be used as a green vegetable, like spinach, and the early flower buds can be eaten like broccoli. The rosettes grow from perennial taproots and have leaves with rounded lobes. From each rosette grow several erect, branched, leafy stems with terminal inflorescences of bright yellow flowers followed by ellipsoidal pods.

The genus *Brassica* is one that has produced many of the most important crop members of the family. *Brassica oleracea* has produced cabbages, cauliflowers, broccoli, Brussels sprouts, and kale; *B. rapa* is the turnip; *B. napus* has produced rape and rutabaga.

Black Mustard, *Brassica nigra* (p. 59), has been cultivated for centuries for its seeds. These are used to make the kitchen condiment, and also in herb medicine to make mustard plasters, and as an emetic. Mustard flour, made from the ground seeds, is also an excellent deodorizer and antiseptic. The plant is an annual one, with a much-branched stem up to 3ft tall. It has large, bristly, lobed lower leaves and smaller toothed upper leaves. The flowers are bright yellow and followed by upright, quadrangular pods pressed against the stems. Each pod has strongly keeled valves, a short beak, and constrictions between the dark red-brown seeds. In Europe this plant is widely cultivated, but in North America it is usually found as a weed in fields and waste places.

Field Mustard, *Brassica rapa* (p. 59), is a wild plant belonging to the same species as the turnip, but wild plants usually lack the swollen roots of cultivated varieties. They have become naturalized in many parts of North America, growing in fields and waste places, but come originally from Europe. This is an annual plant with an erect stem, lobed lower leaves, and toothed upper ones. The flowers are bright yellow, and the inflorescence is unusual in this family since it does not lengthen. The result is that open flowers on their long stalks overtop the still-closed buds in the center of the inflorescence. The pods are held more or less erect and have long slender beaks. The seeds are dark reddish-brown.

Charlock, *Sinapis arvensis* (p. 59), is a European plant also known as Wild Mustard. It was at one time a serious weed of

Whitlow Grass
Draba verna

Watercress
Nasturtium officinale

Comb Draba
Draba oligosperma

Yellow Cress
Rorippa islandica

Rose Rock Cress
Arabis blepharophylla

Hairy Rock Cress
Arabis hirsuta

Tower Mustard
Arabis glabra

vegetable and grain crops, for it produced an abundance of seed, took over large areas, and also acted as a host for insect and fungal pests which attacked other cruciferous crop plants. With the advent of chemical weedkillers, Charlock has been effectively controlled, so that is is now confined to roadsides, waste ground, and field edges, with Corn Cockles and Red Poppies. It is an annual, with an erect, often branched, stiffly hairy stem and roughly hairy leaves. The lower leaves are coarsely toothed, the upper leaves becoming progressively simpler. The bright yellow flowers produce long, beaked pods held upright and away from the stem, and containing 6–12 dark red-brown seeds. The seeds can be used as a substitute for those of Black Mustard.

Hare's-ear Mustard, *Conringia orientalis* (p. 59), grows as a weed of dry places in northern areas of the U.S., especially in the northwest. It comes originally from Europe. This small, annual plant has an erect stem, with characteristic leaves—elliptical with bases clasping the stem—and pale yellow-white flowers. The pods are long and four-angled.

The genus *Draba* has about 300 arctic and alpine species, the majority in North America and Eurasia. They are mostly small, low-growing plants with tufts of simple, often lance-shaped leaves, and little, erect flowering stems. **Whitlow Grass**, *Draba verna* (p. 60), is an annual plant with a small clump of hairy, spoon-shaped leaves, and a flowering stem only 8in tall at most. Its minute flowers are white, each one with deeply notched petals, and they are followed by little, elliptical pods. Whitlow Grass grows on roadsides and in fields, in lawns and gardens, often in bare, poor soil, throughout much of North America. It is a species originally native to Europe.

Comb Draba, *Draba oligosperma* (p. 60), forms tiny cushions of narrow, gray and hairy leaves. In early summer 4-in tall stems grow from the cushion to bear yellow flowers. This is a Rocky Mountain plant, one of many cushion-forming *Draba* species in the mountains.

Watercress, *Nasturtium officinale* (p. 60), is one of the most familiar members of the family, a plant with a distinctive biting taste, eaten in salads and rich in Vitamins A and C. It has become naturalized in quiet streams in many parts of the U.S. and southern Canada. This is a dark green plant with hollow stems which root in the mud and then grow up toward the light to float on the surface. It has compound leaves with 5–9 leaflets. The racemes of white flowers appear in summer and are followed by erect, curving, cylindrical pods.

Yellow Cress or Marsh Cress, *Rorippa islandica* (p. 60), is one of several species related to Watercress and often placed in the same genus. They grow in wet places, on sandy shores and swamps in many parts of North America. Some are annual plants, others are perennials, and they vary in the shape of their

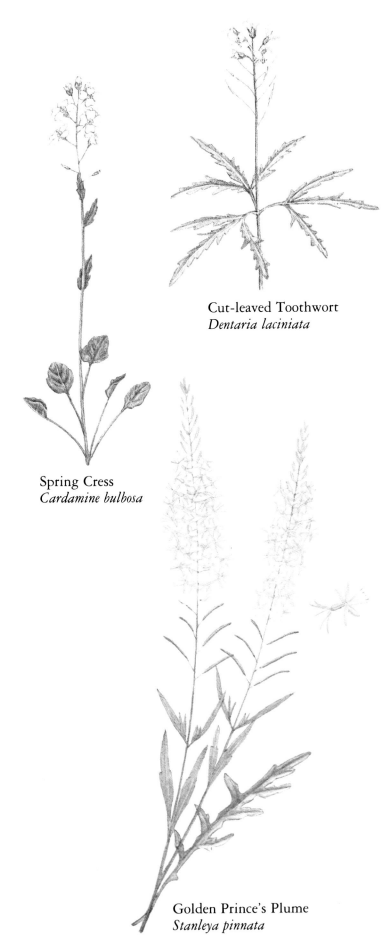

Cut-leaved Toothwort
Dentaria laciniata

Spring Cress
Cardamine bulbosa

Golden Prince's Plume
Stanleya pinnata

leaves and fruits, and in the size of their yellow flowers. They are not edible.

The **Rock-cresses** are a large group of North American and Eurasian plants belonging to the genus *Arabis*; some are grown in rock gardens. There are over 50 species in North America, many growing in the Rocky Mountains and Pacific Coast Ranges in a variety of habitats. **Rose Rock Cress**, *Arabis blepharophylla* (p. 61), is one such western mountain plant which is grown in rock gardens.

Hairy Rock Cress, *Arabis hirsuta* (p. 61), is a biennial plant with a rosette of simple basal leaves and an erect flowering stem. In this species the leaves are hairy and cover the flowering stalk as well as forming the rosette; the flowers are white. The pods are cylindrical and held erect close to the stem. Hairy Rock Cress grows all around the North Pole, on slopes and hillsides, in woods and meadows, sometimes as a weed, south in North America to California and Louisiana.

Tower Mustard, *Arabis glabra* (p. 61), is an annual or biennial plant, forming a rosette of linear, toothed leaves which wither before the flowering stem appears. This grows up to 6ft tall, has arrow-like clasping leaves, and pale yellow flowers, followed by long, slender pods. The plant grows in dry and stony places, in light woods and on banks, becoming a weed on roadsides and waste places all around the North Pole, south to California and North Carolina.

The **Bitter Cresses**, belonging to the genus *Cardamine*, are a group of about 25 species found throughout North America. Most are smooth, hairless plants, and many flower in spring and early summer; they are edible and may be eaten in salads, Pennsylvania Bittercress, *C. pensylvanica,* being the American equivalent of watercress. **Spring Cress**, *C. bulbosa*, is a slender plant, with a crisp white tuber and an erect stem about 20in tall. Its tuber can be grated like horseradish, and its early spring leaves can be added to salads. It has white flowers in late spring. This plant grows, like many of the bitter cresses, in wet places, this species in shallow water and wet woods from Quebec to Minnesota, and south to Florida and Texas.

Toothworts are a group of about 10 northern hemisphere species in the genus *Dentaria*, the majority found in North America. They get their name from the tooth-like scales on their fleshy rhizomes. **Cut-leaved Toothwort**, *D. laciniata*, appears in springtime in rich eastern woods, with four other species. It is found from Quebec to Minnesota, south to Florida and Oklahoma. It has deeply toothed leaves growing from its rhizome, and separate flowering stems 15in tall, with a whorl of three similar leaves halfway up each stem, and a raceme of white or pink flowers. These are attractive plants and some species are grown in gardens.

Prince's Plumes are a group of about six species in the genus *Stanleya*, found in the west and midwest. They have dense, plume-like spikes of flowers, all but one species bright yellow in color. **Golden Prince's Plume**, *S. pinnata* (p. 62), is a perennial, almost shrubby, blue-green plant, with branched leafy stems up to 5ft tall. Its leaves are pinnately lobed or divided with lance-shaped segments. The flowers are rather different to those of most cruciferous plants: the yellow sepals enclose the buds but become bent backward as the flowers open, and the four petals have a distinct brownish base, densely hairy on the inside, and spreading, yellow linear blades. The stamens are long and project out of the flower. The pods are very slender.

Jewel Flowers are a group of about 25 species in the genus *Streptanthus*, found in dry, often rocky places in the southwestern U.S. Their flowers grow in racemes or cymes, and have flask-shaped calyces formed from sepals which are often brightly colored and larger than the petals. The petals are narrow and often crisped or channelled. **Mountain Jewel Flower**, *S. tortuosus*, has erect stems up to 3ft tall, with heart-shaped leaves clasping the stems, and a terminal raceme of flowers which vary in color from cream or yellow to dark purple. The sepals are almost always purple and it is the petals which vary. The pods are long and slender, curved and spreading. This is a very variable plant which grows in dry, rocky places in the Sierra Nevada and Coast Ranges in southern Oregon and California.

Stonecrop family

Crassulaceae

There are about 35 genera and 1500 species of herbs and small shrubs in this family, mostly found in dry, warm temperate regions of the world, many in South America. Some of the stonecrops, *Sedum* species, and houseleeks, *Sempervivum* species, are grown in rock gardens; *Crassula* and *Kalanchoe* species are grown as house plants.

Family Features Members of this family are almost all adapted to life in arid conditions, and many are succulent. They often form dense leaf rosettes with fleshy stems, all with a waxy covering to cut down water loss. The leaves are opposite or alternate, and lack stipules. The flowers are frequently star-like and borne in cymes, often densely packed together. They are regular and hermaphrodite, with four or five sepals and petals, either free or united. They may have as many stamens as petals, the stamens alternating with the petals, or twice as many stamens as petals. The flowers have a superior ovary with as many carpels as petals; the carpels may be free or united at the base. The fruits are follicles or capsules.

The **Stonecrops** are a large group of about 600 species belonging to the genus *Sedum*, found, with one or two exceptions, in the northern hemisphere. About 40 grow wild in North America; many are native species but some are aliens from Europe. These are all succulent plants, small annual or perennial herbs or subshrubs, with fleshy leaves.

Mountain Jewel Flower
Streptanthus tortuosus

Lanceleaf Stonecrop
Sedum lanceolatum

Roseroot
Sedum rosea

Powdery Dudleya
Dudleya farinosa

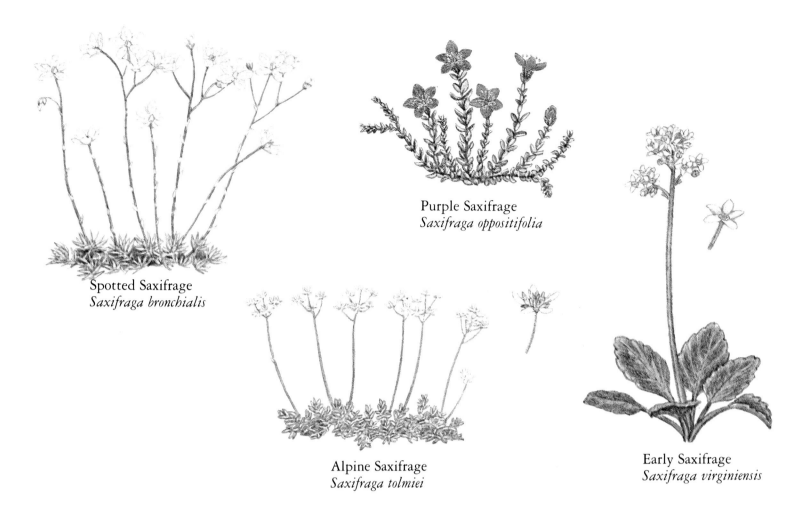

Spotted Saxifrage
Saxifraga bronchialis

Purple Saxifrage
Saxifraga oppositifolia

Alpine Saxifrage
Saxifraga tolmiei

Early Saxifrage
Saxifraga virginiensis

Many are small, mat-like plants with prostrate stems and leaves in rosettes, the leaves all held close together or overlapping to reduce water loss. The plants often grow in the poorest of soils, on dry, stony ground, or clinging to rocks; in periods of drought their fleshy leaves become more and more puckered as they lose water, but they recover almost miraculously after rain. Several are found in the western cordillera. **Lanceleaf Stonecrop**, *Sedum lanceolatum* (p. 63), has rosettes of fleshy, linear leaves and erect stems up to 8in tall, bearing terminal clusters of yellow flowers in summer. Sierra Sedum, *S. obtusatum*, has fleshy, spoon-shaped leaves, often red-tinged and held in cupped rosettes; the yellow flowers grow on stems adorned with reddish leaves.

Other stonecrops are larger plants, with more or less erect leafy stems. The **Roseroot**, *Sedum rosea* (p. 63), is a desirable garden species, but is also found wild all around the North Pole. This is an alpine and mountain plant, growing on cliffs and ledges across northern Canada, south in the Sierra Nevada in the west, and to Maine in the east, especially near the sea. It is a perennial, with a thick, scaly rhizome, and several fleshy stems up to 1ft tall, with many stalkless, flat and broadly lance-shaped leaves often crowded along the stems. The flowers appear in early summer, forming a terminal cluster to crown the stems. The star-like flowers vary in color; European and eastern plants tend to have yellow-green flowers, while plants in the western mountains have maroon or purple ones.

The **Live-forevers**, *Dudleya* species, have rosettes of fleshy, often flattened leaves, and the flowering stems grow from the sides of these rosettes, not from the tips like those of sedums. There are about 40 species of *Dudleya*, all found in the southwest, but hybridizing freely so that it is difficult to determine species accurately. **Powdery Dudleya**, *D. farinosa* (p. 63), forms a cluster of rosettes of fleshy, pointed-ovate leaves, all dusted with powdery meal. In summer it produces erect, 1-ft tall, leafy stems ending in flat, terminal clusters of lemon yellow flowers. It grows on coastal cliffs in California and Oregon. Canyon Dudleya, *D. cymosa*, is a similar species from the Sierra Nevada and Coast Ranges, but it has yellow or red flowers borne in arching cymes. Chalk Dudleya, *D. pulverulenta*, is a huge species, with powdered rosettes 2ft across. It has dark red flowers borne on stout, leafy, 2-ft tall flowering stems in early summer. It is found near the coast of California and in Baja California.

Saxifrage family

Saxifragaceae

This family has about 30 genera and 580 species of herbs, mainly from the temperate regions of the northern hemis-

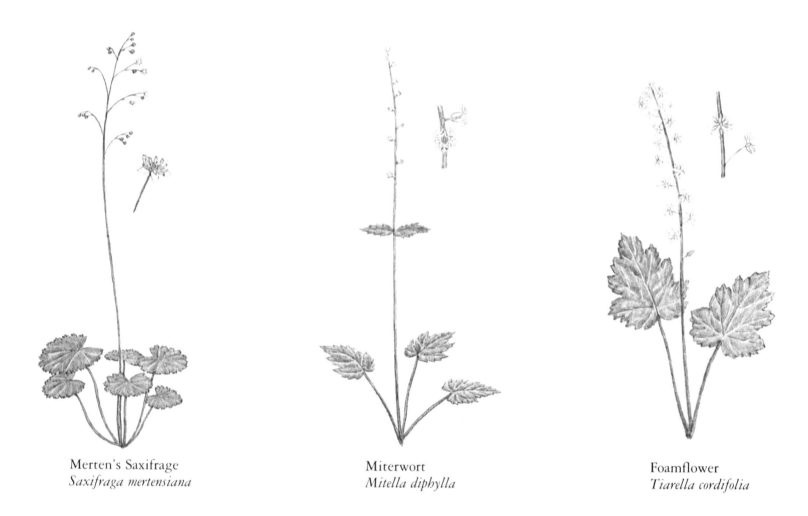

Merten's Saxifrage
Saxifraga mertensiana

Miterwort
Mitella diphylla

Foamflower
Tiarella cordifolia

phere, and is well represented in North America. Many family members are beautiful plants. Saxifrages, *Saxifraga* species, are sought after plants for the rock garden; some are grown in woodland gardens and borders along with other choice members of the family, like Elephant's Ears, *Bergenia* species, and Astilbes *Astilbe* species.

Family features The flowers are usually regular and hermaphrodite, with five sepals, and five petals alternating with the sepals; in some species petals are absent. There are 5–10 stamens, and 1–3 carpels (usually two) in the ovary, often joined together at the base but with free styles and stigmas. The flowers are usually described as perigynous, that is with a flat ring around the ovary on which the stamens, petals, and sepals are inserted. The whole of this ring may glisten with nectar. The fruits are capsules. The leaves are alternate and lack stipules.

The **Saxifrages**, belonging to the genus *Saxifraga*, are by far the largest group in the family, with over 300 species. Most people associate them with cracks and crevices in the high mountains, but they also grow at lower altitudes in mountain woods and meadows.

Spotted Saxifrage, *Saxifraga bronchialis* (p. 64), is a northwestern and Rocky Mountain species, growing among rocks at sea level in the far northwest, and in mountains further south. It is like many alpine saxifrages in form, with rosettes of

spine-tipped, rigid, entire leaves forming moss-like mats; each rosette is less than half an inch across (in some saxifrages they are even smaller). In summer leafless flowering stalks grow from some of the rosettes, bearing purple-spotted, white, star-like flowers; these rosettes die after flowering but others survive and the plant spreads slowly by forming new rosettes each year.

Purple Saxifrage, *Saxifraga oppositifolia* (p. 64), forms loose mats or tufts of stems with opposite fleshy leaves, so close together at the stem tips that they look like rosettes. This is a very small plant, growing at most 3–4in high, and often just creeping over the surface of the ground; its solitary purple flowers look disproportionately large since they measure half an inch across. They are borne at the tips of the stems in late summer. Purple Saxifrage grows in limestone soils, among rock debris, and on slopes in the high mountains of the Arctic around the northern hemisphere, south into Wyoming in the U.S. It can be grown in rock gardens but needs special care.

Alpine Saxifrage, *Saxifraga tolmiei* (p. 64), is another mountain species, with mats of tiny, rounded leaves. It produces white flowers on red stems in late summer. This plant grows in moist places and meadows in the Coast Ranges and Sierra Nevada from California to Alaska.

Early Saxifrage, *Saxifraga virginiensis* (p. 64), is a much bigger plant with toothed, ovate leaves measuring 3in long and growing in basal clumps. Its white flowers appear in spring on leafless flower stalks up to 15in tall, the inflorescences at first dense but becoming looser as the flowers open. It grows in thin woodland, on hillsides, and among rocks from New Brunswick to Manitoba, and south to Georgia and Oklahoma. **Merten's Saxifrage**, *S. mertensiana* (p. 65), is a similar plant from the west. It has a basal clump of large, lobed leaves with hairy leaf stalks, and erect stems with many white flowers in spring and summer. This saxifrage grows in wet, rocky places in coniferous woods along the Coast Ranges and Sierra Nevada, from California to Alaska.

Among the many woodland plants belonging to the family is the **Miterwort** or Bishop's Cap, *Mitella diphylla* (p. 65). It forms spreading clumps of long-stalked basal leaves, shallowly lobed and rather hairy. In early summer the slender, erect flowering stems develop, reaching a height of about 15in; each has a pair of three-lobed, stalkless leaves about halfway up and an elongated cluster of white flowers with elaborately fringed petals. The flowers are followed by capsules shaped like bishops' hats or miters. Plants may be found in rich woods from Quebec to Minnesota, south to Georgia and Missouri, in uplands in the south. A related smaller species, *M. nuda*, has yellow-green flowers and has no leaves on the flowering stems. It grows in bogs and wet woods, usually in moss. Other species grow in the west.

Foamflower, *Tiarella cordifolia* (p. 65), is another plant of rich woods, and is also grown in gardens. It is native from Nova Scotia to Ontario, and south to Georgia and Alabama. It makes spreading colonies of basal leaves, growing from underground rhizomes which creep about underground. The leaves are lobed and toothed, and rather hairy. In late spring and early summer its many flowering stems bear flowers with white petals and white protruding stamens resembling the foam of its name.

Coral Bells, *Heuchera sanguinea*, is a plant that many people grow in their gardens for its attractive leaves and wiry stems with small, but bright pink flowers in early summer. The species is native to the mountains of Arizona and Mexico. There are nearly 40 *Heuchera* species growing wild in North America, most with much less brightly colored flowers than Coral Bells, and some plain dull. Their petals are small, and the sepals form the most conspicuous part of the flower, being fused to form bell-shaped or urn-shaped flowers, sometimes green, sometimes colored.

One of the most common and widespread is the **Alumroot**, *Heuchera americana* (p. 66), another plant grown in gardens, but more for its handsome leaves than for its greenish flowers. It forms clumps of lobed, rather maple-like, somewhat floppy, long-stalked leaves, those of garden varieties often flushed with red or brown. It flowers in spring or early summer,

Alumroot
Heuchera americana

Jack-o'-the-rocks
Heuchera rubescens

Poker Heuchera
Heuchera cylindrica

Coast Boykinia
Boykinia elata

sending up slender stalks with many drooping, bell-shaped, yellow-green flowers, growing in loosely branching clusters. Alumroot grows in dry woods and on shaded slopes from Ontario to Michigan, and south to Georgia and Oklahoma. Midland Alumroot, *H. richardsonii*, is a midwestern species, growing in dry woods and prairies; it is a much hairier plant, with green flowers.

There are several *Heuchera* species in the west, mostly with white or greenish flowers. **Jack-o'-the-rocks**, *H. rubescens* (p. 66), is a mountain plant, growing on rocky slopes in the Sierra Nevada and in the Mojave Desert. It forms clumps of long-stalked, leathery leaves, with leafless inflorescences in early summer. The flowers are white or pale pink, narrowly bell-shaped, with tiny petals emerging from the calyces. **Poker Heuchera**, *H. cylindrica* (p. 66), is rather different. It has dense spikes of creamy flowers topping erect flower stalks which grow well above the leathery, maple-like leaves. It grows on rocky slopes in the Rocky Mountains.

The **Coast Boykinia**, *Boykinia elata* (p. 66), is one of several *Boykinia* species in the west. These are attractive plants, with clumps of handsome, lobed, maple-like leaves on long stalks; the stalks have many brown-tipped hairs on them. In summer the plants produce erect, branched stems, also covered with glandular hairs, and with many white flowers. The flowers have narrow petals. This species grows in wet, shady places,

beside springs, in coastal scrub, coniferous woods, and chaparral in the Coast Ranges and Sierra Nevada from California to Washington. Mountain Boykinia, *B. major*, is a similar species which grows in wet, shady, rocky places in the mountains from California to Washington. Its white flowers have broad, oval petals.

The **Astilbes**, genus *Astilbe*, are well known to many gardeners for the bright splashes of color they bring to damp flower borders in summer. There are a host of varieties in shades of pink and red, as well as white. Most astilbes come from Asia, but one grows wild in North America. This is **False Goatsbeard**, *A. biternata*, its name a reference to its similarity to the Goatsbeard, *Aruncus sylvester*, a member of the Rose family. False Goatsbeard is a plant of moist mountain woods from Virginia to Georgia, and west to Tennessee. It forms a loose clump of stems up to 6ft tall, with large, long-stalked, compound leaves. Each leaf is divided into three sections, each one further subdivided into three toothed leaflets. Individually the flowers are small and may be male or female, or hermaphrodite. The female flowers often lack petals, or have very tiny petals. The flowers are gathered into branched, often drooping, terminal clusters.

The **Prairie Star** or Starflower, *Lithophragma parviflora* (p. 67), is one of about 12 species, perennial plants confined to western and midwestern areas of North America, and known

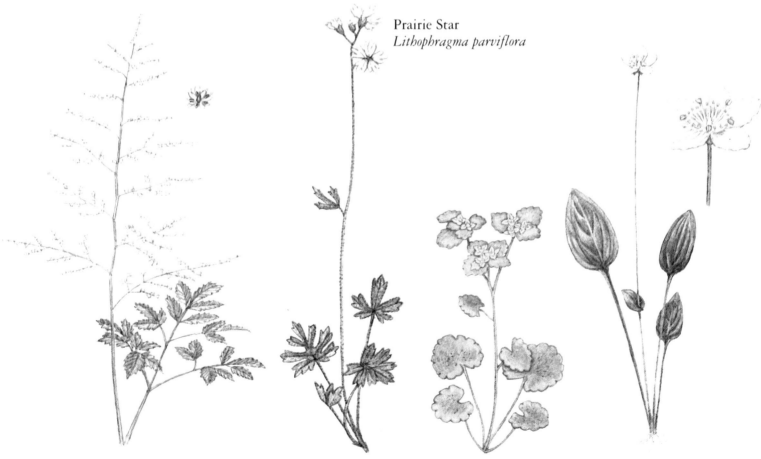

Prairie Star
Lithophragma parviflora

False Goatsbeard
Astilbe biternata

Alternate-leaved Golden Saxifrage
Chrysosplenium alternifolium

Grass of Parnassus
Parnassia glauca

more generally as Woodland Stars. Prairie Star grows on the lower slopes of the Rocky Mountains and on the prairies, on open slopes, in dry woods, and among sagebrush, from British Columbia to Alberta, south to California and Nebraska. Its erect leafless stems bear star-like flowers in early spring at the same time that the leaves are emerging and enlarging; the flowers are distinctive since each white or pinkish petal is cleft into three or five lobes. The leaves are basal and rounded, with three or five lobes, and rather hairy.

Golden Saxifrages are a group of about 55 species in the genus *Chrysosplenium*, found mainly in eastern Asia but with about five species in North America, mostly in Canada or the northern U.S. **Alternate-leaved Golden Saxifrage**, *C. alternifolium* (p. 67), is a circumpolar species, growing in wet and shady places, beside springs and streams across Canada. It has creeping, leafless stems and clumps of long-stalked, rounded leaves. The leaves are thick, with rounded teeth on their margins, and they grow alternately on the flowering stalks, as well as in the basal clumps. The flowers are small and yellow, borne in open clusters at the tops of the stems, and surrounded by greenish-yellow bracts like yellowish leaves. They appear in summer.

Grass of Parnassus is a name given to a group of about 50 *Parnassia* species growing in the northern hemisphere, with about 10 in North America. They grow in wet meadows, beside streams, in bogs and on shores, mostly on calcareous soils. These are perennial plants, with long-stalked leaves forming a basal rosette, and solitary white flowers on erect flowering stalks. There is a single leaf on each stalk. The flowers have five fertile stamens between the petals, and five three-pronged, sterile ones opposite the petals. *Parnassia glauca* (p. 67), is an eastern species with ovate blades on its leaves and heavily veined petals. *P. fimbriata* is a western one, with kidney-shaped leaf blades and fringed petals.

Rose family

Rosaceae

A large and important family in many respects, with about 100 genera and 2000 species found throughout the world, but especially in the temperate regions. Many fruit trees belong to this family, including apple, pear, cherry, peach, and plum. Almond trees provide nuts. Other trees, such as mountain ash, crab apple, serviceberry, and ornamental cherry, are used in gardens, city parks, and streets for ornamental planting. The family is also rich in shrubs: the roses themselves provide a bewildering array of species, hybrids, and varieties, so that there is one to suit any garden; other ornamental shrubs include the many species of *Spiraea*, *Potentilla*, *Cotoneaster*, *Pyracantha*, and *Crataegus*. Herbs for the garden include geums, potentillas, and strawberries.

Goatsbeard
Aruncus dioicus

Queen of the Prairie
Filipendula rubra

Bowman's Root
Gillenia trifoliata

Honeydew
Horkelia cuneata

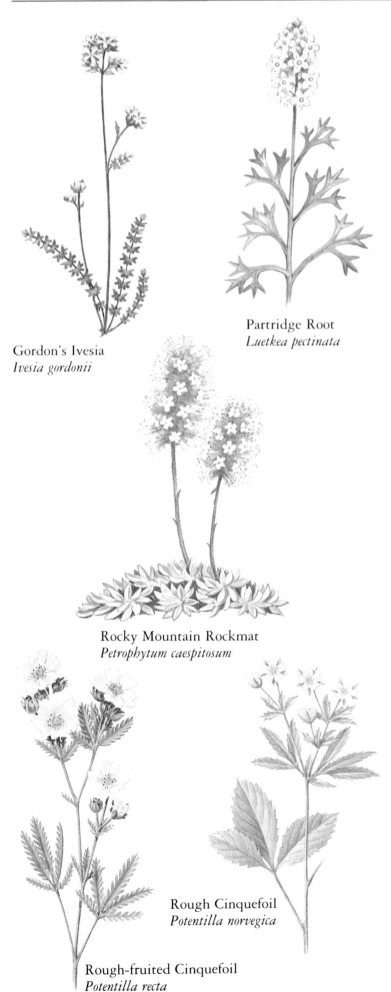

Gordon's Ivesia
Ivesia gordonii

Partridge Root
Luetkea pectinata

Rocky Mountain Rockmat
Petrophytum caespitosum

Rough Cinquefoil
Potentilla norvegica

Rough-fruited Cinquefoil
Potentilla recta

Family features The flowers are regular and hermaphrodite, with five separate, often overlapping sepals, and five separate, often overlapping petals. The flowers have numerous stamens. The ovary is usually superior, with the floral parts in rings around its base, or it is inferior, with the floral parts in rings above it. The ovary has one to many carpels, variously free or united; the styles usually remain free. The fruits are achenes, drupes or pomes. The leaves are simple or compound, usually alternate, frequently with a pair of stipules attached to the leaf stalk.

Goatsbeard, *Aruncus dioicus* (p. 68), is an impressive perennial plant, with several erect leafy stems up to 6ft tall, topped in early to mid-summer with plumes of white fluffy flowers. It has large compound leaves up to 20in long, with long stalks and pointed-oblong, doubly serrated leaflets. The branched, softly spike-like flower plumes have separate male and female flowers, the males with many stamens, and the females with three pistils each. The plant grows in rich woods from Pennsylvania to Iowa, and south to Alabama and Arkansas. It is also grown in flower borders.

Queen of the Prairie, *Filipendula rubra* (p. 68), is grown as an ornamental plant in wet places in gardens, but needs a lot of space. In the wild, plants grow in wet meadows and prairies, and in low-lying woods from Vermont to Minnesota, and south to Kentucky and Georgia, but they are less common in the east and south, and may have escaped from cultivation in these areas. This is a showy species that forms a large clump of leafy, erect stems up to 6ft tall. The leaves are dark green and compound, pinnate in form, with many toothed, deeply lobed leaflets. From midsummer onward, the plants produce terminal sprays of tiny, fluffy pink, sweetly scented flowers. A related European species, *Filipendula ulmaria*, with white flowers, has escaped from gardens in the northeast to grow wild in similar habitats.

Bowman's Root or Indian Physic, *Gillenia trifoliata* (p. 68), is a plant of upland woods in the east, found mostly in the mountains from southern Ontario to Alabama. It is a perennial plant with several branched, leafy stems up to 3ft tall, and palmately compound leaves, each with three leaflets and two narrow stipules. In early summer flowers appear in loose clusters at the tops of the stems; they are white or pale pink with five narrow petals. The related *G. stipulata*, also known as Indian Physic, grows in similar places in the east and midwest, but has much longer and larger stipules, so that the leaves appear to have five leaflets. Both species contain an emetic and have been used in herb medicine.

In the western U.S. and Canada are several Rose family genera found nowhere else in the world. There are, for instance, the 17 *Horkelia* species. **Horkelias** are perennial plants with clumps of pinnate leaves, the upper leaflets joined together. The flowers are usually white, saucer-shaped or cup-shaped, borne in clusters on erect stems separately from the leaves. Each flower has 10 stamens and many carpels arranged on a conical receptacle. **Honeydew**, *H. cuneata* (p. 68), is a Californian species with hairy glandular leaves and saucer-shaped flowers. It grows in sandy fields and woods.

Gordon's Ivesia, *Ivesia gordonii* (p. 69), is one of about 20 *Ivesia* species, also found only in western North America. These are perennial plants which form tufts or clumps of basal pinnate leaves, and dense clusters of yellow, white or purple flowers on separate stalks. Many grow within the broad area covered by the Rocky Mountains and the Great Basin, either at low elevations or in the high mountains. Gordon's Ivesia grows among rocks, on hillsides and ridges well above the timberline. It has a woody base with many crowns, and dense clumps of compound, almost fern-like leaves, the whole plant no more than 8in tall. In the latter half of summer it bears open, yellow flowers in tight heads on almost leafless stalks. Each flower has five sepals and petals, the sepals being longer than the petals, and five stamens.

Partridge Root, *Luetkea pectinata* (p. 69), is another westerner, the only species in its genus. This little plant is found on damp, rocky slopes in the high mountains near and above the timberline, in the Rockies from California to Alaska. It grows 6in tall at most, has woody, creeping stems, and erect stems with fan-shaped, dissected leaves mostly crowded near the base. The effect produced is of dense patches of leaves. The stems also bear flowers in summer: dense terminal spikes of white flowers with yellow anthers.

Rocky Mountain Rockmat, *Petrophytum caespitosum* (p. 69), is one of only three species, all found in the west. It forms dense mats of silky gray leaves on barren limestone rocks and ledges in the high mountains of Oregon and California, east to Montana and Texas. In the latter half of summer erect flowering stalks grow from the mats to bear dense terminal spikes of white flowers with many long stamens. The other two rockmats are both found in Washington state, one in the Coast Range and the other in the Olympic Mountains.

The **Cinquefoils**, members of the genus *Potentilla*, are a large group of over 300 species found in the temperate regions of the northern hemisphere. There are over 70 species in North America. They are mostly small, perennial plants, with a few shrubby species and a few annuals. Their flowers have five petals, cupped not only in a calyx of green sepals, but also in an epicalyx; this looks like a second set of sepals beneath the true sepals. Most have yellow flowers, although a few have white or dark red petals. Their fruits are clusters of dry achenes, often partly enclosed by the persistent calyx.

They are often confused with buttercups, and do have a strong superficial resemblance to those plants, with their yellow, five-petalled flowers and their dark green leaves. But buttercups have simple or divided leaves, not compound ones

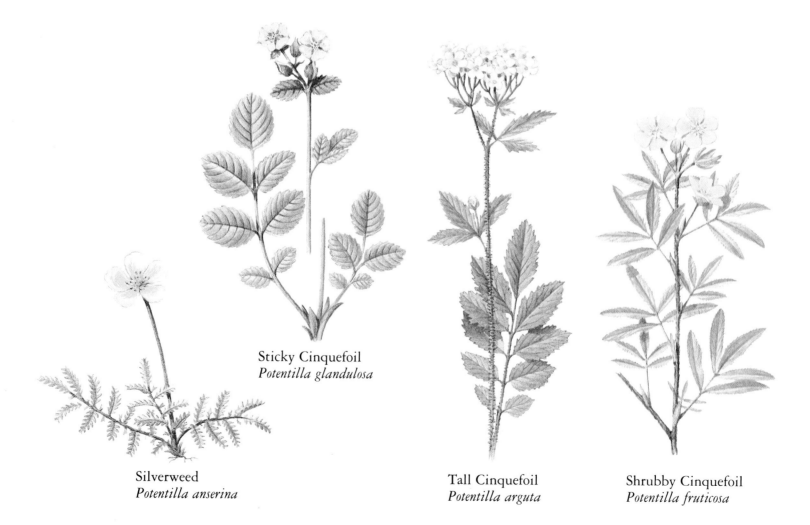

Sticky Cinquefoil
Potentilla glandulosa

Silverweed
Potentilla anserina

Tall Cinquefoil
Potentilla arguta

Shrubby Cinquefoil
Potentilla fruticosa

Wild Strawberry
Fragaria virginiana

Barren Strawberry
Waldsteinia fragarioides

Prairie Smoke
Geum triflorum

Water Avens
Geum rivale

with separate leaflets; buttercups lack stipules, whereas all members of the Rose family have conspicuous stipules; buttercups do not have an epicalyx; and buttercups have a superior ovary, like all members of that family, while cinquefoils have an inferior one. These last two factors give the flowers of buttercups and cinquefoils quite a different appearance on close inspection, so that they become easy to distinguish from one another with a little practice.

Rough-fruited Cinquefoil, *Potentilla recta* (p. 69), has leaves typical of the Five-finger Cinquefoils; there are several species of these, all with leaves that are long-stalked and palmately compound, with several toothed leaflets (often five, hence cinquefoil and five-finger). This one is an alien from Europe, growing in waste ground, on roadsides, and in fields from Nova Scotia to Ontario, south throughout much of the eastern U.S., and west into the prairies of Nebraska and Kansas. It does not have a natural range since it has been introduced, but is spreading rapidly. It is a hairy plant, with flowering stems up to 2ft tall, and large, pale yellow flowers; several varieties of it are grown in gardens. Common Cinquefoil, *P. simplex* and the dwarfer Canadian Cinquefoil, *P. canadensis*, are similar eastern and midwestern species that grow in dry woods and fields.

Rough Cinquefoil, *Potentilla norvegica* (p. 69), is a short-lived plant, almost an annual. It forms 3-ft tall clumps

of stout, branched stems with compound leaves, and is the only cinquefoil species to have leaves with three leaflets. In summer the plant bears many yellow flowers in branched clusters ending the stems. It is a circumboreal species, and is found through much of Canada and the U.S. It grows in a variety of habitats: woods and clearings, in waste places and yards, usually in moist conditions.

Silverweed, *Potentilla anserina* (p. 70), is a lover of damp places, growing in moist meadows, on wet banks and roadsides, and on wet, sandy shores. This plant, like several other cinquefoils, is circumboreal, found right across the northern hemisphere. And like many other cinquefoils, it has leaves that are pinnately compound. In the leaves of this plant, pairs of small, toothed leaflets alternate with pairs of larger ones. It is a hairy, creeping plant with stems that root at the nodes, and leaves that are silvery-hairy beneath. The flowers are the usual cinquefoil ones, with yellow petals. A similar species, Pacific Silverweed, *P. egedei*, is found along the coastal strand of the Pacific.

The roots of Silverweed have a flavor reminiscent of parsnips, but as they are very small, they are often not worth the effort of cooking. However, they can be ground into meal.

Sticky Cinquefoil, *Potentilla glandulosa* (p. 70), is a western species, growing in open places from British Columbia to California, and at lower elevations through the mountains to

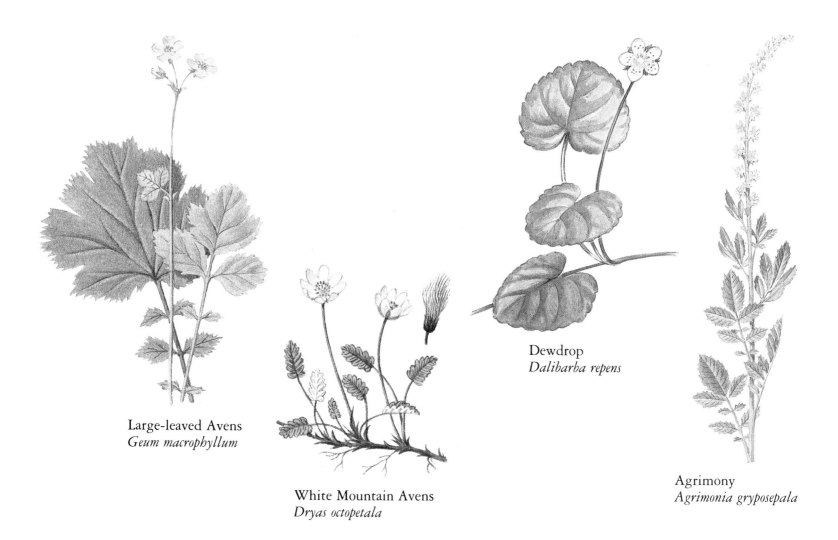

Large-leaved Avens
Geum macrophyllum

White Mountain Avens
Dryas octopetala

Dewdrop
Dalibarba repens

Agrimony
Agrimonia gryposepala

Montana and Arizona. It is well-named, for it has a sticky texture to it, a result of the many glands that cover its stems, and to a lesser extent its leaves. It is a perennial plant, forming a clump of basal pinnate leaves, each with 5–9 toothed leaflets, and several erect, reddish, leafy flowering stems. The flowers vary from creamy white to pale yellow; they are borne in loose terminal clusters.

Tall Cinquefoil, *Potentilla arguta* (p. 70), has white flowers. It is a perennial plant, growing on prairies and in dry woods from Quebec to Alberta and into the Northwest Territory, south to the District of Columbia in the east, and to Arizona in the west. The plant forms a clump of pinnate leaves, rather like those of Silverweed in shape, but with only 7–11 leaflets, covered in sticky brown hairs like the whole plant. It has stout, erect flowering stems up to 3ft tall, topped with dense clusters of typical potentilla-shaped flowers, but white in color.

Shrubby Cinquefoil, *Potentilla fruticosa* (p. 70), has typical cinquefoil flowers, but is a shrub growing about 3ft tall. It has much- branched, woody stems clothed with small, compound leaves. These have 5–7 narrow leaflets, the three terminal ones often joined together. Plants may be found in wet meadows and thickets, in bogs and on shores all around the North Pole, through Canada and Alaska and into the northern U.S., south in the Rockies to Arizona.

Wild Strawberries are smaller, but sweeter and tastier than cultivated varieties. There are two widespread species in North America, the native *Fragaria virginiana* (p. 71), and the introduced European Wild Strawberry, *F. vesca*. They are both perennial plants with small clumps of compound leaves, each leaf with three toothed leaflets. The plants produce runners— long stems which grow out around the mother plant; these root at the nodes and then grow on, so that spreading mats of plants develop. The flowers, and then fruits, grow in small clusters on leafless stalks directly from the base of the clump. The flowers are white with five separate, round petals alternating with the sepals. In the center of the flower are many pistils inserted on a conical receptacle, which enlarges to produce the fruit—not a real fruit at all, but a false fruit since it forms from the receptacle rather than the ovary. The real fruits are the "seeds."

Barren Strawberry, *Waldsteinia fragarioides* (p. 71), grows in woods from Maine to Minnesota, north into Quebec and south to North Carolina, in mountains in the southern parts of its range. It resembles true strawberries in its three-leaflet leaves, but has no runners and its flowers are yellow. Its fruits are dry achenes.

There are about 40 *Geum* species in the northern hemisphere, known collectively as **Avens**. One of the most eye-catching is **Prairie Smoke**, *G. triflorum* (p. 71), not when

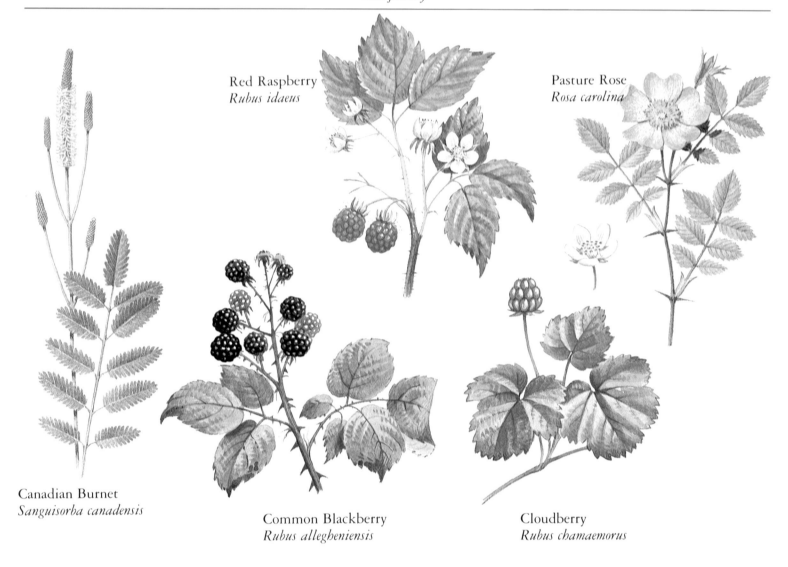

Red Raspberry
Rubus idaeus

Pasture Rose
Rosa carolina

Canadian Burnet
Sanguisorba canadensis

Common Blackberry
Rubus allegheniensis

Cloudberry
Rubus chamaemorus

in flower but when in fruit. This plant grows in dry, open prairies and woods, across southern Canada and the northern U.S., most commonly in the prairies and more locally in the east, south in the Rocky Mountains to California. It is a hairy perennial, with a clump of pinnate, compound leaves, in which small leaflets alternate with larger ones, the whole leaf becoming broader from base to tip. It produces several flowering stems with terminal clusters of nodding, urn-shaped flowers; stalks, sepals, and petals are all usually reddish, although in some plants the petals may be yellow. The center of each flower contains many ovaries with long styles; as the fruits develop, the styles become enormously elongated and feathery, the whole effect being of a purple "feather duster." The name of Prairie Smoke is well earned, but the plant is also called Old Man's Whiskers and Purple Avens.

Water Avens, *Geum rivale* (p. 71), is another mainly northern plant, found from Newfoundland to Alberta, south to Pennsylvania and Indiana in the east, and to New Mexico in the west. It grows in wet meadows and marshes, bogs and swamps, forming a clump of compound, pinnate leaves, each one with a very broad terminal leaflet. The flowers are borne on leafy flowering stems in loose, terminal clusters; they are nodding, with purplish sepals and paler yellowish petals suffused with purple. The center of each flower, like those of all avens, contains many ovaries which enlarge into numerous

achenes. In Water Avens the styles are hooked in fruit, and the fruit forms a burr which can become lodged in the fur of mammals and distributed. The fruits break up when caught in clothing, so each has to be removed individually, a tedious process but an effective dispersal mechanism!

Several *Geum* species have yellow flowers, rather like smaller versions of cinquefoil flowers. **Large-leaved Avens**, *G. macrophyllum* (p. 72), is one of these. It has a clump of hairy, compound leaves with many small leaflets and one large terminal leaflet. The flowers grow on separate stalks adorned with smaller leaves and terminal clusters of the small yellow flowers. This plant grows in woods across Canada and Alaska, south to Maine, Minnesota, and California. Similar species include Yellow Avens, *G. aleppicum*, found in wet meadows across Canada, and Rough Avens, *G. virginianum*, found in upland woods in the east.

White Mountain Avens is not a *Geum* species at all, but is *Dryas octopetala* (p. 72). This little northern and mountain plant grows in rocky places from Alaska to Labrador, south in the western mountains to Colorado. It has prostrate, semi-woody stems, and many dark green, leathery leaves, like miniature White Oak leaves, but with a pale underside. The white flowers grow singly on erect stalks in early summer, and are followed by plumed achenes with white feathery styles. The plant is attractive at all times of year, in flower and in fruit, and even in winter, for it is evergreen. It can be grown in rock gardens but is a true rock plant, only happy when draping its trailing stems over rocks or walls.

Dewdrop or False Violet, *Dalibarba repens* (p. 72), is a creeping plant found in moist woods and swamps from Nova Scotia to Minnesota, south to New Jersey and Ohio. It has prostrate stems and rounded leaves on long stalks, like those of violets. Solitary white flowers are borne on separate reddish stems in the latter part of summer. They are usually sterile, and the plant produces seeds from petal-less flowers borne on recurved stalks.

Agrimony is a name given to a group of 15 similar species, found throughout the northern hemisphere and in South America. One of the most widespread species in North America is *Agrimonia gryposepala* (p. 72). It grows in open woods, on woodland edges, and in disturbed areas from Nova Scotia to Ontario, south to the Carolinas and Tennessee, in mountains in the southern part of its range. It is also found in California and New Mexico. It forms an erect, leafy stem, with dark green, compound leaves in which large leaflets are interspersed with small ones; the leaflets have toothed margins. Terminating the stems and growing from the axils of the upper leaves are sparse spikes of small yellow flowers produced in the latter half of summer. The fruits form gradually, the lower ones maturing, while further up the flowering spike new flowers are still opening. The fruits are quite distinctive—top-shaped with several rows of hooked bristles on the top surface, an aid to dispersal since they become entangled in the hair of passing animals.

Canadian Burnet, *Sanguisorba canadensis* (p. 73), is a wetland plant, growing in swamps and bogs, marshes, wet meadows, and prairies from Newfoundland to Manitoba, and south to Delaware and Indiana; it is also found in the mountains south to Georgia. It is a perennial plant, forming a handsome clump of compound leaves, each with 7–15 toothed leaflets. The stems branch to bear white, poker-like spikes of fluffy white flowers; each flower has four spreading, white, petal-like sepals and four long stamens. The flowers lack petals. This plant is grown in gardens, where it is often known under its old name of *Poterium canadense.*

Bramble is a name given to many of the seemingly innumerable *Rubus* species, a group found mainly in the north temperate regions of the northern hemisphere. The present count is thought to be about 250 species, but new ones are described every year and the naming problem is complicated by hybridization and apomixis (the production of seeds without pollination). The group includes brambles and blackberries, raspberries, black raspberries, dewberries, wineberries, thimbleberries, and cloudberries.

Many of the *Rubus* species follow a distinctive growth pattern. They are shrubby, perennial plants that nevertheless have a biennial pattern of growth. Each year new shoots grow from the perennial base of the plant; these first-year shoots remain unbranched, have compound leaves, and do not flower. In the second year the shoots produce side shoots with smaller, often simpler leaves, then flowers and fruits. The whole shoot dies after fruiting.

Common Blackberry, *Rubus allegheniensis* (p. 73), follows this growth pattern, its more or less erect shoots growing to about 9ft tall. Like many other blackberries, this is a prickly plant; its shoots bear many straight prickles and the leaves bear hooked ones. The white flowers appear around midsummer, and are followed by typical blackberries—sweet and juicy, glossy black fruits made up of many single-seeded sections. It is found on roadsides, in thickets and woodland margins, on old fences and in fields from Nova Scotia to Minnesota, and south in the mountains to North Carolina. Other blackberries grow in other parts of North America.

The **Red Raspberry**, *Rubus idaeus* (p. 73), is found across Canada from Newfoundland to Alaska, south in the U.S. to Pennsylvania, Indiana, and Arizona. It also grows across Europe and Asia. It can be found on roadsides and woodland edges, in clearings and old fields. Its first-year shoots grow up to 6ft tall, and are densely armed with slender prickles and stiff bristles. Around midsummer the second-year shoots produce side shoots with clusters of white flowers, followed by globular red raspberries. Black Raspberry, *R. occidentalis*, has black fruits, less glossy than blackberries, and more like raspberries in appearance. This plant grows in disturbed areas and woods in the northeast and upper midwest.

Cloudberry, *Rubus chamaemorus* (p. 73), is a rather different plant—a creeping herbaceous plant that grows in *Sphagnum* bogs and on wet mountain slopes all around the North Pole, across Canada, extending south in the east to Maine and New Hampshire but not in the west. It has erect stems with long-stalked, shallowly lobed leaves, and no prickles. Its solitary white flowers appear around midsummer, the male and female flowers on separate plants. They are followed by edible orange fruits. These are considered a great delicacy in northern Europe, especially as their season is short and they are difficult to gather.

There are many species of **Roses** in North America, and the Cherokee Rose, *Rosa laevigata*, is the state flower of Georgia. The **Pasture Rose**, *R. carolina* (p. 73), is one of the smaller species, rarely more than 3ft tall. It is found in prairies and pastures, in dry woods, fields, and rocky areas, from Maine to Minnesota, and south to Florida and Texas. It forms slender arching branches armed with the stiff hairs and curved or straight prickles that are characteristic of so many roses. It has compound leaves, each with 3–7 oval leaflets, and loses its leaves in winter. The solitary pink flowers grow on the current year's stems in spring or early summer; each flower has five petals and numerous stamens. The hips which follow are red and globular, and edible.

The fruits of roses are hips; they are formed from the inferior ovary, which swells up and becomes fleshy and brightly colored. The dried remains of the sepals can be seen on the top of each hip. Hips are rich in Vitamin C and minerals, and the flesh can be eaten raw, or made into syrups or wine once the central seeds and hairs have been removed. These hairs are used by children as itching powder.

Midwestern prairies in early summer, with Prairie Smoke (*Geum triflorum*) in the foreground.

Pea and Bean family

Leguminosae

This is the third largest family of flowering plants in the world, with about 600 genera and 12,000 species. It has a bewildering variety of plants, including herbs, shrubs, trees, climbers, water and desert plants, many economically important crops and timber plants, ornamental garden plants, poisonous species, and weeds.

Important crop plants in this family include peas and beans, peanuts, soybeans, lentils, licorice, and alfalfa. Timber derives from tropical trees like the Acacias and the Ironwood from India. Gum arabic comes from *Acacia senegal*, senna comes from several species of *Cassia*, the insecticide derris comes from species of *Derris* from India and Malaya, and other plants yield dyes, bark for tanning leather, fibers, and resins. Among the many decorative garden plants are the Tree of Heaven, redbuds, and laburnums, mimosas, sweet peas, and wisterias, brooms and lupines.

There are three subfamilies in the Leguminosae: the Mimosoideae, the Caesalpinoideae, and the Papilionoideae. Sometimes these are given family status and are then called the Mimosaceae (Mimosa family), the Caesalpiniaceae (Senna family), and the Papilionaceae or Fabaceae (Bean family).

Most members of the **Senna subfamily**, the Caesalpinioideae, are tropical trees or shrubs; few are herbs. Most have pinnate or twice pinnate leaves, and showy flowers in racemes. The flowers have five sepals, five overlapping petals—the upper one (the standard) inside the others—and five or 10 stamens. The ovary is superior with one cell. The fruits are legumes (pods) and often winged.

There are about 35 **Senna** species in North America; some are herbs, others shrubs, usually with yellow flowers. In many the petals are unequal. Two similar species are both known as **Wild Senna**, *Cassia hebecarpa*, and *C. marilandica*. They are perennial plants about 6ft tall, with large pinnate leaves and racemes of yellow flowers in the leaf axils. The pods of the first species are densely hairy; those of the latter almost hairless. The first is a more northern plant, growing in moist woods and along roadsides from Massachusetts to Michigan and south to North Carolina, much rarer in the south. The latter species grows in similar habitats from Pennsylvania to Florida and Texas. *Cassia marilandica* can be used in herb medicine as a laxative. Commercial senna is obtained from Alexandrian Senna, *C. acutifolia*, which comes from the Middle East.

Hog Potato, *Hoffmannseggia glauca*, grows in patches, forming erect stems about 1ft tall from creeping rhizomes. The rhizomes bear edible tubers. The plant has blue-green, twice pinnate leaves, mostly growing from the base of the

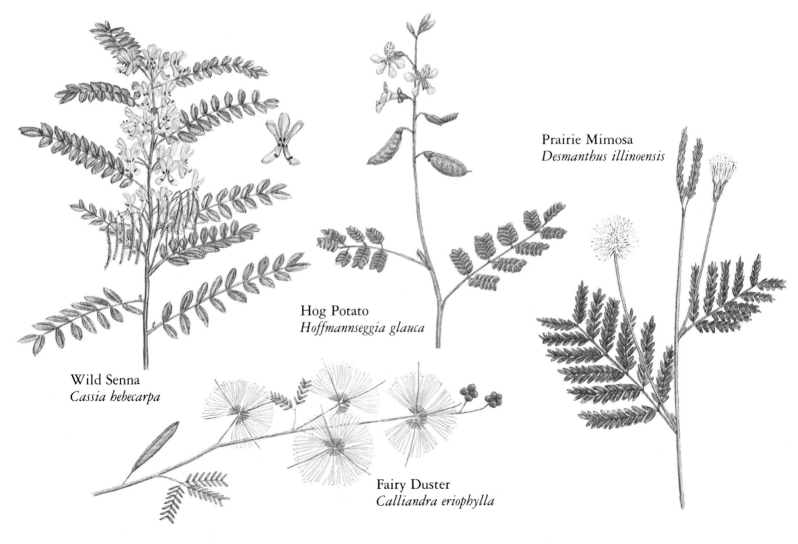

Wild Senna
Cassia hebecarpa

Hog Potato
Hoffmannseggia glauca

Prairie Mimosa
Desmanthus illinoensis

Fairy Duster
Calliandra eriophylla

stems, and long, leafless flower stalks with racemes of yellow-orange flowers. The flowers have five unequal petals and are followed by flattened, curved pods. These plants grow in alkaline soils, in open areas, along roadsides and railroads, from southern California to Texas, south into Mexico, and north to Colorado.

Most members of the **Mimosa subfamily**, the Mimosoideae, are tropical or subtropical trees and shrubs, many found in arid regions. Most have twice pinnate leaves, and their flowers are small and regular, borne in racemes or heads. Each flower has a tubular calyx of five fused sepals—five petals which are either free but not overlapping, or united at the base into a short tube. Each has as many stamens as sepals, or numerous long stamens, and a superior ovary with one cell. The fruit is a legume.

Mesquite, *Prosopis glandulosa*, belongs to this subfamily. This is a common tree or shrub of western rangeland and deserts; it has spreading branches with many feather-like leaves and sharp spines. In summer it produces long edible pods and seeds which can be ground into meal.

Fairy Duster, *Calliandra eriophylla* (p. 76), is a dense, low-growing shrub with many gray branches. It grows only about 1ft high. The leaves are pinnate, with 5–10 pairs of oblong leaflets, but it is the flowers which catch the attention. The pink balls, made up of tiny reddish petals and long pink stamens, are scattered along the twigs. This attractive shrub may be found in sandy washes and gullies, in dry grassland and Creosote Bush scrub below 1000ft from California to Texas, and south into Mexico.

Prairie Mimosa, *Desmanthus illinoensis* (p. 76), is one of the few herbaceous mimosas. It has an erect stem, usually 2–4ft tall, and almost hidden by the twice pinnate leaves; these are sensitive to light and touch, folding up when touched or in strong sunlight. The flowers grow on long stalks from the upper leaf axils; they form small, fuzzy balls made up of many flowers with tiny petals and long stamens. The pods which follow are curved and flattened, leathery in texture, and borne in clusters of about 20 together. This is an important, protein-rich food plant for livestock on rangeland. It may be found on plains and prairies, more commonly on moist soils and on river banks, from Ohio to North Dakota and Colorado, south to Florida and New Mexico.

Sensitive Briar, *Schrankia nuttallii*, is a trailing plant, with branched, ribbed stems armed with many hooked prickles. It has sensitive, 6-in long, twice pinnate leaves, with prickly stalks and bright pink flower balls made up mostly of the long stamens; the balls grow on long stalks in the axils of the leaves throughout the summer. The pods are narrow and four-angled with many prickles; they split open along the four margins. This is one of several *Schrankia* species, all known as Sensitive

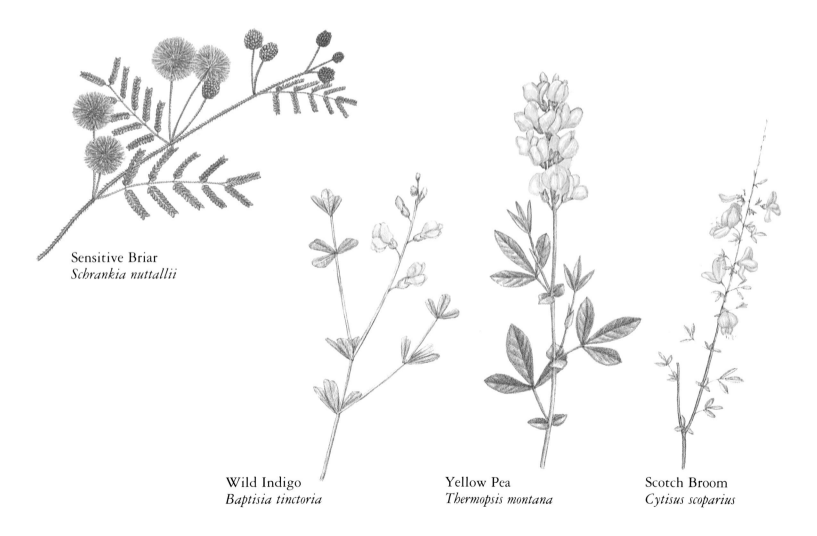

Sensitive Briar
Schrankia nuttallii

Wild Indigo
Baptisia tinctoria

Yellow Pea
Thermopsis montana

Scotch Broom
Cytisus scoparius

Showy Rattlebox
Crotalaria spectabilis

Blue-pod Lupine
Lupinus polyphyllus

Silvery Lupine
Lupinus argenteus

Miniature Lupine
Lupinus bicolor

Briars; they grow in dry, sandy places and prairies, in the east and across the prairie states.

The **Bean subfamily**, the Papilionoideae is by far the biggest subfamily of the Leguminosae in the temperate regions of the world. It is this group that has the flowers, considered typical of the Pea and Bean family, with five unequal petals: one standard petal at the back, one wing petal each side of the standard, and two lower petals often joined together and forming the keel which encloses the stamens and ovary. There are 10 stamens, which may all be free, or more often, nine are fused and one is free. The ovary is superior and enlarges to form the characteristic fruit of the family—the legume, a pod which splits open along one or both seams to release the seeds. The flowers have five sepals fused into a five-toothed tube. The leaves may be simple or compound, the latter often having leaflets modified as tendrils. Stipules are present and may be large and leaf-like, small, or modified to form spines.

Most plants need a supply of nitrogen which they use in the synthesis of proteins; since they cannot obtain nitrogen from the air, they absorb it as soluble nitrates from the soil and are dependent on soil bacteria to fix nitrogen from the air into nitrates. Artificial fertilizers are a substitute for this process. However, members of the Papilionoideae have special nodules on their roots which contain nitrogen-fixing bacteria, and the nitrates are thus directly available to the plants. Leguminous

plants are often planted in poor soils and then dug in as a natural way to enrich the soil. In the same way, wild plants enrich the soil where they are growing.

Wild Indigo, *Baptisia tinctoria* (p. 77), is one of several *Baptisia* species that grow mainly in the east and midwest. It is called Wild Indigo because a dye can be extracted from it that is a poor substitute for true indigo, which comes from a leguminous Asian plant, *Indigofera tinctoria*. As well as providing the dye, an infusion of Wild Indigo can be used as a gargle and antiseptic for use on cuts and wounds, but is poisonous if taken internally. It is a smooth, bushy, perennial plant about 3ft tall, growing from a woody rhizome. It has many palmately compound, clover-like leaves, each with three ovate, rounded leaflets and bristle-like stipules. The plant bears loose clusters of bright yellow, pea-like flowers terminating most of the branches in midsummer. These are followed by short, round pods. Wild Indigo grows in dry or sandy soils, in open woods or burned fields from southern Ontario to Michigan, and south to Florida and Tennessee.

Yellow Pea or False Lupine, *Thermopsis montana* (p. 77), is a perennial plant with several hollow stems 3–4ft tall, and clover-like leaves with broad stipules at the base of the stalks. The flowers are yellow and pea-like, borne in racemes in the axils of the leaves. They are followed by slender, hairy pods. This plant grows in meadows and grassy clearings in coniferous woodland on lower mountain slopes from British Columbia to California, east to Montana and Colorado. Other species are found on the prairies and in the east.

Scotch Broom, *Cytisus scoparius* (p. 77), is a European plant that was introduced into North America as a garden plant. It now grows wild in dry, sandy soils from Nova Scotia to Virginia in the east, and on the Pacific coast. This is a shrub, with branched, green, flexible stems and small, three-leaflet leaves. In early summer its green stems are transformed by the many yellow, pea-like flowers that open in the leaf axils. They are followed by black pods.

Rattleboxes, *Crotalaria* species, have inflated pods in which the dry seeds rattle as they mature. There are about 10 species, mostly from the east and midwest. They are poisonous, annual or perennial plants, with simple leaves and racemes of yellow, pea-like flowers. **Showy Rattlebox**, *C. spectabilis* (p. 78), is found in fields, roadsides, and waste places from Virginia to Florida and Missouri, naturalized in these areas but really a tropical, Old World plant. It has erect stems up to 3ft tall, with ovate leaves and large flowers, followed by inflated, 2-in long pods. Rabbit-bells, *C. angulata*, is a perennial plant only just over 1ft tall, with a clump of sprawling stems, broadly oval leaves at the base, and showy, yellow, pea-like flowers at the tops of the stems. It grows in sandy, open places in the southeast.

There are over 100 species of **Lupines** in North America, belonging to the genus *Lupinus*. The name means "wolf" and refers to the old belief that lupines impoverish the soil, behaving like wolves and "devouring" the land. However, most grow naturally in poor soils, not because they have made them so. In fact, they enrich the soil, for they have root nodules like other leguminous plants and thus trap nitrogen. Lupines are annual or perennial plants with alternate, palmately compound leaves, and racemes of showy flowers terminating the usually erect stems. Most have blue flowers, but some have yellow, white or reddish ones. The flowers are pea-like, the standard with its sides bent backward.

Blue-pod Lupine, *Lupinus polyhyllus* (p. 78), is typical of very many lupines in its general form, but is one of the largest. It has stout, erect stems up to 5ft tall, and its large palmate leaves have 9–13 broadly lance-shaped leaflets, each leaflet up to 4in long. Its stems bear long, dense terminal racemes of blue flowers. This lupine is unusual in growing, not in poor, sandy places, but in lush, damp meadows, beside streams, and in moist woods. It is found from British Columbia to Colorado and Alberta, south to California. This has been one of the most important species in the development of garden varieties.

Other blue-flowered lupines include **Silvery Lupine**, *Lupinus argenteus* (p. 78), which has silvery stems and narrow leaflets on its leaves; it is found in dry places in the Great

Tree Lupine
Lupinus arboreus

Yellow Sweet Clover
Melilotus officinalis

White Sweet Clover
Melilotus alba

Alfalfa
Medicago sativa

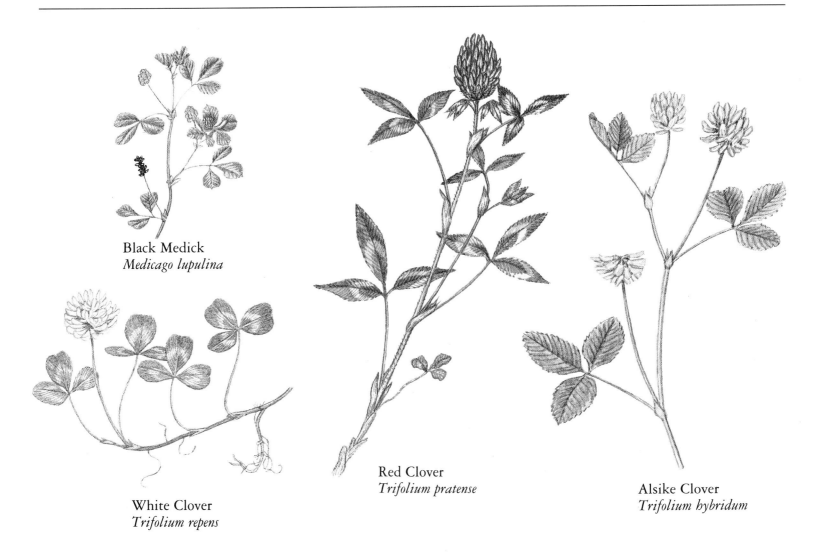

Black Medick
Medicago lupulina

Red Clover
Trifolium pratense

Alsike Clover
Trifolium hybridum

White Clover
Trifolium repens

Basin. Stinging Lupine, *L. hirsutissimus*, has stinging yellow hairs all over and should not be touched; it grows in woods on the Coast Ranges from California to Baja California. **Miniature Lupine,** *L. bicolor* (p. 78), grows only about 1ft tall, and its deep blue flowers have white spots on the standards; this plant grows in the Pacific states. Many other lupine flowers have spots or bands of yellow or white, especially on the standard petals.

The **Tree Lupine,** *Lupinus arboreus* (p. 79), is a semi-shrubby plant, with many erect, branched stems up to 6ft tall, and more or less silky, palmate leaves. Each one has 5–12 leaflets. The flowers grow in loose racemes and are usually yellow, but may be lilac or a mixture of the two colors. Tree Lupines grow wild in sandy places on the coast of California. This plant does well on the infertile soil of old industrial waste land and spoil heaps, and is often used in land reclamation schemes. Sulphur Lupine, *L. sulphureus*, and Butter Lupine, *L. luteolus*, also have yellow flowers. They are both Pacific states species, the first from the Great Basin and the second from the Coast Ranges. Sulphur Lupine has narrow, silvery leaflets, and Butter Lupine broad, bright green ones.

Yellow Sweet Clover, *Melilotus officinalis* (p. 79), is a tall, biennial plant up to 5ft in height, with many slender racemes of yellow, pea-like flowers in late summer. It has clover-like leaves with toothed, elliptical leaflets, and a scent of coumarin (new-mown hay), especially when drying. It comes from Eurasia and is naturalized in waste places and fields throughout much of North America, although much less commonly in the south. The closely related **White Sweet Clover,** *M. alba* (p. 79), with white flowers, grows in similar places across North America.

Alfalfa, *Medicago sativa* (p. 79), is cultivated in many parts of the U.S. and southern Canada, and escapes to grow wild on roadsides and in waste land. It is an Asian plant originally, a perennial with erect or sprawling stems up to 3ft tall, clover-like leaves, and racemes of blue-violet, pea-like flowers in the leaf axils and terminating the stems. The pods are spirally twisted.

Black Medick, *Medicago lupulina*, although closely related to Alfalfa, more nearly resembles Hop-clovers in its appearance. However, it is easy to distinguish in fruit because its ripe pods resemble tiny, black, coiled, kidney-shaped shells. This is another Eurasian plant which grows as a weed in North America. It is a small annual, with prostrate spreading stems, clover-like leaves, and many tiny heads of yellow flowers.

Some of the **Clovers** and **Hop-clovers**, members of the genus *Trifolium*, are among the most familiar of wild flowers. White Clover, with its creeping stems, white-banded leaflets, and heads of white flowers is known to everyone who has played in grass as a child, especially in lawns or picnic sites; or

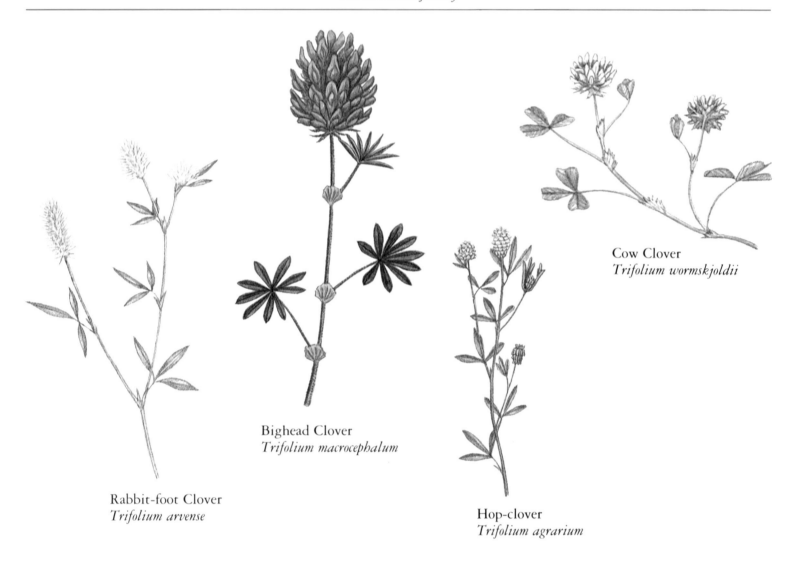

Bighead Clover
Trifolium macrocephalum

Cow Clover
Trifolium wormskjoldii

Rabbit-foot Clover
Trifolium arvense

Hop-clover
Trifolium agrarium

to anyone who has searched for the proverbial lucky leaf with four leaflets instead of three. Red Clover is almost as familiar, with its much bigger clumps of leafy stems and large red flower heads on roadsides and rough grassland. There are nearly 300 *Trifolium* species, mostly found in north temperate regions, with about 90 in North America. In addition, many European species are cultivated in the U.S. and Canada.

Clovers are, in general, distinguishable from other leguminous plants by their leaves with three leaflets, and by their heads or dense, head-like spikes of flowers. The flowers are rich in nectar and much sought out by bees. Honey made from clover nectar is one of the best kinds. The petals, and often the sepals, persist on the flower heads when pods are formed, so that the whole thing looks like a brown, withered parody of its former self.

The seed of **White Clover**, *Trifolium repens* (p. 80), is often added to lawn seed mixes, since the presence of its root nodules improve the soil. Even when not planted, it often establishes itself anyway, and is common throughout North America in lawns and on roadsides, naturalized from its native Europe. It is a small, creeping plant, with stems which penetrate through the grasses and root at the nodes. The leaves grow on long stalks from these prostrate stems; each has three rounded leaflets, and a white, angled band partly encircles the base of each leaflet. The globular heads of white or pink flowers grow

on long stalks from the leaf axils all summer; each head has numerous flowers and, as in many clovers, the petals are more or less united into a tube with the standard folded around the wings. As the flowers fade, they wither and droop around the pods, so that the whole head seems to droop.

There are many varieties of **Red Clover**, *Trifolium pratense* (p. 80), grown as field crops, each variety depending on a different bumblebee for pollination. This is because they flower at different times of the summer, when different species of bees are flying, and because the bees can only pollinate the flowers if their tongues are long enough to reach the bottom of the flower tube. There are basically two kinds of bumblebee: short-tongued and long-tongued. Short-tongued bumblebees are often big and strong, and will "cheat" by boring a hole in the bottom of the flower, robbing it of its nectar without pollinating it. Red Clovers are found in the wild in fields and on roadsides throughout the temperate areas of North America. This is a perennial plant, forming a straggling clump up to 2ft tall, with thin stems and many leaves. The leaves have narrow pointed leaflets, each one with a whitish, crescent-shaped mark toward the base. The pink-purple, ovoid heads of flowers are terminal, borne between two leaves.

Alsike Clover, *Trifolium hybridum* (p. 80), is grown as a forage crop, and also grows wild in fields and on roadsides, more commonly in the north. It has creamy pink or white

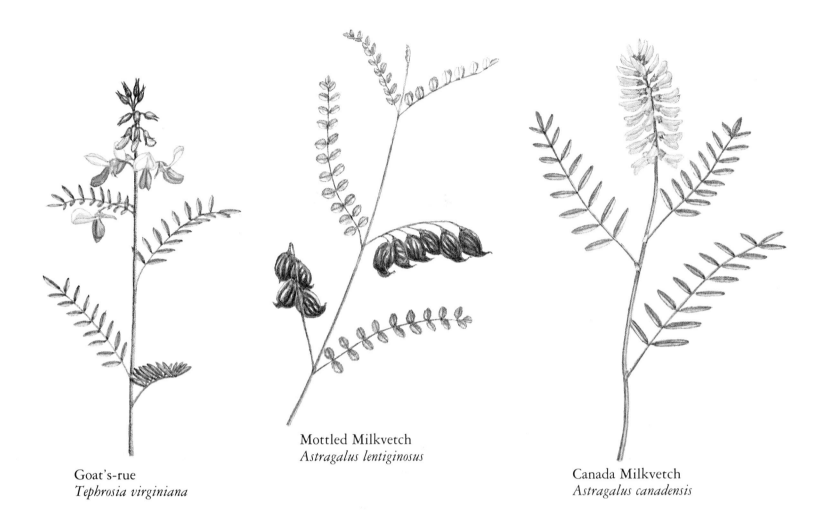

Goat's-rue
Tephrosia virginiana

Mottled Milkvetch
Astragalus lentiginosus

Canada Milkvetch
Astragalus canadensis

flowers and its leaflets have no white markings. **Rabbit-foot Clover**, *T. arvense* (p. 81), is another introduced species, an annual plant found in dry, open areas across the U.S. and southern Canada. It has particularly attractive flower heads, pinkish or white, with long silky hairs—hence the name of Rabbit-foot.

Bighead Clover, *Trifolium macrocephalum* (p. 81), is a native clover found in sagebrush and pine woods from Washington to California, east to Idaho and Nevada. It is a low-growing plant with a spreading rosette of stems, only 1ft tall at most, palmately compound leaves, and particularly large, terminal, reddish flower heads. By contrast, Maiden Clover, *T. microcephalum*, has tiny, pale pink flower heads in bowl-like bracts; it grows in open, grassy places from California to British Columbia.

Cow Clover, *Trifolium wormskjoldii* (p. 81), is another western species, a common plant which grows in damp meadows and beside mountain streams from the Pacific coast east to Idaho and New Mexico, south into Mexico. It has prostrate stems which form spreading mats, leaves with narrow leaflets, and large, round, red-mauve flower heads. Bull Clover, *T. fucatum*, has pink flowers inflated like small balloons at their bases. It is found in grassy places in Oregon and California.

Hop-clovers are small, straggling, annual, much-branched plants, with clover-like leaves and tiny heads of yellow flowers in summer. There are three similar species in North America, all weeds from Europe, like *Trifolium agrarium* (p. 81), growing in lawns, on roadsides and in waste places. They have one-seeded pods enfolded in the dried remains of the petals; the whole head is supposed to resemble a hop flower, hence the name hop-clover.

Goat's-rue, *Tephrosia virginiana*, is a perennial plant with erect, more or less unbranched stems 1–2ft tall, and pinnate leaves. The leaves have an odd number of narrow leaflets, usually 15–25, and may be densely hairy. Bicolored, pea-like flowers grow in clusters at the tops of the stems; they have yellowish-white standards, pink wings, and a pink keel. This plant grows in dry, poor soils, in old fields, and open woods from New Hampshire to Minnesota, south to Florida and Texas. Several related species grow in the coastal plain in the southeastern area of the U.S.

The **Milkvetches** (sometimes called locoweeds), the *Astragalus* species, form one of the largest genera in the Pea family in North America, with about 400 species, most found in the west. A few are excellent forage plants but many are toxic, either because they contain poisonous alkaloids, or because they become toxic by concentrating the element, selenium, from the soil. Horses and other stock generally avoid locoweeds and will only graze on them when other food is scarce, but once started they may succumb to "loco disease," become listless, lose weight, and die. Milkvetches are herbaceous plants, with compound pinnate leaves formed of an odd number of leaflets. The flowers are pea-like, growing in racemes in the leaf axils. They are followed by ovoid or oblong pods, which are often two-celled, and which may be woody or leathery in texture.

Many of the *Astragalus* species have inflated pods and are then called rattleweeds; one such is **Mottled Milkvetch,** *Astragalus lentiginosus* (p. 82), a highly variable plant found throughout the west from western Canada to Mexico. It is almost a group of plants rather than a single species, with many varieties, and it grades into related species. It is usually perennial, but may be erect or prostrate, and varies from completely hairless to densely silky-hairy. Its flowers are borne in racemes, but these may be dense or sparsely flowered, and the flowers may be purple, pink, yellow, or white. The pods are inflated with upturned beaks—this is a constant feature of the species—but they vary in texture from membranous to leathery. Mottled Milkvetches grow in a variety of habitats, from sagebrush, creosote bush, and juniper scrub, to pine forests and mountain slopes, to sandy flats, alkaline soils, and deserts.

Canada Milkvetch, *Astragalus canadensis* (p. 82), grows across the U.S. and most of southern Canada in many moist habitats, from damp meadows and grassy forest clearings to ditches, river banks, and shores. It is a perennial plant, with creeping rhizomes and strong, erect and leafy stems. Its leaves contain 15–29 elliptical leaflets. The pea-like flowers are pale yellow or white, borne in dense racemes above the leaves in summer. They are followed by numerous, densly crowded, pointed-oblong pods held erect.

Many milkvetches have pink, red-purple or blue flowers. **Woolly Locoweed,** *Astragalus mollissimus*, is one such species. It has pinnate leaves with many rounded, woolly leaflets, and pink-purple flowers. It is found in prairies and plains from Nebraska to Wyoming, south to Texas and New Mexico. Nuttall's Locoweed, *A. nuttallianus*, has purple flowers on sprawling stems, and small leaves with elliptical leaflets. It grows in deserts and scrub from California to Utah and Arizona. Missouri Locoweed, *A. missouriensis*, has small clusters of blue-violet flowers and silvery, elliptical leaflets on pinnate leaves. It grows on hillsides and prairies from Minnesota to Alberta, south to Texas and New Mexico.

The *Oxytropis* species, also called **Locoweeds** or Crazyweeds, are a closely related group of similar plants, with about 20 species in North America, mostly in the midwest and Rocky Mountain areas. Several *Oxytropis* species, like the *Astragalus* species, are notoriously poisonous to stock. Among the poisonous species is the common and widespread **Purple**

Woolly Locoweed
Astragalus mollissimus

Purple Locoweed
Oxytropis lambertii

Showy Locoweed
Oxytropis splendens

Late Yellow Locoweed
Oxytropis campestris

Locoweed, *O. lambertii* (p. 83). This plant forms tufts of leaves and stems only about 15in tall. Each leaf has 11–17 narrow leaflets covered with silvery, silky hairs. The bright reddish-purple, pea-like flowers are borne in loose, elongated racemes, on long stalks above the tuft of leaves in spring and summer. The pods are plump and oblong, and held almost erect. This locoweed is found in plains and prairies from Manitoba south to Texas, and west through the mountains to Montana and Arizona.

Showy Locoweed, *Oxytropis splendens* (p. 83), also has spikes of purple flowers, their color showing up vividly against the long, dense, silvery hairs which cover this tufted plant. It grows in prairies and plains, beside roads and rivers from Ontario to Alaska, south to New Mexico.

In the prairie grasslands and open woods of the northern midwestern states and in the Canadian provinces, **Late Yellow Locoweed**, *Oxytropis campestris* (p. 83), opens its yellowish-white flowers from midsummer onward. It is a perennial, silky-hairy plant, variable in appearance. It grows 6–24in tall and has 19–31 lance-shaped leaflets on its leaves. The flowers are borne in many-flowered racemes on erect stalks. They are followed by oblong, semi-membranous pods, often adorned with black and white hairs.

Silver Scurf Pea, *Psoralea argophylla*, is one of about 30 *Psoralea* species, found mostly in the western and midwest regions of the U.S. It grows in plains and prairies from Wisconsin to southern Alberta, south to Missouri and New Mexico. The plant has creeping rhizomes and branched, 2-ft tall stems, with compound leaves. The leaves each have 3–5 oval leaflets densely covered with silky white hairs, at least on the undersides. The very dark blue flowers are borne in small, interrupted spikes at the tops of long stalks in the upper leaf axils; they have silvery-hairy calyces. The pods are also silky and each contains one seed. This plant is reported to be poisonous, although the related Indian Breadroot, *P. esculenta*, has starchy edible taproots which were eaten by the Indians. This plant has dense spikes of blue-purple flowers.

Purple Prairie Clover, *Petalostemum purpureum*, and White Prairie Clover, *P. candidum*, often grow together in dry places throughout the prairies of the midwest. They are perennial plants, often growing in patches, with erect or sprawling stems 1–2ft tall. They have pinnate leaves with narrow leaflets, those of Purple Prairie Clover with 3–5 leaflets, and of White Prairie Clover with 5–9 leaflets. Their flowers are unusual, each one with a single, large standard and four small, separate petals representing wings and keel; all the petals are clawed. The flowers grow in dense, cylindrical heads; they begin to open in a ring at the bottom of the head and gradually work their way upward as time goes on. The plants flower in early summer. Other similar species grow in the east.

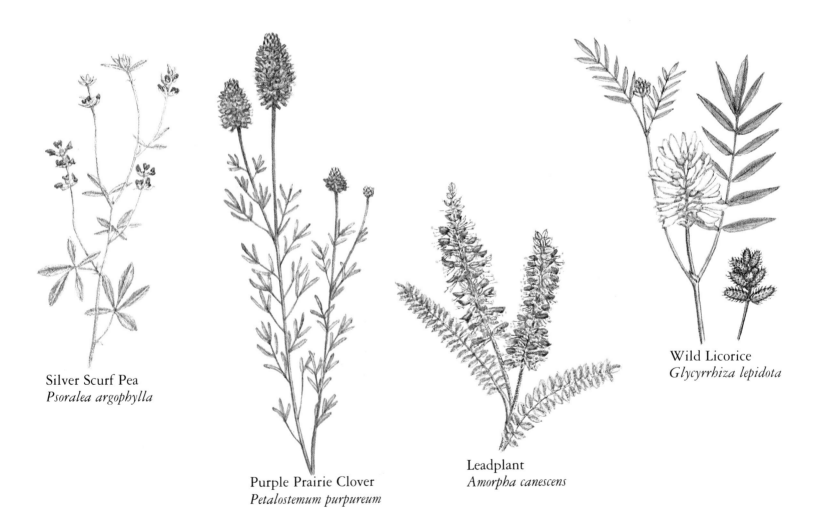

Silver Scurf Pea
Psoralea argophylla

Purple Prairie Clover
Petalostemum purpureum

Leadplant
Amorpha canescens

Wild Licorice
Glycyrrhiza lepidota

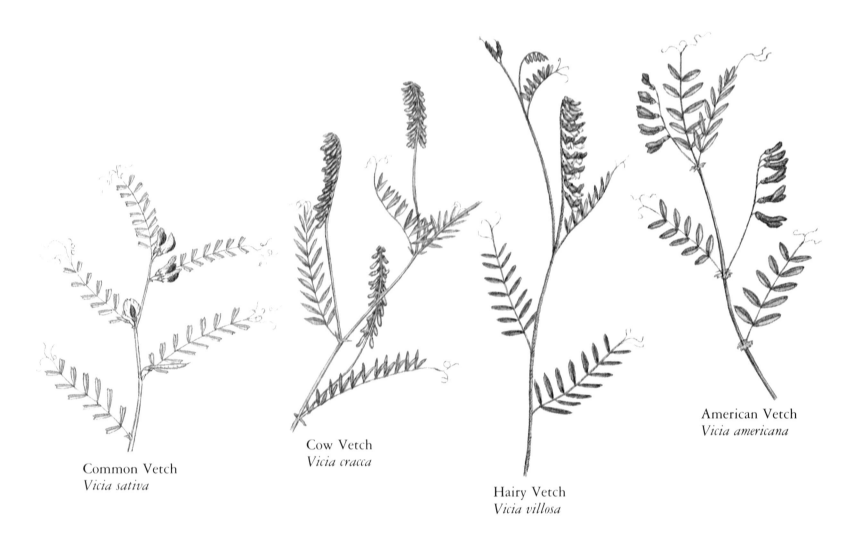

Common Vetch
Vicia sativa

Cow Vetch
Vicia cracca

Hairy Vetch
Vicia villosa

American Vetch
Vicia americana

Leadplant, *Amorpha canescens* (p. 84), is unusual among members of the Pea family because its flowers have only one petal—the standard. This is a characteristic plant of the dry plains and prairies, growing from Michigan to Saskatchewan, south to Arkansas and New Mexico. It is a perennial, with shrubby stems up to 3ft tall, and many leaves, each with 15–45 crowded leaflets covered with dense white hairs. The flowers grow in dense, spike-like racemes from the axils of the upper leaves and terminating the stems; the inflorescences are conspicuous but each individual flower is small, with a single blue petal and 10 bright orange stamens. The pods which follow are hairy.

Wild Licorice, *Glycyrrhiza lepidota* (p. 84), is closely related to the European species of Licorice, *G. glabra*. This latter plant is cultivated for its rhizomes from which licorice is extracted. Licorice is effective as a cough medicine, as a mild laxative, and is used as a flavoring for drugs, candy, and root beer. Wild Licorice rhizomes have much the same flavor and have the same properties; they are chewed by North American Indians for their taste and to ease toothache. Wild Licorice grows in patches in moist ground in a variety of habitats— waste places, river bottoms, meadows, and prairies—from western Ontario to British Columbia, and south to California and Texas. Further east it has become naturalized to grow wild along railroads and in waste places.

Wild Licorice is a perennial plant with deep-growing, sweet-tasting rhizomes. It forms erect, often rather viscid stems up to 3ft tall, with many compound leaves. These have 11–19 lance-shaped leaflets. The flowers are yellowish or greenish-white and borne in dense, bottlebrush-like racemes on long stalks in the leaf axils. The flowers are followed by characteristic brown, oblong pods which are covered by hooked prickly hairs. Each pod contains several seeds but does not split open.

The **Vetches** and tares, *Vicia* species, and the **Wild Peas** or vetchlings, *Lathyrus* species, are both groups of climbing or scrambling plants. They cling to anything within reach— other plants, fences, stones—with modified leaflets which have become tendrils. There are about 130 *Vicia* species in the world, found in northern temperate regions and in South America. Some are crop plants, like the **Common Vetch**, *V. sativa*, which is cultivated for fodder and often escapes to grow wild. It is an annual plant, with slender stems, and pairs of violet flowers in the leaf axils.

Cow Vetch, *Vicia cracca* (p. 85), has an army of names: it is variously called Tufted Vetch, Bird Vetch, Blue Vetch, Tare Vetch, Cats Peas, Tinegrass, together with variations on these names. It is probably not native to North America, but naturalized from European plants. It grows in meadows and fields, along roadsides and in woods throughout much of the

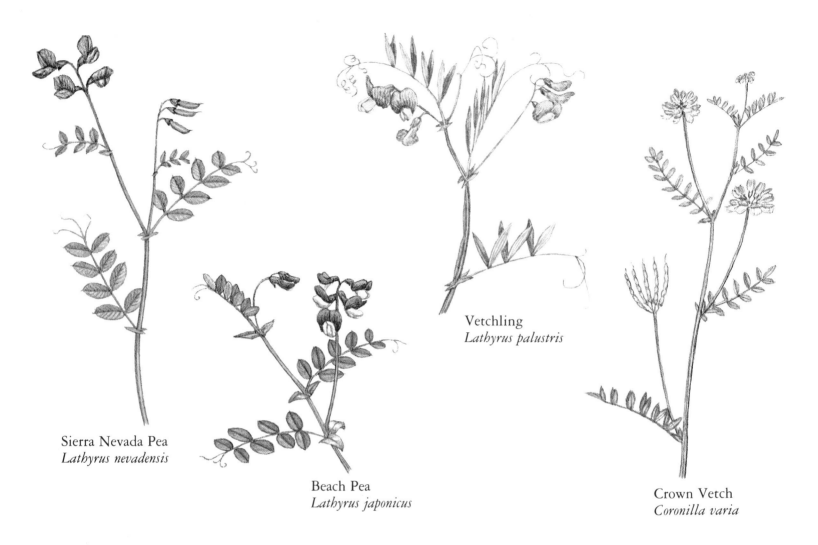

Sierra Nevada Pea
Lathyrus nevadensis

Beach Pea
Lathyrus japonicus

Vetchling
Lathyrus palustris

Crown Vetch
Coronilla varia

continent. It is a small, scrambling plant up to 3ft tall, relying on others for support; it twines around other plants with forked tendrils. It has showy racemes of bright bluish-purple, pea-like flowers on long stalks in the axils of the leaves. They are followed by squarish pods which crack open in hot sun to release the seeds.

Hairy Vetch, *Vicia villosa* (p. 85), is similar to the Cow Vetch in appearance. It has hairy stems, leaves with 5–10 pairs of linear or lance-shaped leaflets, and racemes of 10–30 blue or purple flowers. In some plants the flowers are bicolored, with blue standards and whitish wings. It grows in waste places, fields, and roadsides throughout much of the U.S. and southern Canada, introduced from Europe.

American Vetch, *Vicia americana* (p. 85), is a native species, growing in much of North America, widespread in many different habitats in the west but less so in the east, and mostly found in moist woods in the mountains from Ontario south to West Virginia. It is a climbing, perennial plant, with tendrils which cling to surrounding vegetation, and showy, blue-purple flowers in early summer. Each leaf has 8–14 oblong leaflets, as well as tendrils. The pea-like flowers are borne in loose racemes on stalks in the leaf axils; the racemes are shorter than the leaves.

Sweet Peas and the Everlasting Pea of gardens both belong to the genus *Lathyrus*. There are about 100 wild species in this genus in North America; they are similar to the vetches and have tendrils on their leaves. The **Sierra Nevada Pea**, *L. nevadensis*, is one of many found in dry places in the Pacific states. It grows on dry slopes in coniferous woods, in the western foothills and mountains of the Sierra Nevada and Coast Ranges. It is a perennial, with erect, angled stems, and 4–8 leaflets on its pinnate leaves. Its red-purple or blue flowers are borne in racemes on long stalks in the leaf axils.

Most *Lathyrus* species are poisonous, but the **Beach Pea**, *L. japonicus*, is an exception and its seeds can be eaten like cultivated peas, if gathered while young and tender. This plant grows on sandy beaches and shores on the Atlantic and Pacific coasts, and around the Great Lakes. It has slightly fleshy, often bluish foliage on prostrate, angled stems. The pinnate leaves have 3–6 pairs of leaflets and a terminal coiled tendril. In the axils of the leaves grow racemes of flowers on long stalks; eastern plants have purple flowers, but western ones often have flowers with a purple standard, whitish keel, and wings. The flowers are produced in the latter part of the summer.

Vetchling, *Lathyrus palustris* (p. 86), grows in marshes and swamps, wet meadows, and shores across northern North America, south to Pennsylvania, in the west to California. Coastal plants on both sides of the continent tend to be hairier than inland plants. This is a slender, climbing plant with

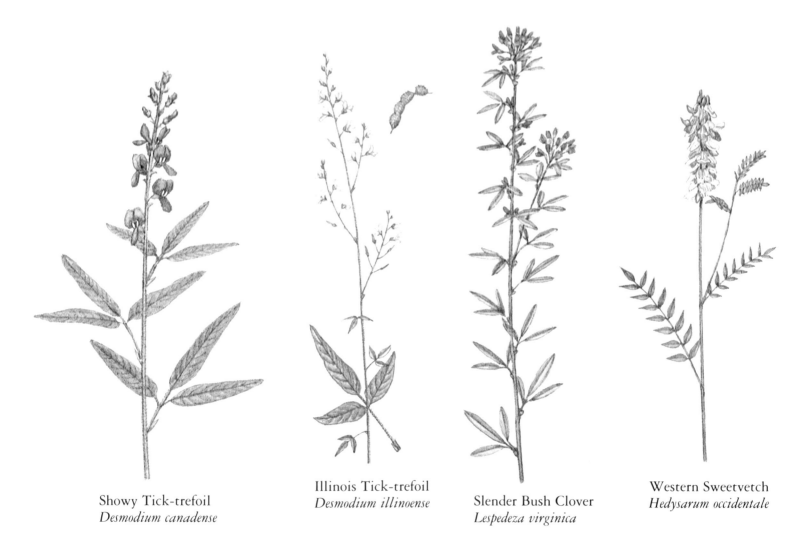

Showy Tick-trefoil
Desmodium canadense

Illinois Tick-trefoil
Desmodium illinoense

Slender Bush Clover
Lespedeza virginica

Western Sweetvetch
Hedysarum occidentale

winged stems; its compound leaves have 4–6 leaflets and a terminal branched tendril. In midsummer it bears small racemes of red-purple flowers in the leaf axils.

Crown Vetch, *Coronilla varia* (p. 86), is an alien on the North American continent, where it has escaped after introduction as a garden plant from Europe and Asia. It is a small, straggling, perennial plant up to 20in tall, with umbels of pink, pea-like flowers growing on long stalks in the leaf axils in summer.

The **Tick-trefoils**, *Desmodium species*, are another group of herbaceous leguminous plants, with nearly 50 species in North America. **Showy Tick-trefoil**, *Desmodium canadense*, is one of the showiest species, with terminal racemes of pink or purple, pea-like flowers in late summer. It is also one of the most common, growing in thickets, on river banks, and in moist soil across southern Canada from Quebec to Alberta, south to the Carolinas and Arkansas. This is a bushy plant up to 6ft tall, with many compound, clover-like leaves, each with three long-oval leaflets. The pods which follow the flowers contain 3–5 seeds and are characteristic of tick-trefoils. They do not split open like those of most pea family species; instead they become transversely segmented into one-seeded sections and eventually split up. The pods are covered in hooked hairs which become attached to animals, so dispersing the seeds. They also become attached to clothes!

The **Illinois Tick-trefoil**, *Desmodium illinoense*, has erect, spindly stems covered with hooked hairs, with roughly hairy, clover-like leaves and terminal racemes of white flowers. The flowers darken to pink or purple as they age. The pods break into 2–5 flattened segments. This plant grows in prairies, often in moist places, from Ontario to Nebraska and Ohio, and on south to Oklahoma.

Slender Bush Clover, *Lespedeza virginica*, is one of about 20 species of bush clovers in eastern North America, all small herbaceous plants. This is one of the tallest, with erect, branched stems growing up to 3ft high. It is found in dry upland woods and thickets from Massachusetts to Wisconsin, and south to Georgia and Texas. It also extends into southern Ontario and west into Kansas. This is a very leafy, downy plant; its many compound leaves are each divided into three narrow leaflets. Like some of the other bush clovers, the plant has two kinds of flowers, petal-less ones growing in small clusters from the leaf axils in the middle of the stems, and showy clusters of purple petalous flowers growing from the upper leaf axils. The pods do not split open and contain only one seed.

Western Sweetvetch, *Hedysarum occidentale* (p. 87), is a perennial plant, with several erect, leafy stems growing about 2ft tall from a thick, edible taproot. It has pinnate leaves with 9–21 ovate leaflets covered with minute brown glands on the upper surface. The flowers are showy, pink or purple in color, and arranged in long, dense racemes at the tops of the stems. The pods of this and other sweetvetches split into one-seeded sections, like those of the tick-trefoils. The plant is found in rocky soils and meadows quite high in the Cascades, the Olympic Mountains, and the Rockies from Washington to Idaho and south to Colorado. Other *Hedysarum* species grow in the Rocky Mountains and across Canada.

Bird's-foot Trefoil, *Lotus corniculatus*, is a European plant widely naturalized in North America. In Europe Bird's-foot Trefoil is only one of over 70 common names given to this plant; its many others include Eggs-and-bacon, Cat's Claw, Devil's Fingers, Shoes-and-stockings, Tom Thumb, Pig's-foot, and many variations on these themes. The question of why such a small plant has merited such attention seems to have no answer. For this is a small, more or less prostrate, trailing plant with no economic significance, nor any medicinal folklore. It is a perennial with a clump of slender, leafy stems which grow erect if supported by surrounding vegetation; the leaves are compound, each with three leaflets. In summer the plant bears many heads of bright yellow, often red-tinged, pea-like flowers, growing from the leaf axils. These are followed by pods, which twist and split open when ripe and dry to release the seeds.

This is one of about 45 *Lotus* species found in North America, many of them very local and confined to the west and southwest. They include the **Hill Lotus**, *L. humistratus*, an annual, sprawling plant with tiny, solitary, yellow flowers in the axils of gray-haired leaves; it is common in the foothills of the southern Rockies. **Spanish Lotus**, *L. purshianus*, has solitary, pale pink flowers in the leaf axils of its erect stems. It is an annual, much-branched plant with only three leaflets on each leaf. It grows in disturbed, dry places and fields from British Columbia to California. Deer Weed, *L. scoparius*, is more like a bushy shrub with erect, green stems, small, tough leaves, and yellow, red-tinged flowers; it grows on dry slopes and fans among brush in California, thriving in after-burn areas for several years.

The **Butterfly Pea**, *Clitoria mariana*, is a perennial plant, with branched, twining or trailing stems growing about 3ft tall. It has compound leaves divided into three elliptical or ovate leaflets, and a few showy flowers in the leaf axils. The flowers are large in proportion to the rest of the plant, up to 2in long and like sweet peas, with a large, oval standard, pale blue or lavender in color with dark streaks in the center. This plant grows in dry upland woods and barrens from New York to Iowa, south to Florida and Texas.

The similar **Climbing Butterfly Pea**, *Centrosema virginianum*, always has twining stems, with clover-like leaves and showy violet flowers in the leaf axils. Each flower has a broad

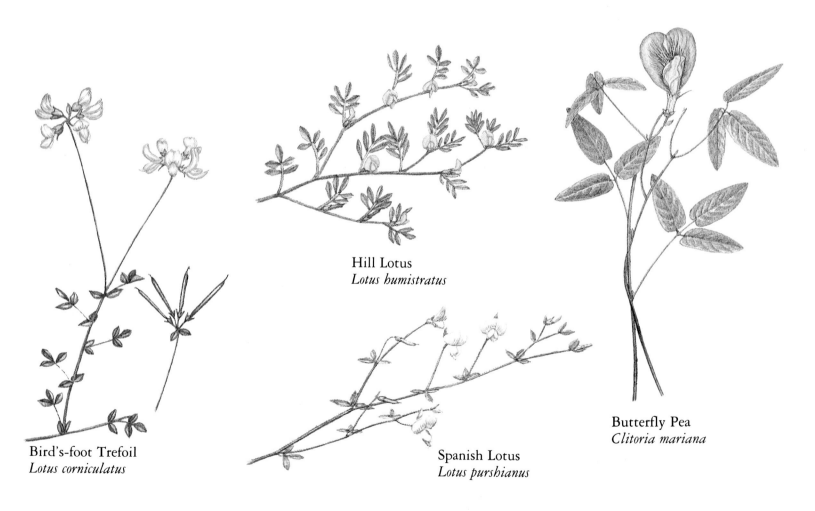

Hill Lotus
Lotus humistratus

Bird's-foot Trefoil
Lotus corniculatus

Spanish Lotus
Lotus purshianus

Butterfly Pea
Clitoria mariana

standard with a white patch in the center. This plant grows in dry woods and barrens from Florida to Texas, north to New Jersey and Virginia, more commonly in the southeast. The flowers of both Butterfly Pea and Climbing Butterfly Pea are unusual in that the standard petal is held beneath the keel. However, Butterfly Pea flowers are held more or less erect, while those of Climbing Butterfly Pea generally hang down.

Groundnut, *Apios americana*, is another twining, vine-like plant, with stems up to 10ft long and pinnate leaves, each with 5–7 ovate leaflets. In the axils of the leaves grow dense clusters of curious, brownish-purple flowers; each flower has a reflexed standard petal, two wing petals which become turned back beneath the keel, and a horseshoe-shaped, upturned keel. The pods which follow contain several seeds, edible when they are young. The roots of the plant develop a string of small white tubers along their length; these are edible, with a turnip-like flavor, and may be gathered at any time of year. Groundnut can be found in moist woods and thickets from Nova Scotia to South Dakota, and south to Florida and Texas.

Coral Bean, *Erythrina herbacea*, is an erect and prickly plant, the prickles formed from stipules at the leaf-stalk bases. Its stems grow up to 5ft tall and bear many thin, papery, compound leaves, each one with three triangular leaflets. The flowers grow in showy, spike-like inflorescences terminating the stems; they are red, with red calyces and scarlet petals, the

standards folded around the keels so that the flowers appear long and narrow. Coral Bean grows in sandy soils in hummocks and open pine woods from Florida to Texas, north to Missouri and the Carolinas.

The **Hog-peanut**, *Amphicarpa bracteata*, produces edible seeds. However, the pods which contain these seeds are usually underground; seeds produced by the "normal" pods, which grow on the aerial parts of the plant, are inedible! This perennial plant has twining, vine-like stems and compound leaves, each with three pointed-ovate leaflets. Flowers grow in clusters on long stalks from the leaf axils; they are followed by curved pods, usually with three inedible seeds. In contrast to these "normal" flowers and pods, the plant also produces petal-less flowers on thin runners growing from the base of the stem, from which develop small, one-seeded, often subterranean pods. These seeds are edible when boiled. Hog-peanut vines are common in thickets and moist woods from Nova Scotia to Manitoba and Montana, south to Florida and Texas.

Milk-peas, *Galactia* species, are twining or trailing perennial plants, with pinnate leaves (mostly with three leaflets) and short racemes of white, pink or purple, pea-like flowers in the axils of the leaves. They grow in woods and barrens, mostly in the southeast. Trailing Milk-pea, *G. regularis,* is found as far north as New York. It has trailing stems, clover-like leaves, and reddish-purple flowers.

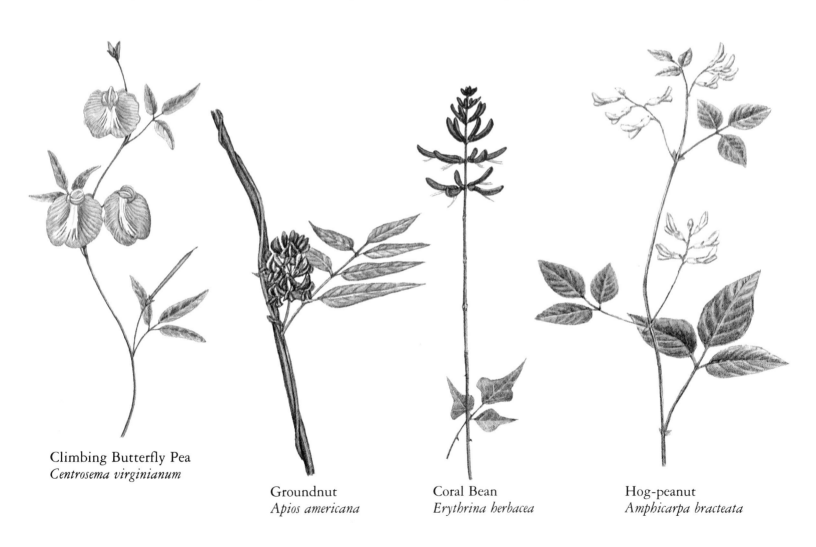

Climbing Butterfly Pea
Centrosema virginianum

Groundnut
Apios americana

Coral Bean
Erythrina herbacea

Hog-peanut
Amphicarpa bracteata

Wood Sorrel family

Oxalidaceae

There are 3 genera and nearly 900 species in this family, mainly tropical plants but also found in temperate regions. They are mostly herbs, several are grown in gardens and rock gardens. Others are weeds.

Family features The flowers are hermaphrodite and regular, with five sepals and petals, 10 stamens, and a superior ovary with five carpels. They are either solitary or borne in cymes. The fruits are usually capsules. The leaves are compound and clover-like, with three rounded leaflets jointed to the leaf stalk; they often exhibit sleep movements by folding downward at night.

By far the majority of the plants in this family belong to the genus *Oxalis*, with about 800 species. **Violet Wood Sorrel**, *Oxalis violacea*, is a native American plant of dry woods and prairies, found from Maine to South Dakota, and south to Florida and Texas. It is a small plant with several underground bulbs and a clump of basal, long-stalked, clover-like, bright green leaves. In early summer it produces a succession of leafless flower stalks, much taller than the clump of leaves and still not much more than 1ft tall, with terminal umbel-like clusters of rose-violet flowers.

This plant, like other wood sorrels, is edible in small quantities, and its leaves can be added to salads, to which they give a sour taste. However, they should not be eaten in large amounts or over an extended period of time, for they contain oxalic acid, the source of their sour flavor. They can also be made into a very refreshing drink if the leaves are steeped in hot water, sugar added, and the liquid chilled.

Common Wood Sorrel, *Oxalis montana*, forms patches of clover-like leaves with heart-shaped leaflets, spreading gradually over the ground in rich, moist woods from Nova Scotia to Saskatchewan, in the Great Lake states, south in the mountains to North Carolina and Tennessee. Its single flowers grow on separate stalks; they are white, veined with pink. The whole plant is only 6in tall at most. **Redwood Sorrel**, *O. oregana*, is a similar western species, growing in the shade of the Redwood forests from California to Washington. It has white or pink, funnel-shaped flowers, often veined with purple.

Yellow Wood Sorrel, *Oxalis europaea* (p. 91), is a cosmopolitan weed, probably native to North America originally (in spite of its specific name) but now found throughout Europe, and in Asia as well. It grows as a weed in gardens and waste land, in fields and on roadsides, as well as in natural habitats like woods, in much of southern Canada and the U.S. It is a perennial, spreading by means of long, slender,

Redwood Sorrel
Oxalis oregana

Common Wood Sorrel
Oxalis montana

Violet Wood Sorrel
Oxalis violacea

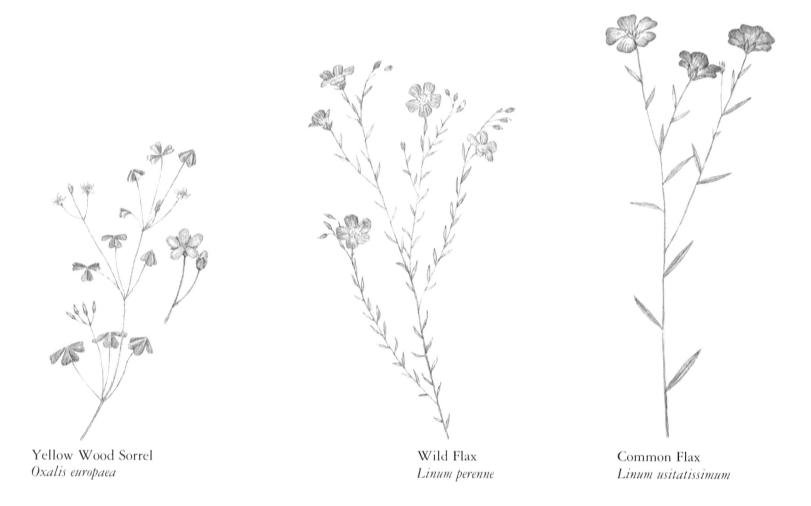

Yellow Wood Sorrel
Oxalis europaea

Wild Flax
Linum perenne

Common Flax
Linum usitatissimum

underground stems, and with more or less upright, leafy stems. The leaves are clover-like, folding down at night, and the yellow flowers grow in small clusters on long stalks from the leaf axils. The seed pods which follow are borne on erect stalks, a feature which serves to distinguish this species from the very similar Upright Yellow Sorrel, *O. corniculata*, which bears its pods on deflexed stalks. This latter species is a common weed in the south, where it grows in gardens and greenhouses.

Flax family

Linaceae

There are about 12 genera and nearly 300 species in this small but important family, important in that linen and linseed oil come from one species, Common Flax, *Linum usitatissimum*. It is a family of herbs and shrubs growing in tropical and temperate regions. Many of them have flowers similar to those of the Oxalidaceae, but flaxes have simple entire leaves, a feature which immediately distinguishes them from the wood sorrels.

Family features The flowers are hermaphrodite and regular, with five sepals, five contorted, often fleeting petals, and five or 10 stamens, often joined into a ring at the base of the filaments. The ovary is superior, with 2–6 carpels. The flowers are usually borne in cymes or racemes. The fruits are generally capsules. The leaves are simple and entire, usually alternately arranged, with or without stipules.

There are several good garden plants in the family, including the North American **Wild Flax**, *Linum perenne*, which has flowers of sky blue. This is a perennial plant, 2–3ft tall, which grows in the prairies and plains from Manitoba and Wisconsin to Alaska, and south to Texas and California. It has several erect stems clothed with numerous erect, linear leaves and bearing many loosely branched clusters of flowers in midsummer. This is one of over 30 *Linum* species found in North America, with flowers in various shades of blue, yellow or white.

Common Flax, *Linum usitatissimum*, is an annual plant, with slender stems up to 3ft tall, and lance-shaped, more or less erect leaves. It has pale blue flowers. It is widely cultivated and escapes to grow wild on roadsides and in waste places. Linen is produced from the fibers in the stems; the fibers are made into thread after they have been extracted, and then woven into cloth, or used to make canvas. Shorter fibers are used to make fine papers. The heated seeds are crushed to produce linseed oil, used in the manufacture of paints and varnishes, inks and soaps. The residue from these seeds is used for cattle feed.

Spotted Cranesbill
Geranium maculatum

Richardson's Cranesbill
Geranium richardsonii

Small-flowered Cranesbill
Geranium pusillum

Geranium family

Geraniaceae

There are about 5 genera and 750 species, mostly herbs, in this small but familiar family. Almost everyone has grown potted geraniums in the house or garden at some time or another, and the bright red or pink flowers of the most common varieties are seen in millions of window boxes. Their leaves have a peculiar, distinctive scent which clings to the hands. Many geraniums have scented leaves, and the scents vary with species, ranging from lemon to apple, mint or eucalyptus. An oil extracted from *Pelargonium graveolens* and *P. odoratissimum* is used in perfumery as a less costly substitute for "Attar of Roses"; it is used in soaps, shampoos, and toilet water.

Family features The flowers are more or less regular and hermaphrodite, with parts in fives: five free overlapping sepals, five free overlapping petals, 10–15 stamens, often joined at the base, and 3–5 carpels in the ovary. The fruits are lobed capsules in which the stigmas elongate to form long beaks, one to each lobe, and with one seed in each lobe. The leaves are alternate, simple or compound, often palmately lobed, and they have stipules.

Wild Cranesbills are annual or perennial herbs, about 300 of them in the genus *Geranium*. (The houseplants known as "geraniums" actually belong to the mostly tropical genus *Pelargonium*). The **Spotted Cranesbill**, *G. maculatum*, grows in woods and meadows from Maine to Manitoba, south to Georgia, and west to Tennessee and Kansas. It is a perennial plant with a thick, creeping rhizome and clumps of palmately compound leaves. The basal leaves of the clump are all long-stalked, with 5–7 deeply cut lobes on the large blades. The rose-pink flowers are borne on separate flowering stalks in loose terminal clusters on long stalks growing from the axil of a pair of leaves, which are formed about halfway up each flowering stalk. Within each flower cluster the flowers grow in pairs. This arrangement of leaves and flowers is characteristic of cranesbills.

The fruits of Spotted Cranesbill are distinctive and characteristic of many cranesbills. Each fruit consists of five spoon-shaped sections, with the bowls of the spoons at the bottom and containing the seeds, and all the handles of the spoons forming a "beak." When the seeds are ripe, they are ejected explosively as the handle of each spoon contracts and pulls the bowl of the spoon upward, flinging out the seeds. Afterward the spoons are left curled about the central axis of the fruit.

Richardson's Cranesbill, *Geranium richardsonii*, is a perennial western species growing in damp woods and meadows in many parts of the west, from British Columbia to California, and through the mountains to Saskatchewan and New Mexico. It grows about 2–3ft tall, has a clump of deeply cleft basal leaves, and several flowering stems with clusters of white or pinkish, purple-veined flowers.

Carolina Cranesbill, *Geranium carolinianum*, has the same general form, with long-stalked basal leaves and flowering stems, but is typical of another kind of cranesbill, in that it is an annual. It is a small, hairy plant, only about 1ft tall, with many branched stems and clusters of small pink or red-purple flowers with very separate, notched petals. It grows in dry and sandy soils, in barren, open places and waste ground across southern Canada and throughout much of the U.S.

Several similar European cranesbills are established as weeds in North America; they are admirably suited to life as weeds, thriving in open disturbed places and producing prolific seeds. **Small-flowered Cranesbill**, *Geranium pusillum* (p. 92), is one such plant. It has a clump of deeply divided leaves on long stalks, and much branched, leafy, flowering stems with small lilac or red-purple flowers. It is found throughout much of the U.S. and southern Canada, and flowers all summer.

Herb Robert, *Geranium robertianum*, has become widely naturalized in northeastern North America, from Newfoundland to Manitoba, and south to West Virginia. It has some of the most deeply dissected leaves of all the cranesbills, almost ferny in appearance. They have a disagreeable scent when handled but are very attractive in appearance, especially when they turn red in the sun or late in the season. This is an annual, often hairy plant, with a rosette of many branched, straggling stems growing about 1ft tall. It produces bright pink flowers throughout the summer. The fruits are rather different to those of most other cranesbills in the way the seeds are projected away. In Herb Robert the whole spoon-shaped section comes away with the seed, leaving the central axis of the fruit naked. Seed and "spoon" separate in the process.

The **Storksbills**, from the genus *Erodium*, come mostly from the Mediterranean, and a few have become established as weeds in North America. **Filaree** or Common Storksbill, *E. cicutarium*, is now found throughout most of the continent in disturbed and open areas, in fields and on roadsides. It is an annual, forming rosettes of pinnate, ferny leaves at first, and then prostrate, branched stems with similar leaves and terminal umbels of pink flowers. The fruits are similar to those of cranesbills, but with much longer "handles" to the "spoons." When ripe, the fruits split into single-seeded sections, the beaks remaining attached to the seeds and becoming spirally coiled like a corkscrew. On the ground this corkscrew unwinds or winds closer with changes in humidity, and the movements screw the seed into the ground; it is prevented from re-emerging by backward-pointing hairs. The seeds are thus "planted" at exactly the right depth!

Carolina Cranesbill
Geranium carolinianum

Herb Robert
Geranium robertianum

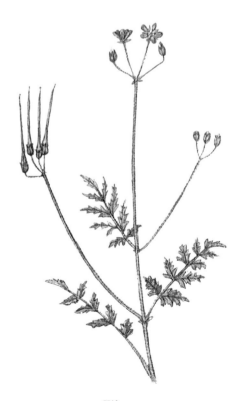

Filaree
Erodium cicutarium

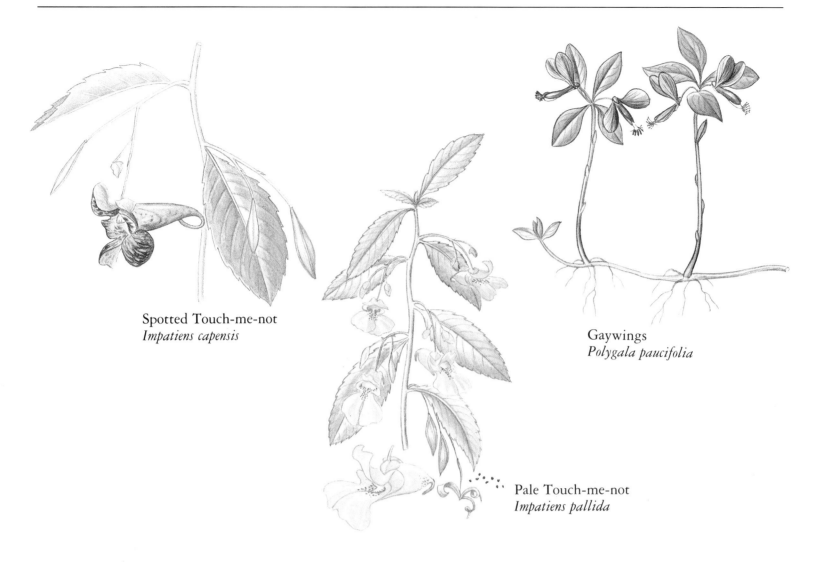

Spotted Touch-me-not
Impatiens capensis

Gaywings
Polygala paucifolia

Pale Touch-me-not
Impatiens pallida

Touch-me-not family

Balsaminaceae

This family has 4 genera and 600 species, 500 of them in the genus *Impatiens*. They are mostly rather succulent herbs with watery, translucent stems found in tropical Asia and Africa, but a few species are native to temperate North America and Europe. Many have large, showy flowers, and plants like Busy-Lizzy, *Impatiens wallerana*, are popular garden, greenhouse, and house plants.

Family features The flowers are bilaterally symmetrical and hermaphrodite. Each has 3–5 sepals, one larger than the others and forming a spur at the back of the flower; the sepals are often petal-like. Each flower has five petals, the uppermost the largest, and two on each side usually fused together. Five stamens alternate with the petals. The ovary is superior with five cells. The flowers are often drooping, solitary or borne in racemes in the leaf axils. The fruits are capsules with elastic sides, so that when they are ripe a light touch or raindrop will trigger them into sudden opening. The leaves are simple, alternate, opposite, or in whorls.

Jewelweed is a name given to two *Impatiens* species from eastern North America. One of these is also known as **Spotted Touch-me-not**, *I. capensis*, and it grows in wet, shady places,

along streams and by springs from Newfoundland to Saskatchewan, south to South Carolina and Oklahoma. It is a hairless annual plant up to 5ft tall, with succulent, translucent stems, which exude watery juice when broken. It has thin, elliptical leaves with wavy margins. The flowers are large and helmet-shaped, hanging in clusters in the axils of the leaves in summer; they are orange-yellow with red-brown spots.

The other Jewelweed is also known as **Pale Touch-me-not**, *Impatiens pallida*. It has pale yellow flowers with few red-brown spots. It grows in wet woods and meadows, in shady places from Quebec to Saskatchewan and south to North Carolina and Missouri, but is less common than Spotted Touch-me-not.

Milkwort family

Polygalaceae

There are about 12 genera and 800 species of herbs, shrubs, and climbers in this family, found in temperate and tropical regions throughout the world except New Zealand, Polynesia, and the Arctic.

Family features The flowers are hermaphrodite and bilaterally symmetrical, often borne on jointed stalks. Each flower has five free, overlapping sepals, the two inner ones often colored like petals and resembling wings. There are

Whorled Milkwort
Polygala verticillata

White Milkwort
Polygala alba

Field Milkwort
Polygala sanguinea

usually three petals, the outer two free or united with the lowermost (this is often boat-shaped and known as the keel). The flowers generally have eight stamens, their filaments often joined together into a sheath which is split above and joined to the petals. The ovary is superior, usually with two cells. The fruit is a capsule or may be fleshy. The leaves are simple and frequently alternate, and they lack stipules.

About 50 **Milkworts,** *Polygala* species, grow in North America. **Gaywings** or Fringed Polygala, *Polygala paucifolia* (p. 94), is a creeping plant with slender, underground stems. From these grow erect stems about 6in tall, with several oval leaves alternately arranged near the top. In summer the stems end in a cluster of showy, rose-purple flowers, with broad, winged sepals and a fringed keel. This is a plant of moist, rich woods, found from New Brunswick to Saskatchewan, south to New York and Wisconsin, in the mountains to Georgia. The leaves may be evergreen and the plant is sometimes called Flowering Wintergreen.

Whorled Milkwort, *Polygala verticillata*, is one of several North American species with whorled leaves. This plant has erect, branched stems about 15in tall, with whorls of 2–5 linear leaves, and terminal, dense, tapering spikes of white or greenish flowers. It grows in moist, sandy soils, in fields, woods and grasslands from Maine to Manitoba, and south to Florida and Texas.

Seneca Snakeroot, *Polygala senega*, has looser spikes of white flowers; its erect stems are unbranched and have alternate, lance-shaped leaves. This perennial plant grows in woods and prairies from New Brunswick to Alberta, south to Georgia and Arkansas. It was used as a snakebite remedy by the Seneca Indians, and is still used in herb medicine to treat asthma and bronchitis. **White Milkwort,** *P. alba*, is a western plant with similar spikes of white flowers, but its numerous, long, wiry stems have linear leaves. It grows in rocky hills and dry plains from Montana to Minnesota, and south to Arizona and Texas.

Field Milkwort, *Polygala sanguinea*, is one of several species with pink or purple flowers. In Field Milkwort the flowers are tiny and borne in dense, rounded or cylindrical heads, most of the color provided by large bracts beneath the flowers. The heads are borne on 1-ft tall stems with alternate, linear leaves. This plant grows in meadows and woods from Nova Scotia to Minnesota, south to South Carolina and Louisiana. Cross-leaved Milkwort, *P. cruciata*, also has heads of purple flowers but its narrow leaves grow in whorls. It is found in marshes, pine barrens, and wet woods on the coastal plain in the east.

Orange Milkwort, *Polygala lutea*, has dense heads of orange flowers and alternate, narrow leaves on erect or sprawling stems. It grows in acid bogs and pine barrens in the coastal plain. Several other species have yellow flowers.

Spurge family

Euphorbiaceae

A large and varied family of trees, shrubs, and herbs found throughout the tropics and temperate regions of the world, with the majority in the tropics. It contains 300 genera and 5000 species, some of great economic importance. Rubber trees come from this family, as do several tropical crop plants, including cassava and tapioca. Castor Oil, which comes from *Ricinus communis*, is used in paints, textiles, and dyes, as well as medicinally. The family also supplies ornamental plants, including poinsettias and crotons.

Family features The flowers are regular. Male and female flowers are separate, usually on the same plant. The flowers generally have sepals but no petals, but both may be missing. The flowers contain one to many stamens and a superior ovary with three cells. The fruits are capsules or drupes. The leaves are usually simple, alternate, often with stipules.

The **Spurges**, *Euphorbia* species, are a vast group of 2000 herbs, shrubs, and trees. Their flowers are reduced, the male ones consisting of a single stamen, the females of a single pistil. Several male flowers are arranged around one female, and together they form the center of a cup-like bract, the whole arrangement looking like a single flower. These are grouped in clusters with special leaves beneath, sometimes green, sometimes colored. Spurges have milky sap, often caustic and sometimes poisonous.

Some spurges are weeds. **Cypress Spurge**, *Euphorbia cyparissias*, is a European plant that has escaped from gardens to grow in waste places, on roadsides, and in cemeteries, mostly east of the Rockies. This is a perennial, hairless plant, with creeping rhizomes and many erect, branched stems up to 1ft tall, with dense linear leaves. Umbels of typical spurge flowers grow at the tops of many of the stems, the round, yellow-green leaves of the umbels turning red in the sun or with age. Its white sap is caustic and poisonous.

Sun Spurge, *Euphorbia helioscopia*, is a common weed in waste places from Ontario to Kansas, and elsewhere in North America. It is an annual, with a single leafy stem 8–20in tall ending in umbels of spurge flowers cupped in broad, leafy, often bright yellow bracts.

Fire-on-the-mountain or Wild Poinsettia, *Euphorbia heterophylla*, is a different sort of annual, with an erect, branched stem up to 3ft tall. Its leaves vary from linear to ovate, some with serrated edges. The upper leaves are often lobed, and those just beneath the flowers are blotched with red or white at the base, resembling those of Poinsettias. Flowers appear in late summer, the male flowers remaining within cups while the females hang outside like little balls. This plant grows in

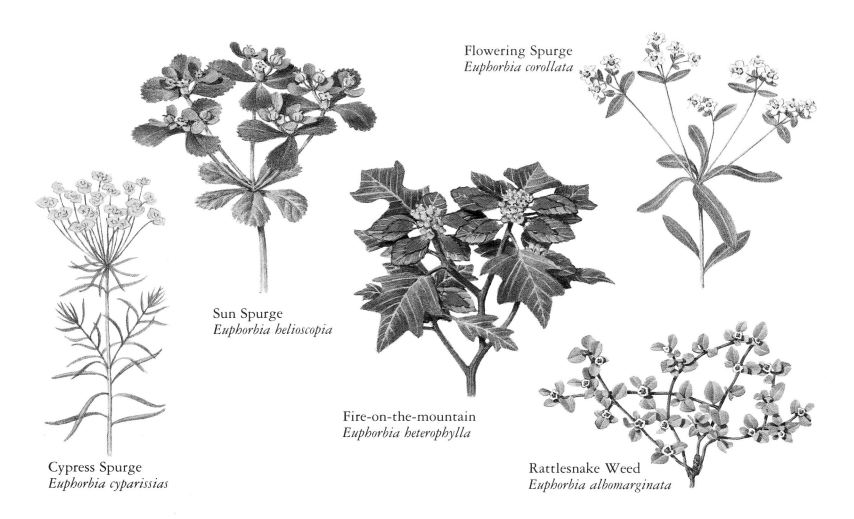

Flowering Spurge
Euphorbia corollata

Sun Spurge
Euphorbia helioscopia

Fire-on-the-mountain
Euphorbia heterophylla

Cypress Spurge
Euphorbia cyparissias

Rattlesnake Weed
Euphorbia albomarginata

sandy soil, in open and disturbed places from Wisconsin to South Dakota, south to Florida and Arizona. It is grown in gardens in the east. Snow-on-the-mountain, *E. marginata*, is a related plant with white or white-edged bracts. It grows in open waste places in the east and in the prairies.

Flowering Spurge, *Euphorbia corollata* (p. 96), is a perennial, with clumps of 3-ft tall stems; these have scattered, oval leaves near the base, and whorls of leaves beneath umbels of flowers at the top. The "flowers" look as if they have five white petals each, but these are the bracts, and the true flowers are the typical spurge ones. This plant grows in dry woods and prairies, roadsides and old fields from Ontario to Minnesota, south to Florida and Texas. Its sap is caustic; the plant was used by Indians to burn off warts, and also as an emetic.

Some spurges are creeping plants with prostrate stems. **Rattlesnake Weed**, *Euphorbia albomarginata* (p. 96), is a western plant found in deserts, arid grassland, scrub, and chaparral from California to Texas, north to Utah and south into Mexico. Its prostrate stems have rounded, opposite leaves, each one with an attractive, thin white margin. The flowers are borne in the middle of small white, maroon-centered cups formed of bracts. **Prostrate Spurge**, *E. supina*, grows in gardens and waste places from southern Quebec and Maine to Florida and Texas, forming a small mat of prostrate stems. Its opposite, elliptical leaves are often purple-stained.

Tread-softly or Spurge Nettle, *Cnidoscolus stimulosus*, is well named. It is covered with stinging hairs which inflict a painful rash if they are touched. This is a perennial plant, with erect or sprawling stems up to 3ft tall, and large, palmately lobed leaves. The fragrant, showy flowers grow in clusters at the top of the plant, the central flower in each cluster an inconspicuous female, the outer flowers male with white, trumpet-like sepals. Tread-softly grows in sandy woods and fields from Virginia to Florida and Texas.

Three-seeded Mercury, *Acalypha gracilens*, is one of several species given this common name. It is an annual plant, with branched stems up to 3ft tall, alternate, lance-shaped leaves, and minute male and female flowers in spikes in the leaf axils. The spikes contain several female flowers near the base, and male flowers along most of its length. This plant grows in sandy soils, in open woods, fields, and meadows from Maine to Wisconsin, south to Florida and Texas.

Crotons, *Croton* species, belong to a large genus of about 750 herbs and shrubs found in tropical and warm temperate regions in all parts of the world except Europe. They have a characteristic way of branching, with two or more stems arising at every node, and are covered with star-shaped hairs. Many are used in medicine, particularly in Central and South America. They are used to treat skin and eye diseases, to kill worms, and reduce fever.

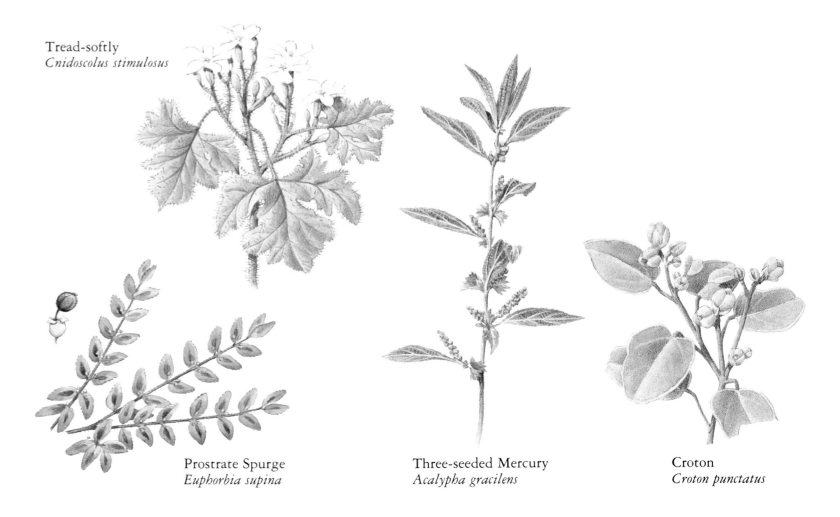

Tread-softly
Cnidoscolus stimulosus

Prostrate Spurge
Euphorbia supina

Three-seeded Mercury
Acalypha gracilens

Croton
Croton punctatus

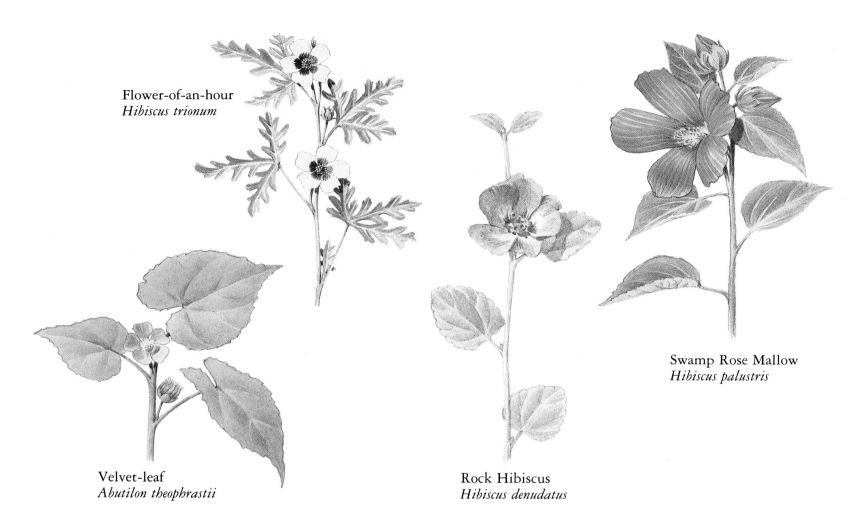

Flower-of-an-hour
Hibiscus trionum

Swamp Rose Mallow
Hibiscus palustris

Velvet-leaf
Abutilon theophrastii

Rock Hibiscus
Hibiscus denudatus

About 30 species come from the U.S., most from the south and southeast. *Croton punctatus* (p. 97), is usually an annual. The whole plant, except the upper surface of the leaves, is covered with clusters of hairs, each cluster with a red tubercle in the center. The flowers are borne in small recemes at the tops of the stems, the female flowers at the base of each raceme, and the male flowers at the apex. Plants grow in coastal sand dunes from North Carolina to Florida and Mississippi. Texas Croton, *C. texensis*, grows in the midwestern prairies. It has 3-ft tall stems with lance-shaped leaves, and male and female flowers on separate plants. It is used in Indian medicine as a skin wash, as an insecticide, and for treating eye diseases.

Mallow family

Malvaceae

This family has about 40 genera and 900 species of herbs, shrubs, and trees growing in tropical and temperate regions of the world, many found in tropical areas of America. Many of the plants in the family are grown in tropical and temperate gardens, from shrubs like hibiscus to perennial plants like the mallows and hollyhocks. Cotton comes from this family. It is a source, not only of cotton, but also of oil, which is extracted from the seeds and used in soap and cosmetics; the residue from

the seeds is used in paper and cellulose manufacture.

Family features The flowers are regular and hermaphrodite with five petals and sepals, the sepals often united and the petals more or less separate. There are numerous stamens joined at the base to form a tube, and the ovary is superior with five to many carpels. The fruit may be a capsule or schizocarpic, i.e. splitting into many one-seeded sections when ripe. The flowers may be borne singly in the leaf axils or in branched clusters. The leaves are alternate, entire or palmately lobed, with stipules. The plants are often velvety with star-shaped hairs, or scaly.

Abutilon is a mainly tropical genus of shrubs and herbs, with about 100 species. **Velvet-leaf**, *Abutilon theophrastii*, also called Pie-maker and Indian Mallow, is native to southern Asia, but has escaped from cultivation to become naturalized in disturbed and waste places, and on roadsides in many parts of North America, most commonly in the south. This is a velvety, annual plant, with an erect, branched stem up to 6ft tall, and large, heart-shaped leaves up to 8in across. It has yellow flowers with wedge-shaped petals, borne singly in the axils of the leaves. The fruits consist of 10–15 hairy, one-seeded sections with conspicuous horizontal beaks.

Hibiscus is another large genus, with about 200 species of shrubs and herbs from the warmer regions of the world. **Flower-of-an-hour**, *H. trionum* (p. 98), comes from southeastern Europe but has become naturalized in much of North America, growing in disturbed and waste places, on roadsides and in fields. It is a branched, annual plant, with an erect stem up to 2ft tall, and three-lobed, wavy-margined leaves. Solitary flowers grow in the leaf axils in summer; the flowers are quite large, pale yellow with purple centers, and they last for only a few hours, then quickly wilt. The fruits which follow are hairy capsules divided into five sections, each enclosed in the bristly, five-angled calyx, which becomes inflated and papery.

Rock Hibiscus, *Hibiscus denudatus* (p. 98), grows in rocky places in the deserts from southern California to Texas, and into Mexico. It is a straggling plant, with long stems and a few velvety, ovate leaves, all covered with whitish hairs. The bowl-shaped flowers are small, white or pale pink, borne in the leaf axils and terminating the stems.

Swamp Rose Mallow, *Hibiscus palustris* (p. 98), has showy, bright pink flowers like those of hollyhocks, each one about 6in wide and borne in the axils of the upper leaves. The plant is a coarse perennial, with stems up to 6ft tall, and yellow-green, ovate leaves. It grows in coastal marshes from Massachusetts to Florida, and in the Great Lakes region. The similar *H. moscheutos* grows in the same places, and has yellowish flowers with purple centers.

The **Mallows** are a group of about 30 species belonging to the genus *Malva*. They are Old World plants from Europe and Asia, and several have become widely naturalized as weeds in North America. Like many of the genera in this family, mallows have distinctive fruits, earning them the common name of Cheeses. Each fruit resembles a round cheese cut into segments. The base of the fruit is formed from the receptacle cupped in the calyx, and the segments are formed from a flat ring of a one-seeded nutlets.

Probably the most widespread and abundant mallow in North America is the **Common Mallow**, *Malva neglecta*, which grows as a weed in gardens and waste places. It is one of the smallest species, an annual with prostrate or sprawling, branched stems growing up to 2ft tall. It has many downy hairs on the stems, and long-stalked, rounded, palmately lobed leaves. The flowers are white, veined or tinged with pink or purple, with notched petals, and they grow in clusters in the leaf axils in summer. The fruits each contain 12–15 finely hairy sections.

Another common mallow is **Musk Mallow**, *Malva moschata* (p. 99), which grows in waste places and on roadsides from Quebec to British Columbia, south in the east to Virginia and Nebraska, in mountains further south. This is a perennial plant up to 4ft tall, with branched, hairy stems. It has a clump of kidney-shaped basal leaves and the stem leaves are more deeply divided the higher up they grow on the stems. The rose pink or purple flowers are mostly borne in dense terminal

Musk Mallow
Malva moschata

Cheeseweed
Malva parviflora

Common Mallow
Malva neglecta

Marsh Mallow
Althaea officinalis

clusters; they have triangular, notched petals. The dark fruits are rounded and densely hairy. **Cheeseweed**, *M. parviflora* (p. 99), is a common weed in Californian orchards and in waste places. It is an annual, with branched stems, rounded, lobed leaves, and whitish or pinkish flowers in the leaf axils.

Marsh Mallow, *Althaea officinalis* (p. 99), is a European plant which can now be found in salt marshes from Massachusetts to Vermont. It is an erect, branched plant up to 6ft tall, with velvety, lobed leaves, and clusters of pink flowers in the axils of the upper leaves. The roots of this plant are rich in mucilage, and were used to make the original marshmallows. They can still be used in this way, and can also be cooked as a vegetable.

Wheel Mallow, *Modiola caroliniana*, is a southern species found as a native plant as far north as South Carolina, but now naturalized further north in the east and in California. It grows as an annual or biennial weed in lawns and waste places. This is a spreading, prostrate plant with stems up to 2ft long, which lie on the ground and root at the nodes. It has palmate, maple-like leaves with 3–5 coarsely toothed lobes and small, solitary, reddish-purple flowers in the leaf axils. Like the mallows, this plant has a cheese-like fruit, with 14–25 kidney-shaped nutlets each containing one seed.

Sida, *Sida rhombifolia*, is a branched, annual or biennial plant, with tough stems and diamond-shaped, toothed leaves.

Its solitary, small, creamy-white flowers grow on long stalks in the leaf axils. Plants may be found in spring and summer, in waste places and on roadsides from North Carolina and Virginia to Florida and Texas. This is one of about 20 *Sida* species in North America, many with yellow flowers. Some are tropical weeds, extending north as far as Virginia, and growing in waste places and on roadsides.

Alkali Mallow, *Sida hederacea*, is a western species, a perennial with prostrate stems and small, whitish-yellow flowers in the axils of the leaves. It is velvety in texture, with whitish, star-shaped hairs, and has rounded, kidney-shaped leaves. This plant grows in many wet and alkaline places in the southwest and Pacific states.

There are several genera and many species in this family which are native to western North America. They include the Globe Mallows, *Sphaeralcea* and *Iliamna* species, the Checkermallows, *Sidalcea* species, several *Hibiscus* species, and the Bush Mallows, which are shrubs belonging to the genus *Malacothamnus*. Many are mountain plants growing in lush, mountain meadows and beside springs, while others are found in the arid areas and deserts.

The **Poppy Mallows** are a small group of southern and midwestern species in the genus *Callirhoë*. **Winecups**, *C. involucrata*, is the most widely distributed, growing in prairies and plains from Minnesota to Wyoming, and south to Texas.

Wheel Mallow
Modiola caroliniana

Alkali Mallow
Sida hederacea

Sida
Sida rhombifolia

Winecups
Callirhoë involucrata

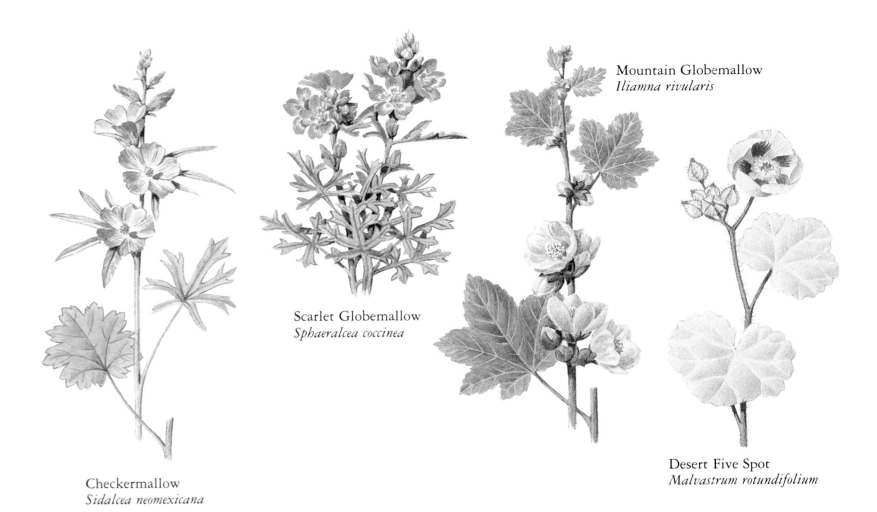

Scarlet Globemallow
Sphaeralcea coccinea

Mountain Globemallow
Iliamna rivularis

Checkermallow
Sidalcea neomexicana

Desert Five Spot
Malvastrum rotundifolium

It is a perennial plant, with trailing, hairy stems. Its leaves are palmately cleft into 5–7 toothed lobes and it bears a few large, bowl-shaped, crimson flowers on long stalks in the leaf axils. The flowers have broadly truncated petals and three bracts immediately beneath the calyx, two features which are typical of poppy mallows. The fruits have the typical ring-form of the mallow family, with 10–20 carpels.

Checkermallows, *Sidalcea* species, are another group of mostly western mallows; most have pink flowers and are difficult to distinguish from each other. Some are grown as ornamental garden plants. *Sidalcea neomexicana*, is one of the most widespread, growing in wet, often alkaline, places, beside streams and springs, in mountain valleys and scrub, from California to Oregon, and east to New Mexico and Wyoming. It is a perennial, with a clump of shallowly lobed leaves and narrow flowering spikes up to 3ft tall crowded with deep pink flowers. White Checkermallow, *S. candida*, is one of the few mallows with white flowers; it grows in wet places in the Rocky Mountains.

The **Globemallows** belonging to the genus *Sphaeralcea* are a group of about 20 western species, difficult to separate from each other. They are perennial plants with palmate leaves and erect flowering spikes (like that of a hollyhock) with reddish flowers. Many of them are densely covered with soft, velvety hairs; even the backs of the fruits are densely hairy — with star-shaped hairs. **Scarlet Globemallow**, *S. coccinea*, grows in plains and dry prairies from Manitoba to Alberta, south to Texas and New Mexico. It is a spreading plant with creeping rhizomes; in early summer its weakly erect stems and brick-red flowers form patches of color on roadsides.

Another group of plants, also known as Globemallows, belongs to the genus *Iliamna*. **Mountain Globemallow**, *I. rivularis*, is also sometimes called Mountain Hollyhock; it grows in moist soil, beside springs, and along the sides of rivers and streams in the mountains from British Columbia to Oregon, east to Montana and Colorado. It is a large, perennial plant with clumps of large, maple-like leaves less deeply dissected than the leaves of many mallows; in summer it has erect, leafy spikes of pink, hollyhock-like flowers 3–6ft tall. The fruits of *Iliamna* species are formed in a ring, like those of many mallows, but they differ from other species in having more than one seed in each segment.

Desert Five Spot, *Malvastrum rotundifolium*, is an annual plant about 12–18in tall, with branched stems and rounded, heart-shaped leaves all covered with bristly hairs. Even the sepals are bristly on the conspicuous buds, and the flowers are globe-shaped when fresh, pink in color with a deeper spot at the base of each petal. This little plant grows in open places in Creosote Bush scrub and in the Mojave and Colorado deserts from California to Arizona and Utah.

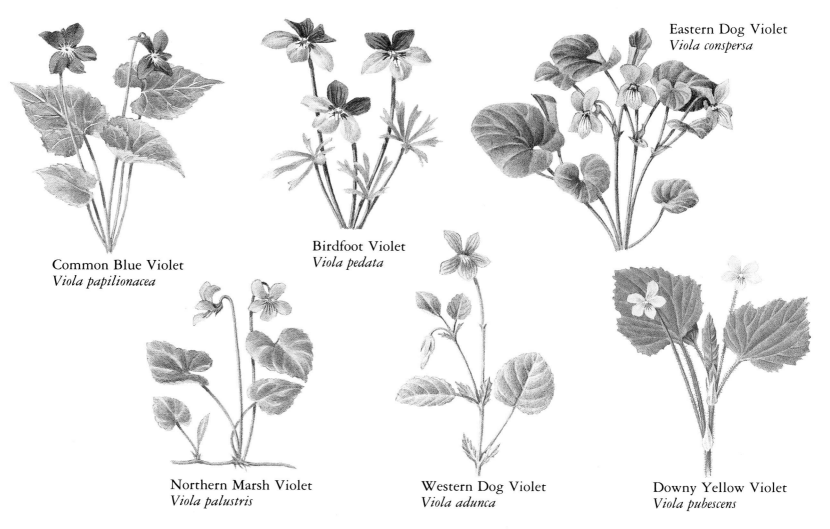

Eastern Dog Violet
Viola conspersa

Common Blue Violet
Viola papilionacea

Birdfoot Violet
Viola pedata

Northern Marsh Violet
Viola palustris

Western Dog Violet
Viola adunca

Downy Yellow Violet
Viola pubescens

Violet family

Violaceae

For many people this family is synonymous with pansies and violets, *Viola* species, although there are actually 22 genera and 900 species in the family, and only 500 of them are in the genus *Viola*. They are found in temperate and tropical regions, and are mostly herbaceous plants, although a few of the tropical species are shrubs. Violets and pansies are grown in gardens, and some violets are also used in herb medicine and perfumery.

Family features The flowers are solitary or borne in racemes; they are regular or bilaterally symmetrical. Each has five persistent, overlapping sepals and five petals; these are usually unequal, and the lowermost is spurred. There are five stamens, the lowermost often spurred, and with the anthers of all five joined in a ring around the ovary. The ovary is superior with one cell. The fruits are capsules or berries. The leaves are simple and alternate with leafy stipules.

Violets are beautiful, small plants with distinctive flowers like faces. There are over 80 species in North America, growing in a variety of habitats, especially in damp or shady places. Many are grown in gardens. Often their main flowering season appears to be spring but in fact they flower through the spring and summer. This apparent discrepancy comes from the fact that they produce two kinds of flowers. The familiar ones, with bright petals, are spring flowers, and the summer flowers remain hidden beneath the foliage, do not open, and are self-pollinated. It is these flowers that form most of the seed.

Violet flowers are quite distinctive, with five petals forming a bilaterally symmetrical and spurred flower. They come in three colors—blue-violet, yellow, and white—are often veined, and the two lateral petals are frequently bearded. Plants may form rosettes of leaves with flowers on separate stalks, or may have long, leafy stems with flowers in the leaf axils. Many species are widespread and common, others are confined to small areas, some are rare.

Common Blue Violet or Meadow Violet, *Viola papilionacea*, is a low-growing plant with rosettes of leaves, and flowers on separate stalks. The leaves are smooth and hairless, with long stalks and pointed, heart-shaped blades. The flowers are blue-violet with white beards on the two lateral petals, the lowest petal boat-shaped with a long spur. The plant grows in low-lying fields, damp woods, and meadows, and on damp roadsides from Massachusetts to Minnesota, and south to Georgia and Oklahoma.

There are many blue-flowered, rosette-forming violets similar to Common Blue Violet in eastern North America.

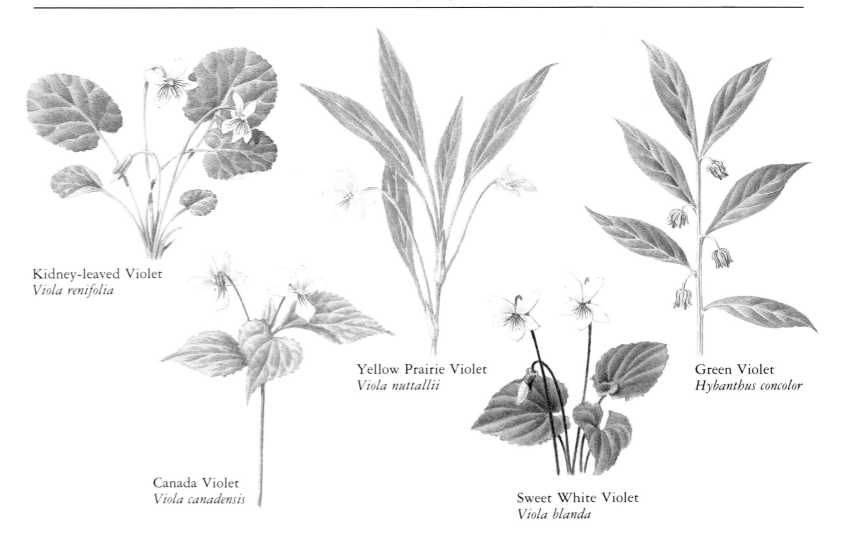

Kidney-leaved Violet
Viola renifolia

Yellow Prairie Violet
Viola nuttallii

Green Violet
Hybanthus concolor

Canada Violet
Viola canadensis

Sweet White Violet
Viola blanda

Northern Marsh Violet, *V. palustris*, has rosettes of thin, rounded leaves and pale lilac, blue-veined flowers. The **Birdfoot Violet**, *V. pedata* (p. 102), and the Prairie Violet, *V. pedatifida*, have leaves deeply divided into linear segments; the first grows in dry woods and fields in the east, the second on the prairies.

Western Dog Violet, *Viola adunca* (p. 102), has a different form, for it has erect stems up to 8in long, with rounded, scallop-edged leaves. In the axils of these grow the flowers, pale to dark violet in color, with a spur on the lowest petal. This plant is found in open woods, in meadows, and on hillsides from Canada to California, and on the Great Plains. The similar **Eastern Dog Violet**, *V. conspersa* (p. 102), grows in damp meadows and woods from Quebec south in the mountains to Georgia.

The majority of the yellow violets have leafy stems rather than leaf rosettes. **Downy Yellow Violet**, *Viola pubescens* (p. 102), grows in rich, dry woods from Quebec to North Dakota, and south to Georgia and Oklahoma. It is a softly hairy plant, large for a violet, with stems reaching 16in long, and 5-in wide leaves. Its flowers are clear yellow with purple-brown veins. **Yellow Prairie Violet**, *V. nuttallii*, has many, more or less upright stems, and lance-shaped or ovate leaves. Its yellow flowers are brown-veined with very little beard, and often tinged with purple. This violet grows in plains and prairies, dry woods and slopes from Minnesota to Missouri, west to British Columbia and California.

Many of the white violets are very small plants of the northern woods, 6in tall at most, with little rosettes of leaves. **Sweet White Violet**, *Viola blanda*, is found in moist, shady places; it has creeping stems, rosettes of heart-shaped leaves, and fragrant white flowers. The lower petals are brown-veined and the upper ones twisted backward. **Kidney-leaved Violet**, *V. renifolia*, is similar but lacks the creeping stems; it grows in swamps and woods throughout much of Canada, into the northern U.S., south in the mountains of the east and west.

Canada Violet, *Viola canadensis*, is a rather different plant with stems up to 15in long, and pointed, heart-shaped leaves. Its white flowers have a central yellow blotch. It grows in moist woods across southern Canada, into the northern U.S., and south in the mountains.

The **Green Violet**, *Hybanthus concolor*, is so different as to be hardly recognizable as a violet. It is a coarse plant with erect, leafy stems up to 3ft tall. Its leaves are broadly elliptical, with pointed tips and short stalks. In the axils of these leaves grow the little drooping flowers, with greenish-white petals shorter than the linear sepals. The lowermost petal is wider than the others and is spurred. This perennial plant grows in rich woods and ravines from Ontario to Michigan, south to Georgia, Arkansas, and Kansas.

Gourd family

Cucurbitaceae

Also called **Cucumber family**. A family of about 100 genera and 900 species, mostly herbs with trailing stems, or vines, mainly from the tropical regions of the world. There are many economically important food species in this family, including vegetables and fruits like squashes, melons, water melons, pumpkins, and cucumbers. Gourds and calabashes are used as containers in tropical countries.

Family features The flowers are regular, with male and female flowers separate, either on the same plant or on separate plants. Each flower has 4–6 sepals more or less united into a tube, and five free or united petals. Each male flower has 1–5 stamens, usually more or less united; each female flower has an inferior ovary with 1–3 cells. The fruit is generally a fleshy, spongy berry with a leathery rind. The plants are often stiffly hairy and have watery juice. They have alternate, simple, often palmately lobed leaves, and many species have spirally coiled, often branched tendrils growing opposite the leaves.

Wild Pumpkin, *Cucurbita foetidissima*, is known by several other names, including Buffalo Gourd, Stinking Gourd, and Bigroot, references to its large inedible fruit, bad smell, and immense taproot. It is a perennial plant, with rough, trailing stems up to 20ft long, separate but hidden by large, gray-green, lobed, triangular leaves. It has funnel-shaped, yellow flowers beneath the leaves, male and female on the same plant. The female flowers give rise to the fruits — hard, spherical, inedible pumpkins striped in light and dark green when young, ripening to lemon yellow. This monstrous plant grows in dry, gravelly, and sandy places from Missouri to California, and south into Mexico. Further east it has spread along the railroads.

Wild Cucumber or Balsam-apple, *Echinocystis lobata*, is a more northern species of moist woods and meadows, found from New Brunswick to Saskatchewan, south to Florida and Texas, but rare in the south. It is an annual vine which clings to vegetation with tendrils opposite its maple-like leaves. It has sprays of small white flowers on long stalks in the leaf axils, male and female separate but on the same plant. Each flower has six petals. The fruits are solitary, greenish berries covered with weak prickles and drying as they ripen. Each fruit contains four seeds.

Bur-cucumber, *Sicyos angulatus*, is a similar plant, also a climbing vine with palmately lobed leaves. But it has five-petalled flowers and small clusters of bristly, single-seeded fruits. It grows in moist places, in woods, on river banks and roadsides from Quebec to Minnesota, and south to Florida and Arizona.

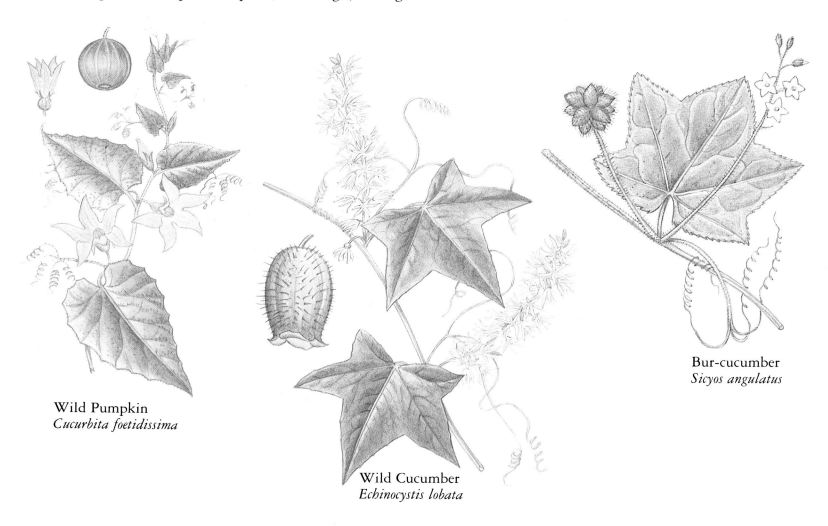

Wild Pumpkin
Cucurbita foetidissima

Wild Cucumber
Echinocystis lobata

Bur-cucumber
Sicyos angulatus

Stickleaf family

Loasaceae

A small family of herbs, with about 15 genera and 250 species, mostly from the warm, dry regions of America.

Family features The flowers are hermaphrodite and regular, solitary or borne in heads or clusters. Each flower has 4–5 sepals fused into a tube, which is often ribbed and persistent. The 4–5 petals are sometimes clawed and the stamens are usually numerous, free or in bundles opposite the petals. The ovary is inferior with 1–3 cells. The fruit is a capsule. The leaves are opposite or alternate, simple or divided, without stipules. These are hairy plants, with rough bristly, barbed or stinging hairs.

There are about 50 species in the genus *Mentzelia*, many found in the west, some growing in dry, sandy or gravelly places, others on rocky hillsides and on the plains. Some are called **Blazing Stars** because of their bright yellow, star-like flowers, others are called **Stickleafs** because their barbed hairs make them cling to clothes or animal hair. Many are annual plants, with branched, often white stems, and rigid leaves.

The **Giant Blazing Star**, *Mentzelia laevicaulis*, has large, lemon-yellow flowers at the top of shining white stems. It is a biennial with a rosette of sinuate leaves in the first year, and a flowering stem up to 5ft tall in the second, with stiff hairs near the top of the stem and irregularly toothed, rough, grayish leaves. It grows in dry, gravelly places in arid areas from California to British Columbia, and through the interior to Utah and Montana.

Other members of the genus, like **White-stemmed Stickleaf**, *Mentzelia albicaulis*, have small, tubular, yellow flowers. These are borne on slender, shining white stems in the axils of small, narrow leaves. This annual plant grows in dry, sandy places, in pine woods and scrub east of the Sierra Nevada from California to British Columbia, and east to New Mexico and Nebraska.

White-bracted Stickleaf, *Mentzelia involucrata*, is a low-growing, leafy plant 6–12in tall, with rough, coarsely toothed leaves. It has pale, creamy yellow, cup-like flowers on the ends of its branches. This hairy plant grows in rocky places, on hillsides and in washes from California to Arizona, and south into Mexico.

Desert Rock Nettle, *Eucnide urens*, is a perennial, spreading, bushy plant with yellowish, often sprawling stems, and ovate, toothed leaves, the whole plant covered with stinging hairs. It grows up to 2ft tall, but is often broader than high. In early summer it produces many clusters of attractive, pale yellow flowers. This plant grows in dry, rocky places in the deserts from southern California to Utah and Arizona.

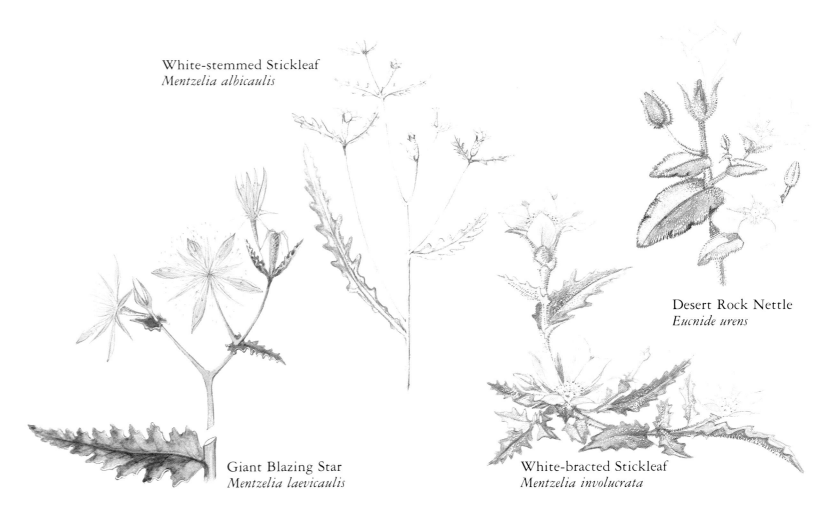

White-stemmed Stickleaf
Mentzelia albicaulis

Desert Rock Nettle
Eucnide urens

Giant Blazing Star
Mentzelia laevicaulis

White-bracted Stickleaf
Mentzelia involucrata

Passion Flower family

Passifloraceae

There are about 12 genera and 600 species in this mainly tropical family of trees, shrubs, and vines. The most familiar are the Passion Flowers of the genus *Passiflora*, several of which are grown in gardens for their spectacularly unusual flowers and for their edible fruits.

Family features The flowers are regular and hermaphrodite, or have male and female flowers separate. They have five overlapping, free or partially joined sepals, and five overlapping petals, often joined at the base. There are five or more stamens, and a superior ovary with 3–5 styles, often on a stalk. In addition, the flowers often have a corona—one or more rows of thread-like filaments at the base of the petals. The fruits are capsules or berries. The leaves are alternate, entire or lobed, and with glands on the leaf stalks. The small stipules soon fall.

Passion Flowers are climbers, clinging by means of tendrils. Many, but not all, have bizarre flowers with a striking corona, large, club-shaped anthers, and a large, trifid stigma, often in contrasting colors. *Passiflora incarnata*, from the eastern U.S. is no exception, and its large, wheel-like flowers have white sepals and petals often obscured by the purple and pink corona, creamy anthers on brown filaments, and creamy stigma. Its edible yellow berries are known as maypops. The flowers are solitary, growing in the axils of three-lobed leaves. This plant grows in open woods, fields, and roadsides, unlike *Passiflora lutea*, another eastern species which hides its yellow flowers in moist shady places.

Rockrose family

Cistaceae

There are about 8 genera and 200 species in this small family of herbs and shrubs, the majority found in the Mediterranean region. Some of them are highly decorative shrubs for dry, sunny places in the garden. The various species and varieties of *Cistus* are small, evergreen shrubs with distinctively crinkled pink or white flowers. *Helianthemum* species are mostly creeping plants for the rock garden.

Family features The flowers are hermaphrodite and regular, with 3–5 contorted, free sepals, five often contorted, overlapping petals which soon fall, many free stamens, and a superior ovary. The fruits are capsules with several cells. The leaves are usually opposite and entire with stipules. These plants often have star-shaped hairs.

Frostweed, *Helianthemum canadense*, grows in dry, sandy soil in open places or open woods from Maine to Minnesota,

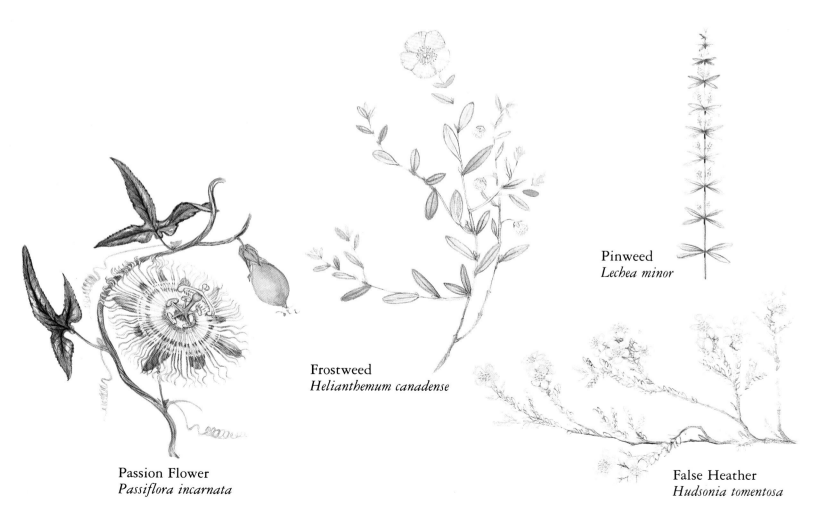

Passion Flower
Passiflora incarnata

Frostweed
Helianthemum canadense

Pinweed
Lechea minor

False Heather
Hudsonia tomentosa

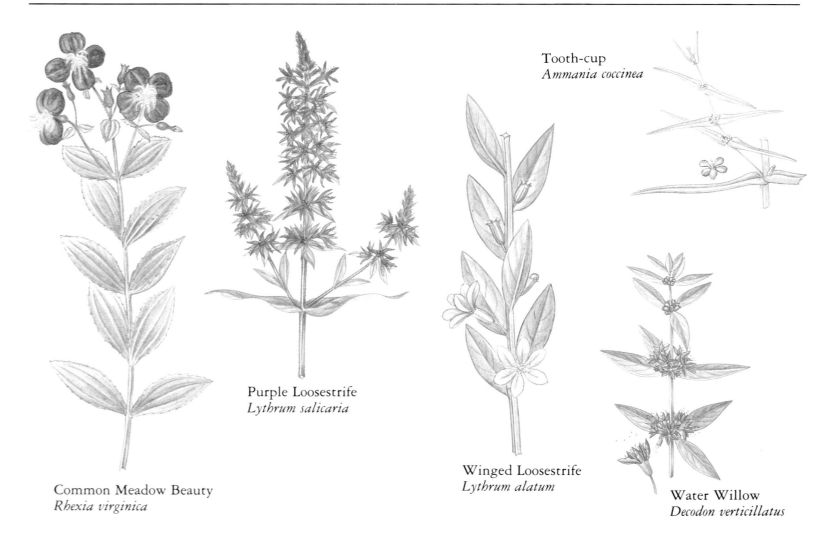

Purple Loosestrife
Lythrum salicaria

Tooth-cup
Ammania coccinea

Common Meadow Beauty
Rhexia virginica

Winged Loosestrife
Lythrum alatum

Water Willow
Decodon verticillatus

south to North Carolina and Tennessee. It is a perennial, with thin, wiry stems and many linear leaves. The yellow flowers are borne singly, terminating the main branches of the stems; they open in early summer, each flower lasting for only a day. Late-season flowers mostly lack petals and grow on side shoots lower down the stems, soon overtopping the terminal flowers. A similar species, *H. bicknellii*, grows in dry, sandy places from South Dakota to Texas, west into the prairies.

False Heather, *Hudsonia tomentosa* (p. 106), is a matted, low-growing plant with woody stems covered by tiny, overlapping, evergreen leaves, gray-woolly in color and texture. In early summer the plants produce sulfur-yellow flowers in the axils of the leaves at the tops of the branches. Plants may be found on coastal beaches and dunes from New Brunswick to North Carolina, and in sandy places in the prairies around the Great Lakes. Golden Heather, *H. ericoides*, is greener, with spreading leaves; it grows on beaches and dunes from Newfoundland to Virginia.

The **Pinweeds** are a small group of eastern species in the genus *Lechea*. They are small plants with erect stems and many small leaves. In late summer they produce numerous, long clusters of minute red flowers. Most have alternate leaves but *Lechea minor* (p. 106), has whorled ones. It grows in sandy fields and open woods from New Hampshire to the Great Lakes region, south to Florida and Texas.

Meadow Beauty family

Melastomataceae

This is a large family of tropical and subtropical plants, with about 240 genera and 3000 species of trees, shrubs, and herbs, many of them very beautiful and some grown in gardens. The family is represented in North America by only one genus and about 10 species.

The **Meadow Beauties**, *Rhexia* species, are all found in eastern and southern North America, mostly in the U.S. They are perennial plants with erect, branched stems, opposite, more or less stalkless leaves, and large, usually pink or purple flowers. The flowers are regular and hermaphrodite, with four sepals fused into a tube, four large petals, and eight stamens. The fruit is a capsule enclosed by the persistent calyx-tube, which becomes distended to accommodate it, the terminal part of the calyx becoming a flaring neck, so that the whole thing resembles an urn.

One of the most widespread is **Common Meadow Beauty**, *Rhexia virginica*. It grows in moist meadows, beside bogs and ditches, in wet, sandy pinelands from Nova Scotia to Wisconsin, and south to Florida and Texas. Although most species have pinkish flowers, *R. lutea*, the Yellow Meadow Beauty, has yellow flowers.

Common Evening Primrose
Oenothera biennis

Showy Evening Primrose
Oenothera speciosa

Tufted Evening Primrose
Oenothera caespitosa

Beach Primrose
Oenothera cheiranthifolia

Loosestrife family

Lythraceae

There are about 25 genera and 550 species of herbs and shrubs in this family, distributed all over the world, except in the cold regions. Some are grown as ornamentals in the garden. Henna, the hair dye, comes from the Middle Eastern species, *Lawsonia inermis*.

Family features The flowers are hermaphrodite and regular, with 4–8 sepals joined to form a tube, and 4–8 free petals, often crumpled in bud. There are 4–8 stamens, as many as or twice as many as the petals. The ovary is superior, with 2–6 cells and many seeds. The flowers are borne singly or in complex clusters. The fruits are usually capsules. The leaves are generally opposite or whorled and lack stipules, or the stipules are minute.

Lythrum is a genus of about 30 species of herbs and shrubs found throughout the world. **Purple Loosestrife**, *L. salicaria*, is found throughout most of the northern hemisphere beside streams and lakes, and in marshes. It is a perennial plant with tall, unbranched clumps of flowering stems, conspicuous in the late summer landscape with their reddish-purple flowers. The flower spikes are made up of many whorls of flowers, each with six crumpled petals.

There are three different flower forms in this species, found on separate plants. In the first type the flower has short styles, with long and medium-length stamens; the second kind has medium-length styles, with short and long stamens; the third kind has long styles, with short and medium-length stamens. The three kinds of stamens produce different size pollen. This complex arrangement is designed to ensure cross-pollination, a mechanism to maintain the vigor of the species—and this plant can be very vigorous in conditions that suit it, swamping other smaller plants in the area.

Several other *Lythrum* species grow in marshes in northeastern areas. **Winged Loosestrife**, *L. alatum* (p. 107), has erect, branched, four-angled stems with thick, pointed leaves, and solitary flowers in the axils of the upper leaves. It grows in moist soil on the prairies from southern Ontario to Kentucky and Texas.

The **Water Willow** or Swamp Loosestrife, *Decodon verticillatus* (p. 107), grows in arching tangles of stems, often leaning over the water of bogs or swamps, from Quebec to Illinois, south to Florida and Louisiana. It has slender stems with lance-shaped leaves in pairs or whorls. Its pink-purple flowers grow in clusters in the upper leaf axils; each flower has a cup-like calyx, five narrow petals, and styles and stamens like those of Purple Loosestrife.

Tooth-cup, *Ammania coccinea* (p. 107), is a much-branched

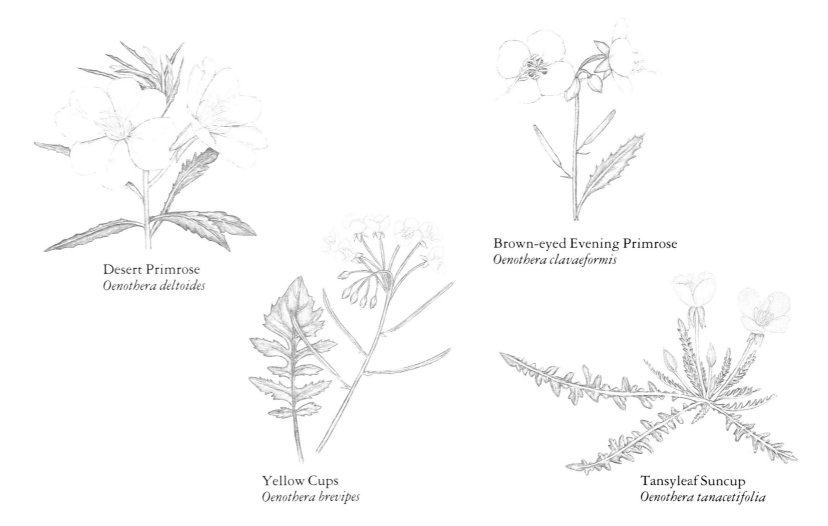

Desert Primrose
Oenothera deltoides

Brown-eyed Evening Primrose
Oenothera clavaeformis

Yellow Cups
Oenothera brevipes

Tansyleaf Suncup
Oenothera tanacetifolia

annual found in marshes and beside ponds from tropical America to Ohio and Iowa. It has succulent stems and opposite, long, lance-shaped leaces with clasping bases. In late summer small clusters of flowers grow in the leaf axils, their pink or purple petals mostly concealed within the sepals.

Evening Primrose family

Onagraceae

There are about 20 genera and 650 species in this family of herbs and shrubs, found throughout the world, but most commonly in the temperate regions. There are some highly ornamental garden plants in the family, including fuchsias, whose exotic flowers make them favorites with many people.

Family features The flowers are hermaphrodite and regular. Each has 4–5 sepals fused to form a calyx-tube which is attached to the ovary, and 4–5 free, often contorted or overlapping petals. There are as many stamens or twice as many stamens as calyx-lobes. The ovary is usually inferior, with 2–6 cells and few to many seeds. The fruits are usually capsules. The leaves are simple, opposite or alternate, usually without stipules.

The **Evening Primroses**, members of the genus *Oenothera*, are a large group of about 200 New World species, mostly

found in the temperate regions, many in the western U.S. One of the most widespread is the **Common Evening Primrose**, *O. biennis* (p. 108), found throughout much of the U.S. and southern Canada. It is a biennial, with a rosette of lance-shaped, often wavy leaves in the first year, and a leafy flowering spike up to 5ft tall in the second. The showy yellow flowers open in the evening a few at a time. Each flower has four reflexed sepals, four petals, eight prominent stamens, and a cross-shaped stigma. The fruits are large, oblong capsules held more or less upright.

This is the plant from which comes Evening Primrose oil, now the focus of much research. It soothes inflammation and eczema, helps wounds to heal, and eases coughs. The first-year plant is edible; the taproots can be cooked and eaten like carrots, and the young leaves of the rosette can be used as a green vegetable or in salads.

One of the most attractive evening primroses, a plant often grown in gardens, is the **Showy Evening Primrose**, *Oenothera speciosa* (p. 108), with white or pink flowers. This is a perennial, with a clump of erect, branched stems up to 2ft tall, and lobed, lance-shaped leaves. The flowers grow in the axils of the upper leaves during early summer, opening in the evening. The plant grows naturally in dry, open places, in the prairies and plains from Missouri and Kansas to Texas and into Mexico, but has also become naturalized farther east.

In the west there are many evening primroses and suncups, as some of them are called. Some are rosette-forming plants, like **Tufted Evening Primrose**, *Oenothera caespitosa* (p. 108), which has a rosette of linear leaves with lobed margins. Its flowers may grow directly from this rosette, or on a stem up to 8in tall. The flowers are large, fragrant, and white, aging to pink. This plant grows on dry and stony slopes in pinyon and juniper woodland, in the deserts and mountains of California, north to Washington and Utah. **Beach Primrose**, *O. cheiranthifolia* (p. 108), has a rosette of thick, grayish-hairy leaves, and radiating, more or less prostrate stems, which bear upward-facing yellow flowers on their ends. It grows on Pacific beaches.

Some botanists split the genus *Oenothera* into two separate genera: *Oenothera* and *Camissonia*. The *Oenothera* species have flowers which open in the evening, and the flowers have a four-lobed stigma; *Camissonia* species open in the morning and the flowers have a ball-shaped stigma. Other botanists think all these plants belong in the one genus *Oenothera*. In the first scheme, the following *Oenothera* species would belong to the genus *Camissonia*.

The **Desert Primrose** or Birdcage Evening Primrose, *Oenothera deltoides* (p. 109), is given this name because its dead stems resemble a birdcage. It grows as a winter or spring annual in sandy places and Creosote Bush scrub, in the Mojave and Colorado deserts, and into Arizona. It forms sprawling, pale stems, 1ft tall at most, with peeling skin, and long-stalked, ovate leaves on the stems and in a basal rosette. Large white flowers open from nodding buds in the axils of the upper leaves; their petals turn pink as they age. The fruits are cylindrical, woody capsules, also with peeling skin, light brown in color with purple spots.

Yellow Cups, *Oenothera brevipes* (p. 109), grows in the Mojave and Colorado deserts, in Nevada and Arizona, in Creosote Bush scrub, and on dry slopes and washes. It is an annual, with a reddish, erect stem up to 15in tall growing from a rosette of deeply toothed, basal leaves. Its flowers are bright yellow, borne in a terminal cluster on the erect stem, and followed by linear capsules.

Brown-eyed Evening Primrose, *Oenothera clavaeformis* (p. 109), is also known simply as Brown Eyes. Its name comes from the brown spot at the base of each petal. This is an annual plant with a rosette of irregularly toothed leaves and a single stem, only 15in tall, topped by a raceme of white flowers. The flowers darken to reddish as they age and dry. Brown Eyes grows in sandy soils from the Great Basin to California, in the Mojave and Colorado deserts.

Tansyleaf Suncup, *Oenothera tanacetifolia* (p. 109), grows in open places in meadows and sagebrush scrub, where the soil is moist in spring, from California to Washington, and east in

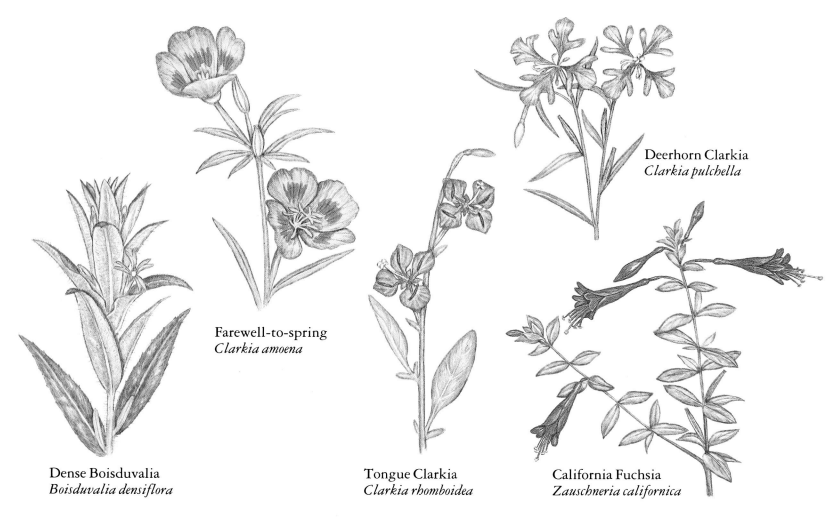

Farewell-to-spring
Clarkia amoena

Deerhorn Clarkia
Clarkia pulchella

Dense Boisduvalia
Boisduvalia densiflora

Tongue Clarkia
Clarkia rhomboidea

California Fuchsia
Zauschneria californica

the Great Basin. It forms rosettes of feathery leaves and in summer bears yellow, four-petalled flowers, each one on a separate stalk growing from the center of the rosette. The flowers darken to red as they age.

The *Boisduvalia* species are a group of about 10 annual plants found in western areas of North and South America, and in Tasmania. **Dense Boisduvalia**, *Boisduvalia densiflora* (p. 110), has erect, leafy stems up to 3ft tall, with lance-shaped lower leaves. In the dense inflorescence at the top of the stem grow rose-purple flowers in the axils of pointed-ovate bracts. The flowers have notched petals, and are followed by capsules which develop beneath the petals from inferior ovaries. This plant is found in moist places in a variety of habitats on the western slopes of the Californian mountains, north to British Columbia and Idaho.

There are about 33 *Clarkia* species in western North America and Chile, all annuals, most with showy flowers, and some grown in gardens. **Farewell-to-spring** or Herald-of-summer, *C. amoena* (p. 110), flowers as the green of the spring landscape begins to turn gold in summer. It has erect or sprawling stems up to 3ft tall, with lance-shaped leaves, like many clarkias, and terminal flowers opening from erect buds. The sepals are joined at the tips and are pushed to one side when the flowers open. The flowers are bowl-shaped, with four petal-lobes, pink or lavender with red blotches in the center of each petal. Farewell-to-spring grows on slopes and bluffs near the sea, in coastal scrub and grassland from southern British Columbia to central California.

Many clarkias have flowers with lobed petals, like the **Tongue Clarkia**, *Clarkia rhomboidea* (p. 110), which grows on open slopes and in chaparral from California and Arizona to Washington and Montana. Its simple or somewhat branched stem grows up to 3ft tall, and has a few ovate leaves with flowers near the top. The stem is curved while the buds are forming, and the buds droop, the stem straightening as the flowers open. Each petal has a narrow base with a small lobe on each side, and a diamond-shaped tip; they are pink or lavender, with darker flecks and often with a red base.

Some of the clarkias have truly elaborate flowers, like **Deerhorn Clarkia**, *Clarkia pulchella* (p. 110), with four petals arranged in a cross, each one trilobed. This species has erect stems with linear leaves and mauve-pink flowers; it grows in the Great Basin. In the flowers of Elegant Clarkia, *C. unguiculata*, each petal has a narrow base and a round lobe at the tip; the petals are pink with a deeper spot where the lobe meets the base. This plant grows in dry, shaded slopes in the mountain foothills of California.

California Fuchsia, *Zauschneria californica* (p. 110), is an attractive native plant which is also grown in gardens. It is rather shrubby, with many branches and linear leaves, often

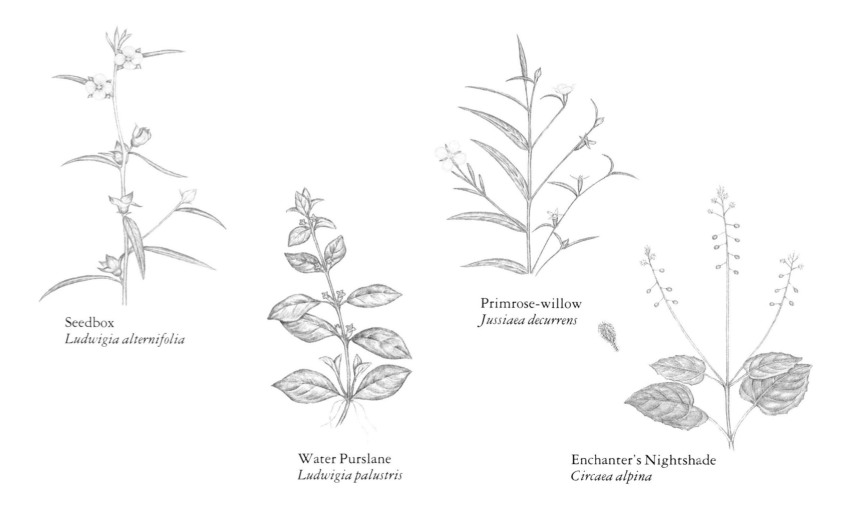

Seedbox
Ludwigia alternifolia

Water Purslane
Ludwigia palustris

Primrose-willow
Jussiaea decurrens

Enchanter's Nightshade
Circaea alpina

with matted, grayish hairs. In late summer and fall it covers itself with brilliant red, trumpet-shaped flowers growing in the upper leaf axils. Hummingbirds are attracted by the nectar secreted by the flowers, and the flowers are followed by erect, linear, four-angled capsules. In the wild the plant grows on dry, lower slopes, in chaparral and in coastal sage brush from southern Oregon to Baja California, and east to New Mexico.

Several *Ludwigia* species are found in North America, many in the east. They are perennial, aquatic or marsh plants, with erect, creeping or floating stems, their flowers resembling those of evening primroses. **Seedbox**, *L. alternifolia* (p. 111), is an erect plant, with many branched stems and lance-shaped leaves. Solitary, bright yellow flowers grow in the upper leaf axils; each flower has four petals alternating with four broad sepals, which are longer than the petals. The flowers are followed by squarish capsules opening by a pore at the top—the seedboxes. This plant grows in swamps and wet places from southern Ontario to Florida and Texas.

Water Purslane, *Ludwigia palustris* (p. 111), has flaccid stems, either creeping on muddy shores or floating in shallow water. The stems are often reddish and are leafy, with many opposite, lance-shaped, ovate leaves. In the latter half of summer tiny, petal-less flowers appear in the leaf axils. The plant is found in suitable habitats from Nova Scotia to Oregon, and south into Mexico.

Primrose-willow, *Jussiaea decurrens* (p. 111), is one of several species often placed in the genus *Ludwigia*. However, it has eight stamens, whereas the *Ludwigia* species have four. Primrose-willow grows in shallow water and swamps, usually in the coastal plain from Maryland to Florida and Texas, and north to Indiana. It has erect, branched stems up to 3ft tall, with narrow wings formed from the bases of the lance-shaped leaves. In the latter half of summer yellow flowers appear in the leaf axils; each one has four petals arranged in the form of a cross. *Jussiaea repens* is a related species with creeping or floating stems; it may form dense mats in ponds and swamps.

Enchanter's Nightshade, *Circaea alpina* (p. 111), is a little woodland plant growing in cool, damp woods across Canada, south as far as New York and South Dakota, farther south in the mountains to Tennessee in the east and New Mexico in the west. It has soft, weak stems, 1ft tall at most, and toothed, pointed, heart-shaped leaves with winged stalks. In late summer this plant forms sparse racemes of tiny white flowers, each flower pointing downward on a long stalk; each flower has two sepals, two notched petals, and two stamens. The fruits are bristly capsules pointing downward on long stalks like the flowers before them.

Fireweed, *Chamaenerion angustifolium* is one of the most easily recognizable and familiar willowherbs, forming great drifts of purple-red flowers in late summer, especially after

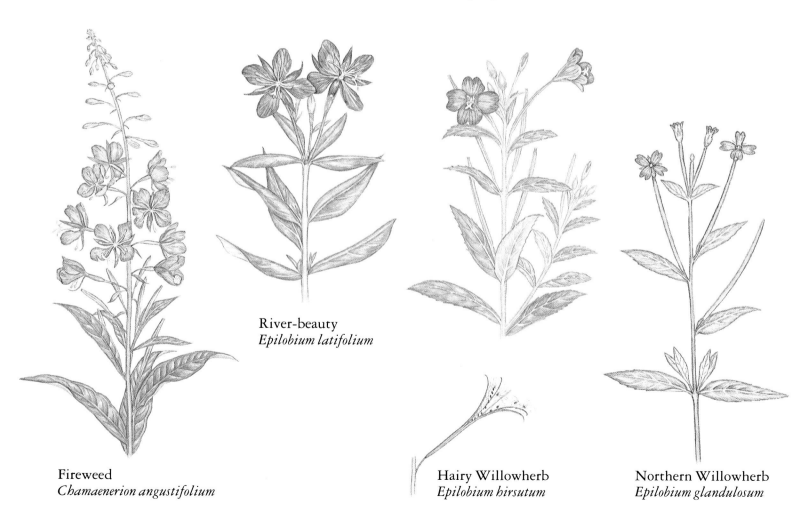

River-beauty
Epilobium latifolium

Fireweed
Chamaenerion angustifolium

Hairy Willowherb
Epilobium hirsutum

Northern Willowherb
Epilobium glandulosum

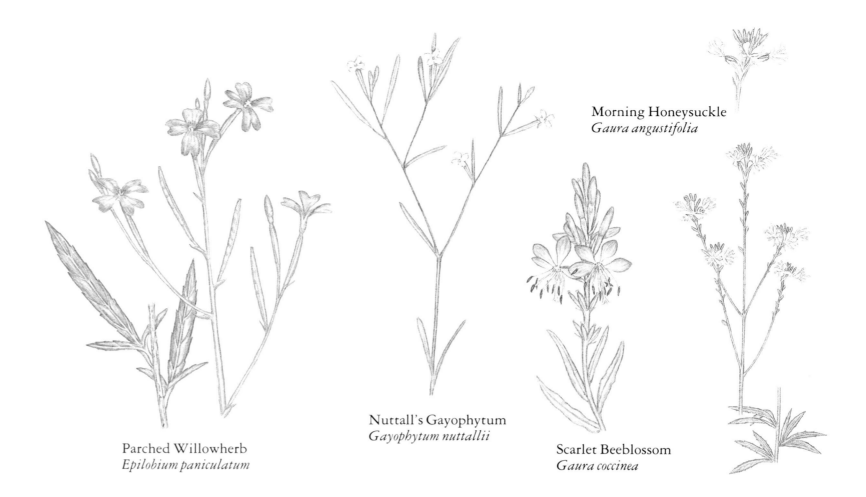

Morning Honeysuckle
Gaura angustifolia

Parched Willowherb
Epilobium paniculatum

Nuttall's Gayophytum
Gayophytum nuttallii

Scarlet Beeblossom
Gaura coccinea

fires, for it rapidly colonizes burned-over areas. It forms wide colonies, spreading by means of creeping underground rhizomes, forming many erect, leafy stems up to 6ft tall. These are topped by long spikes of showy, red-purple flowers in mid and late summer. The inferior ovaries develop into 3in long capsules, which split open to reveal silky-haired seeds. These are blown by the wind in huge numbers to invade new areas.

Most of the **Willowherbs** belong to the genus *Epilobium*, a large group with over 100 species found throughout the world, except in the tropics. They are annual or perennial plants with pink or purple flowers. **River-beauty**, *E. latifolium* (p. 112), is a northern willowherb which grows on river banks and in streams from Quebec to Alaska, and in the Rocky Mountains. It has short, often arching stems up to 20in tall, forming tangled masses, with fleshy, often whitish leaves, and clusters of magenta flowers in the upper leaf axils. Its young shoots can be eaten like asparagus.

Many other willowherbs also grow in wet places. **Hairy Willowherb**, *Epilobium hirsutum* (p. 112), is an introduced species, originally from Europe and Asia and now found in wet soils, especially in disturbed places, from Quebec to Illinois and New York. It forms patches of erect, leafy stems growing up to 6ft tall, with lance-shaped, toothed leaves all covered with soft hairs, and with large, rose-purple flowers in summer. **Northern Willowherb**, *E. glandulosum* (p. 112), grows in

wet places from Newfoundland to Alaska, south in the west to Colorado and California. It forms clumps of stems about 3ft tall, with tiny pink flowers in the axils of lance-shaped leaves.

Parched Willowherb, *Epilobium paniculatum*, is a mainly western species, a common plant of dry places from British Columbia to California, through the mountains to South Dakota and New Mexico. It is an annual, hairless plant growing up to 6ft tall. Its stem has shredding skin near the base, and is very much branched above, with alternate linear leaves and flowers on all the branches. The small flowers have notched petals above an elongated ovary, which elongates even more in fruit to form a four-angled, linear capsule.

Nuttall's Gayophytum, *Gayophytum nuttallii*, is a slender plant, with much-branched, threadlike stems and linear leaves. It has minute white flowers with reflexed sepals growing in the axils of the upper leaves. It is found in dry places on slopes and ridges, usually in coniferous forests, from California to Washington, east to New Mexico and South Dakota, south into south America.

Scarlet Beeblossom, *Gaura coccinea*, has flowers that open white in the evening (when they may be pollinated by moths), remain open till morning, and then gradually turn pink, becoming darker as the day progresses, but falling before evening, when new flowers open. This is a perennial, bushy plant, with more or less toothed, linear or lance-shaped leaves.

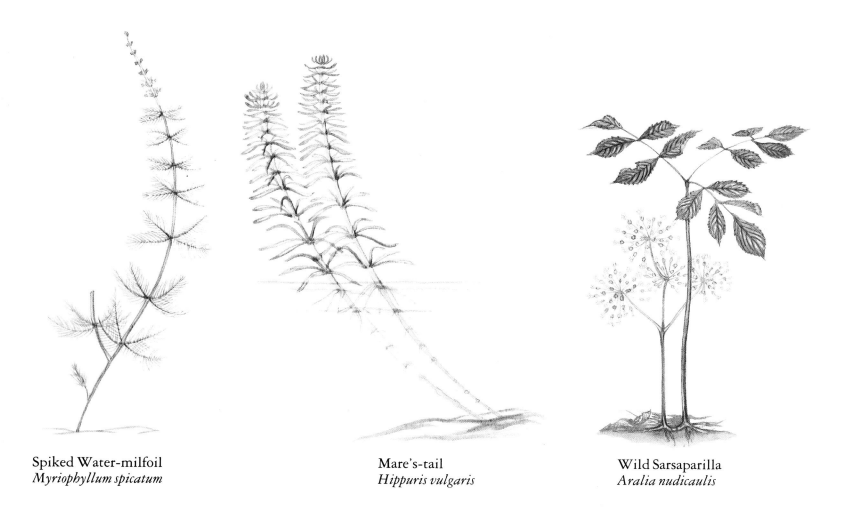

Spiked Water-milfoil
Myriophyllum spicatum

Mare's-tail
Hippuris vulgaris

Wild Sarsaparilla
Aralia nudicaulis

The flowers grow in terminal spikes at the tops of the stems; each has four unequal, clawed petals all spreading upward, and eight stamens with long filaments. This plant grows on dry limestone slopes, among pinyon and junipers, in the plains and prairies, and in the mountains of the Mojave Desert. It has a wide distribution, from Manitoba to Indiana and Texas, into Mexico, west to Alberta and California.

Morning Honeysuckle, *Gaura angustifolia*, (p. 113), is an eastern species found in sandy woods, fields, and roadsides from North Carolina to Florida. It has erect stems up to 6ft tall and narrowly elliptical leaves, becoming smaller toward the top of the stem and often growing in clusters. The flowers open at sunset; they are borne in untidy spikes, and have pink or white clawed petals.

Water-milfoil family

Haloragaceae

A small family of herbaceous plants, with 7 genera and about 170 species found throughout the world. Most of them are aquatic or marsh plants.

Family features The flowers are solitary or borne in clusters. They are regular and usually hermaphrodite, often very small, with 2–4 fused sepals forming a calyx-tube, and either with 2–4 petals or no petals at all. There are 2–8 large stamens and an inferior ovary with 1–4 cells. The fruit is a small, indehiscent nut or drupe. The leaves are alternate, opposite or whorled and may be very large. Submerged leaves are divided. Stipules are absent.

Water-milfoils belong to the genus *Myriophyllum*. They are aquatic herbs, found in shallow water or on muddy shores, with erect stems and dissected leaves, often in whorls. About 12 species are found in North America. **Spiked Water-milfoil**, *M. spicatum*, is a circumboreal species, found in clear, calcium-rich waters across Canada and south across much of the U.S., to Maryland in the east and California in the west. It has erect stems with whorls of 3–4 leaves beneath the water, and flowering stems emerging from the water. These are almost leafless, with whorls of tiny, reddish flowers. Whorled Water-milfoil, *M. verticillatum*, has leafy flowering spikes projecting above the water, the leaves similar to, but smaller than, the dissected underwater leaves.

Mare's-tail family

Hippuridaceae

There is one species in this family, the **Mare's-tail**, *Hippuris vulgaris*, a plant which is found in lakes and ponds, in quiet streams and sometimes in marshes, especially in base-rich water, all around the North Pole, in northern Africa and the far southern areas of South America. In North America it is found as far south as New York, Indiana, and New Mexico. This is a perennial plant, with creeping rhizomes at the bottom of the water and erect stems which project well above the surface. The stems are hairless and leafy, with many whorls of 6–12 linear leaves both above and beneath the water. In summer the plants bear tiny flowers in the axils of the upper leaves. They have no sepals or petals, and either have a single stamen with a one-celled ovary beneath, or a single stamen alone. The fruits are smooth green achenes.

Ginseng family
Araliaceae

A mostly tropical family of 55 genera and about 700 species, chiefly trees and shrubs. Some are grown in gardens, by far the most familiar being the many varieties of ivy, *Hedera* species. One of the most famous members of the family is Ginseng, a Chinese plant whose roots were believed to be a cure for all ills. It has curiously misshapen roots, some resembling the human body, and these were thought to be the most valuable. Myths usually have some basis in fact and this is no exception;

Ginseng does have some medicinal properties and can be used in herb medicine, like its American counterpart which is described overleaf.

Family features The flowers are hermaphrodite and regular, with a small, toothed calyx. There are three to many, often five, petals which may be free or united. The stamens are free, as many as the petals and alternating with them, and the ovary is inferior, usually with as many cells as the petals. The fruit is a drupe or berry. The flowers are small and arranged in heads, umbels, spikes or compound clusters. The leaves are simple or compound, usually alternate, with barely distinguishable stipules and often covered with star-shaped hairs.

Several species of *Aralia* are found in North America, the majority perennial herbs. The long rhizomes of **Wild Sarsaparilla**, *A. nudicaulis* (p. 114), were used by many Indian tribes for their tonic and stimulant properties, and were also brewed into tea or root beer. The plant grows in upland and mountain woods from Newfoundland to British Columbia, south to Georgia and Colorado. From its rhizomes grow tall stems bearing umbrella-like leaves. Each leaf has three long-stalked sections, and each section is further subdivided pinnately into leaflets. Greenish-white flowers appear beneath the leaves in early summer, borne in rounded umbels on long stalks growing from the rhizome. The fruits are clusters of blue-black berries.

Spikenard
Aralia racemosa

American Ginseng
Panax quinquefolium

Dwarf Ginseng
Panax trifolium

Spikenard, *Aralia racemosa* (p. 115), is a related plant, also used by American Indians in their herbal medicine, and for making tea and root beer. It has erect stems up to 6ft tall, each stem bearing a few large, spreading leaves. The leaves have the same form as those of Wild Sarsaparilla, divided into three sections, each section further subdivided pinnately into oval, toothed leaflets. In addition, the stems bear terminal compound inflorescences composed of many umbels of tiny green flowers. The flowers are followed by dark purple berries.

The *Aralia* species are little used in herb medicine today, in contrast to **American Ginseng**, *Panax quinquefolium* (p. 115). This is a popular herbal remedy, although it is far from clear what for. The Chinese species of *Panax* is reputed to be a panacea for all ills, and an aphrodisiac as well. The same virtues are attributed to American Ginseng, and quantities are exported to China each year. In fact, it seems only to stimulate appetite and to alleviate digestive disorders arising from nervous exhaustion. American Ginseng is grown commercially in Wisconsin, but is not easy to cultivate and wild plants are becoming rare or extinct in many parts of their formerly wide range. At one time the plant grew in rich woods from Nova Scotia to Minnesota, south to Indiana and in the mountains to Georgia and Oklahoma.

It is a perennial plant, with a fleshy, slow-growing, spindle-shaped root. From this grows an erect stem up to 2ft tall, with a circle of three compound leaves at the top. Each leaf is about 1ft across, with five toothed leaflets. Around midsummer an umbel of small, greenish flowers appears at the center of this circle, followed by bright red berries.

Dwarf Ginseng, *Panax trifolium* (p. 115), looks like a miniature version of American Ginseng, only 4-8in tall. It has an umbel of white flowers above compound leaves, followed by a cluster of yellowish berries. This little plant grows in rich woods from Nova Scotia to Quebec and Minnesota, south to Georgia, in mountains in the south.

Carrot family
Umbelliferae

Also known as the **Parsley family** and the **Apiaceae**. A large family of herbaceous plants, with about 270 genera and 2800 species, mostly found in northern temperate regions. This family is economically important, contributing vegetables like celery, carrots, and parsnips, and culinary herbs like parsley, caraway, fennel, coriander, and dill. Some family members are grown in flower gardens, notably the *Eryngium* species. Others are among the most poisonous plants known, including Hemlock and American Water Hemlock.

Family features The flowers are tiny, regular, and

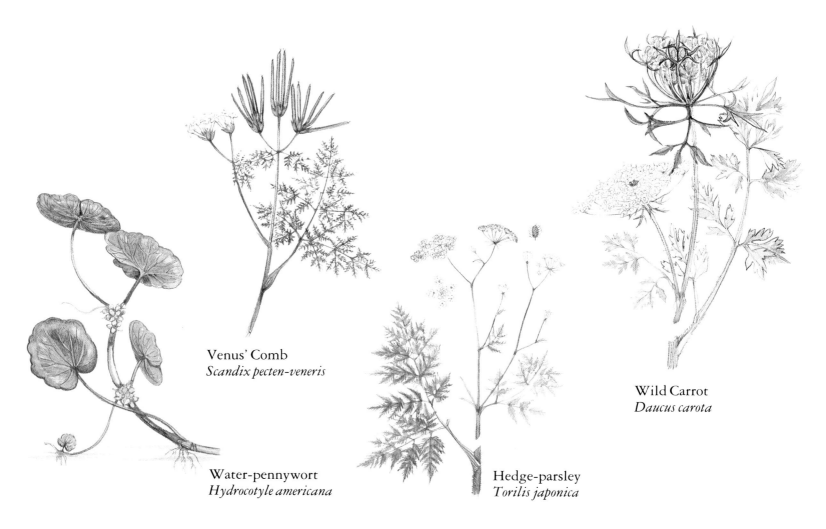

Venus' Comb
Scandix pecten-veneris

Water-pennywort
Hydrocotyle americana

Hedge-parsley
Torilis japonica

Wild Carrot
Daucus carota

hermaphrodite, borne in simple or compound umbels. Each flower has a five-lobed calyx fused to the ovary, and five free petals. Five stamens alternate with the petals, and the ovary is inferior with two cells. The fruit is quite distinctive, consisting of two sections, one each side of the central axis of the fruit, and often joined together and suspended across the top of this central axis. When the fruit is ripe it splits open from the bottom, so that each section swings from the top, exposing the seeds which are attached to the central axis. Many umbellifers have furrowed stems, either with soft pith or hollow in the center. Their leaves are alternate, usually compound, and often much divided, with sheathing bases. Many species are aromatic.

The **Water-pennyworts** are a small group of species belonging to the genus *Hydrocotyle*. They are rather different to most umbellifers, small perennial plants growing in wet places or water, with creeping or floating stems and rounded leaves, like "pennies." *Hydrocotyle americana* (p. 116) has very slender, creeping stems rooting at the nodes, and long-stalked, shallowly lobed, rounded leaves. Unlike many *Hydrocotyle* species, this plant may sometimes grow erect, even though its stems are weak. It has small umbel-like clusters of greenish-white flowers in the axils of the leaves. It grows in wet woods, bogs, and meadows from Newfoundland to Wisconsin, south to North Carolina and Tennessee.

Venus' Comb, *Scandix pecten-veneris* (p. 116), is native to the Mediterranean region of Europe. In the northeastern U.S. it grows as a weed in fallow fields and on roadsides and, although widely naturalized, has become rarer as a result of modern weed-killers and techniques for producing cleaner seed. It is a winter annual, with an erect, branched stem up to 2ft tall, and dissected, ferny leaves. The small white flowers are borne in simple umbels, usually growing in pairs in early summer. The plant becomes highly distinctive when the fruits form, as they are 2-3in long with extremely long beaks. This plant has many names, for it has been familiar to farm workers for centuries; the names mostly describe the fruits, which are formed at harvest time when the wheat is gathered. Names range from Venus' Comb and Ladies' Comb, to Shepherd's Needles, Darning Needles, and Devil's Needles.

Hedge-parsley, *Torilis japonica* (p. 116), is another Eurasian weed found in fields and waste places from New York to Illinois and Kansas, south to Florida and Texas, and also in California. It is a hairy, annual plant, with stiff, ridged stems and pinnately divided leaves. The leaflets are lance-shaped and toothed. Its white or pinkish flowers grow in compound umbels with 5–12 rays; the fruits which follow are egg-shaped, with hooked bristles.

Wild Carrot, *Daucus carota* (p. 116), is a common weed, growing in waste places, on roadsides, and in fields nearly

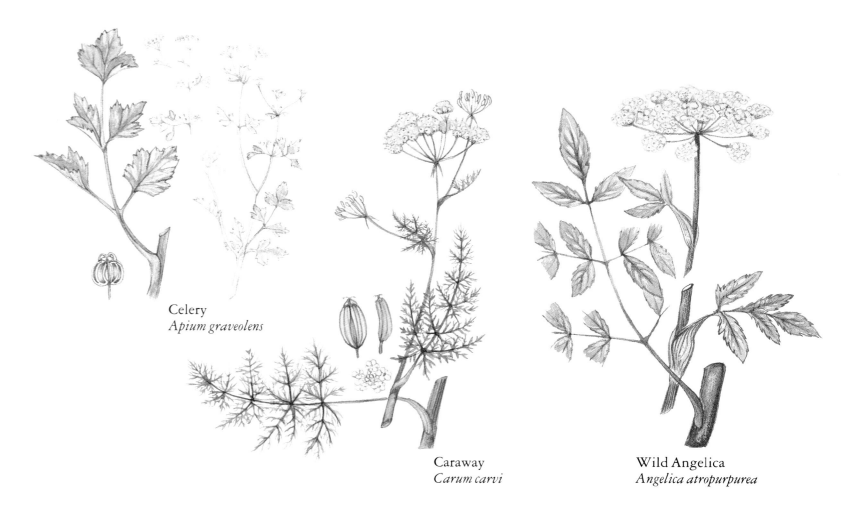

Celery
Apium graveolens

Caraway
Carum carvi

Wild Angelica
Angelica atropurpurea

Sweet Cicely
Osmorhiza claytoni

Black Snakeroot
Sanicula marilandica

Hemlock
Conium maculatum

throughout the continent. It is not a native plant, coming originally from Europe and Asia, and wild plants do not usually have edible roots unless they come from garden plants that have gone to seed. Cultivated carrots belong to the subspecies *sativa* and have fleshy roots, whereas true wild carrots are subspecies *carota*, and have thin, tough roots. They all have the characteristic carroty scent.

Carrots are biennial plants, forming the familiar clumps of ferny leaves in the first year and overwintering at the end of the year by taproots. From these grow the flowering stems in the second year. They have divided, fern-like leaves and dense, flat-topped umbels of creamy white flowers, usually with one central purplish or red flower in each umbel. The fruiting umbels close up and come to resemble birds' nests containing many spiky fruits.

Celery, *Apium graveolens* (p. 117), is widely cultivated, but much less persistent as a weed than Wild Carrot, and rarely found growing in an area for more than a season or two. It is a biennial plant, with erect, grooved stems and pinnate leaves. The leaves have lobed, toothed leaflets and the plant has the characteristic scent of celery. Its flowers are greenish-white, borne in dense compound umbels on short stalks, subtended by small leaves.

Caraway, *Carum carvi* (p. 117), was presumably introduced for its seeds, which are used in baking, in sauerkraut, and for

making liqueurs. The plant is still cultivated in North America, and also grows as a weed in waste places across southern Canada and much of the U.S. It is a biennial, with a rosette of finely dissected leaves in the first year. In the second year the flowering stems develop; they are ridged and hollow, with dissected leaves and compound umbels of white or pinkish flowers, each umbel with 5–16 rays. The fruits (the caraway "seeds") are elliptical and ribbed, with an aromatic scent when crushed.

Wild Angelica, *Angelica atropurpurea* (p. 117), is one of about 20 *Angelica* species in North America. They are stout perennial plants, with clumps of long-stalked, pinnate leaves, and thick stems with reduced leaves, the uppermost often bladeless. Wild Angelica has purple stems up to 6ft tall; its compound leaves have sharply toothed leaflets and large sheathing bases to the leaf stalks. The umbels of white flowers are dense, up to 8in across, with 20–45 rays. The plant grows in wet woods, beside streams, and in swamps from Labrador to Minnesota, south to Delaware and Indiana. The stems of this plant can be candied, like those of the European Angelica, *A. archangelica*, which is usually used in baking.

Sweet Cicely, *Osmorhiza claytoni*, is one of several *Osmorhiza* species found in North America. It grows in moist woods from Nova Scotia to Saskatchewan, south to North Carolina and Arkansas. It is a hairy, perennial plant with a root smelling of

Cow Parsnip
Heracleum lanatum

Water Parsley
Oenanthe sarmentosa

Water Parsnip
Sium suave

Water Hemlock
Cicuta maculata

anise, branched, erect stems, and spreading, bluntly divided leaves. The small white flowers grow in sparse, flat-topped, compound umbels borne above the leaves, and they are followed by dark, hairy, narrowly elliptical fruits. The related species, *O. longistylis*, is much more strongly scented with anise, and its roots and fruits can be used as a flavoring for candy and medicines. It is also used in herb medicine to alleviate indigestion.

Black Snakeroot or American Sanicle, *Sanicula marilandica* (p. 118), was used in herb medicine, first by Indians and then by settlers, to treat fevers and St Vitus' Dance, more recently as a remedy for sore throats. It is a perennial plant with a thick rhizome (the part used in medicine), and a clump of palmately cleft leaves, each with five toothed leaflets. The flower stalks have few leaves, but bear dense, compound umbels of greenish-white flowers. The fruits are ovoid, with many hooked bristles.

One of the risks involved in eating wild umbellifers or using them in herb medicine is that some of the most poisonous of all flowering plants belong to this family and often resemble the useful species. **Hemlock**, *Conium maculatum* (p. 118), is poisonous, and can cause paralysis and death. Originally a Eurasian plant, it is now widely naturalized in waste ground and on roadsides, usually in damp places, throughout much of the U.S. and southern Canada. It looks like many umbellifers,

with upright stems, fern-like leaves, and umbels of white flowers in summer. Its distinguishing features are its smooth, furrowed, grayish, hollow stems covered with purplish spots, and its scent, often likened to that of cat's urine. It is a biennial plant, with a clump of leaves in the first year, flowering stems up to 6ft tall in the second. Its dark brown fruits are globular, with wavy, pale brown ridges.

An equally poisonous native species is the **Water Hemlock**, *Cicuta maculata*, which grows in swamps and wet meadows, in ditches and wet thickets from Quebec to Wyoming, south to Florida and Mexico. It may be mistaken for Water Parsnip, for it has thickened roots and a scent like parsnips. Its roots are its most poisonous parts; even small quantities may cause convulsions and death. This is a perennial, with a branched stem up to 6ft tall, compound, pinnate leaves, and domed compound umbels of white flowers. It can be recognized by its hollow, purple-streaked stems, and yellow, oily sap which smells of parsnips. Other species of *Cicuta* are equally poisonous, and all grow in wet places. The others do not have spotted stems, but do have the scent, and generally have thickened roots.

In contrast to this poisonous lookalike, **Water Parsnip**, *Sium suave*, has edible roots but is so similar in appearance to Water Hemlock that it is better not to risk eating wild, parsnip-scented roots. It is a perennial plant, with a tall,

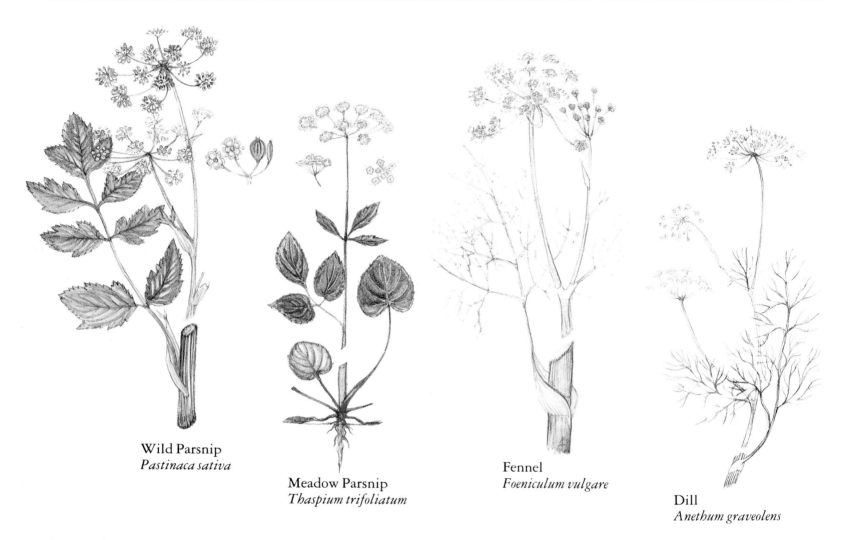

Wild Parsnip
Pastinaca sativa

Meadow Parsnip
Thaspium trifoliatum

Fennel
Foeniculum vulgare

Dill
Anethum graveolens

branched, angular stem and once-pinnate leaves with lance-shaped leaflets. Its umbels of white flowers appear in late summer. The plant grows in wet meadows and swamps across much of North America.

Water Parsley, *Oenanthe sarmentosa* (p. 119), is an apparently harmless western species found in slow-moving water and marshes from California to British Columbia and Idaho. It has succulent, sprawling stems up to 5ft tall, and once-pinnate leaves with broad, serrated leaflets. In summer it bears umbels of white flowers growing from the leaf axils; each umbel has 10–20 rays. The fruits are purplish, oblong in shape, with prominent, broad ribs.

Cow Parsnip, *Heracleum lanatum* (p. 119), is a large, hairy, perennial plant, one of the largest umbellifers, and up to 9ft tall. It has an erect, hollow stem, ridged and woolly in texture. The leaves are huge, each divided into three, often deeply toothed leaflets up to 2ft across, and the leaves have greatly inflated sheathing bases on their stalks where they are attached to the stems. The white flowers are borne in giant, compound umbels, 6-12in across. The flowers in each umbel are not all the same, those on the rim with enlarged, notched outer petals pointing toward the outside. This magnificent but rankly scented plant grows in moist places in mountains and lowlands, in meadows and beside streams throughout much of North America, except in southern states like Texas and New

Mexico. Young stems and roots can be eaten as a vegetable, but must not be mistaken for those of Water Hemlock.

The true, edible **Wild Parsnip**, *Pastinaca sativa*, has yellow flowers. It is a biennial plant with a strong scent of parsnip, a clump of pinnately divided leaves in the first year, and erect flowering stems up to 5ft tall in the second. The taproots are the edible vegetables. The flowering plant has hollow, furrowed stems, and pinnate, bright green leaves with serrated leaflets. It also has dense, compound umbels of tiny yellow flowers in late summer. Each flower has five inrolled petals. Wild Parsnip is native to Europe and Asia but has become thoroughly naturalized over most of North America, growing in waste places, on roadsides, and in fields.

Meadow Parsnip, *Thaspium trifoliatum*, grows in woods from New York to Minnesota, and south, mostly in the Mississippi River valley. It is a perennial plant—unusual in this family because its basal leaves are simple—with heart-shaped blades on long stalks. The only other similar plant is one of the Golden Alexanders, *Zizia aptera*. The leaves on the flowering stalks have three ovate leaflets each, and the flowers are yellow or purple, borne in umbels with 6–10 unequal rays. Yellow-flowered plants are more common in the western parts of the range, purple-flowered ones in the east. Two other *Thaspium* species grow in woods and prairies of the east and midwest; they have twice-pinnate leaves and yellow flowers.

Fennel, *Foeniculum vulgare* (p. 120), is a familiar salad plant and vegetable, with a distinctive anise-like scent and taste. The young shoots are usually eaten fresh, and the stems and leaves can be dried and chopped for flavoring sauces that are especially good with fish. It is native to Mediterranean Europe, but is now naturalized over much of the U.S., especially in the south, growing in waste places and on roadsides, in fields and grasslands. It is a perennial plant, but individuals seldom live for more than a few years, and they produce many seeds. Each plant has an erect, solid stem up to 6ft tall, with many extremely finely divided, ferny leaves; opposite the upper leaves are umbels of yellow flowers.

Dill, *Anethum graveolens* (p. 120), is one of several umbellifers grown for their seeds, which are used as kitchen herbs. Dill is also an ingredient of gripe water, given to infants to relieve colic; other active constituents are Fennel and Anise, both also umbellifers. All relieve indigestion. Dill is native to Mediterranean Europe, but has escaped from cultivation in many parts of the U.S. to grow wild in waste places and on roadsides. It is a branched, annual plant up to 5ft tall, hairless and blue-green in color, with compound leaves so finely divided that their segments appear threadlike. The flowers are greenish-yellow and borne in large, compound umbels above the leaves, with 30–40 small umbels in each compound one. The fruits are flattened, elliptical, and strongly ridged.

Three species of **Golden Alexanders** grow in moist woods and meadows. They are hairless, perennial plants, with fleshy roots, branched stems up to 3ft tall, and loose, compound umbels of golden yellow flowers. *Zizia aurea* is found in the east and midwest from Quebec to Saskatchewan, and south to Florida and Texas. All its leaves are compound, with lance-shaped, serrated leaflets, and it has 10–18 little umbels in each compound umbel. *Z. aptera* grows in most of southern Canada, south in the east to Georgia, and in the Rocky Mountains to Colorado. It can be distinguished from the other Golden Alexander species by its simple, heart-shaped, not compound, basal leaves. The third species, *Z. trifoliata*, is only found in mountain woods of the southeastern U.S.; it has compound leaves and 4–10 umbels in each compound umbel.

Gray's Lovage, *Ligusticum grayi*, is one of about nine species of Lovage found in North America. This is a western plant found in mountain meadows and on the slopes of the Sierra Nevada and Cascades. It forms a clump of pinnate leaves with toothed leaflets, and an almost leafless flowering stem about 2ft tall. This bears a loose, compound umbel of white flowers, with 5–14 rays; the flowers are followed by narrowly winged, oblong fruits.

There are about 80 species of **Prairie Parsleys** in the genus *Lomatium*, all from western North America. They are perennial plants, with compound, often ferny leaves, and with yellow or

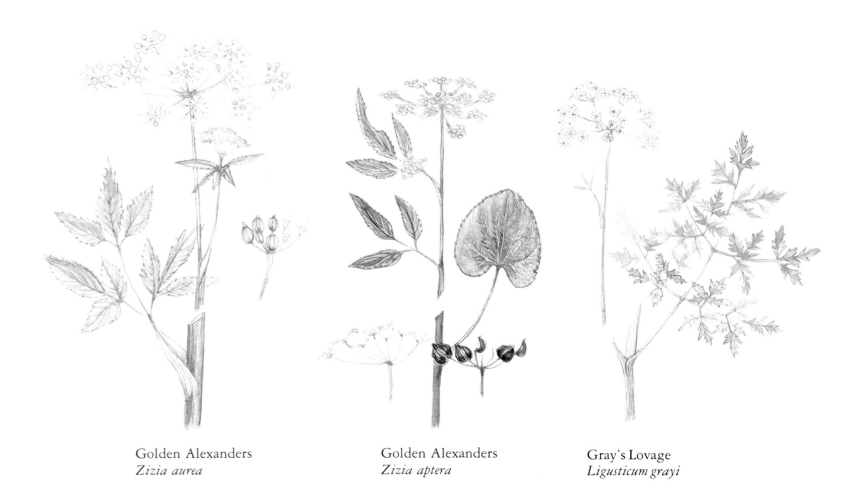

Golden Alexanders
Zizia aurea

Golden Alexanders
Zizia aptera

Gray's Lovage
Ligusticum grayi

purple flowers in compound umbels; many have very short stems and some lack stems altogether. Their leaves often smell like parsley, a feature which can be used to identify them. Many Prairie Parsleys have edible roots, and these were well known to the Indians who called them cous. The roots were eaten raw like celery, or ground into flour and made into biscuits. This gave them the settlers' name of biscuitroots.

One of several species still called **Biscuitroot** is *Lomatium macrocarpum*, a widely distributed plant growing in dry, open places from British Columbia to Alberta, and south to California. It has pinnate leaves divided two or three times into small segments, and may be quite densely hairy and purplish in color at the base. Its tiny, white or yellow flowers grow in dense, compound umbels, 5–25 small umbels in each compound one. The fruits are flattened oblongs, each one up to 1in long with narrow wings.

Cous, *Lomatium cous*, is another species with edible roots. It grows in dry, open places, often with sagebrush, or in foothills from Washington and Oregon to Montana and Wyoming. Pestle Parsnip, *L. nudicaule*, has pinnate leaves with large, rounded leaflets. It also grows in dry, open places from British Columbia to Alberta, south to California and Utah. It, too, has edible roots.

Ranger's Button is a name that describes very well the flowers of *Sphenosciadium capitellatum*, for they do resemble white buttons borne on "furry" shoots in umbels at the tops of the stems. This is a stout, perennial plant, with erect stems up to 7ft tall, and pinnate leaves with linear leaflets and sheathing leaf bases. It grows in the foothills and mountains, in swampy places, beside streams, and in wet meadows from California to Oregon and Idaho.

Beach Silvertop, *Glehnia leiocarpa*, is a prostrate species which grows on the coastal strand of the Pacific Ocean, on beaches and dunes from Alaska to northern California. It has rosettes of fleshy, compound leaves, with leaf stalks often buried in the shifting sands, and ovate leaflets in threes. The leaves are shiny above, hairy beneath. In early summer dense umbels of white flowers appear on short stems in the centers of the rosettes.

Rattlesnake-master, *Eryngium yuccifolium*, is not readily recognizable as an umbellifer; its flowers are borne in heads rather than umbels and its leaves are like those of a yucca. It is a perennial, with a clump of linear, spine-edged leaves, and a single flowering stem up to 5ft tall, branched near the top to bear the flower heads. These heads consist of about 30 densely packed flowers with white or greenish petals, each cupped in a green bract. The plant grows in woods and prairies from New England to Minnesota, south to Florida and Texas. It is used in Indian medicine to treat snakebite and as a remedy for venereal disease.

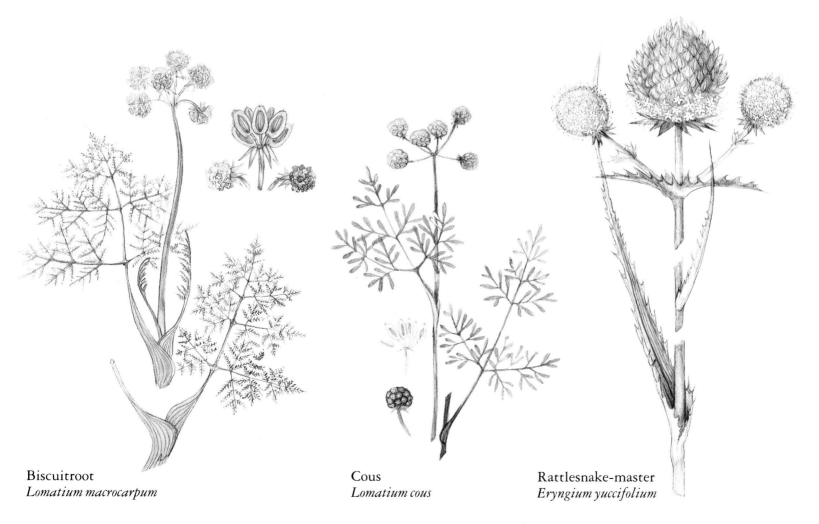

Biscuitroot
Lomatium macrocarpum

Cous
Lomatium cous

Rattlesnake-master
Eryngium yuccifolium

Summer in the Rocky Mountains, with Cow Parsnip (*Heracleum lanatum*) and Giant Red Paintbrush (*Castilleja miniata*) in the foreground.

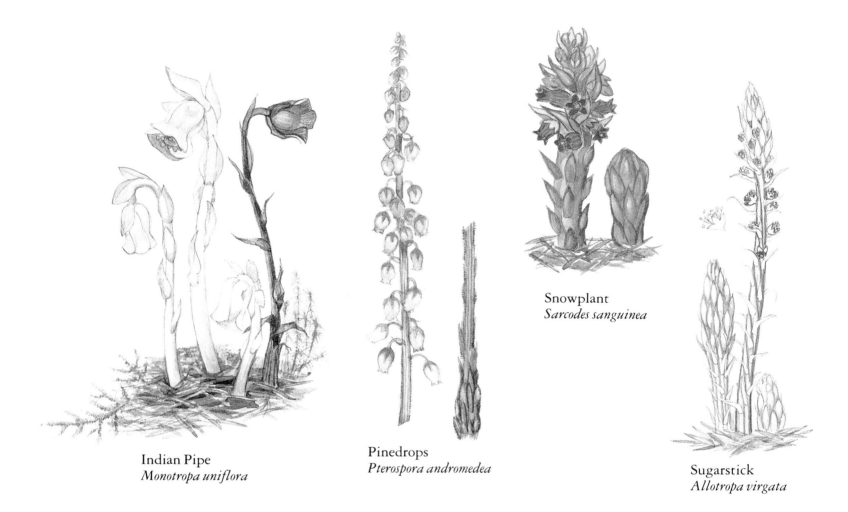

Indian Pipe
Monotropa uniflora

Pinedrops
Pterospora andromedea

Snowplant
Sarcodes sanguinea

Sugarstick
Allotropa virgata

Indian Pipe family

Monotropaceae

These are specialized plants, lacking chlorophyll and feeding as saprophytes, growing in soils rich in raw humus, often in coniferous woods. They may be white, pink or brownish in color, with roots covered in mycorrhizal fungi. The fungi presumably enable them to absorb their nutrients from the humus in the soil. There are about 12 genera and 30 species in the north temperate regions. They are closely related to the Wintergreen family.

Family features The flowers are solitary or borne in racemes on erect stems. They are regular and hermaphrodite, usually dull in color. Each has 2–6 free sepals and usually 4–5 petals, which may be free or united into a lobed corolla. There are twice as many stamens as petals, and the ovary is superior with 1–6 cells. The fruits are capsules with minute seeds. The leaves are reduced to scales.

Indian Pipe, *Monotropa uniflora*, is a small, distinctive plant, with a clump of white, fleshy stems, only 9in tall at most, which may be found growing in the humus-rich litter of moist woodland in summer. Each stem has transparent, scale-like leaves and is bent over at the top, where the single, bell-like flower hangs. A related plant, *M. hypopitys*, known as

Pinesap, is also found in woodland, but usually in acid soils, and often in upland woods. It has a fleshy, erect stem with a cluster of flowers at the top, and varies in color from pink or red to yellow or creamy white. Both are found throughout North America.

Pinedrops, *Pterospora andromedea*, follows the family pattern, forming a clump of reddish-brown, erect stems in the deep, dry humus of coniferous woodland. The stems grow up to 3ft tall, are covered in glandular hairs, and bear many drooping, yellowish, bell-like flowers that glisten translucently. They persist for several years after flowering, becoming dried and dark brown in color with hanging capsules.

Snowplant, *Sarcodes sanguinea*, has stout, fleshy, unexpectedly bright red stems up to 2ft tall, appearing as the snow disappears in the coniferous woods of the Cascades and Sierra Nevada. It grows only where there is deep humus to supply its nutrients. Each stem has translucent, overlapping bracts, with bell-shaped flowers in the axils of the upper ones.

Sugarstick, *Allotropa virgata*, looks like a striped peppermint stick, with stems striped vertically in red and white, and long, white, scaly leaves. The whitish flowers grow in the axils of leaves, in racemes terminating the stems. Plants are not common, but may be found in deep humus in coniferous woods of the Coast Ranges and Sierra Nevada from California to British Columbia.

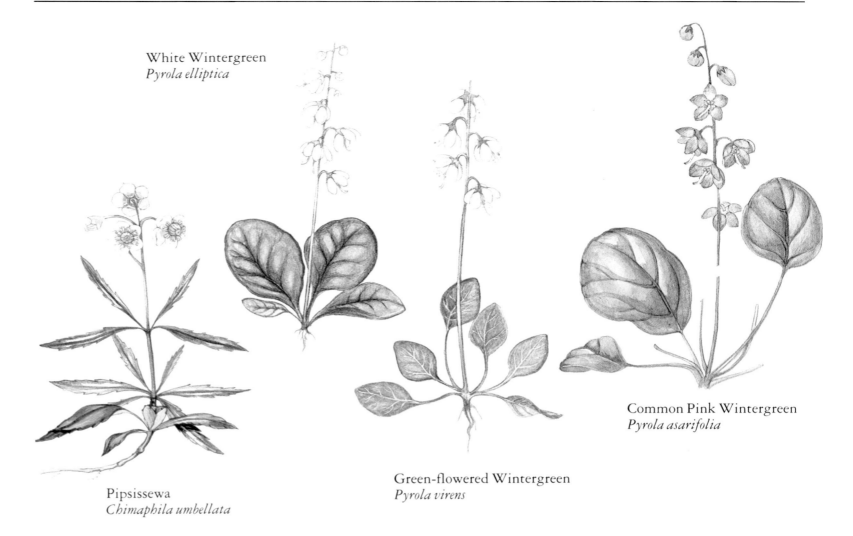

White Wintergreen
Pyrola elliptica

Pipsissewa
Chimaphila umbellata

Green-flowered Wintergreen
Pyrola virens

Common Pink Wintergreen
Pyrola asarifolia

Wintergreen family

Pyrolaceae

A small family with 4 genera and about 40 species of evergreen herbs, mostly found in Arctic and northern temperate regions. They are closely related to and sometimes included in the Ericaceae, the Heath family.

Family features The flowers are solitary or borne in clusters, often nodding, and may be white, pink or purple. They are regular and hermaphrodite, each with four or five sepals fused to form a calyx, and usually with five petals, free or joined at the base. There are usually 10 stamens, and the ovary is superior with 4–5 cells. The fruit is a globular capsule. The leaves are simple, in basal rosettes or, if on the stems, alternate or in whorls; they lack stipules.

Pipsissewa or Prince's Pine, *Chimaphila umbellata*, is a small, perennial, sub-shrubby plant, with creeping rhizomes and whorled clusters of leathery, toothed leaves. In early or midsummer, the flowering stems develop, about 1ft tall, with whorls of leaves and 4–8 nodding, fragrant, waxy flowers; each flower has five white or purplish petals and 10 radially arranged stamens. The plant is found in dry woodland, especially in coniferous woods, across southern Canada and much of the U.S., north to Alaska, and south in the Rocky Mountains to California and Colorado, most commonly in the west, and absent from parts of the south. It is a used as a herbal remedy by many Indian tribes to alleviate rheumatism and kidney problems. The related Spotted Wintergreen, *C. maculata*, is an eastern plant, with nodding umbels of 2–5 flowers and white-striped leaves.

The 12 *Pyrola* species, commonly known as the **Wintergreens**, are woodland plants, usually found in coniferous woods. They have rosettes of evergreen leaves and erect, leafless flowering stalks with terminal clusters of nodding flowers. **White Wintergreen** or Shinleaf, *P. elliptica*, is typical, growing in rich woodland and in dry, upland woods from Newfoundland to British Columbia, south in the east to West Virginia, and into Montana and Idaho in the west. It has a rosette of broadly ovate leaves and a raceme of nodding, white, fragrant flowers in summer. **Green-flowered Wintergreen**, *P. virens*, is a smaller plant, with white, green-veined flowers. It grows in dry woods from northern Canada south to Maryland and Indiana, and in the Rocky Mountains.

Common Pink Wintergreen, *Pyrola asarifolia*, differs from the others in having pink or pale purple flowers, and rounded or kidney-shaped leaves. It grows in moist, boggy woods, near springs and streams, usually under conifers, from Newfoundland to Alaska, and south to New York, Indiana, and New Mexico.

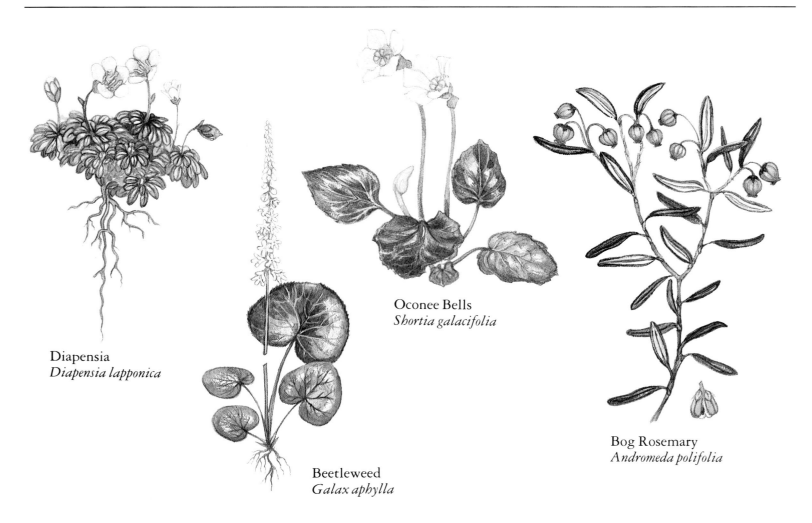

Diapensia
Diapensia lapponica

Beetleweed
Galax aphylla

Oconee Bells
Shortia galacifolia

Bog Rosemary
Andromeda polifolia

Diapensia family
Diapensiaceae

A very small family related to the heaths, with 6 genera and about 20 species of evergreen herbs or dwarf shrubs found in the north temperate and Arctic regions of the world. Some are grown in rock gardens.

Family features The flowers are solitary or borne in heads. They are regular and hermaphrodite, with a deeply five-lobed, persistent calyx and a deeply five-lobed corolla. Each flower has five stamens inserted on the corolla and alternating with the lobes; the stamens may be free or joined into a ring with five staminodes (sterile stamens). The ovary is superior with three cells, and the fruit is a capsule. The leaves are simple.

Diapensia, *Diapensia lapponica*, is a matted, evergreen plant, with branched stems and crowded, overlapping leaves. It forms dense mats on gravel and mountain ledges, and is found all around the North Pole, but only on mountain summits in the southern reaches of its range, in Maine and New York. In spring white, bell-shaped flowers appear on short, erect branches all over the mat.

Beetleweed, *Galax aphylla*, is a very different plant, forming a clump of long-stalked, evergreen leaves with heart-shaped, glossy blades. The plant grows in woods, mainly in the mountains from Maryland to Kentucky, south to Georgia and Alabama. In spring it produces attractive spikes of white flowers on long stalks 2–3ft tall.

Oconee Bells, *Shortia galacifolia*, is similar in forming clumps of evergreen, glossy leaves, in this plant growing from creeping rhizomes. The leaves have rounded blades with toothed margins. In spring solitary, white, bell-shaped flowers appear among the leaves. In the wild this plant is very rare, growing only in ravines and along streams in the woods of the southern Appalachians. It has become a popular garden plant for woodland gardens.

Heath family
Ericaceae

This is a large family, with about 70 genera and 1500 species, found throughout the world, except in desert regions, and confined to mountains in the tropics. They all have roots associated with mycorrhizal fungi. Many grow in acid soils where other plants cannot survive; heath family members probably thrive in these soils because their mycorrhizal fungi help them absorb nutrients. All members of the family are woody to a greater or lesser extent, and some are large shrubs or trees. Others are small, creeping, subshrubby plants. There are many fine garden plants among them, including rhododendrons, azaleas, and heathers. Cranberries and blueberries come from *Vaccinium* species.

Family features The flowers are often showy, usually regular and hermaphrodite, with four or five sepals united to form a tubular calyx, and four or five petals united to form a tubular or bell-like corolla. There are usually twice as many stamens as petal-lobes, and the ovary is superior with several cells. The fruits are capsules, berries or drupes. The flowers are borne singly or in clusters. The leaves are usually evergreen. They are mostly simple and usually arranged alternately; they lack stipules.

Bog Rosemary, *Andromeda polifolia* (p. 126), is a dwarf, evergreen shrub, only 1ft tall, with spreading stems and narrow, evergreen leaves, white on the underside when they are young. In early summer the plants produce umbel-like clusters of bell-shaped, pink or white flowers on the ends of the stems. The plant grows in acid bogs from Newfoundland to Saskatchewan, south to New Jersey and Minnesota.

Known to the Indians as **Kinnikinnick**, and to the Europeans as Bearberry, *Arctostaphylos uva-ursi*, grows around the North Pole, south in North America to Virginia, New Mexico, and California. It is found in exposed, sandy and rocky ground, like pine barrens, where it may cover large areas. This is a prostrate, shrubby plant with woody stems and leathery, spoon-shaped leaves. In early summer it bears white, pink-tinged, bell-like flowers, and from these are formed the bright red, mealy berries. The berries are edible, although not particularly good to eat. They are said to be palatable if cooked and eaten with cream and sugar. The Indians used the leaves as a herbal remedy for kidney and bladder infections, and they dried and smoked them as a tobacco substitute. The leaves are rich in tannins and were also used for tanning leather.

Many other species of *Arctostaphylos* grow in central America and in California, where they are known as Manzanitas. They are woody plants, varying from small shrubs to crooked trees.

Wintergreen, *Gaultheria procumbens*, is another creeping plant, also known as Checkerberry and Teaberry. It is the source of Oil of Wintergreen, used to flavor cough drops, candy, and toothpaste. The oil can be used in compresses to alleviate pain from sprains and rheumatism, but care is needed as the oil can be irritating, and is poisonous if taken internally. Wintergreen grows in woodlands in acid soil, from Newfoundland to Manitoba, south to Virginia and Kentucky, and in the mountains to Georgia. It has creeping rhizomes from which grow many erect, green stems. These have evergreen leaves crowded near the tops and white, bell-shaped flowers drooping from the leaf axils. The berries ripen to their full red color by late summer and often remain on the plants in winter.

Mountain Heather, *Cassiope mertensiana*, is one of several

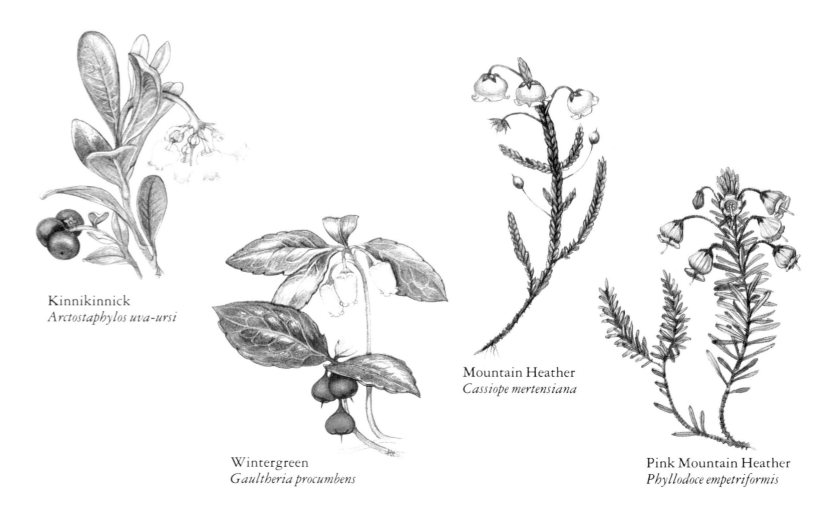

Kinnikinnick
Arctostaphylos uva-ursi

Wintergreen
Gaultheria procumbens

Mountain Heather
Cassiope mertensiana

Pink Mountain Heather
Phyllodoce empetriformis

moss heathers, *Cassiope* species, found in the north and northwest. The name moss heather is descriptive of these creeping, matted shrubs, with their flat, linear, evergreen leaves crowded close to the stems. Mountain Heather grows near the timber line in the mountains from Alaska to California and Nevada. In late summer it bears small, white, bell-like flowers in the leaf axils.

Pink Mountain Heather, *Phyllodoce empetriformis* (p. 127), is another creeping shrublet, with needle-like, evergreen leaves closely covering the stems. In the latter half of summer it bears pink urn-shaped flowers in the axils of leaves near the ends of the branches. This plant grows on slopes and in alpine meadows in the Rocky Mountains from Alaska to California and Colorado. Cream Mountain Heather, *P. glandulifera*, grows in the mountains from Oregon and Wyoming northward; it has yellowish or greenish-white flowers.

Trailing Arbutus, *Epigaea repens*, has prostrate, trailing stems with oval, leathery, evergreen leaves. Clusters of fragrant, pink flowers appear in the leaf axils and on the ends of the stems in early spring. The plant grows in sandy or rocky places on acid soils, in woodland from Newfoundland to Saskatchewan, south to Florida and Alabama.

Alpine Azalea, *Loiseleuria procumbens*, is an attractive, far northern plant growing all around the North Pole, from northern Canada south to the mountains of New York in North America. It forms bushy mats in exposed, rocky or peaty areas, with much-branched, woody stems and opposite, evergreen leaves. These leaves are typical of those on many plants found in conditions where water may be scarce; they are leathery, with hairs on the undersides, and they have inrolled margins—all ways of conserving water. The plant bears small, terminal clusters of white or pink, bell-shaped flowers in summer, followed by ovoid capsules.

Labrador Tea, *Ledum groenlandicum*, is a densely branched shrub, no more than 3ft tall. Its evergreen, leathery leaves also have inrolled margins, and white or rusty, woolly hairs beneath. The leaves are fragrant and may be dried and steeped in boiling water to make a pleasant drink—Labrador tea or Hudson Bay tea. The plant bears white flowers in dense, terminal clusters around midsummer. It grows in bogs from Greenland to Alaska, south into the U.S. as far as New Jersey, Michigan, and Minnesota.

There are over 30 species of *Vaccinium* in North America, about 150 throughout the world. They include the cranberries, bilberries, and huckleberries, together with many less well known species, plus hybrids. Among the best known is *Vaccinium macrocarpon*, the **Cranberry**, a trailing shrub with slender stems and small, evergreen, elliptical leaves. It bears clusters of nodding, pinkish-white flowers in the lower leaf axils, recognizable from their four backward-pointing petals

Trailing Arbutus
Epigaea repens

Alpine Azalea
Loiseleuria procumbens

Labrador Tea
Ledum groenlandicum

Cranberry
Vaccinium macrocarpon

and cone of fused stamens. The flowers are followed by the familiar, dark red cranberries. Plants grow in bogs and along lake shores from Newfoundland to Manitoba, south to Virginia, and in the mountains to Tennessee.

Small Cranberry, *Vaccinium oxycoccus*, is a similar species, with pointed leaves and smaller, pink to red berries. It grows in bogs around the North Pole, south to New Jersey and Minnesota in North America.

Cowberry, *Vaccinium vitis-idaea*, is sometimes called Mountain Cranberry; it grows in bogs and among rocks throughout boreal North America, south to the mountains of New England, Minnesota, and British Columbia. It is also found in northern Europe and Asia. This creeping, low-growing shrub has many arching branches and leathery, evergreen leaves. It bears little, drooping clusters of bell-shaped, pink-tinged white flowers terminating the stems in midsummer, then red, edible berries in the fall.

Dwarf Bilberry, *Vaccinium myrtillus*, grows in mountain forests from British Columbia to western Alberta, south in the Rockies to Colorado. It forms spreading patches of erect stems only 1ft tall, with oval leaves; in summer drooping, pink, urn-shaped flowers appear in the leaf axils, followed by edible, bluish-red berries.

Many of the *Vaccinium* species are taller woody shrubs, up to 12ft tall. Blueberries are borne by one such shrub, *V.*

corymbosum, which grows in swamps in the eastern U.S. and Canada. California Huckleberry, *V. ovatum*, is a western species that grows in dry slopes and woods near the Pacific coast. It grows up to 7ft tall, and has leathery leaves, urn-shaped, pink flowers, and sweet, black, edible berries.

Crowberry family
Empetraceae

A very small family, with 3 genera and 9 species, found in north temperate and Arctic regions, southern South America, and the island of Tristan da Cunha.

Crowberry, *Empetrum nigrum*, is the only widespread or common member of the family in North America, although five other family species are found on the continent. Crowberry is a low-growing, evergreen shrub with small, leathery, needle-like leaves alternately arranged on the prostrate, slender stems. The leaves have strongly inrolled margins to reduce water loss. Tiny pink flowers grow in the axils of the leaves, male and female flowers on separate plants, and the female plants go on to produce juicy black berries. Crowberry grows on acid, peaty soils throughout the boreal regions of North America, south to the mountains of New England and northern Minnesota.

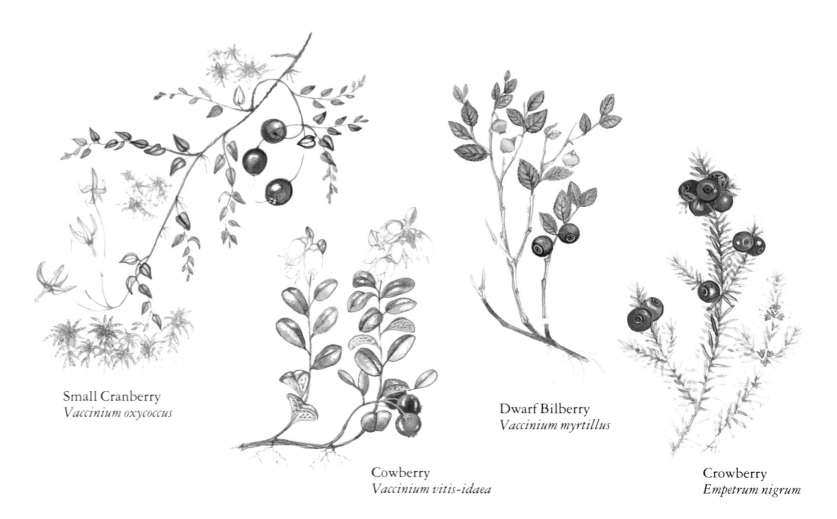

Small Cranberry
Vaccinium oxycoccus

Dwarf Bilberry
Vaccinium myrtillus

Cowberry
Vaccinium vitis-idaea

Crowberry
Empetrum nigrum

Primula family

Primulaceae

There are about 28 genera and 800 species of herbs in this family, mostly found in the northern hemisphere and many restricted to the mountains. They include numerous choice garden plants, such as the popular primroses and polyanthus, cyclamens for the greenhouse, androsaces and soldanellas for the rock garden, lysimachias for flower borders, and dodecatheons for the bog garden.

Family features The flowers are hermaphrodite and regular, with a toothed calyx formed of five fused sepals, and a lobed corolla formed of five fused petals. Each flower has five stamens opposite the petal-lobes, and a superior ovary with one cell and a single style. The fruits are capsules. The flowers may be solitary, or borne in branched clusters or umbels. The majority of plants have their leaves in basal rosettes. Others have leafy stems with simple or lobed leaves.

The **Primulas**, genus *Primula*, are a large group of species centered in Asia, and beloved of gardeners throughout the temperate world. Primroses and polyanthus are favorites for spring gardens, drumstick and candelabra primulas for bog gardens, auriculas for the greenhouse, and several Asiatic species are grown as pot plants.

In North America there are relatively few native *Primula* species, and none of them are grown in gardens. They follow the pattern of the genus in being perennial plants with rosettes of basal leaves and separate, leafless flower stalks carrying the flowers. **Parry's Primrose**, *P. parryi*, is a western species, growing, like many of the American plants, in mountain crevices and on wet screes. It has large, rather fleshy leaves, and an umbel of bright pink or purple, yellow-eyed flowers in midsummer. It is unusual among primulas in having an unpleasant, rank scent.

Some primroses are given the name of Bird's-eye Primrose, an allusion to the contrasting center of the flower. The American **Bird's-eye Primrose** is *Primula mistassinica*, a northern and eastern species of cliffs, rocks, and shores found from Labrador to Alaska, south to New York and Minnesota. It has a rosette of toothed leaves, dusted on the underside with white or yellow powder, a characteristic seen in many primroses. It has umbels of pink or white flowers with yellow eyes and notched petals.

The **Shooting Stars** are a group of about 14 species mostly found in western North America, and belonging to the genus *Dodecatheon*. They are beautiful plants and quite easy to recognize, for their dart-like flowers are distinctive, with their swept-back corolla lobes and fused stamens forming a beak. They are perennials, with rosettes of smooth, lance-shaped or

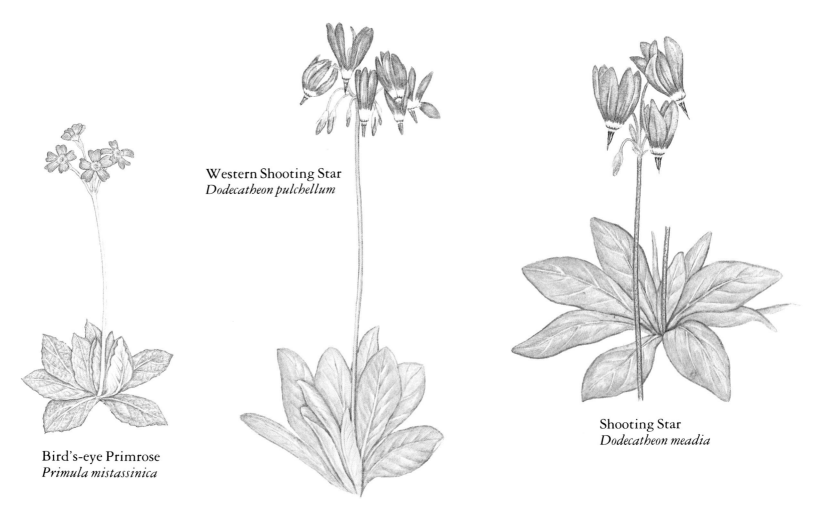

Western Shooting Star
Dodecatheon pulchellum

Bird's-eye Primrose
Primula mistassinica

Shooting Star
Dodecatheon meadia

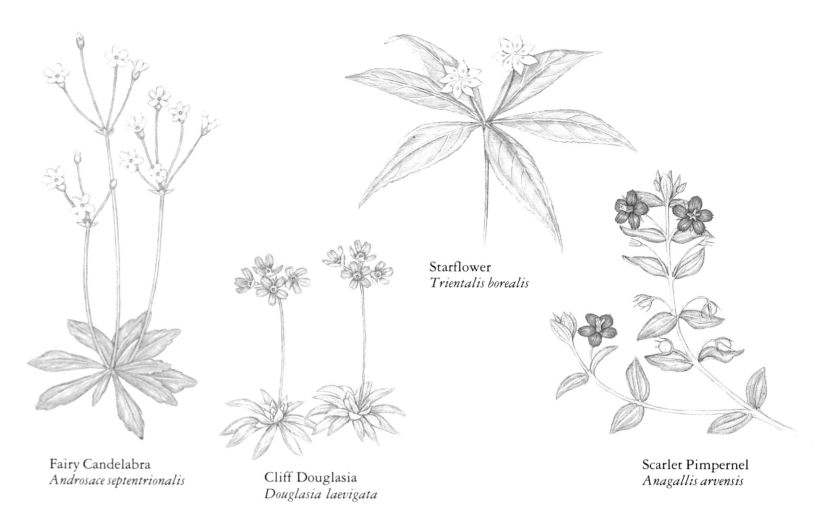

Fairy Candelabra
Androsace septentrionalis

Cliff Douglasia
Douglasia laevigata

Starflower
Trientalis borealis

Scarlet Pimpernel
Anagallis arvensis

ovate leaves, and leafless stalks with umbels of drooping flowers. Most of them have pink or magenta flowers banded with white or yellow, although the Northwestern Shooting Star, *D. dentatum*, has white flowers. The **Western Shooting Star**, *D. pulchellum* (p. 130), is one of the most widely distributed, growing in meadows and grassland, on the coast and in the mountains, from Alaska to Mexico and east to Wisconsin. The similar *D. meadia* (p. 130) is an eastern and midwestern species found in moist woods and prairies from Maryland to Wisconsin, south to Georgia and Texas.

There are about 60 species of *Androsace* in the northern hemisphere, many of them confined to the mountains, and some grown in rock gardens. They are small plants which form a basal rosette of leaves and several leafless flowering stems with umbels of small flowers. The **Fairy Candelabra**, *Androsace septentrionalis*, is more widely distributed than many, growing in dry, rocky places in the Rocky Mountains, and in sandy places on the northern prairies and plains. It is an annual plant, no more than 10in tall at most, with a rosette of lance-shaped leaves and umbels of pale pink or white flowers. The name of Fairy Candelabra is particularly appropriate for this delicate plant.

Cliff Douglasia, *Douglasia laevigata*, is another mountain plant, one of several related species found in the Rocky Mountain area. This one grows on ledges and river bluffs in the western Cascades. It forms a mat of prostrate stems, with rosettes of leaves all over the stems, and leafless flowering stems with umbels of pink flowers in spring and summer. This is an attractive plant for a rock garden.

The **Starflower**, *Trientalis borealis*, is a flower of the humus-rich soils of cool northern woods. It is found from Nova Scotia and Labrador to Alberta, south to Pennsylvania and Minnesota. This is a perennial plant, with creeping rhizomes from which grow erect stems in spring. Each stem has a whorl of five or six shiny, dark green leaves at the top, with two white, star-like flowers on long stalks growing from the center of the whorl.

Scarlet Pimpernel, *Anagallis arvensis*, is an attractive little European plant grown in gardens in North America; it has escaped to grow wild in yards, roadsides, and waste places throughout much of the continent. It has sprawling, often prostrate, stems with opposite, pointed-ovate leaves, and many solitary red flowers on long stalks in the leaf axils. These flowers open only in the morning, closing at about 3 o'clock in the afternoon, and remaining closed or closing early in dull weather. Because of this the plant has many folk names relating to time and the weather, such as Poor Man's Weatherglass, Shepherd's Clock, Jack-go-to-bed-at-noon, and Weatherflower, together with innumerable variations and combinations of these.

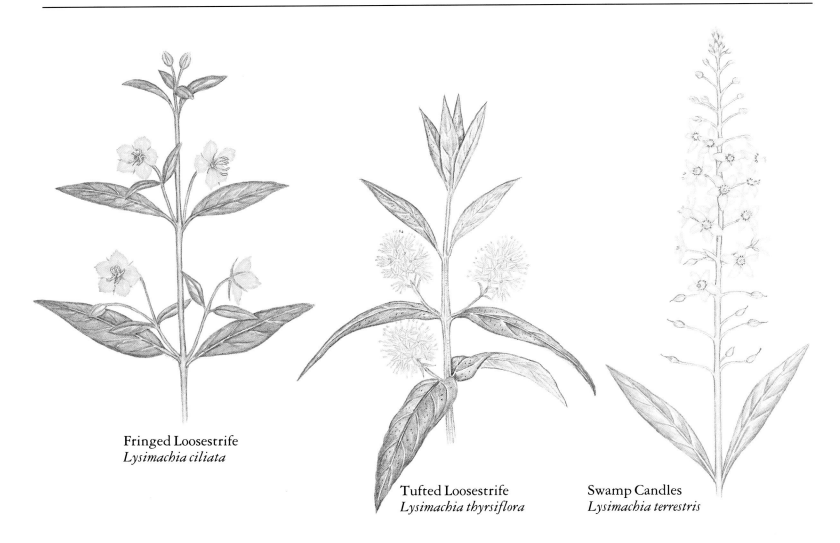

Fringed Loosestrife
Lysimachia ciliata

Tufted Loosestrife
Lysimachia thyrsiflora

Swamp Candles
Lysimachia terrestris

The **Loosestrifes**, the *Lysimachia* species are rather different, mostly erect plants with leafy stems and flowers in the axils of the upper leaves. There are nearly 100 species in the temperate regions of the world, with several familiar wild flowers in the U.S. and Canada. Typical species include **Fringed Loosestrife**, *L. ciliata*, which grows in marshes and along streamsides from Nova Scotia to British Columbia, south to Florida and New Mexico; and **Tufted Loosestrife**, *L. thyrsiflora*, which grows in swamps, lakes, and ditches throughout Canada and much of the U.S. Both species have yellow flowers growing in the axils of the upper leaves, those of Fringed Loosestrife in loose clusters, those of Tufted Loosestrife in dense tufts.

By contrast, the flowers of the plant known as **Swamp Candles**, *L. terrestris*, grow in showy, terminal racemes on erect stems up to 3ft tall. They are bright yellow marked with red lines and spots. The plant grows in open swamps and wet places, where it spreads rapidly by means of special buds produced in the leaf axils. They drop to the ground as the plant dies back for the winter and form new plants in the spring. This species is found from Newfoundland to Minnesota, and south to South Carolina and Tennessee. It hybridizes with yet another species, the Whorled Loosestrife, *L. quadrifolia*, which has whorls of narrow leaves and whorls of yellow flowers. It grows in wet places, especially on the prairies.

Hybrids also form between Swamp Candles and Tufted Loosestrife. These hybrids are all attractive plants but are sterile and can only spread by vegetative means.

Moneywort, *Lysimachia nummularia* (p. 133), is a different kind of plant, with prostrate, creeping stems gradually spreading out as summer goes on, until it forms a leafy mat studded with the typical yellow loosestrife flowers in midsummer. The leaves are opposite, rounded, and are supposed to resemble coins, hence the name of Moneywort. The plant is originally native to Europe, but was introduced into North America to occupy wet places in gardens; it never was a plant to respect boundaries and now grows more or less wild in wet pastures and woods in many parts of the continent, more commonly in the east where it may become a weed.

Water Pimpernel, *Samolus floribundus* (p. 133), grows on the banks of streams and ponds inland, and on shores, often in brackish places, on the coastal plain from tropical America north to New Brunswick and Michigan. It forms tufts of spoon-shaped leaves, and in spring and summer produces leafy stems with racemes of tiny, white, bell-shaped flowers.

Featherfoil, *Hottonia inflata* (p. 133), is one of those unpredictable plants that is abundant one year and disappears the next, to reappear five years later. It grows in the water of ponds and ditches, in swamps and slow-moving rivers in the east, from Maine to Florida in the coastal plain, and up the

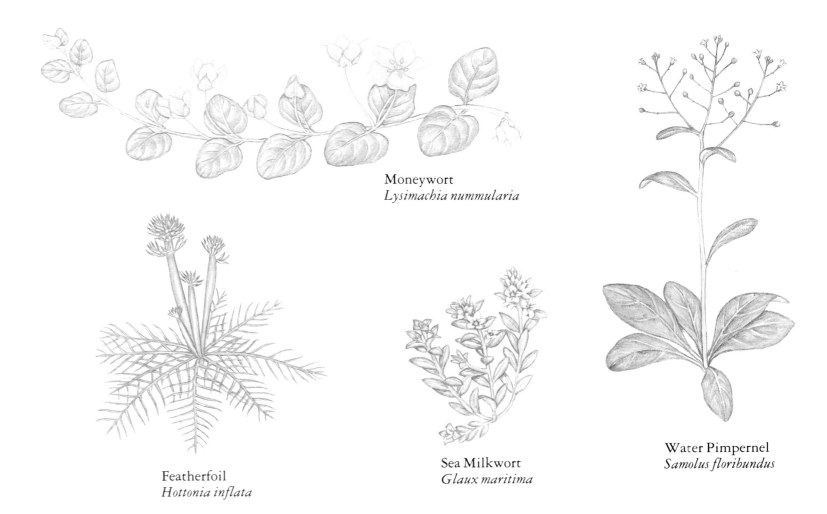

Moneywort
Lysimachia nummularia

Featherfoil
Hottonia inflata

Sea Milkwort
Glaux maritima

Water Pimpernel
Samolus floribundus

Mississippi River valley. It has a submerged stem with many feathery leaves, and a terminal umbel of flowering stalks which emerge from the water. These flowering stalks act as flotation devices; they are hollow and inflated, constricted at the nodes where the whorls of flowers grow with leafy bracts. The flowers are tubular with white petals barely emerging into view from the large green sepals.

Sea Milkwort, *Glaux maritima*, grows in very different conditions. Although a widespread plant, this is not a familiar one. It may be found all around the coasts of the north temperate regions, in grassy salt marshes, on rocks and cliffs, and in estuaries, also in alkaline places inland. It is a small, perennial plant, hairless and succulent in appearance, with prostrate stems rooting at the nodes and bearing many pairs of pointed-ovate, blue-green leaves. The solitary flowers grow in the leaf axils in summer; they have no petals but the bell-shaped calyx is white or pink and looks like a corolla. The fruits are globular capsules which split into five valves.

Leadwort family

Plumbaginaceae

A relatively small family of herbs and shrubs, with 10 genera and 300 species, many associated with the coast and some with mountains. They are especially numerous in the Mediterranean region of Europe, and in Asia. Others grow in the Arctic.

Family features The flowers are hermaphrodite and regular, with five sepals fused to form a ribbed, often papery calyx, and five fused petals which often persist around the fruits. There are five stamens opposite the petals, and the ovary is superior with one cell and five styles. The fruits are nuts or capsules opening by lids. The flowers are borne in one-sided inflorescences or in heads, with sheathing, often dry, papery bracts. The leaves are simple and often borne in a basal rosette. They lack stipules.

There are some good garden and decorative plants in this family, with the *Statice* and *Limonium* species being the best known. These are Everlasting Flowers, whose papery flowers feel dry even when fresh, and which are often used in dried flower arrangements.

Sea Lavender, *Limonium carolinianum* (p. 134), is not a garden plant, but a wild flower that grows in salt marshes from Newfoundland to Quebec, south to Florida and Texas. It is a perennial, with basal clumps of elliptical or spoon-shaped leaves from which grow strikingly large, branched inflorescences in late summer. The flowers are lavender, borne along one side of the stems only.

Thrift, *Armeria maritima* (p. 134), is another maritime plant found in salt marshes, on coastal bluffs, and in sandy

Sea Lavender
Limonium carolinianum

Thrift
Armeria maritima

Dogbane
Apocynum androsaemifolium

Indian Hemp
Apocynum cannabinum

places around the northern and Arctic coasts of North America from Newfoundland in the east to California in the west. It is a very attractive, little, cushion-forming plant, spreading into carpets as it grows older, and often becoming bare in the center. The carpets are formed of many tufts of narrow, rather fleshy leaves growing from the branches of a woody rootstock. In the summer the flowers appear: heads of fragrant, red-purple flowers with papery bracts, waving on long stalks. They are rich in honey and nectar and visited by bees. This plant has been grown in gardens for centuries, its neat cushions adorning narrow flower beds between paths.

Dogbane family

Apocynaceae

This is a mostly tropical and subtropical family, with about 180 genera and over 1500 species of herbs, shrubs, and climbing plants. Many species have a rubbery latex as sap, and in some members of the family the sap is very poisonous. The latex from the African Bushman's Poison Tree is used by the bushmen to tip arrows for hunting. This plant is grown in hedgerows in California and Florida. The Oleander and Frangipani, both used as ornamental plants in the tropics, are also poisonous.

Family features The flowers are regular and hermaphrodite, with five sepals fused to form a lobed calyx, and five petals fused to form a funnel-shaped corolla. There are five stamens inserted in the tube of the corolla, and the ovary is superior with two cells. The fruits are variable, but are often two pods. The leaves are usually opposite or in whorls.

The several species of *Apocynum* found in North America are perennial herbs with erect stems and fibrous bark. They hybridize freely with each other. The most widely distributed, growing in woods, fields, and on roadsides in much of North America, is **Dogbane**, *A. androsaemifolium*. Its erect, bushy stems bear drooping, ovate leaves growing in opposite pairs, and numerous clusters of bell-like flowers. The flowers are pink, striped with darker pink inside, and each is followed by a pair of drooping, narrow seed pods containing linear, hairy seeds. Like other members of the family, this plant has poisonous, milky sap and mammals eating the leaves have died. However, its rhizome has been used in herbal medicine as a heart tonic.

Its relative, *Apocynum cannabinum*, known by the common name of **Indian Hemp**, is much more poisonous, its action on the heart being much more powerful. Although it is used in medicine, the drug from this plant is only used with great caution in cases of heart failure, and as a diuretic to combat water retention that can result from heart failure. The plant is abundant on woodland edges, roadsides, fields, and waste places in the southern U.S. from coast to coast, and is also found in the northern U.S. and southern Canada, but much less commonly. It is similar to Dogbane, but has cylindrical, greenish-white flowers and its elongated seed pods are even longer and narrower, up to 8in long.

Blue Star, *Amsonia tabernaemontana*, gets its name from its clusters of blue, star-like flowers. This is a perennial plant, with erect, little-branched stems filled with milky sap, and alternate ovate leaves. The flowers are followed by erect, cylindrical pods. It grows in rich deciduous woods and bottomlands from New Jersey southward in the coastal plain, and westward to Kansas. There are several other *Amsonia* species found in a variety of habitats, from the dry deserts and scrub of the west to the river banks of the prairies and the eastern woods.

Rather different in appearance and habit are the two **Periwinkles**, *Vinca minor* and *Vinca major*, little and large versions of a creeping plant with bright blue flowers. They are both European natives introduced as garden plants, which have escaped to grow along roadsides, in waste places, and woods in many parts of North America. The **Lesser Periwinkle**, *V. minor*, is a low-growing plant with thin, prostrate stems, which root at the nodes, and upright, leafy stems little more than 1ft high. Greater Periwinkle, *V. major*, has trailing

stems which grow up to 3ft tall. Both have funnel-shaped, blue flowers which have a curious wheel-like appearance, an effect created by the petals, which all curve in the same direction, and by a white ring at the "hub."

Buckbean family
Menyanthaceae

This is a small family of aquatic herbs, with 5 genera and 33 species, found throughout many parts of the world. They are often included in the Gentian family.

Family features The flowers are regular and hermaphrodite, with five fused sepals forming a lobed calyx, and a five-lobed corolla. Each flower has five stamens and a superior, one-celled ovary. The fruit is a capsule with many seeds.

Buckbean, *Menyanthes trifoliata*, grows on the edges of lakes and ponds, and also in marshes and bogs, where it may spread into wide patches among other like-minded plants. It is found throughout the boreal regions of the northern hemisphere, south in North America into the southern Sierra Nevada in the west, and into Missouri in the east. It spreads in the mud by means of long, creeping rhizomes, producing many leaves which grow above the surface of the water; each leaf has three broad leaflets. In early summer the pink-tinged

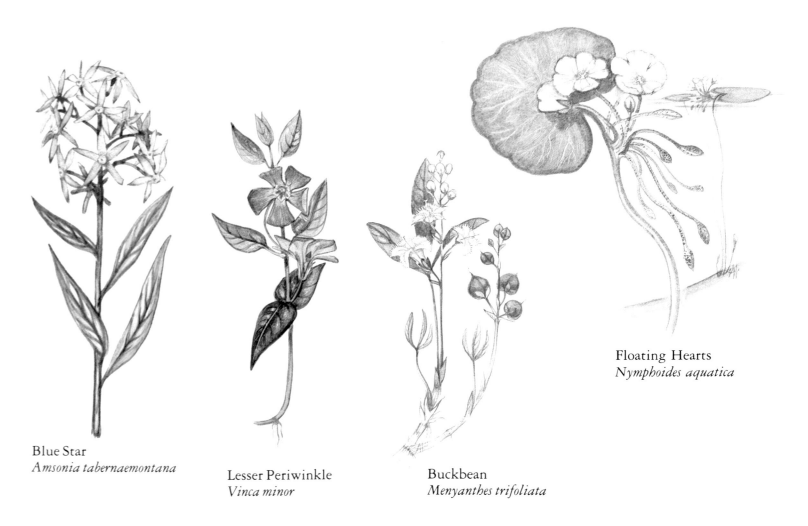

Blue Star
Amsonia tabernaemontana

Lesser Periwinkle
Vinca minor

Buckbean
Menyanthes trifoliata

Floating Hearts
Nymphoides aquatica

white flowers grow in terminal clusters on separate leafless stalks; the flowers have delicately fringed petals and bring an exotic feel to the northern bogs.

There are two species of *Nymphoides* or **Floating Hearts** in North America, both similar to Water Lilies. *Nymphoides aquatica* (p. 135) grows in ponds and slow-moving streams in the coastal plain in the east. Its floating, heart-shaped leaves are green above and purple beneath, with prominent veins. *Nymphoides cordata* grows in similar places across southern Canada and in the eastern U.S.; it too has floating leaves but they are variegated with purple on the upper surface and lack the prominent veins beneath. In summer they produce their floating white flowers; these have only five petals, a feature which immediately separates them from the multi-petalled water lily blooms.

Gentian family

Gentianaceae

A family of beautiful herbaceous plants, with about 80 genera and 900 species. Many people think of this as a mountain family, but in fact its members occupy an array of habitats, from brackish marshes to lowland woods and grassland, as well as mountain slopes and valleys. They are found mostly in the temperate regions of the world. Some of the gentians from the genus *Gentiana* are grown in rock gardens; none of them are easy to grow, and some provide even experienced gardeners with a great challenge.

Family features The flowers are borne singly or in clusters; they are hermaphrodite and regular, usually showy, with 4–12 sepals frequently fused to form a calyx-tube, and 4–12 brightly colored petals fused to form a tubular or wheel-shaped corolla. There are as many stamens as petal-lobes, inserted on the corolla tube alternately with the petal-lobes. The ovary is superior, usually with one cell. The fruit is a capsule with many small seeds. The leaves are opposite and entire, often connected to each other in pairs across the stem.

The **Gentians** are by far the biggest group in the family, with about 400 species, mainly growing in the mountains and cool regions of the northern hemisphere, with over 30 in North America. They all contain bitter substances used in herb medicine, some species to a much greater extent than others. The European Yellow Gentian, *G. lutea*, is the most useful in this respect, and its rhizomes are the source of Gentian Bitter, used to flavor liqueurs, and in herb medicine as a tonic for the digestive system.

Gentians are mostly perennial plants, the majority found in moist woods and meadows and in the mountains. They have erect stems, opposite leaves, and clusters of showy flowers in

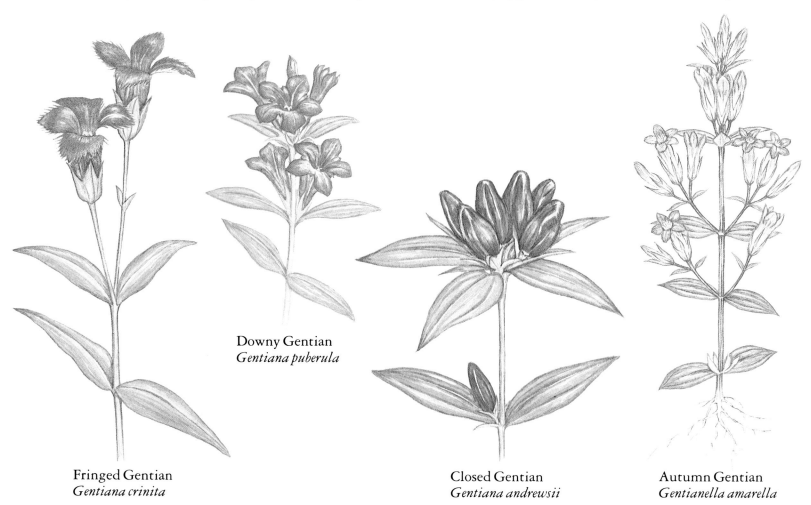

Fringed Gentian
Gentiana crinita

Downy Gentian
Gentiana puberula

Closed Gentian
Gentiana andrewsii

Autumn Gentian
Gentianella amarella

the upper leaf axils. The flower parts are usually in fives. **Fringed Gentian**, *Gentiana crinita* (p. 136), is one of the most attractive species in this genus of attractive plants. It grows in wet meadows and seepage areas, in woods and prairies from Maine to Manitoba, and south in the mountains to Georgia. Unusually among gentians, it is an annual or biennial plant that relies on seed for its renewal and is now becoming rare, so its flowers should not be picked. The flowers have only four petal-lobes each.

The **Downy Gentian**, *Gentiana puberula* (p. 136), is much more typical in having open, funnel-shaped flowers with five corolla-lobes. Its blue flowers are borne in dense, terminal clusters on 2-ft tall, unbranched, leafy stems in late summer and fall. This species grows in dry prairies and upland woods from Ohio to Manitoba, south and west to Kentucky and Kansas. Some gentians have flowers that never open, kept closed by a membrane joining the corolla lobes; such a plant is the **Closed Gentian**, *Gentiana andrewsii* (p. 136). Others have tubular flowers, like the Stiff Gentian, *G. quinquefolia*. Both these species may be found in wet woods and meadows in the eastern U.S. and Canada.

The **Autumn Gentian** or Northern Gentian, *Gentianella amarella* (p. 136), grows in moist places throughout the north, south into Vermont in the east, and down through the Rockies to Mexico in the west. It is an annual or biennial plant, with erect, 2-ft tall, branched and leafy stems, and bluish or purple flowers in the leaf axils. The flowers are smaller and duller than those of the gentians, trumpet-shaped with a fringe of long hairs in the throat.

Monument Plant, *Frasera speciosa*, is one of the Green Gentians, the *Frasera* species. They have erect stems, thick, opposite or whorled leaves, and a terminal inflorescence. Their flowers have two fringed glands on each petal-lobe. They grow mostly in dry places, on slopes, in chaparral, and coniferous woodland in the west. Monument Plant grows about 5–6ft tall, a stout plant with thick, very leafy stems, and a spike-like inflorescence with many greenish-white flowers. It is found in coniferous woods in the Sierra Nevada and Coast Ranges.

The related **Star Swertia**, *Swertia perennis*, is a perennial plant, with a clump of elliptical leaves and an erect, leafy stem ending in a narrow raceme of bluish-purple or greenish flowers. This plant grows in damp, high mountain meadows from Alaska to California.

Prairie Gentian, *Eustoma grandiflorum*, is an attractive wild flower that grows in damp places in open fields and on the prairies from Colorado to Nebraska, south to New Mexico and Texas. It has erect stems up to 2ft tall, opposite, ovate leaves, and terminal clusters of large, chalice-shaped, bluish-purple, white, or pinkish flowers in summer.

Rosita, *Centaurium calycosum*, is a southwestern plant,

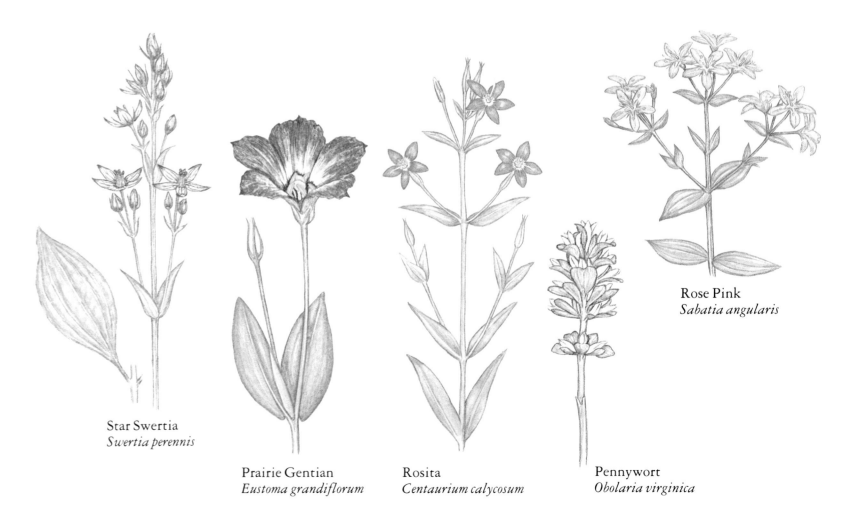

Star Swertia
Swertia perennis

Prairie Gentian
Eustoma grandiflorum

Rosita
Centaurium calycosum

Pennywort
Obolaria virginica

Rose Pink
Sabatia angularis

growing in moist places in prairies and meadows, and along streams from Texas to California, north into Colorado and Utah. It is an annual, with branched stems, opposite, lance-shaped leaves, and trumpet-shaped, pink flowers on the tips of long stalks growing from the axils of the leaves. It flowers in the early part of the summer. Several related plants also grow in the west.

The **Rose Pink**, *Sabatia angularis* (p. 137), sometimes called the Rose Gentian, is one of several *Sabatia* species which grow in the eastern U.S., many in brackish marshes or wet places in the coastal plain. Rose Pink, however, has a wider distribution, growing in many wet places from Connecticut to Florida and Texas, but also west to Michigan and Kansas. It is an annual or biennial plant, with stout stems sharply four-angled at the base. Further up the plant the stems fork. It has many ovate, opposite leaves, and pink flowers in the axils of the upper leaves. This is an attractive, even showy plant, that can be grown in wet places in wild gardens.

Pennywort, *Obolaria virginica* (p. 137), is a fleshy, perennial plant, with erect stems up to 6in tall, and purplish, opposite leaves on the upper parts of the stems. The funnel-shaped flowers are dull white or tinged with dull purple, borne singly or in clusters in the axils of the upper leaves in early summer. This plant grows in rich upland woods from New Jersey to Indiana, south to Florida and Texas.

Milkweed family
Asclepiadaceae

There are about 200 genera and 2000 species in this family of herbs, shrubs, and climbing vines, most commonly found in the warmer regions of the world. They are closely related to the Apocynaceae, and like the members of that family, contain milky juice that is poisonous in many species.

Family features The flowers are hermaphrodite and regular, with five short sepals fused into a calyx-tube, and five petals fused into a corolla, often with a well-developed corona. The five stamens have their anthers fused to the stigma and the pollen grains are united in pollinia, these joined together in pairs by horny bands. The ovary is superior with two cells, two styles, and a single joined stigma. The fruits are pairs of follicles, with many seeds. However, because of the complex pollination mechanism, not many fruits are formed. The leaves are simple and opposite.

The members of this family have extraordinary pollination mechanisms, only rivalled by members of the Orchid family. The flowers all have a central, massive column composed of stamens and style fused together. The pollen is produced in small, discrete sacs known as pollinia, that must be transferred to the correct place on the stigma of another plant from the

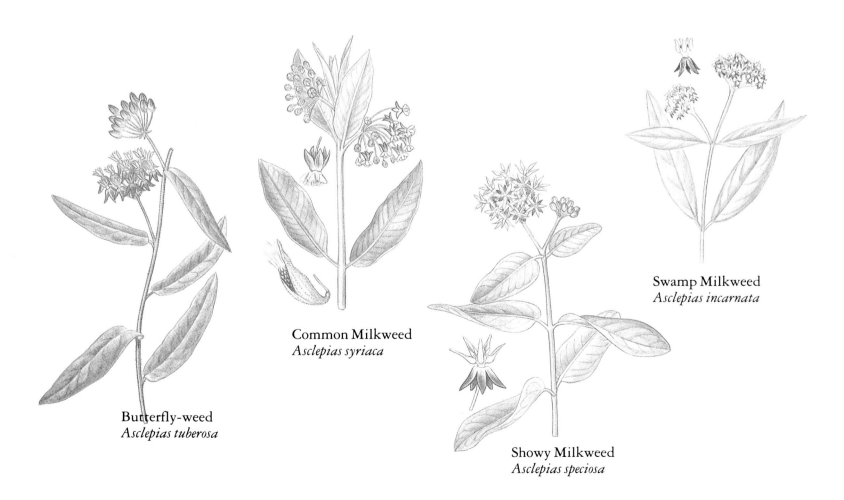

Butterfly-weed
Asclepias tuberosa

Common Milkweed
Asclepias syriaca

Showy Milkweed
Asclepias speciosa

Swamp Milkweed
Asclepias incarnata

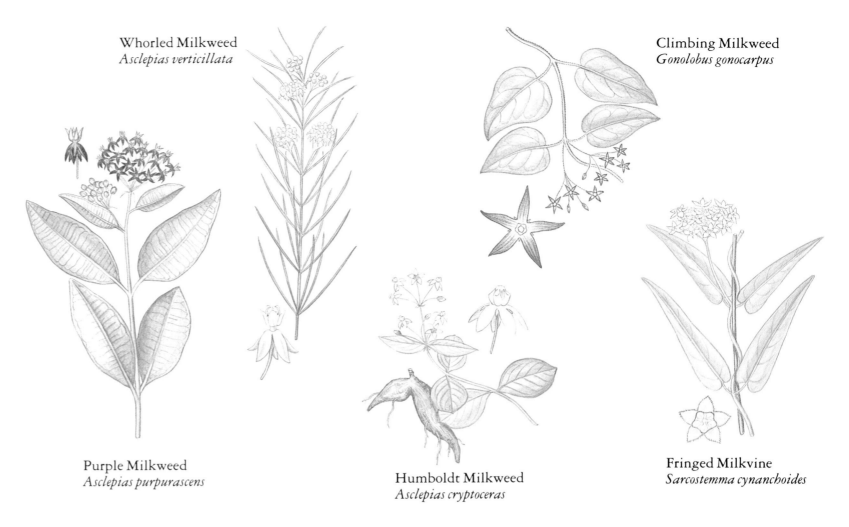

Whorled Milkweed
Asclepias verticillata

Climbing Milkweed
Gonolobus gonocarpus

Purple Milkweed
Asclepias purpurascens

Humboldt Milkweed
Asclepias cryptoceras

Fringed Milkvine
Sarcostemma cynanchoides

same species for pollination to occur. The pollinia are carried from flower to flower by insects, flies, wasps, bees, and butterflies, among others, but usually only members of one insect family will pollinate the flowers of one plant species. The pollinia are formed in pairs, joined together by a horny, jointed band that becomes attached to the legs of the insect. The structure of the flower ensures that the legs of the visitor slip into grooves where the pollinia lie waiting. As the insect flies off, the horny band moves so that the pollinia are re-aligned into the exact position needed to ensure they will catch in a slit in the next flower visited, and become deposited on the stigma.

The **Milkweeds** are a large group of New World species belonging to the genus *Asclepias*, with about 60 species in North America. Their flowers are borne in large, showy umbels and are very distinctive. Each flower has five small, reflexed sepals hidden beneath the petals, which are much larger, brightly colored, and also reflexed. On the stamen tube of the flower is the crown or corona, a structure made up of five hoods which contain nectar to attract insects. The shape of the hood varies with species, and in some species the hoods contain horns. The fruits of milkweeds are large, erect pods which split open to release the seeds. These drift on the wind, carried by a tuft of hairs. Milkweeds are perennial plants, usually with unbranched stems and milky sap.

Butterfly-weed, *Asclepias tuberosa* (p. 138), has bright flowers, usually orange or red, sometimes yellow, borne in large umbels at the tops of the stems, and in the upper leaf axils in summer. It has erect, leafy stems up to 2ft tall. It grows in dry, upland woods and prairies, and in open fields from New Hampshire to South Dakota, and south to Florida and Mexico, most commonly in the south of its range. Its name of Butterfly-weed is an apt one, for many butterflies, including monarchs and swallowtails, are attracted to it. It also has another name, that of Pleurisy Root, from its use in Indian and herb medicine as a remedy for pleurisy and other chest complaints. It is unusual in that it has watery sap, rather than the latex-like, milky sap of many milkweeds.

Common Milkweed, *Asclepias syriaca* (p. 138), is a much stouter, quite downy plant, with a large clump of leafy stems up to 6ft tall. Its flowers are duller, purplish in color, borne in compact umbels which droop slightly from the leaf axils. Like some other milkweed species, this one has edible young shoots, but they are only safe to eat if cooked in several changes of boiling water, so that the slightly poisonous, milky juice is removed. Many milkweeds are much more poisonous and cannot be eaten, so accurate identification is essential. The plant grows in fields and meadows, on roadsides and in waste places from New Brunswick to Saskatchewan, south to Georgia and Kansas.

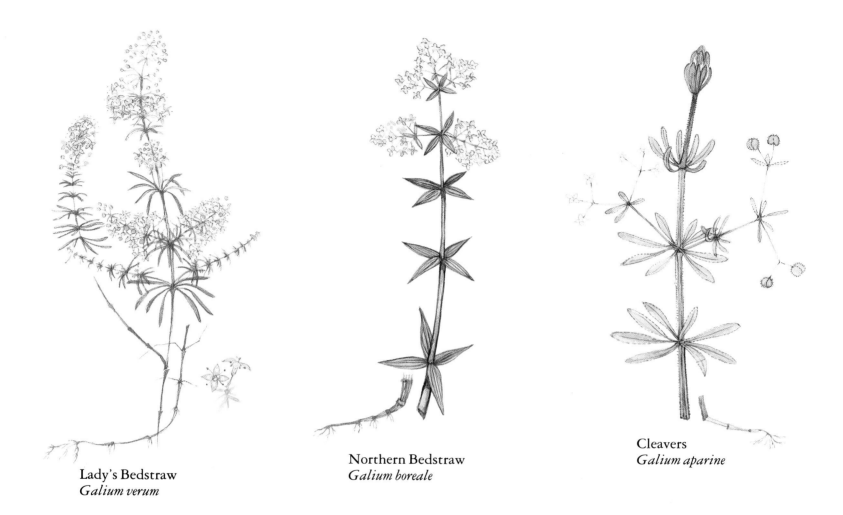

Lady's Bedstraw
Galium verum

Northern Bedstraw
Galium boreale

Cleavers
Galium aparine

Showy Milkweed, *A. speciosa* (p. 138), is a western species, a velvety, gray-white, perennial plant up to 6ft tall, with large, opposite leaves on erect stems, and umbels of pink flowers. It grows in dry, gravelly and sandy soils, in moist valleys and grassland, and along waterways from British Columbia to California, east to the Mississippi valley. Its young shoots are edible if boiled first in several changes of water to remove the milky juice.

Swamp Milkweed, *Asclepias incarnata* (p. 138), is not edible. It grows in wet prairies and swamps from Nova Scotia to Saskatchewan and Utah, south to Florida and New Mexico. It has stout stems up to 4ft tall, with opposite, lance-shaped leaves, and umbels of pink flowers. **Purple Milkweed**, *A. purpurascens* (p. 139), is similar, with purple flowers. It grows in dry places from New Hampshire to Wisconsin, south and west to Kansas and Oklahoma.

Whorled Milkweed, *Asclepias verticillata* (p. 139), is recognizable from its whorls of 3–6 narrow leaves on slender stems. It has greenish-white flowers in umbels growing from the axils of the upper leaves. This is a mainly midwestern species, growing in prairies and fields, on roadsides and in upland woods from Massachusetts to Saskatchewan and south to Florida and Arizona. Similar species are the Horsetail Milkweed, *A. subverticillata*, and the Plains Milkweed, *A. pumila*; both have narrow leaves and white flowers. They grow in the prairie states. The Horsetail Milkweed is very poisonous if eaten by livestock, so they usually avoid it.

The **Humboldt Milkweed**, *Asclepias cryptoceras* (p. 139), is a more or less prostrate plant, with rounded, opposite leaves, and small umbels of greenish-yellow flowers in the leaf axils. It grows on gravelly slopes in the Great Basin.

The **Climbing Milkweeds** or Anglepods, *Gonolobus* species, are vines, mostly from the southeastern states; they have twining stems, broadly heart-shaped, opposite leaves, and clusters of cup-shaped flowers in the leaf axils. *Gonolobus gonocarpus* (p. 139) grows in woods and thickets from Georgia and Alabama, north to West Virginia and Indiana. Its flowers vary in color from yellow to brownish-purple, and it has smooth, angled pods. Several related species are known as Spiny-pods, since they have weak spines on their follicles.

Fringed Milkvine, *Sarcostemma cynanchoides* (p. 139), is another climbing vine, twining in and around bushes in the deserts, plains, and brush of the southwestern U.S. from California to Texas, north into Utah and Oklahoma, south into Mexico. It has opposite, lance-shaped or narrowly triangular leaves, like arrow-heads, and umbels of purplish flowers in the leaf axils. Each flower is star-like, with five furry-edged petals. A similar desert species, *S. hirtellum*, has greenish-white flowers with smooth, rather than furry, edges to the petals.

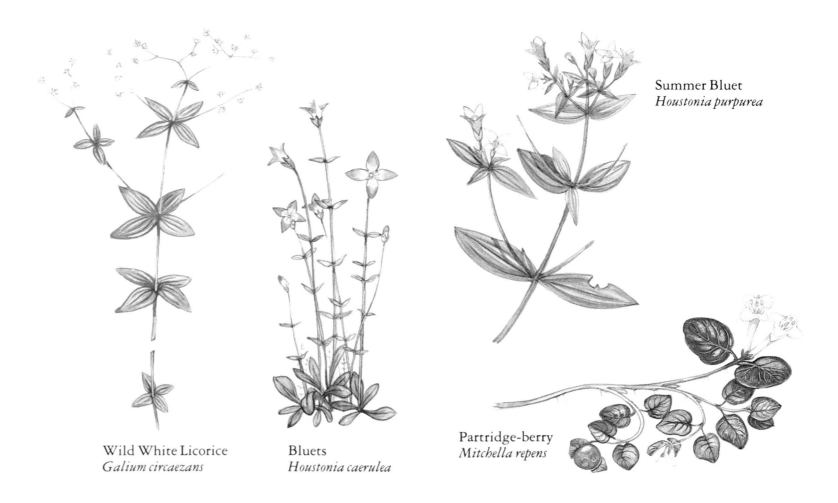

Summer Bluet
Houstonia purpurea

Wild White Licorice
Galium circaezans

Bluets
Houstonia caerulea

Partridge-berry
Mitchella repens

Bedstraw family

Rubiaceae

Also called the **Madder family**. This is one of the largest families of flowering plants, with about 500 genera and 6000 species, mostly found in the tropics. Coffee, quinine, and gardenias all come from members of this family. Madder, *Rubia tinctorum*, has been known since prehistoric times as a source of the madder dye, used to dye fabrics red, until replaced by synthetics.

Family features The flowers are hermaphrodite and regular, with fused sepals and petals. The calyx and corolla both have four or five lobes, and there are as many stamens as corolla-lobes inserted in the tube of the corolla and alternating with the petal-lobes. The ovary is inferior, with two or more cells. The fruits are berries, drupes or capsules. The leaves are simple and usually entire, sometimes toothed, opposite or borne in whorls. They have stipules which may be indistinguishable from the leaves.

There are not that many members of the family in temperate regions, about 140 in North America, the majority small herbaceous plants belonging to the genus *Galium*, commonly known as **Bedstraws**. They are small, slender plants, with four-angled, squarish stems, and leaves in whorls. The flowers are small and either borne in dense clusters on every tiny branch of the stems, or in the leaf axils.

Lady's Bedstraw, *Galium verum* (p. 140), gets its name from the legend that it was present in the straw in the stable where Christ was born; the legend was expanded to include the story that childbirth was easier if this plant was in the mattress straw when women were in labor. The plant contains coumarin, a substance that gives it the scent of new-mown hay. Lady's Bedstraw can be used in cheese-making, for its flowers curdle milk. It is used in herb medicine as a treatment for kidney gravel. And it yields a red dye that was used at one time for dying wool. It is a low-growing, perennial plant, with wiry, much-branched, creeping stems and upright leafy stems, forming dense patches along roadsides and in fields in the northeast and northern midwest regions of the U.S., and across Canada. It has whorls of 8–12 leaves on its squarish stems and dense clusters of yellow flowers in late summer.

Most bedstraws have white flowers. Several are boreal plants distributed in a great circle around the North Pole. The aptly named **Northern Bedstraw**, *Galium boreale* (p. 140), is one of these. It grows in damp places in a variety of habitats, among rocks and screes, beside streams, south to Kentucky in the east and California in the west. It has numerous stems, with many whorls of four lance-shaped leaves, and dense clusters of white flowers in midsummer. Fragrant Bedstraw, *G. triflorum*, is

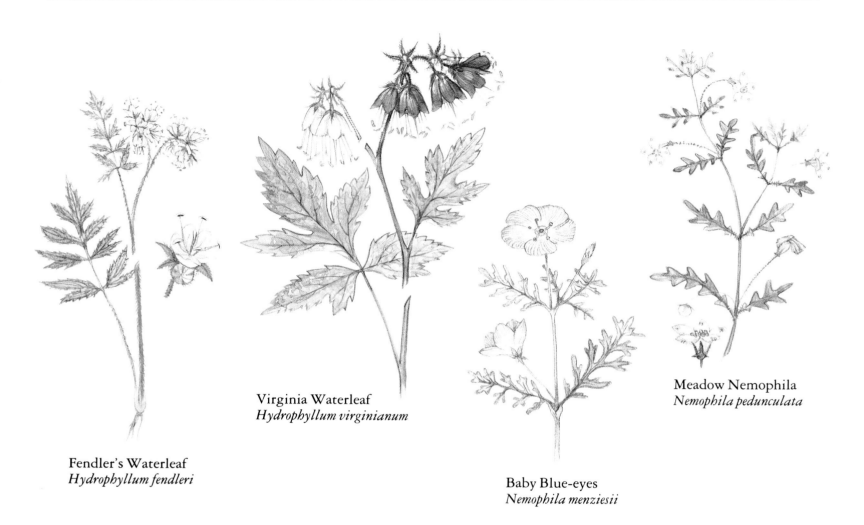

Virginia Waterleaf
Hydrophyllum virginianum

Meadow Nemophila
Nemophila pedunculata

Fendler's Waterleaf
Hydrophyllum fendleri

Baby Blue-eyes
Nemophila menziesii

another boreal species, a scrambling plant with bristly stems, leaves in whorls of six, and a scent of vanilla. Its flowers are borne in small clusters in the leaf axils.

Also found throughout the northern hemisphere, and all over North America, **Cleavers**, *Galium aparine* (p. 140), is an annual plant, with weak, scrambling, angled stems. They cling to vegetation (and clothing!) by hooked bristles on the angles. The narrow leaves grow in whorls of 6–8, and small clusters of tiny, greenish-white flowers grow in the leaf axils. They are followed by globular fruits, produced in pairs and covered in a myriad of tiny hooks. They catch on everything that brushes past them, a superb distribution mechanism and obviously successful. The plant is a nuisance as a weed, but its fruits can be roasted to make a coffee substitute, and its young shoots can be eaten as a green vegetable or in salads. It is also used in herb medicine for purifying the blood.

Wild White Licorice, *Galium circaezans* (p. 141), grows in dry woods and thickets from Maine to Minnesota, south to Florida and Texas. It has whorls of four, broadly oval or elliptical leaves on its stems, and sparse clusters of greenish-white flowers in summer.

Bluets is a name given to several dainty plants, species of *Houstonia*, which grow in the east. *Houstonia caerulea* (p. 141) is typical, a hairless, perennial plant with slender rhizomes from which grow little, branched stems, only 8in tall at most, with

opposite, ovate leaves. In spring and early summer they produce small, blue, yellow-eyed flowers growing on long stalks from the upper leaf axils. This plant is found in moist soil in meadows, woods, and fields from Nova Scotia to Wisconsin, south to Georgia and Arkansas. **Summer Bluet**, *H. purpurea* (p. 141), is a more robust plant, up to 18in tall, with several stems, opposite leaves, and clusters of flowers varying in color from purple to white. It grows in dry, open places in the eastern U.S.

Partridge-berry, *Mitchella repens* (p. 141), is a creeping plant with trailing stems that root at the nodes, and opposite, shiny, evergreen leaves. It is sometimes grown as an ornamental ground-cover plant in shady places in gardens, especially in a form with white-veined leaves. In early summer it bears twinned, pink or white tubular flowers in the axils of the uppermost leaves; the flowers are joined at the base and together produce a single red berry in late summer. The berries persist into winter and are edible, but rather tasteless and dry.

Waterleaf family
Hydrophyllaceae

A small family with about 20 genera and 250 species of herbs, many from western North America. Some of the annual species of *Nemophila* and *Phacelia* are grown as bedding plants in flower borders. Otherwise the family is economically unimportant, though it has some lovely wild flowers in it.

Family features The flowers are borne in cymes. They are hermaphrodite and regular, with five sepals joined at least at the base, and a tubular or flat corolla with five petal-lobes. There are five stamens inserted on the corolla, alternating with the petal-lobes. The ovary is superior with one or two cells. The fruits are capsules. The leaves are entire or pinnate, borne in basal rosettes or alternately on the stems. The plants are often hairy.

The **Waterleafs**, *Hydrophyllum* species, are perennials found in moist and shady places, often in woods, throughout the U.S. and in southern Canada. They have underground rhizomes from which grow clumps of broad, pinnately lobed or divided leaves, often with lighter patches of green, as if stained by water, hence the name of waterleaf. The stems bear similar, but smaller leaves, and terminal clusters of bell-shaped flowers with long, projecting stamens; the flowers vary from greenish-white to blue-violet in color, and open in summer, early or late depending on species.

Fendler's Waterleaf, *Hydrophyllum fendleri* (p. 142), is a western species which grows in damp, shady places in the Rocky Mountains from British Columbia to California, and east to Idaho and New Mexico. It is a rather coarse plant, with a single hairy stem up to 3ft tall, large, pinnately divided leaves with broad toothed leaflets, and loose, terminal clusters of white or violet flowers. **Virginia Waterleaf**, *H. virginianum* (p. 142), is a similar eastern species found in rich, moist woods or open, wet places from Quebec to North Dakota, and south to North Carolina and Arkansas. Waterleafs are edible, their basal leaves making a good vegetable when gathered young and boiled in water.

Baby Blue-eyes, *Nemophila menziesii* (p. 142), is a well-known Californian wild flower, flowering in spring with California Poppy and Tidy Tips. It can be grown in wild-flower gardens with these two species, the orange, yellow, and blue complementing each other beautifully. Baby Blue-eyes is a little, annual plant, only 6in tall, with several slender, somewhat succulent, branched stems, and pinnately divided leaves. Its bowl-shaped, bright blue flowers have lighter centers and may measure over an inch across; they are borne singly on thin stalks near the tops of the stems. Plants grow in moist places, in flats, and on grassy hillsides, in chaparral and coastal sage scrub, on the coast and in foothills from southern California to Oregon.

There are several other *Nemophila* species in the west. **Meadow Nemophila**, *N. pedunculata* (p. 142), is a weak plant, often with prostrate stems, and pinnately divided leaves. Its flowers are tiny, white or pale blue, dark-veined

Suksdorf's Romanzoffia
Romanzoffia suksdorfii

Dwarf Hesperochiron
Hesperochiron pumilus

Whispering Bells
Emmenanthe penduliflora

with a purple blotch on each petal-lobe; they grow on long stalks in the leaf axils. This plant grows in moist and shaded places west of the Sierras, from California to British Columbia. Fivespot, *N. maculata*, is a similar plant that has larger, bowl-shaped flowers; it grows in moist places on the western slopes of the Sierra Nevada.

Suksdorf's Romanzoffia, *Romanzoffia suksdorfii* (p. 143), is a low-growing, perennial plant with a tuft of long-stalked basal leaves. These leaves have rounded, kidney-shaped blades with lobed margins. In spring the plants produce slender, branched flowering stems up to 15in tall, with a few reduced leaves and funnel-shaped flowers; these are white with a pale yellow band in the throat. The plants grow in moist coniferous forests near the coast, often among rocks or on cliffs, from California to Washington.

Dwarf Hesperochiron, *Hesperochiron pumilus* (p. 143), is a tiny perennial plant only 2in tall. It has a tuft of narrow, oblong leaves, and in early summer produces a few solitary flowers growing on long stalks directly from the center of the tuft. The flowers are white and saucer-shaped, very hairy within the corolla-tube. The plant grows in moist meadows and flats from Washington to Montana, south to California and Arizona.

Whispering Bells, *Emmenanthe penduliflora* (p. 143), is related to the phacelias. It is a delicate, annual plant, hairy and with a pleasant scent. It has slender, erect stems, narrow, pinnately lobed leaves, and bears yellow, bell-shaped flowers dangling from the tops of the stems in early summer. The flowers persist for a long time, drying to become like tissue-paper bells that rustle in the wind—the whispering bells. The plant is found in dry places, in chaparral, and sage scrub, especially after burns or disturbance, in the Coast Ranges and Sierra Nevada, and in the deserts from California to Utah and Arizona.

There are over 200 *Phacelia* species in North America, many from the west. These are annual or perennial herbaceous plants, usually hairy and often glandular. Their flowers are tubular, funnel-shaped or bell-shaped, often with protruding stamens. Most species have blue, purple or white flowers, but some have wholly yellow flowers, or ones with yellow markings. The flowers are borne in coiled clusters, which uncurl as the flowers open to become straight in fruit. In this feature they resemble members of the Borage family.

Wild Heliotrope or Common Phacelia, *Phacelia distans*, is a typical member of the genus, with its coils of blue flowers and divided leaves. It is an annual plant, 2–3ft tall, with finely hairy stems which may be simple and erect, or branched and sprawling, decorated with alternate, divided, almost fern-like leaves. Its flowers are borne in early summer in a few terminal clusters; individually they are quite large and broadly bell-

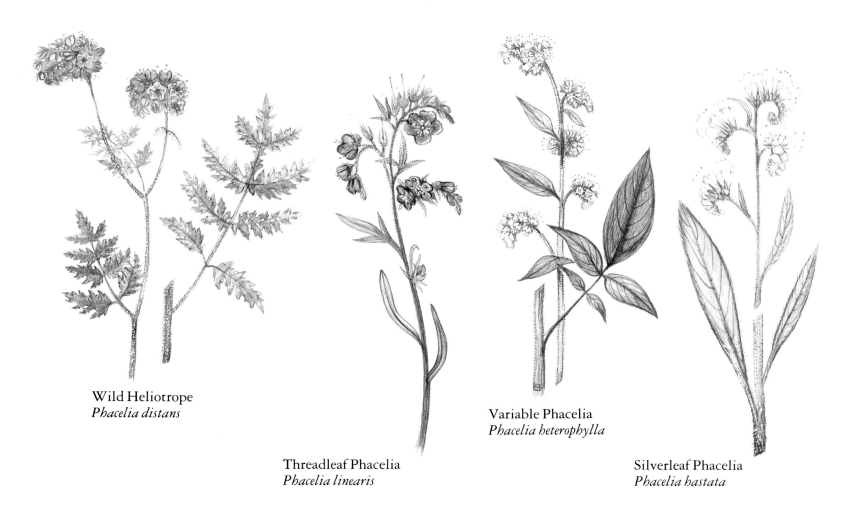

Wild Heliotrope
Phacelia distans

Threadleaf Phacelia
Phacelia linearis

Variable Phacelia
Phacelia heterophylla

Silverleaf Phacelia
Phacelia hastata

shaped. Wild Heliotrope grows in fields, on slopes, and among brush, in deserts in much of California, and into Nevada and Arizona. **Threadleaf Phacelia**, *P. linearis* (p. 144), has stiff stems up to 2ft tall, with narrow leaves, and large, open, violet or white flowers in early summer. It grows on dry, gravelly slopes and in open flats from California to British Columbia.

Variable Phacelia, *Phacelia heterophylla* (p. 144), is a much more widespread species found in dry, rocky places throughout the Rocky Mountains from British Columbia to California. It usually has a single erect, rather coarse stem growing up to 6ft tall, with many gray-green, three-lobed leaves, each leaf having one large, ovate leaflet and two much smaller ones at the base. The flowers grow in coiled clusters in the leaf axils; they are white to greenish-yellow in color, with hairy calyces, bell-shaped corollas, and projecting stamens. **Silverleaf Phacelia**, *P. hastata* (p. 144), also grows in dry, rocky places in the Rocky Mountains. It is a perennial, with lance-shaped, silvery leaves, and coils of white or lavender flowers.

Sagebrush Bells, *Phacelia glandulifera*, has yellowish flowers in long, coiled sprays terminating the stems, and pinnately lobed gray leaves. It is covered with conspicuous dark glands. The plant grows in dry, sandy places among sagebrush scrub, in pinyon-juniper, and pine woods from California to Washington and Wyoming in the Great Basin.

Miami Mist, *Phacelia purshii*, is an eastern and midwestern species, distinctive for the fringed edges to its white or blue petals. It is an annual, with sprawling stems growing up to 2ft tall, and pinnately lobed leaves. It grows in moist woods from Pennsylvania to Illinois, south to Georgia and Alabama.

There are about 45 *Nama* species found in southwestern areas of North America, in Mexico and South America, many of them appearing in desert areas after rainfall. They are low-growing, branched, annual or perennial plants, with well-spaced leaves on their stems. **Purple Mat**, *N. demissum*, is an annual with a few prostrate stems forming an open mat spreading from the center of the plant. It is never much more than 1ft across, and may be minute in a dry year. The stems branch toward their ends and form clusters of spoon-shaped leaves with red-purple, bell-shaped flowers growing in the axils of the leaves and branches. The plant grows in desert flats and washes, and in Creosote Bush scrub from California to Utah and Arizona, south into Mexico.

Rothrock's Nama, *Nama rothrockii*, is a perennial plant, with erect stems up to 1ft tall, growing from slender rhizomes. It has serrated leaves, and ball-like clusters of red-purple or lavender, funnel-shaped flowers at the tops of the stems. It is covered with sticky hairs. The plant grows in sandy flats and slopes, in pinyon scrub and coniferous woods in the Sierra Nevada and San Bernardino Mountains.

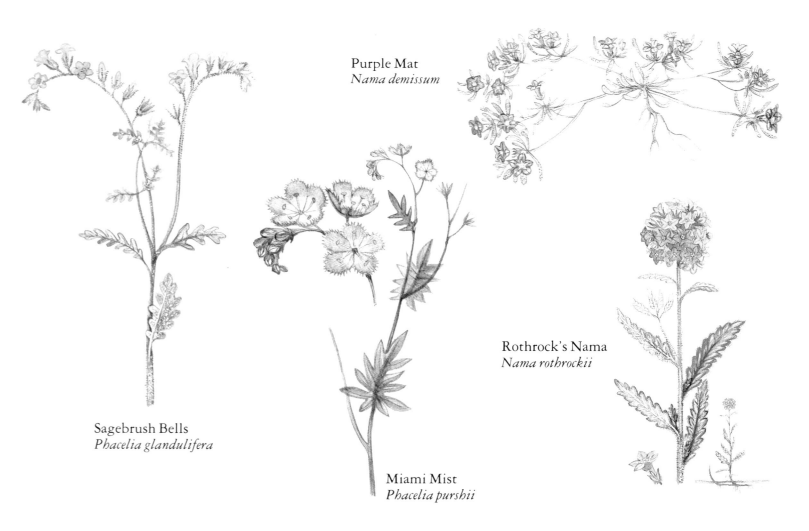

Purple Mat
Nama demissum

Sagebrush Bells
Phacelia glandulifera

Miami Mist
Phacelia purshii

Rothrock's Nama
Nama rothrockii

Phlox family

Polemoniaceae

A small family with about 15 genera and 300 species, most from North America, especially from the west. The majority are herbs. Many species and varieties of phlox are grown in flower gardens.

Family features The flowers are usually solitary or borne in terminal clusters; they are hermaphrodite and regular. Each has a five-lobed calyx formed of five fused sepals, often with membranous sections between the lobes, and a funnel-shaped or bell-shaped corolla formed of five fused petals. There are five stamens inserted on the corolla, alternating with the corolla lobes, and the ovary is superior, usually with three cells. The fruit is usually a capsule. The leaves are alternate or opposite, and may be simple, dissected or compound.

Phloxes, *Phlox* species, come in several kinds—large, erect, perennial, herbaceous plants, with tall, leafy stems and terminal clusters of showy flowers; smaller annual plants, but still with leafy, erect stems and showy flowers; trailing or creeping plants, often woodland or alpine species, with a woody base, prostrate stems and linear, sometimes almost prickly leaves, studded with flowers in spring; or cushion-forming mountain plants.

Garden Phlox, *Phlox paniculata*, is of the first type, a large, herbaceous, perennial plant which has given rise to many of the large garden varieties. This species is native to the U.S., and truly wild plants may be found from New York to Illinois, south to Georgia and Arkansas, in moist places, woods, and thickets; elsewhere they are likely to have escaped from gardens. This is a handsome plant, with leafy stems up to 6ft tall, and a cluster of showy pink flowers at the top of each stem in the latter half of summer. Annual Phlox, *P. drummondii*, is a much smaller species, only 18in tall at most, and annual instead of perennial. It also has many garden varieties used in summer bedding at the front of flower borders. It is native to Texas but may be found wild in Florida and north into Missouri, growing in open, sandy places.

Blue Phlox, *Phlox divaricata,* is another species grown in gardens, this one in rock gardens. It has many trailing, leafy, non-flowering shoots, from which grow flowering shoots in late spring. These are erect, up to 18in tall, and bear opposite, ovate to lance-shaped leaves, with terminal clusters of blue or purple flowers. The flowers have wedge-shaped petals. In its native habitats, the plant grows in rich woods from Quebec to Minnesota, south to Georgia and Texas.

Long-leaved Phlox, *Phlox longifolia*, is a western species, one of many found in the Rocky Mountain area. It forms clumps of slender, leafy stems, often only 6-12in tall, with

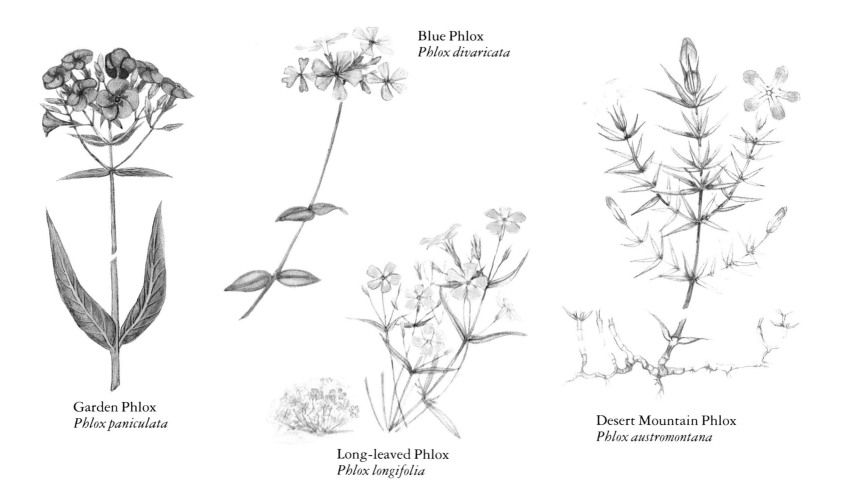

Garden Phlox
Phlox paniculata

Blue Phlox
Phlox divaricata

Long-leaved Phlox
Phlox longifolia

Desert Mountain Phlox
Phlox austromontana

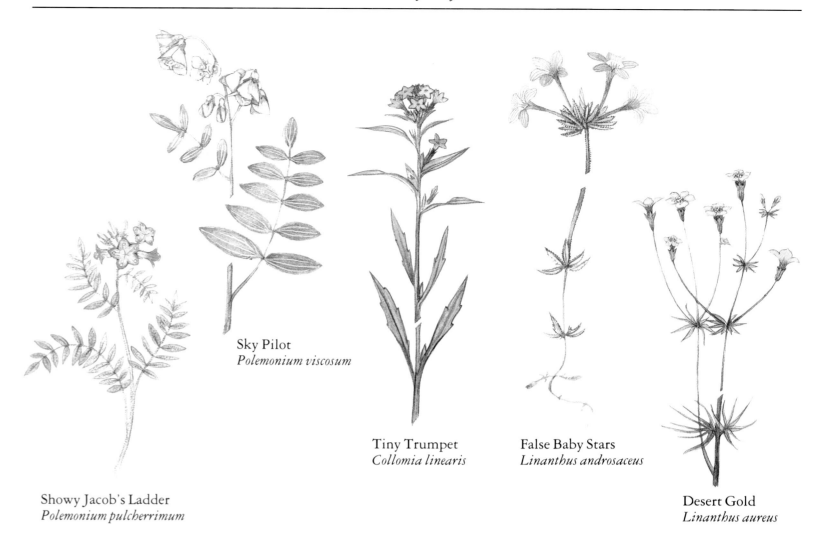

Sky Pilot
Polemonium viscosum

Tiny Trumpet
Collomia linearis

False Baby Stars
Linanthus androsaceus

Showy Jacob's Ladder
Polemonium pulcherrimum

Desert Gold
Linanthus aureus

opposite, linear leaves. In early summer pink or white, salver-shaped flowers appear on long stalks in the upper leaf axils. This phlox grows in dry, open flats and on slopes in the Great Basin.

Desert Mountain Phlox, *Phlox austromontana* (p. 146), grows in dry, rocky places in the high mountains from California to Arizona, and north to Oregon and Idaho. It is a perennial, with a woody base and many short, branched stems only 4in long, densely covered with linear, gray-green, pungently scented leaves. Its white or pink flowers grow at the tips of the stem branches in early summer.

Jacob's Ladder is a name given to many *Polemonium* species because of the ladder-like aspect of their leaves, which are compound with many opposite leaflets. **Showy Jacob's Ladder**, *P. pulcherrimum*, is one such species from the Rockies, common in dry, rocky places throughout the mountains. Its leaves have a skunk-like scent when crushed, like several of the other species. This plant forms clumps of ladder-like leaves growing from a woody, branched base, and flowering stems bearing terminal clusters of blue, yellow-throated, funnel-shaped flowers. The similar *P. reptans* is found in the east. Several species are grown in gardens.

Sky Pilot, *Polemonium viscosum*, forms spreading clumps of leaves only 6in tall, distinctive for their many whorls of tiny, divided leaflets; the leaves have a strong, lingering, skunk-like odor if crushed. The blue-violet, funnel-shaped flowers are borne in nodding terminal clusters on taller stems up to 15in high in the latter half of summer. Sky Pilot grows in dry, rocky places from Washington and Oregon east into Alberta, south through the mountains to New Mexico.

Tiny Trumpet, *Collomia linearis*, is one of several western *Collomia* species. It is common in dry places in the Rocky Mountains, but is also found from British Columbia to Ontario and Nebraska, growing as a weed in waste places and along roadsides. It is a small, annual plant, with an erect, leafy stem up to 1ft tall, and head-like clusters of pink-purple, tubular flowers terminating the stem and on branches growing from the leaf axils. Its leaves are alternate and linear or lance-shaped.

There are about 40 species of *Linanthus*, mostly from western North America and Chile, with many in California. They are annual or perennial plants, often with branched stems, and opposite leaves divided into linear segments, giving the stems a bottlebrush appearance. Their flowers are borne in clusters or heads at the tops of their stems and are variously colored, usually in shades of white, blue or pink, often with spots or bands of other colors. **False Baby Stars**, *L. androsaceus*, is typical, found in open places, chaparral, and grassland in California. It has long, trumpet-like flowers, white, pink or yellow in color.

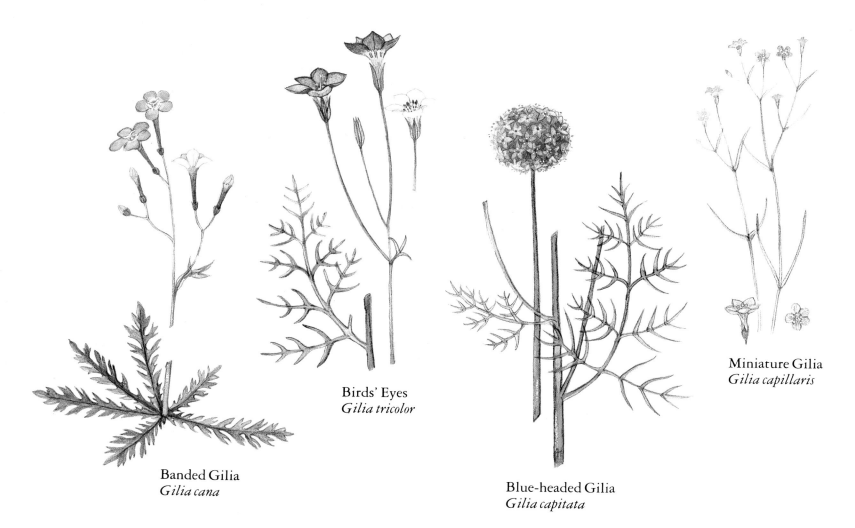

Birds' Eyes
Gilia tricolor

Miniature Gilia
Gilia capillaris

Banded Gilia
Gilia cana

Blue-headed Gilia
Gilia capitata

Desert Gold, *Linanthus aureus* (p. 147), has yellow flowers, like odd members of many Phlox family genera. This is a tiny, annual plant, only 4in tall at most, with several slender stems and well-spaced leaves, each one with 3–7 needle-like segments. Its flowers are funnel-shaped and vary from pale to deep yellow, with a brownish-purple throat. This plant is found in dry places, sandy slopes, and Creosote Bush scrub in the Mojave and Colorado deserts, and scattered through California into Nevada and New Mexico.

There are about 50 *Gilia* species in western North America and South America. Some are grown in gardens. Most are annuals, many with dissected leaves often in a basal rosette or on the lower parts of their stems. Their flowers are usually tubular or funnel-shaped, varying in color from pink to white, blue, lavender or even yellow. The flowers may be solitary, in loose clusters, or dense heads.

Banded Gilia, *Gilia cana*, has a rosette of lobed or toothed leaves, more or less densely covered with cobweb-like hairs. Its flowers are tubular, with spreading corolla-lobes, pinkish-purple in color, with a band of yellow around the tube. They are borne in loose clusters on branched flowering stems up to 1ft tall in the latter half of summer. This is a variable species found in dry places in a variety of habitats in California, in the Mojave Desert, in canyons and washes, in pinyon and juniper scrub and in the mountains.

Birds-eyes, *Gilia tricolor*, is one of the showier *Gilia* species. Its large, bell-shaped flowers can vary from pale to dark blue-violet in color, with a yellow tube and throat, and five pairs of dark purple spots on the throat. The plant flowers in early spring, the flowers solitary or borne in loose clusters terminating branched flower stalks up to 15in tall. It also has a rosette of dissected leaves. This plant grows in grassland, in open places, and on slopes in the Coast Ranges and in the foothills of the Sierra Nevada of central California.

Blue-headed Gilia, *Gilia capitata*, has a rosette of dissected leaves and branched flowering stalks. But the tubular, blue-violet flowers are gathered into dense, terminal balls of 50–100 flowers. This plant is found on grassy slopes and in pine forests in the western Cascades and Coast Rangers from British Columbia to California. It is one of several *Gilia* species with ball-like heads of flowers.

Miniature Gilia, *Gilia capillaris*, forms patches of erect, often much-branched stems about 1ft tall, with linear leaves and branched inflorescences of tiny, funnel-shaped flowers. The flowers may be white or pink, and are often streaked with purple. This plant grows in sandy places, in foothills and flats, in the Sierra Nevada and Coast Ranges of the U.S.

Pale Trumpets, *Ipomopsis longiflora* (p. 149), forms an open, untidy, much-branched plant, with many stems, thread-like leaves, and trumpet-shaped, pale blue or white

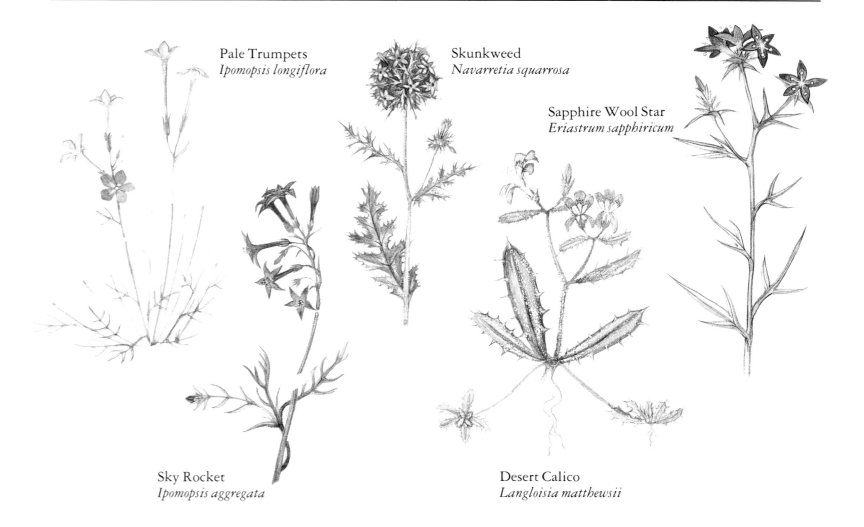

Pale Trumpets
Ipomopsis longiflora

Skunkweed
Navarretia squarrosa

Sapphire Wool Star
Eriastrum sapphiricum

Sky Rocket
Ipomopsis aggregata

Desert Calico
Langloisia matthewsii

flowers. The leaves are actually pinnate, with linear segments, and the flowers grow in the axils of the upper ones. The plant grows in sandy deserts and dry grassland from Utah to Nebraska, south to Texas and Arizona, and into Mexico.

Sky Rocket, *Ipomopsis aggregata,* has several names, including Desert Trumpet and Skunkflower, as well as Scarlet Gilia and Foxfire. The names refer to its bright red or pink flowers and its slight scent of skunk. It is a biennial to perennial plant, with erect, simple or branched stems up to 4ft tall, with dissected leaves mostly near the base. The many tubular flowers are borne on the branches of the upper stems; they are usually red, mottled with yellow, but may be pink, and they have pointed petal-lobes, often bent backward along the long tube of the flower. Skyrocket grows in dry, sandy flats, on dry slopes and rocky ridges, in scrub, pine woods and chaparral, forming patches of bright color in early summer. It is found from British Columbia to California, through the Rocky Mountains and in the plains to North Dakota and Texas, south into Mexico.

Skunkweed, *Navarretia squarrosa*, is another member of this family with a skunky odor to the leaves. It is one of about 30 western species in the genus *Navarretia*, all spiny, annual plants with rigid, usually branched stems, needle-shaped or prickly leaves, and flowers borne in dense heads with spiny bracts. The stems of this species grow up to 2ft tall and have

shiny, prickly-lobed, rigid leaves. Its spiny-bracted clusters of tubular, blue-purple flowers are borne at the tops of the branches. Skunkweed grows in dry flats and woods, in the foothills of the Coast Ranges and Sierra Nevada from British Columbia to California.

Wool Stars are a small group of western species in the genus *Eriastrum*. They grow in the western deserts and plains, and in the mountains. They have star-like flowers and, in some, the flower clusters are woolly, hence the name of wool stars. **Sapphire Wool Star**, *E. sapphiricum*, is an annual, sticky-glandular plant up to 1ft tall, with branched, erect stems and linear or narrowly three-lobed leaves. Its sapphire blue flowers grow with bracts in clusters tipping each branch; each flower is tubular, with blue lobes and a yellow throat and tube. Plants grow in coastal sage scrub, chaparral, pine woods and desert in California.

Desert Calico, *Langloisia matthewsii*, is a tufted annual plant, only 6in high but often broader than tall, with whitish stems hidden by the pinnately toothed, bristly leaves. In early summer flowers nestle among the leaves; they are tubular and two-lipped, white or pink, with elaborate red and white markings on the upper lip. This plant is found in large numbers in sandy and gravelly areas, in scrub and deserts from southern California to Arizona. Several related species grow in the same area; all are tufted annuals with bristle-tipped leaves.

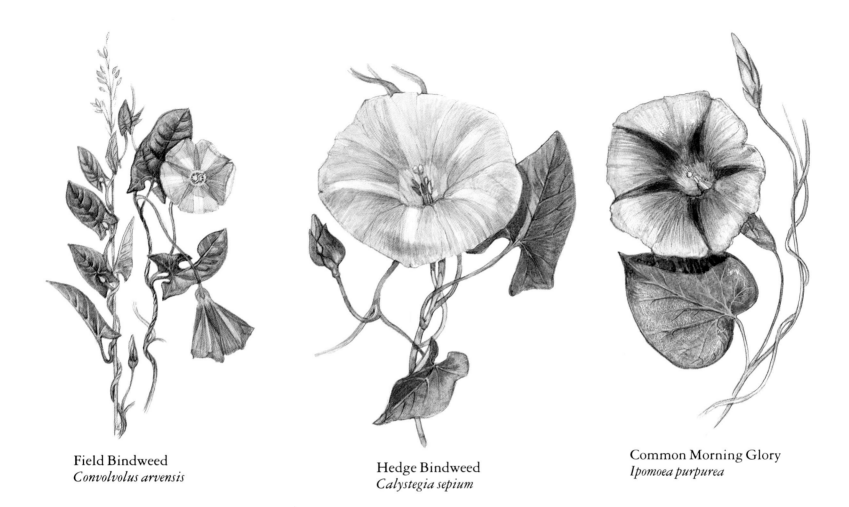

Field Bindweed
Convolvolus arvensis

Hedge Bindweed
Calystegia sepium

Common Morning Glory
Ipomoea purpurea

Morning Glory family

Convolvulaceae

This is a mostly tropical family, with about 55 genera and 1650 species of herbs and shrubs, many of them climbers with twining stems. Some are ornamental garden plants with showy flowers, like morning glories, *Ipomoea* species, but some of the bindweeds, *Convolvulus* species, are pernicious weeds. Sweet potatoes are edible tubers produced by *Ipomoea batatas*, a plant which grows in tropical countries, unlike true potatoes.

Family features The flowers are hermaphrodite and regular, usually with five free, often overlapping sepals, and five fused petals. Each has five stamens inserted at the base of the corolla-tube, alternating with the petal-lobes. The ovary is superior with 1–4 cells. The fruits are usually capsules. The leaves are simple and alternate; they lack stipules. The stems contain milky juice.

Field Bindweed, *Convolvulus arvensis*, is a weed that grows in fields and yards, in waste places and on roadsides in many parts of the U.S. and southern Canada, so common as to seem native, although it has been introduced from Europe. It is a perennial plant with stout, underground rhizomes which penetrate to a depth of 6ft or more, so deeply that they are very difficult to eradicate. The plant spreads into tangles of climbing stems that festoon fences and twist around other plants, strangling them if left alone for long enough. The stems twist in a counterclockwise direction. They bear variably arrow-shaped leaves and many white or pink, funnel-shaped flowers on long stalks opposite the leaves. This is an attractive plant but an invasive, unwelcome one.

Field Bindweed is like a scaled-down version of the **Hedge Bindweed**, *Calystegia sepium*, for its leaves are 1–2in long and its flowers are less than an inch long, whereas the leaves of the latter plant are 2–5in long and its funnel-shaped flowers are about 2in long. In addition, the flowers of Field Bindweed tend to be pink, while those of Hedge Bindweed tend to be white. Hedge Bindweed in just as difficult a weed as Field Bindweed, but its rhizomes do not penetrate as deeply, though they spread far and wide. This is another strangler, with twining stems twisting counterclockwise, but because it is bigger and more vigorous it can damage surrounding plants much more quickly, swamping them with its foliage. It grows in waste places and on roadsides, in disturbed ground and thickets throughout much of the northern hemisphere.

Morning Glory is a name given to many of the plants in this family, some of them *Calystegia* species of the western deserts. These are twining plants with arrow-shaped or triangular leaves, and funnel-shaped white flowers, some of them tinged with pink or purple. **Beach Morning Glory**, *C. soldanella*, from the beaches and dunes of the Pacific coast, is rather different—a trailing plant with fleshy, kidney-shaped leaves, but its pink, funnel-shaped flowers identify it immediately as a member of this family.

Many *Ipomoea* species are also called morning glories. **Common Morning Glory**, *I. purpurea* (p. 150), is grown as an ornamental plant in gardens, introduced from tropical America, but has escaped in many parts of the east to grow wild on roadsides and in waste places, in fields and thickets north into Canada. It is an annual, twining vine with hairy stems, broad, heart-shaped leaves, and funnel-shaped flowers in shades of white, pink, purple, and blue, growing in small clusters in the leaf axils. Other related plants include the southern **Ivy-leaved Morning Glory**, *I. hederacea*, with three-lobed leaves and blue flowers; Red Morning Glory, *I. coccinea*, a plant of the coastal plain, with heart-shaped leaves and red flowers; and Wild Potato-vine, also called the Manroot, *I. pandurata*, a perennial plant of the east and midwest which has enormous, edible, tuberous roots. It has heart-shaped leaves and its flowers are white with purple centers.

Bush Morning Glory, *Ipomoea leptophylla*, is a western species, not a climbing plant but a bushy perennial, growing about 4ft tall. It has erect stems with many narrowly lance-shaped leaves, and funnel-shaped, pink-purple flowers in the axils of the upper leaves. It has enormous, fleshy roots,

which are edible like those of Manroot, and is sometimes given the name of Bigroot. This plant grows in sandy soils in the plains and prairies from South Dakota to Montana, south to Texas and New Mexico.

The **Dodders**, members of the genus *Cuscuta*, are sometimes placed in a separate family because they are parasitic plants, quite unlike any others. They lack roots but have yellow or brown twining stems, with leaves reduced to tiny scales, and clusters of small white or yellow flowers in late summer. The plants spread by seed. When dodder seeds germinate, the seedlings must find a host very quickly or die. The stem of the seedling rotates, and if it finds the stem of another plant, twines around it and develops suckers which penetrate the conduction vessels of the host, from which it can then absorb food and water.

Many Dodder species are found in North America, parasites on a wide variety of plants. One of the most harmful is *Cuscuta epithymum*, introduced from Europe, which grows on clover and alfalfa, and which may cause considerable damage to crops. It seeds are spread in contaminated clover seed. One of the most common native dodders is *C. gronovii*, a parasite of many herbaceous and woody plants, found from Nova Scotia to Manitoba, south to Florida and Arizona. It forms coarse, deep yellow stems with numerous clusters of small, bell-shaped, white flowers.

Bush Morning Glory
Ipomoea leptophylla

Ivy-leaved Morning Glory
Ipomoea hederacea

Dodder
Cuscuta gronovii

Forget-me-not family

Boraginaceae

Also called the **Borage family**. There are about 100 genera and 2000 species of herbaceous plants in this family, found in tropical and temperate regions of the world, but particularly in the Mediterranean region and eastern Asia. There are many ornamental plants in the family, both annuals and perennials, including forget-me-nots, pulmonarias, anchusas, and heliotropes. The roots of Alkanet, *Alkanna tinctoria*, yield a red dye used to color medicines and to stain wood; Comfrey, *Symphytum officinale*, is used in herb medicine; Borage, *Borago officinalis*, is used in herb medicine, as a kitchen herb, in pot-pourris, and as a bee plant.

Family features The flowers are borne in one-sided clusters which are curled tightly at first, uncoiling as the flowers open gradually from the bottom. Each flower is hermaphrodite and regular, with five fused sepals and five petals fused to form a lobed corolla-tube. There are five stamens inserted on the corolla, alternating with the petal-lobes. The ovary is superior with two or four cells, entire or four-lobed, with the style protruding from the middle of the lobes. The fruit consists of four nutlets. The leaves are simple, usually alternate, and stipules are absent. These plants are often bristly.

Salt Heliotrope, *Heliotropium curassavicum*, is a perennial plant with an overall appearance of being smooth, blue-gray, and fleshy. It has prostrate, fleshy stems and alternate, lance-shaped or spoon-shaped, succulent leaves. Its flowers grow in double coiled clusters in the leaf axils, uncoiling and straightening as the season progresses. The flowers are funnel-shaped with five rounded lobes, white or tinged with blue, often with yellow spots in the throat, and a yellow or purple center. This is a widely distributed plant but one restricted in habitat, growing in alkaline and salty soils from British Columbia to Manitoba, south to California and New Mexico, and into South America.

Houndstongue, *Cynoglossum officinale*, is a European plant extensively naturalized in North America, growing in waste places and on roadsides, in open woods and meadows, probably introduced for its use in herb medicine. Its leaves were recommended for wrapping around dog bites; since they resemble dog's tongues it was thought they could cure the bites! It was also used to treat bruises and wounds but is rarely used in modern herb medicine since it can cause dermatitis. This is an upright, leafy plant up to 3ft tall, with large, lance-shaped leaves covered with soft gray hairs. Its stems branch near the top to end in curled clusters of dull red, funnel-shaped flowers, the clusters lengthening and straightening as the flowers open.

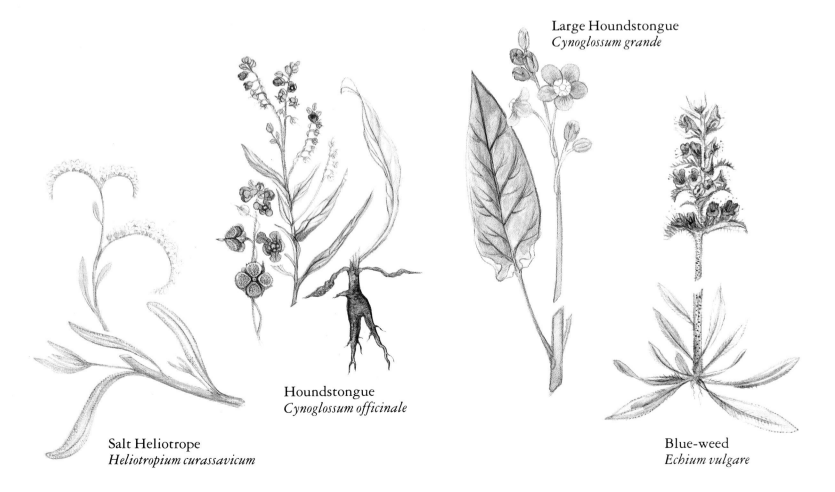

Large Houndstongue
Cynoglossum grande

Houndstongue
Cynoglossum officinale

Salt Heliotrope
Heliotropium curassavicum

Blue-weed
Echium vulgare

Large Houndstongue, *Cynoglossum grande* (p. 152), is a similar plant which is native to western North America, found in dry, shady woods in the Coast Ranges and Sierra Nevada from California to Washington. It forms clumps of large, oblong leaves, with erect, leafy flowering stems in early summer. The flowers are bright blue, with white teeth around the tube at the center of each flower. This plant was used in Indian herb medicine to treat burns.

Blue-weed or Viper's Bugloss, *Echium vulgare* (p. 152), is another European plant naturalized in North America, growing wild in waste places and on roadsides in many parts of the U.S. and southern Canada. It is a roughly hairy, biennial plant, with a rosette of large, lance-shaped leaves in the first year, and an erect, leafy flowering stem up to 3ft tall in the second. The flowers are borne in coiled clusters in the axils of leaves; they are pink in bud, opening blue and funnel-shaped. This was another medicinal herb, used to treat snakebites and scorpion stings, and although this use has fallen into disrepute, an infusion of the leaves still makes a good cordial.

Comfrey, *Symphytum officinale*, is native to Europe but cultivated in many areas of North America; it may grow as an escape in damp waste places for a few years. It is a coarse plant, forming clumps of large, bristly stems and leaves, the stems ending in coiled clusters of tubular, yellowish-white or blue flowers. The bases of the leaves run down the stems, making them appear winged. The plant has a long history of use in herb medicine, especially for healing wounds, sprains, and broken bones, and was often called Knitbone or Boneset in many old herbals.

False Gromwell, *Onosmodium virginianum*, is a stout, hairy, perennial plant with a clump of leafy stems ending in coiled clusters of flowers. The leaves are oblong and the flowers are yellow or orange, tubular with projecting styles, rather similar in shape to those of Comfrey, and produced around midsummer. The plant may be found in sandy places, in dry woods, and pine barrens from Massachusetts and New York, south to Florida and Louisiana.

Puccoon is a name given to several *Lithospermum* species by the Indians, who extracted a red dye from the roots to use as face paint. These plants grow in woods and prairies in the east and midwest. Most are perennials, with erect, leafy stems and curled clusters of funnel-shaped, yellow or orange flowers at the tops of the stems. **Hoary Puccoon**, *L. canescens*, grows in dry woods and prairies from Ontario to Saskatchewan, south to Texas and Tennessee, and east along the Allegheny Mountains. Its erect stems grow up to 18in tall and are unbranched, with many narrow leaves; the whole plant is covered with dense, grayish hairs. In late spring it bears curled sprays of bright yellow flowers. Carolina Puccoon, *L. carolinense*, is a similar plant which has roughly hairy, green leaves.

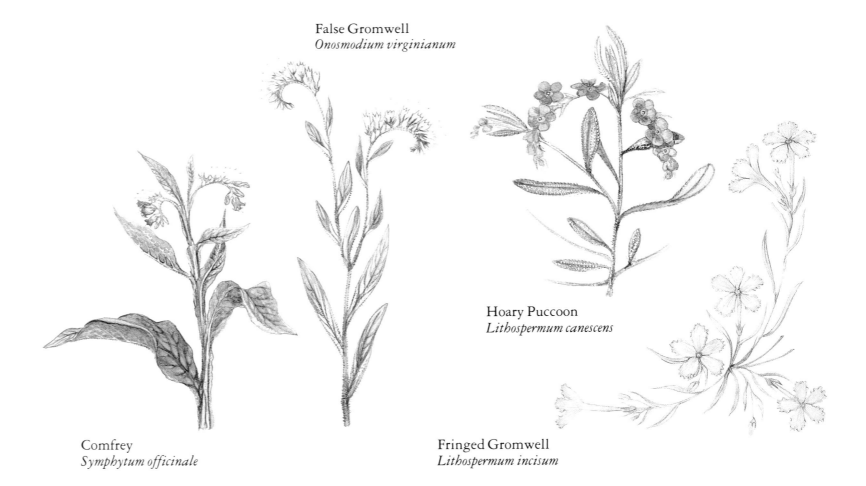

False Gromwell
Onosmodium virginianum

Hoary Puccoon
Lithospermum canescens

Comfrey
Symphytum officinale

Fringed Gromwell
Lithospermum incisum

Fringed Gromwell, *Lithospermum incisum* (p. 153), is a western and midwestern species growing in dry plains and foothills from British Columbia to Ontario, south to Arizona and Texas. It forms a clump of branched stems with narrow leaves; flowers produced in early summer are bright yellow and trumpet-shaped, with long tubes and flaring tips. Flowers produced later in the year often lack petals but produce most of the gray-white, pitted nutlets.

Virginia Bluebell, *Mertensia virginica*, can be spectacular when growing in masses, and is most abundant and most likely to seen in this way in the midwest. It grows in moist places and on stream banks in woodland from New York to Wisconsin, and south to Alabama and Kansas. It is a hairless, perennial plant with a clump of large, lance-shaped leaves, and erect, leafy stems 2–3ft tall. At the tops of the stems hang drooping clusters of beautiful flowers, pink in bud and opening blue, with bell-like corollas. The flowers open in spring. Other similar, but less showy *Mertensia* species occur throughout the U.S. and in Canada.

Oysterleaf, *Mertensia maritima*, is a rather different plant, a coastal species found on the northern Pacific and Atlantic coasts. It forms prostrate mats of stems, with fleshy, spoon-shaped leaves, and numerous bell-shaped flowers, pink at first, later turning bright blue.

There are about 50 **Forget-me-nots**, *Myosotis* species growing in the temperate regions of the world, with about 12 species in North America, some native, others introduced from Europe. *Myosotis sylvatica* is the species grown in gardens. **Water Forget-me-not**, *M. scorpioides*, is a European species found in wet places and water; it is naturalized in eastern and northwestern areas of the U.S. and in Canada. This perennial plant has leafy stems which creep a little and then turn upward to unfurl coiled clusters of blue, yellow-eyed flowers. It is a sprawling plant, only 2ft tall at most, and often smaller. Other forget-me-nots vary in habitat (some grow in dry woods and open, sandy places), and in flower color (some have pale blue or white flowers); some have tiny flowers, some are annuals. A few grow in the west.

There are over 80 species in the genus *Cryptantha*, many found in western North America. They are hairy plants, sometimes known as **White Forget-me-nots**, most of them with white flowers borne in curled clusters. **Common White Forget-me-not**, *C. intermedia*, is a stiff, very hairy, annual plant, which grows up to 2ft tall; it has linear or lance-shaped leaves, and leafless flower stalks in spring and early summer. It is found in chaparral, coastal sage, and pinyon scrub on the western side of the Rocky Mountains from California to British Columbia. **Yellow Cryptantha**, *C. flava*, is an exception, for it has yellow flowers, one of only two such species in the genus. This plant forms clumps of grayish, oblong leaves and erect,

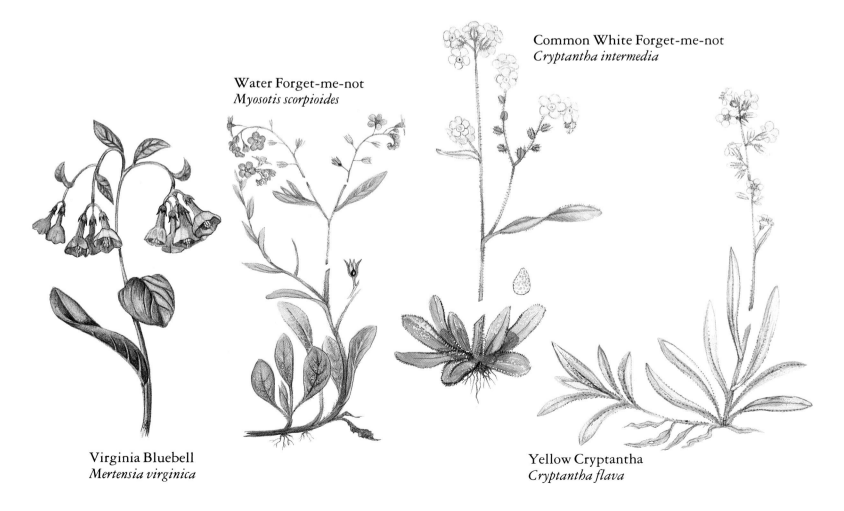

Common White Forget-me-not
Cryptantha intermedia

Water Forget-me-not
Myosotis scorpioides

Virginia Bluebell
Mertensia virginica

Yellow Cryptantha
Cryptantha flava

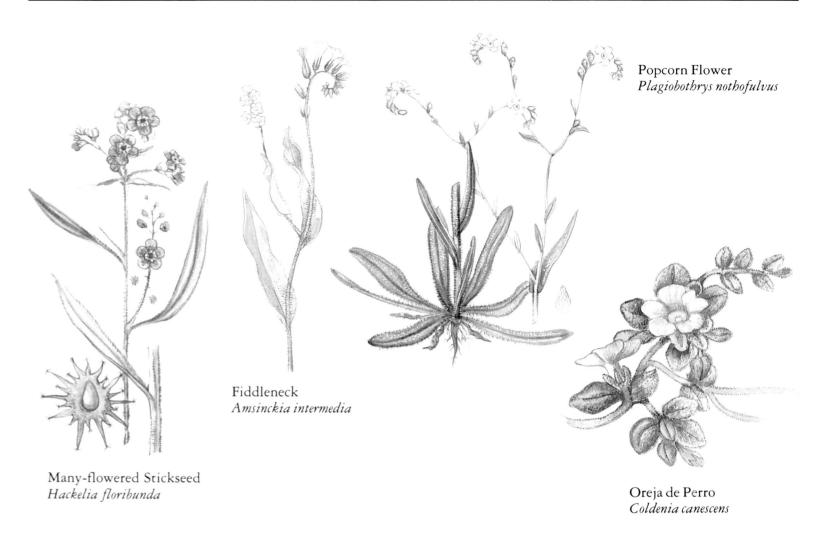

Popcorn Flower
Plagiobothrys nothofulvus

Fiddleneck
Amsinckia intermedia

Many-flowered Stickseed
Hackelia floribunda

Oreja de Perro
Coldenia canescens

leafy flowering stems, with many yellow, funnel-shaped flowers in summer. It grows in sandy plains and among juniper from Arizona and New Mexico, north to Wyoming.

Stickseeds are a group of mostly western species in the genus *Hackelia*; they resemble forget-me-nots and are sometimes called false forget-me-nots. **Many-flowered Stickseed**, *H. floribunda*, is a perennial plant, with an erect stem up to 3ft tall, lance-shaped leaves, and terminal coiled clusters of bright blue, funnel-shaped flowers. The nutlets which follow the flowers have prickly edges, a characteristic of Stickseeds that gives them their common name. The nutlets catch in the fur of animals and so are dispersed; they also catch in clothing. Many-flowered Stickseed grows in coniferous woodland in the Rocky Mountains from Washington to Montana, south to California and New Mexico.

Fiddleneck is a name given to several *Amsinckia* species. They are western plants, bristly-hairy, often acrid annuals, with branched stems, leafy at the base, and terminal, coiled clusters of yellow, funnel-shaped flowers, like fiddlenecks. The yellow color of their flowers is unusual in this family, most of whose members have blue, white or pink blooms. Fiddlenecks grow throughout the west, mostly in grassy places, on lower slopes in the mountain areas and in the plains, but also in deserts and scrub, and one species grows in salt marshes on the Pacific coast. They may be difficult to distinguish from each other. *Amsinckia intermaedia* grows in grassy places from California to Washington, east to Arizona and Idaho.

There are about 100 species of *Plagiobothrys* in western North America and South America. They resemble the *Amsinckia* species but have white flowers and are usually softly hairy, never with acrid hairs. **Popcorn Flower**, *P. nothofulvus*, is an annual plant, with a rosette of lance-shaped leaves and a sparsely leafy, erect stem, branched near the top to end in coiled clusters of flowers. The flowers have dense, red-brown hairs on their calyces, and white funnel-shaped corollas. This plant is common in grassy places, in fields and on hillsides throughout much of California, and north to Washington.

The *Coldenia* species are low-growing or shrubby plants, often densely hairy, and with small, broad leaves. Shrubby Coldenia, *C. greggii*, grows on limestone slopes in New Mexico and Texas; it is a small gray shrub, its most obvious feature being the feathery calyces that surround the reddish-purple flowers. **Oreja de Perro**, *C. canescens*, also grows in Texas; it forms dense, spreading mats, with many branched, prostrate stems covered by tiny, gray leaves, and studded with pink flowers. The older stems become woody and gnarled. *Coldenia plicata* is a similar matted species found in sandy places in California, Arizona, and Nevada. It has distinctive, rounded leaves, grayish-hairy with a pleated appearance, and blue or lavender flowers.

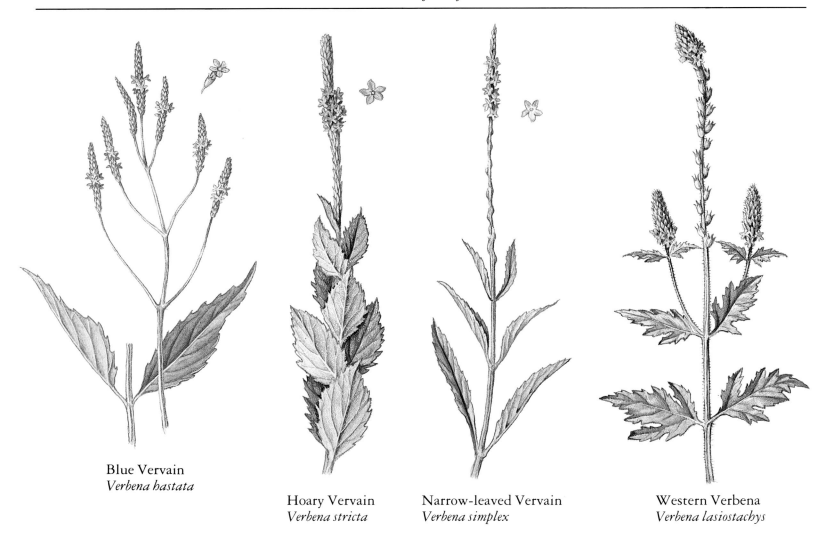

Blue Vervain
Verbena hastata

Hoary Vervain
Verbena stricta

Narrow-leaved Vervain
Verbena simplex

Western Verbena
Verbena lasiostachys

Vervain family

Verbenaceae

This is a mainly tropical and subtropical family, with about 75 genera and 3000 species of herbs, shrubs, and trees. Some members of the family, like verbenas, are ornamental garden plants grown as annuals and perennials in flower borders; clerodendrons, which are shrubs, are grown in tropical borders, or greenhouses in cooler climates. Teak comes from a member of this family—an Asian tree called *Tectona grandis*; the wood is one of the hardest and most durable, and so heavy that it tends to sink in water.

Family features The flowers are usually borne in many-flowered inflorescences; they are bilaterally symmetrical and hermaphrodite. Each flower has 4–5 sepals fused to form a lobed or toothed calyx, and 4–5 petals fused to form a lobed, often two-lipped corolla. There are usually four stamens inserted on the corolla tube. The ovary is superior, most commonly with four cells, and often four-lobed. The fruit is usually formed of four nutlets, but may be a berry. The leaves are opposite or borne in whorls, simple or compound, and they lack stipules. The terminal branches of the stem in these plants are often four-angled.

Blue Vervain, *Verbena hastata*, is one of over 40 vervain species in North America, only a few of which are widely distributed. It grows in wet meadows and prairies, in swamps, ditches, and low fields from Nova Scotia to British Columbia, south to Florida and Arizona. It is a perennial plant, growing up to 5ft tall, with stiffly branched, four-angled stems resembling a candelabrum, and opposite, lance-shaped, roughly textured leaves. Its blue flowers are borne in long spikes terminating the stems; individually they are small and tubular, and they open a few at a time in late summer, from the bottom of the spike upward. Blue Vervain is used in Indian herb medicine as a tranquilizing tea and cold remedy. European Vervain, *V. officinalis*, is much better known in herb medicine as a cold and fever remedy. It is widely naturalized along roadsides in eastern North America and has spikes of lilac or blue flowers.

Hoary Vervain, *Verbena stricta*, is similar to Blue Vervain, but has pale hairy stems, elliptical leaves, and thick, compact spikes of deep blue-purple flowers. It grows in prairies and barrens, and on roadsides in the midwest. **Narrow-leaved Vervain**, *V. simplex*, grows in dry places, in woods, fields, and roadsides in the east and midwest. **Western Verbena**, *V. lasiostachys*, grows in many places on the western side of the mountains in California and Oregon. It has coarsely lobed leaves and usually purple flowers, although they may be pink or white.

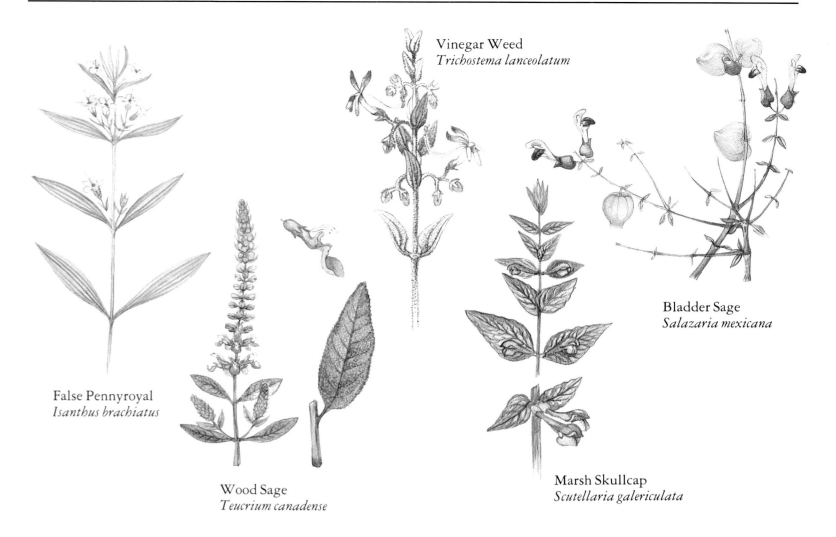

Vinegar Weed
Trichostema lanceolatum

Bladder Sage
Salazaria mexicana

False Pennyroyal
Isanthus brachiatus

Wood Sage
Teucrium canadense

Marsh Skullcap
Scutellaria galericulata

Not all vervains are erect plants with flowers in narrow spikes. Rose Vervain, *V. canadensis*, is a midwestern prairie species, with flat-topped clusters of pink or blue flowers on sprawling stems. Moss Verbena, *V. tenuisecta*, has prostrate stems forming a leafy mat, with narrowly divided leaves, and rounded spikes of showy pink or white flowers. It may be abundant on roadsides in the southeast.

Mint family

Labiatae

Also known as the **Lamiaceae**. A relatively large family, with about 180 genera and 3500 species, mostly herbs and some shrubs, found in tropical and temperate regions of the world, with many in the Mediterranean area. Many contain aromatic oils. Plants like mint, basil, sage, rosemary, and thyme are used as kitchen herbs. Other species have been used for centuries in herb medicine: plants like betony, balm, pepper-mint, and horehound. Lavender, clary, and patchouli are all important in the perfume industry. Bergamot is used to flavor teas, and rosemary, balm, and peppermint are used to flavor liqueurs. Some beautiful garden plants belong to this family, including the annual salvias used in summer bedding schemes, and the perennial lavenders and monardas.

Family features The flowers are often borne in spikes, made up of whorls of flowers in the axils of bracts; they are hermaphrodite and bilaterally symmetrical. The sepals are united into a tubular, often two-lipped calyx with five teeth, and the petals are united to form a tubular, five-lobed, often two-lipped corolla. Each flower has two or four stamens inserted on the corolla-tube. The ovary is superior, with two deeply lobed cells, and the divided style arises from the cleft in the center. The fruit consists of four nutlets, free or in pairs. The stems are usually square and the leaves opposite. Stipules are absent. The plants are often aromatic.

Wood Sage or Germander, *Teucrium canadense*, grows in moist places, especially in woods and thickets, in most of the U.S. and southern Canada. It is a perennial plant, with creeping rhizomes and erect downy, leafy stems, four-angled in the typical labiate way. The leaves are opposite, lance-shaped, toothed, and densely hairy beneath. The pink flowers are borne in a terminal spike; each has four small lobes, and a flattened lip hanging downward.

False Pennyroyal, *Isanthus brachiatus*, is a branched, leafy, annual plant. Its erect stems grow 1–3ft tall, and they have opposite, lance-shaped leaves with small clusters of 1–3 blue flowers in the axils of the upper leaves. The plant grows in dry soils from Ontario to Minnesota, south to Florida and Arizona.

Vinegar Weed, *Trichostema lanceolatum*, in one of several

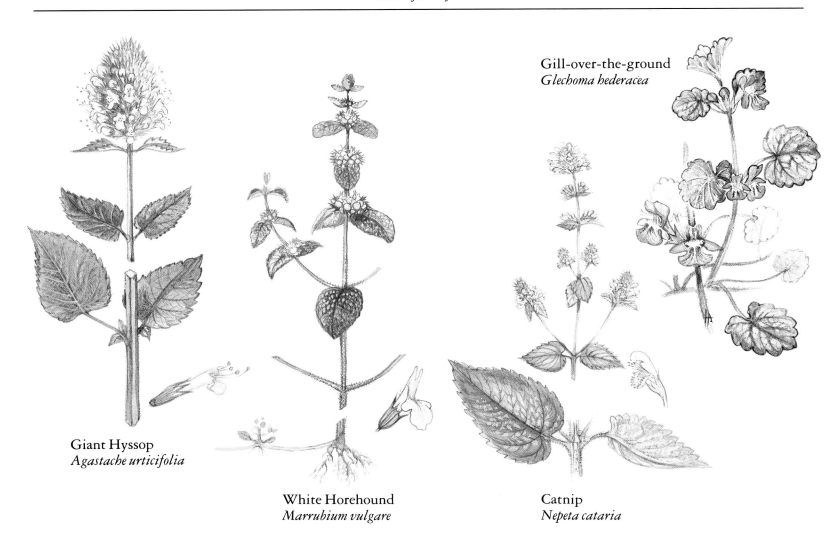

Giant Hyssop
Agastache urticifolia

White Horehound
Marrubium vulgare

Catnip
Nepeta cataria

Gill-over-the-ground
Glechoma hederacea

western species in the genus *Trichostema*, plants known collectively as Bluecurls. The name comes from their blue flowers, which have long, blue, curling stamens. Vinegar Weed grows in dry, open places and fields from Oregon to Baja California. It is a bushy, annual plant, 2ft or more tall, glandular-hairy in texture, with lance-shaped leaves and long spikes of blue flowers. Each flower has a long corolla-tube with four small corolla-lobes spreading outward and upward, and a long lower lip. The whole plant has a strong, unpleasant scent. Other plants in the genus are also scented, some pleasantly aromatic, like the shrubby Woolly Bluecurls, *T. lanatum*, which is native to southern California and a striking plant for the garden. There are also two species found in the east.

Bladder Sage, *Salazaria mexicana* (p. 157), is a dense, low-growing shrub, only 2–3ft tall, with spine-tipped twigs and small, oblong leaves. It flowers in early summer, its two-lipped, deep blue flowers borne in sparse racemes at the tops of the stems. As the fruits develop, the calyces become inflated and papery, so that the plant appears to be covered in orange bladders. It grows in dry washes and canyons, in deserts and Creosote Bush scrub from California to Texas, north to Utah and south into Mexico.

The **Skullcaps** are a group of about 300 species in the genus *Scutellaria*, found throughout most of the world. They are perennial, herbaceous plants, with opposite, entire leaves, and two-lipped, often S-shaped, blue flowers. **Marsh Skullcap**, *S. galericulata* (p. 157), forms patches of erect stems up to 2ft tall, with opposite, lance-shaped leaves, and solitary flowers in the axils of the upper leaves. It grows in swamps, wet meadows, and other wet places all around the North Pole, south to Delaware, Missouri, and California.

Giant Hyssop, *Agastache urticifolia*, is a large, perennial plant, with several branched stems up to 5ft tall, and nettle-like leaves; another name for it is Nettleleaf Horsemint. It grows in the west, in moist soil in the Rocky Mountains from British Columbia to Montana, and southward to California. It has distinctive, dense flower spikes terminating its stems, each spike made up of whorls of pale lavender flowers with protruding stamens. This is one of several *Agastache* species in North America, distinguished by their dense, terminal spikes of flowers.

White Horehound, *Marrubium vulgare*, is found in disturbed places throughout almost the whole of the U.S. and southern Canada, although it is not native to the continent, being introduced from Eurasia. This is a medicinal plant used in cough medicines and teas to treat coughs, bronchitis, and other throat and chest problems. It is an aromatic, perennial plant with erect stems 2–3ft tall, and wrinkled, ovate leaves thickly covered with woolly, white hairs. It bears dense whorls of white, two-lipped flowers in the axils of the upper leaves.

Catnip, *Nepeta cataria* (p. 158), is another medicinal plant, also grown in flower borders in gardens, and native to Europe. It gets its name from the attraction it has for cats, who seem to love its scent and will rub themselves against bruised parts of it. However, rats dislike it, as do many insects, and it can be planted in gardens to protect other plants from their attacks. In herb medicine it is used to promote perspiration, so is useful for treating a fever. It is a perennial plant, noticeably whitened in color by the soft, dense hairs which cover the leaves. It has more or less erect stems, with toothed, ovate leaves, and clusters of red-spotted, white, two-lipped flowers in the axils of the upper leaves and terminating the stems.

Gill-over-the-ground, *Glechoma hederacea* (p. 158), has many names: Ground Ivy in its native Europe, Gill-over-the-ground in the eastern U.S., Creeping Charlie in the west; the names reflect its wandering habit and creeping stems. In Europe it was also called Alehoof since, before the advent of hops, it was used to give the bitter flavor to beer. It is also used in herb medicine as a remedy for diarrhea and colds. It is a low-growing, perennial plant with stems up to 2ft long, and rounded, heart-shaped leaves with wavy margins. Its stems turn upward at the ends to bear blue-purple, two-lipped flowers in twos or fours in the axils of the leaves. In North America it grows in moist, shady places, usually in woods and disturbed habitats.

Selfheal, *Prunella vulgaris*, sounds from its name as if it ought to be a medicinal plant; at one time it was, and highly recommended for the treatment of wounds, but is little used today. It is native to both Europe and North America, growing throughout much of this continent in fields, on roadsides, and as a weed in gardens. It is a small, perennial plant, with erect stems up to 20in tall, and ovate or lance-shaped, irregularly toothed leaves. Its blue-violet, two-lipped flowers are borne in dense clusters amid hairy bracts at the tops of the stems.

Hemp-nettle, *Galeopsis tetrahit*, is another European labiate introduced in North America, so well naturalized that it appears to be native in some areas. It grows in moist places across the continent, much more commonly in the north and absent from the southwest. This is a hairy, annual plant, with a branched stem, and coarse, toothed leaves like those of nettles, but without the stinging hairs. The flowers grow in whorls in the axils of the upper leaves; they are two-lipped, pink or purple with yellow spots in the center of the lower lip.

Henbit, *Lamium amplexicaule*, is an annual plant, with branched, rather sprawling stems, and scalloped, rounded leaves, the lower ones with long stalks, the upper ones clasping the stems. Whorls of two-lipped, purple flowers grow in the axils of the upper leaves; the flowers are hairy on the outside. This plant grows as a weed in waste places, fields, and on

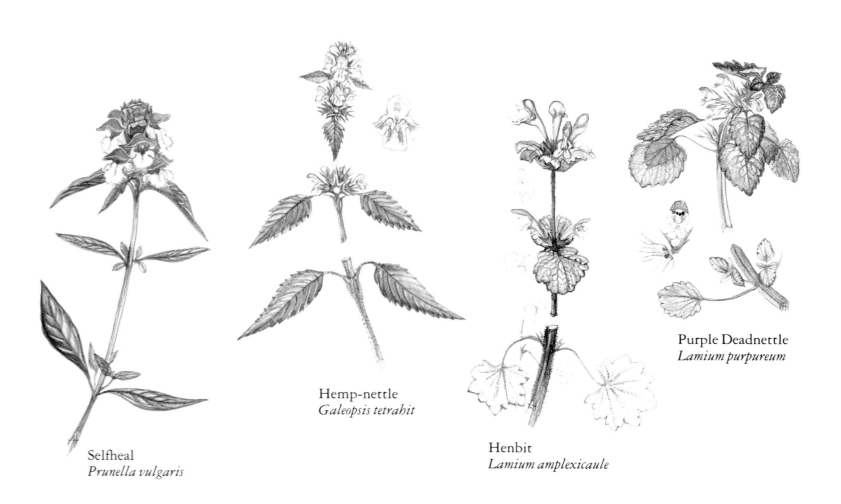

Selfheal
Prunella vulgaris

Hemp-nettle
Galeopsis tetrahit

Henbit
Lamium amplexicaule

Purple Deadnettle
Lamium purpureum

roadsides across much of North America, but is not a native plant, being naturalized from Europe. It is related to the deadnettles: White Deadnettle, *L. album*, with white flowers, and **Purple Deadnettle**, *L. purpureum* (p. 159), with purple flowers, are both European plants also found growing occasionally as weeds.

Motherwort, *Leonurus cardiaca*, is another old medicinal plant, used to treat nervous and heart disorders. It comes from Asia, but now grows as a weed in disturbed and waste places over much of the U.S. and southern Canada. It is a perennial plant, with branched stems up to 4ft tall, and many long-stalked, palmately lobed leaves. The lower leaves have 5–7 irregularly toothed lobes and the upper ones three pointed lobes. The flowers grow in whorls in the axils of the upper leaves; they are pink and two-lipped, with a white-bearded upper lip, and spine-tipped lobes on the calyces.

Obedient Plant, *Physostegia virginiana*, has earned its common name from the story that its flowers will stay in the new position for a short time if they are moved; if so, it is for a very short time, or the plants on which I have tested the theory have not heard the story! The plant is also called False Dragonhead, its flowers similar to those of snapdragons, and resembling the head of a dragon with a large mouth. This is an eastern plant, growing in relatively moist places, in woods and thickets, and in prairies, from Maine to Alberta, south to the

Carolinas and Texas. It is a perennial plant, with a clump of erect, leafy stems with opposite, narrowly elliptical, serrated leaves, and terminal spikes of flowers in the latter half of summer. The flowers are tubular, two-lipped, and vary in color from pale mauve, almost white, to pink or rose purple. This is an attractive plant, which is grown in several color varieties in gardens.

Woundwort, *Stachys palustris*, is a plant that grows all around the northern hemisphere, mainly in the north, across Canada and south into the U.S. as far as New York, Missouri, and Arizona. It is found in moist and wet places, in marshes and swamps. This is a hairy, perennial plant, which has erect stems up to 3ft tall, and opposite, lance-shaped leaves with serrated edges. Its flowers grow in whorls in the axils of the upper leaves; they are two-lipped, with a hooded upper lip, purple in color, with white markings on the spreading lower lip. Woundwort has antiseptic properties and its leaves have traditionally been used to bind wounds (hence Woundwort), stopping the bleeding, and aiding healing.

There are about 700 species of **Sage** in the warmer temperate and tropical regions of the world, belonging to the genus *Salvia*. Some of them are grown as ornamentals in shrub and flower gardens, a few are used in herb medicine and as kitchen herbs. They are a variable group of plants, many being small leafy shrubs, others being small herbs; but they all have

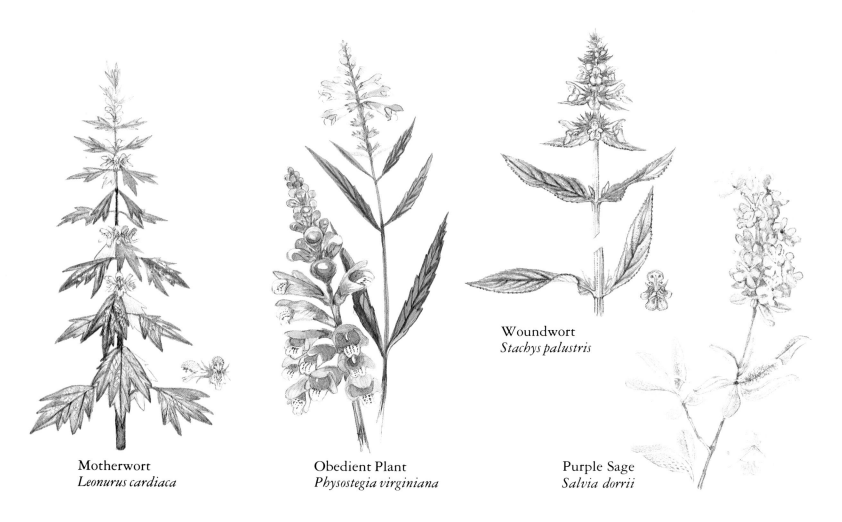

Motherwort
Leonurus cardiaca

Obedient Plant
Physostegia virginiana

Woundwort
Stachys palustris

Purple Sage
Salvia dorrii

flowers which grow in whorls in the axils of the upper leaves forming a terminal spike, and they are usually aromatic. Over 50 of them are found in North America, the majority in the south and west.

Purple Sage or Desert Sage, *Salvia dorrii* (p. 160), is a western species. It is a broad, low-growing, shrubby plant which has spiny branches, silvery leaves, and bright blue, two-lipped flowers growing in the axils of conspicuous purplish bracts. The plant often grows with Sagebrush (which is not a sage, but *Artemisia tridentata*, a member of the daisy family), in western deserts and other dry places.

Chia, *Salvia columbariae*, is one of the herbaceous sages, an annual plant with coarsely toothed leaves mostly forming a basal rosette. Its erect stems bear a few widely spaced whorls of dense blue flowers in the axils of bracts. It grows in dry places, in chaparral, and scrub in the southwest. Not all sages have blue flowers; Lemmon's Sage, *S. lemmonii* has red flowers. Thistle Sage, *S. carduacea*, has lavender flowers; it gets its name from its prickly, thistle-like leaves.

A smaller number of sages grow in the east. **Blue Sage**, *Salvia azurea*, is a perennial plant with erect stems, linear leaves at the base of the stems, and a loose spike of blue flowers terminating the stem. It grows in dry woods from North Carolina to Minnesota, south to Florida and Texas. Nettle-leaved Sage, *S. urticifolia*, from the southeast has violet flowers; and Lyre-leaved Sage, *S. lyrata*, has scarlet flowers.

Bee-balm or Oswego Tea, *Monarda didyma*, is a North American native plant, also grown as a spectacular garden flower. It is the source of Oil of Bergamot, used to flavor tea. It grows wild in moist woods and thickets in the east from Maine to Michigan, south to New Jersey and Ohio, and in the mountains to Georgia, but is also grown in flower borders there and in other parts of the U.S. This is a perennial plant, forming a clump of erect stems up to 5ft tall, four-angled like those of all labiates, with opposite, coarsely toothed, lance-shaped leaves. At the top of each stem is the bright red, head-like cluster of flowers above a circle of reddish bracts. Each flower has a long tube and two lips, the upper lip narrow, the lower lip divided into three narrow lobes. Bees and hummingbirds are attracted to the blossoms, seeking the nectar contained within. Wild Bergamot, *M. fistulosa*, is similar but has pale lavender flowers; it grows in woods and prairies across much of southern Canada and the U.S.

Coyote Mint, *Monardella odoratissima*, is a small, perennial plant, woody at the base with branched stems up to 15in tall, lance-shaped leaves, and a pleasant aromatic scent. The flowers are borne in heads above broad bracts at the tops of the stems; both bracts and two-lipped flowers are purplish and the bracts covered with dense hairs. The plant grows on dry slopes, in sagebrush scrub and coniferous forests, in the mountains from

Chia
Salvia columbariae

Blue Sage
Salvia azurea

Bee-balm
Monarda didyma

Coyote Mint
Monardella odoratissima

Washington to Idaho, south to California and New Mexico. There are about 20 *Monardella* species in western North America, annual or perennial species, most with heads of pale purplish or white flowers; Red Monardella, *M. macrantha*, is a much more spectacular plant, with scarlet or yellow, elongated, funnel-shaped flowers.

Wild Basil, *Satureja vulgaris*, is an erect, perennial plant, with hairy stems up to 2ft tall, and many opposite leaves. The two-lipped flowers vary from rose-purple to white and are borne in dense heads terminating the stems, or in head-like clusters on long stalks in the axils of the uppermost leaves. The heads of flowers appear to be woolly, the texture coming from the hairy bracts mixed with the flowers. This plant grows in upland woods from Newfoundland to Manitoba, south to North Carolina and Kansas. It also grows in Europe. It is not the same plant as the culinary herb known as Basil; that is another labiate species, *Ocimum basilicum*, known properly as Sweet Basil.

Several of the best known culinary herbs are labiates, including Sweet Marjoram, *Origanum majorana*, and **Wild Marjoram** or Oregano, *Origanum vulgare*. Both are European plants, but the former is not found in North America, while the latter grows wild in disturbed sites on calcareous soils in the eastern U.S. and Canada. It forms patches of erect, purplish stems about 2ft tall, with opposite, ovate leaves, and the characteristic marjoram scent. In late summer dense, rounded clusters of reddish-purple to pale pink, two-lipped flowers develop on long stalks in the leaf axils and at the tops of the stems.

Wild Thyme, *Thymus praecox*, is a small, matted, perennial plant, with branched, prostrate stems covered with small, elliptical leaves. In the summer the plants flower, producing rows of side stems along the main shoots, each with a terminal head of small purple, two-lipped flowers. This is a European plant grown in rock gardens. It has escaped from cultivation in North America to grow wild in upland woods from Nova Scotia to Ontario, south to North Carolina and West Virginia. The kitchen herb is the related Garden Thyme, *T. vulgaris*, a small, bushy shrublet from southern Europe, not found wild in North America.

There are about 10 **Mints**, *Mentha* species, in North America, all more or less scented, a few native, others native to Europe and grown on this continent, and now naturalized. **Spearmint**, *Mentha spicata*, and Peppermint, *M.* x *piperita*, are both well known for the flavors extracted from them. They are cultivated and now grow wild in much of North America, probably more commonly in the east than the west. They are important also for their use in medicine, peppermint containing menthol and being one of the best remedies for indigestion and dyspepsia. Spearmint has similar uses, but is less powerful

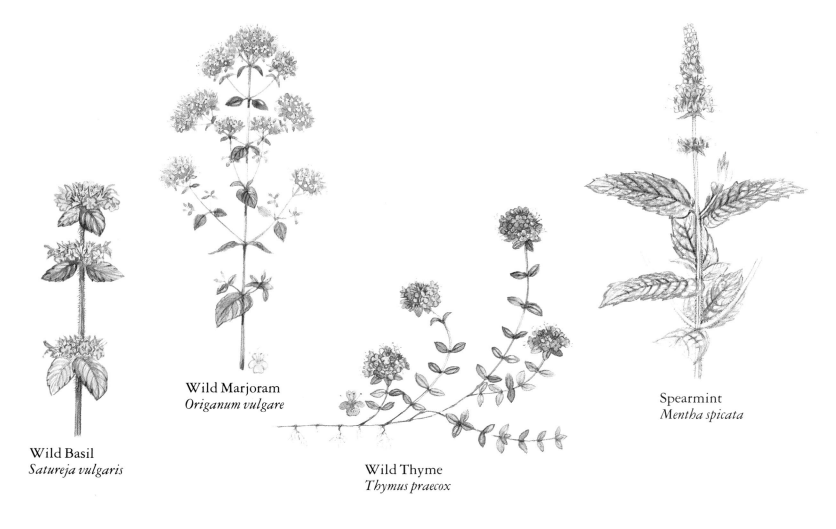

Wild Marjoram
Origanum vulgare

Wild Basil
Satureja vulgaris

Wild Thyme
Thymus praecox

Spearmint
Mentha spicata

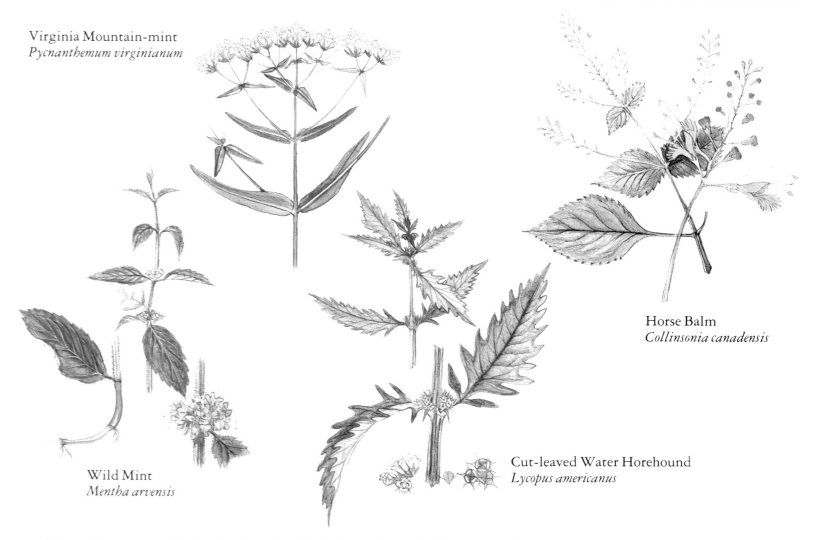

Virginia Mountain-mint
Pycnanthemum virginianum

Horse Balm
Collinsonia canadensis

Wild Mint
Mentha arvensis

Cut-leaved Water Horehound
Lycopus americanus

and is used more as a kitchen herb or in mint jelly. It is a perennial with branched, 3ft tall stems, and serrated, lance-shaped leaves. Each stem bears a terminal flower spike formed of separated whorls of lilac flowers.

Wild Mint, *Mentha arvensis*, has a strong, rather sickly scent. It grows in much the same conditions as peppermint, and has to be removed from fields of cultivated peppermint if it invades them, since its presence spoils the flavor. This is a native plant which grows all around the North Pole, south in North America to Virginia in the east and California in the west, in moist places, especially along streams. It is a perennial plant, with long, creeping roots and erect stems up to 2ft tall, and toothed, ovate or elliptical leaves. Its flowers grow in dense, widely spaced whorls in the axils of the upper leaves; they are very small, tubular in shape, with four lobes, white to pale lavender or pink in color.

Mountain-mints, *Pycnanthemum* species, also have a strong scent of mint, but do not have the same history of use in medicine or cooking as the *Mentha* species. They were, however, used by the Indians as a tonic and as a cooking herb. Most of the 17 species are found in the east and midwest. **Virginia Mountain-mint**, *P. virginianum*, is typical, a stout perennial with branched, leafy stems growing about 3ft tall. In the latter half of summer the plants flower, bearing dense, flat-topped clusters of small, two-lipped flowers in the upper leaf axils. The flowers are white, often spotted with purple on the lower lip, and they open a few at a time in each cluster. This plant grows in prairies and upland woods from Maine to North Dakota, south to Georgia and Oklahoma.

Cut-leaved Water Horehound, *Lycopus americanus*, is one of about six widespread *Lycopus* species in North America related to the mints, but without scent, and known as water horehounds or bugleweeds. They are perennial, spreading plants, with creeping, rooting stems from which grow erect, leafy stems, and are found in wet places. Cut-leaved Water Horehound is one of the most common, found across the U.S. and southern Canada in moist places, but absent from the southwestern deserts. It has elongated rhizomes and erect, four-angled stems up to 2ft tall, with opposite, coarsely toothed or almost lobed leaves. Its white, numerous flowers grow in dense whorls in the axils of the upper leaves; each one is tubular with four lobes.

Horse Balm or Stone Root, *Collinsonia canadensis*, has a thick, woody rhizome, used in herb medicine as a diuretic. It has stout, erect stems 2–4ft tall, and opposite, ovate, serrated leaves, the lower ones on long stalks. The flowers are borne in loosely branched inflorescences at the tops of the stems; they are yellow, two-lipped, and lemon-scented, with long stamens. This plant may be found in rich woods from Quebec to Michigan, and south to Florida and Arkansas.

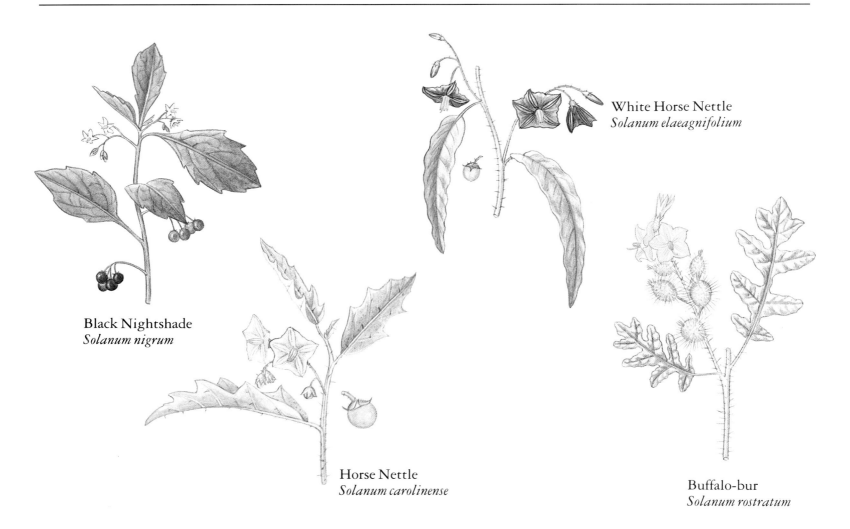

Black Nightshade
Solanum nigrum

Horse Nettle
Solanum carolinense

White Horse Nettle
Solanum elaeagnifolium

Buffalo-bur
Solanum rostratum

Nightshade family

Solanaceae

A large and important family, with about 90 genera and 2000 species, mostly herbs and twining plants, the majority found in the tropics and warm temperate regions, especially in Central and South America. There are several important food plants in this family, including potatoes, tomatoes, chilis, and peppers. Some members of the family, such as Belladonna and Henbane, are very poisonous; they contain powerful alkaloids used in medicine. Atropine, which is extracted from Belladonna, is invaluable in the treatment of eye diseases. Tobacco also belongs to this family. Ornamental plants include petunias and Chinese lanterns.

Family features The flowers are solitary or borne in cymes. They are usually hermaphrodite and regular. The calyx has 3–6 lobes and is persistent; the corolla usually has five lobes. The stamens are inserted on the corolla and alternate with the corolla-lobes. The ovary is superior with two cells. The fruit is a berry or capsule. The leaves are alternate and simple. Stipules are absent.

By far the largest group in the family is the **Nightshades**, with about 1500 mainly tropical species in the genus *Solanum*. Over 40 grow in North America, most commonly in the

south, many of them native but others naturalized from other parts of the world. The flowers of nightshades have characteristic stamens, with short filaments and large anthers; these anthers protrude from the flat or reflexed petal-lobes and their tips are pressed, or even joined, together so that they form a cone around the style. The flowers are followed by berries, black or brightly colored, and often poisonous, especially dangerous to children.

Black Nightshade, *Solanum nigrum*, is a cosmopolitan weed, found in waste places, yards, and fields in much of North America, as well as in other parts of the world. It is a leafy, annual plant, with branched, green stems, and many ovoid or broadly triangular, irregularly toothed leaves. Its flowers grow in drooping clusters opposite the leaves; they have five white, spreading petal-lobes and yellow anthers. The flowers are followed by clusters of dull black berries.

Horse Nettle, *Solanum carolinense*, is a deep-rooted, perennial plant, another weed but more difficult to eradicate than Black Nightshade since its roots go deep and its stems are spiny, so that it is difficult to handle. It is a coarse plant, with branching stems up to 3ft tall, and coarsely lobed, prickly leaves. In summer racemes of star-like, white or pale violet flowers develop opposite the leaves; they have cones of yellow anthers. The berries are yellow, like tomatoes. This plant grows in sandy soil, in fields, and waste places, originally in

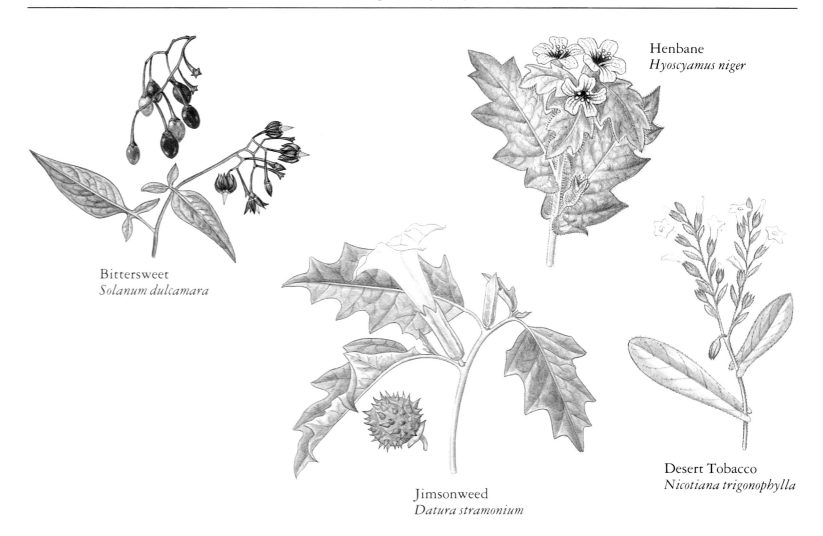

Bittersweet
Solanum dulcamara

Henbane
Hyoscyamus niger

Jimsonweed
Datura stramonium

Desert Tobacco
Nicotiana trigonophylla

the southeast, but now north to Ontario and westward to Idaho, Texas, and Utah.

White Horse Nettle, *Solanum elaeagnifolium* (p. 164), is another weed but an attractive one, a short-lived, perennial plant with weak prickles on the stems. It is sometimes called the Silverleaf Nightshade, for it has silvery-hairy leaves, forming a perfect foil for its violet flowers. The leaves have wavy edges and their hairs are star-shaped. The plant grows in dry places, and has spread east and west from its original range in the prairies to grow on roadsides and cultivated land.

Buffalo-bur, *Solanum rostratum* (p. 164), is a prickly annual, with dense yellow spines on its stems, leaf stalks, and calyces. It has branching stems up to 3ft tall, pinnately lobed leaves with star-like hairs and spines on the veins, and racemes of flat, yellow flowers in summer. The flowers are followed by berries enclosed in the extremely spiny, persistent calyces. This plant is native to dry prairies and plains in the central U.S., but has spread eastward and westward on roadsides and field edges.

Bittersweet, *Solanum dulcamara*, is not a native plant, but an invader from Europe, now naturalized in thickets and woodland throughout much of the U.S. and southern Canada, except in the arid regions of the southwest. It is a climbing plant, woody at the base, with branched stems scrambling over other plants or fences. It has simple or lobed leaves, and

racemes of blue-purple flowers, with reflexed petal-lobes and yellow anthers. These are followed by glossy red berries.

Jimsonweed, *Datura stramonium*, is much more poisonous than the nightshades; a few seeds can be lethal to children. The poison is hyoscyamine, which causes visual disturbance, hallucinations, coma, and death. The leaves of the plant have been used in medicine, mainly for the treatment of asthma. Jimsonweed is a coarse annual, with an unpleasant scent. It has a branched, often purplish stem up to 5ft tall, and large, coarsely toothed leaves. Its flowers have an elongated winged calyx and a funnel-shaped, white corolla, about twice the length of the calyx. The fruits are prickly, egg-shaped capsules containing rough, black seeds. Jimsonweed grows in dry places, waste ground, and pastures throughout the U.S. and southern Canada.

Henbane, *Hyoscyamus niger*, is another poisonous species containing the same poisons and with the same effects as Jimsonweed. This plant is native to Europe, but has become naturalized on roadsides and in waste places in the northern areas of the U.S. and southern Canada. It is another coarse annual with an unpleasant scent, and is stickily hairy. Its erect, branched stems grow to about 3ft tall and are very leafy, with leaves so coarsely toothed they are almost lobed. It bears conspicuous flowers in late summer—funnel-shaped and greenish-yellow, with purple veins.

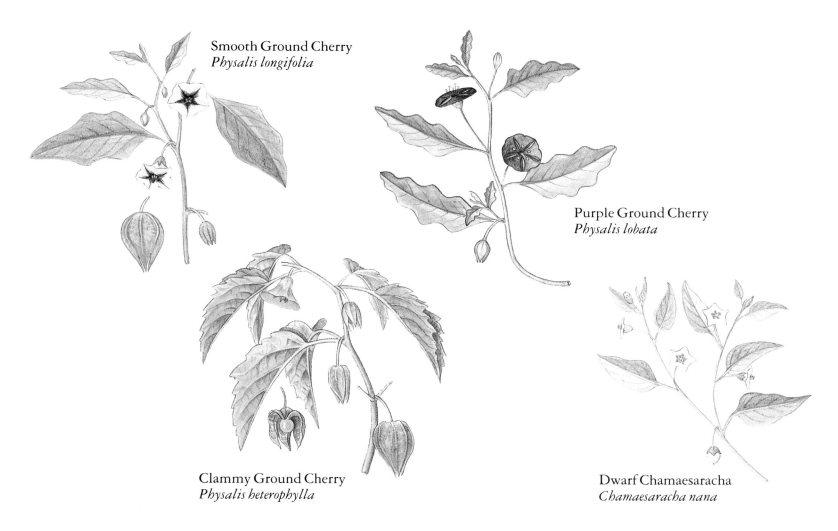

Smooth Ground Cherry
Physalis longifolia

Purple Ground Cherry
Physalis lobata

Clammy Ground Cherry
Physalis heterophylla

Dwarf Chamaesaracha
Chamaesaracha nana

There are about 60 species of **Tobacco** belonging to the genus *Nicotiana*, most native to North and South America, and all poisonous plants with heavy scents. Their poison is nicotine or a related alkaloid, and is extremely toxic whether absorbed through the skin or ingested, causing nausea, sweating, irregular heartbeat, and possibly death. Cultivated Tobacco, *N. tabacum*, comes from South America. **Desert Tobacco**, *N. trigonophylla* (p. 165), is a western species found among rocks, in washes, and in Creosote Bush scrub from the Mojave and Colorado deserts to Texas and Nevada. It is usually perennial, with a sparsely branched stem 2–3ft tall, and lance-shaped leaves with bases clasping the stem; the plant is covered with sticky hairs. In spring and early summer loose clusters of white, trumpet-shaped flowers appear at the tops of the stems. Dried plants are smoked by the Indians.

Ground Cherries, *Physalis* species, are coarse, annual or perennial plants with characteristic fruits—brightly colored berries enclosed in papery sacs formed from the inflated, persistent calyces. The garden plants known as Chinese Lanterns belong to this genus. The berries of many of them are edible when ripe, either raw or made into preserves or pies. However, the berries are poisonous when green.

The berries of **Clammy Ground Cherry**, *Physalis heterophylla*, are some of the best to eat. This is a perennial species, with spreading stems up to 3ft tall, and heart-shaped, toothed leaves, all covered with sticky hairs. It has solitary, bell-shaped, greenish-yellow flowers with purple centers; they grow in the axils of the leaves in the latter half of summer. The yellow, tomato-like berries are enclosed in papery, green sacs. The plant grows in dry, sandy soil, in upland woods and prairies from Nova Scotia to Minnesota and Utah, south to Florida and Texas. **Smooth Ground Cherry**, *P. longifolia*, is a similar but smooth species. It grows in dry woods and prairies, in waste land, and on roadsides from Ontario to Washington, south to Virginia, Louisiana, and Arizona.

Purple Ground Cherry, *Physalis lobata*, has flat, purplish flowers, round or pentagonal in outline, followed by berries enclosed in sharply five-angled, inflated calyces. This is a perennial plant, with branched stems and sinuately lobed leaves; the flowers are solitary, borne on long stalks in the leaf axils. Plants grow on high plains and bluffs from Kansas to Texas and Arizona.

Dwarf Chamaesaracha, *Chamaesaracha nana*, is a western plant found in sandy places and coniferous woods in the Sierra Nevada, from California to Oregon and Nevada. It is a low-growing, perennial plant, with an erect, branched stem only 10in tall, and ovate leaves on long, narrowly winged stalks. Clusters of flat, white flowers grow on long stalks in the leaf axils; they have a single green spot at the base of each petal. The flowers are followed by dull white or yellowish berries.

A Connecticut swamp, with Blue Vervain (*Verbena hastata*), Purple Loosestrife (*Lythrum salicaria*), and Dark Mullein (*Verbascum nigrum*) in the foreground.

Snapdragon family

Scrophulariaceae

Also called the **Figwort family**. A large family of herbs and shrubs, with over 200 genera and nearly 3000 species, found almost throughout the world. Many have large, showy or brightly colored flowers; some, like speedwells, snapdragons, penstemons, and foxgloves, are grown in gardens. Some members of the family are partially parasitic, including rattleboxes, louseworts, and eyebrights; their roots connect with those of grasses and other plants which may be stunted in their growth as a consequence.

Family features The flowers are hermaphrodite and usually bilaterally symmetrical. Each has a five-lobed calyx and a corolla formed of 4–5 fused petals; the corolla is often two-lipped. The flowers normally have two or four stamens inserted in pairs on the corolla. If a fifth stamen is present, it is usually sterile and different from the others. The ovary is superior and two-celled. The fruits are capsules or berries. The leaves are simple or pinnate, and stipules are absent.

The **Mulleins**, *Verbascum* species, are stately plants with tall stems and spikes of many flowers. They are biennials, forming a basal rosette of leaves in the first year and the tall, flowering stem in the second. Several species are grown in gardens.

Common Mullein, *V. thapsus*, is native to Europe but is widely naturalized in North America, growing in disturbed places, on roadsides, and in fields. The stout, 6-ft tall flowering spikes bear many yellow flowers that open over a long period of time, apparently at random. Its gray-woolly leaves have a variety of uses in folk lore: they were used as shoe liners to keep feet warm in winter; they were soaked in saltpetre and used as wicks; women used them as a substitute for rouge, since they redden the cheeks if rubbed against the skin; they were dried and used as a constituent of tobacco; they are used in herb medicine as a remedy for chest diseases; and they were used as poultices. For the plant the leaves have different uses: they are arranged in such a way as to direct water running down the stem into the roots at the base of the plant, and the wool cuts down water loss—both useful functions for a plant that grows in dry places in its native habitats.

Moth Mullein, *Verbascum blattaria*, is a much more slender plant, with stems only 3–4ft tall, and shiny, hairless leaves that do not run down the stem like those of Common Mullein. It has a looser, more graceful raceme of yellow flowers. This is another European alien, one found in disturbed places in many areas of the U.S.

The **Monkey-flowers**, *Mimulus* species, have brightly colored flowers and some are grown in gardens. There are over 80 species in North America, most of them found in the

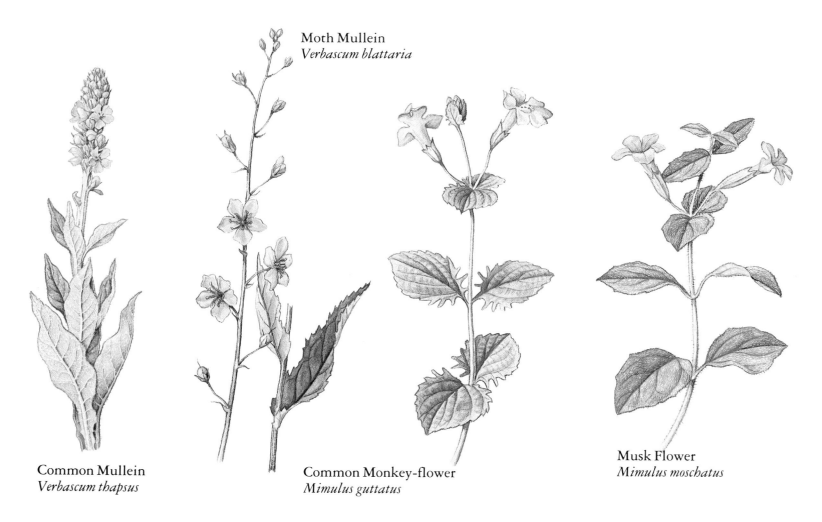

Moth Mullein
Verbascum blattaria

Common Mullein
Verbascum thapsus

Common Monkey-flower
Mimulus guttatus

Musk Flower
Mimulus moschatus

Pacific and southwestern states, many growing in wet places, stream banks and wet gravel, vernal pools, damp forests, and meadows, others in dry, sandy and rocky places, disturbed ground, and chaparral. They are annual or perennial plants, with opposite leaves and flowers in the leaf axils. Each flower has a toothed calyx and a broad, two-lipped corolla, its throat more or less closed by a palate formed of two ridges. These ridges may be covered in hairs (bearded) or hairless.

Common Monkey-flower, *Mimulus guttatus* (p. 168), is typical of many in having yellow flowers and growing in wet places. It is found in a variety of wet habitats throughout the Rocky Mountains from Alaska to California. This is a perennial, hairless plant, with leafy, creeping stems which root at the nodes and form overlapping mats. In summer erect stems develop, with opposite, rounded leaves and yellow, orange-spotted flowers in the upper leaf axils. **Musk Flower**, *M. moschatus* (p. 168), is a similar species, with ovate to oblong leaves, and funnel-shaped, unspotted yellow flowers. It often feels slimy to the touch and has a scent of musk. It grows in wet places, especially beside streams, in coniferous forests in the mountains, and on the coast from California to British Columbia, also from Newfoundland to Michigan, and south along the Atlantic coast.

Lewis' Monkey-flower, *Mimulus lewisii*, is a showy species, the glow of the deep pink or red flowers emphasized by two hairy, yellow blotches on the palate of each bloom. Plants form patches of erect, leafy stems 2–3ft tall, with stalkless, toothed leaves, and the flowers are borne on long stalks in the axils of the upper leaves. They grow along the banks of mountain streams in the Rockies from California to Alaska, east to Colorado and Montana.

Square-stemmed Monkey-flower, *Mimulus ringens*, is often known simply as Monkey-flower in the east, where it does not have to compete for a name with many other species. It grows in wet places, along streams, and in marshes from Nova Scotia to Saskatchewan, south to Georgia and Texas. It has four-angled stems, opposite, lance-shaped leaves, and two-lipped, blue flowers with yellow palates. Its flowers have long stalks and its leaves are stalkless. In contrast, *M. alatus*, which grows in similar places, has short stalks on both leaves and flowers.

Turtlehead, *Chelone glabra*, is a stiff-looking plant, with a dense, terminal spike of two-lipped, white flowers resembling turtles' heads. It is a perennial, with erect stems and narrow toothed leaves in opposite pairs. It grows in wet places, in woods, and beside streams from Newfoundland to Minnesota, and south to Georgia and Alabama. The less common *C. obliqua*, is sometimes grown in gardens; it is a similar plant, with purple flowers, and grows in wet places on the coastal plain in the east.

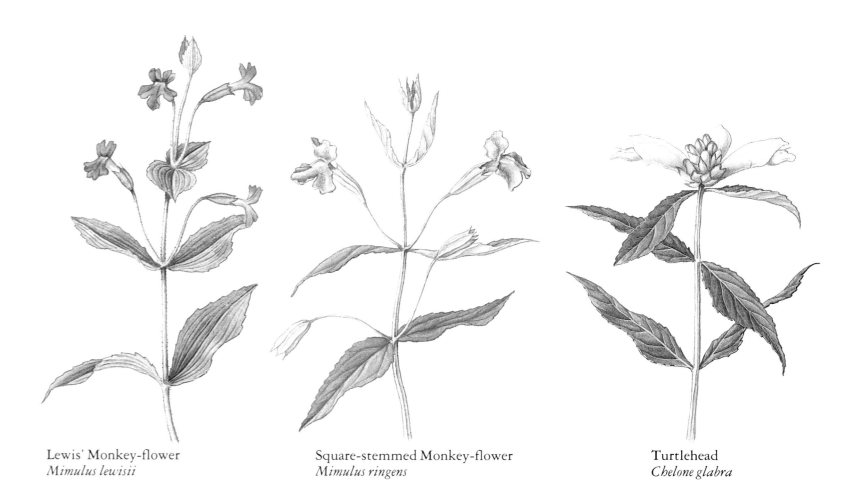

Lewis' Monkey-flower
Mimulus lewisii

Square-stemmed Monkey-flower
Mimulus ringens

Turtlehead
Chelone glabra

The **Beardtongues**, *Penstemon* species, are a large, western North American group, with over 150 species found in a variety of habitats, from mountain meadows to sagebrush and chaparral, pine forests to dry, rocky places, hillsides and plains, washes and canyons. They are perennial plants or shrubs, with opposite leaves and showy flowers, several grown in gardens. The flowers grow in large inflorescences terminating the stems; they are tubular in shape, often with an inflated throat and with a two-lipped opening. The upper lip is often much weaker, with only two lobes; the lower lip is large and has three lobes. The sterile stamen is well developed in these plants and is often bearded (forming the beardtongue).

Some of the most colorful penstemons are those with bright red flowers. There are several such species in the west and southwest, including the **Southwestern Penstemon**, *Penstemon barbatus*, a plant which is attractive enough to be grown in gardens. It forms a clump of erect stems up to 3ft tall, with grass-like, linear leaves, and many drooping flowers in a long, terminal inflorescence. It grows in open, rocky areas in the forests of the southwestern mountains, from Colorado to Texas, and into Mexico.

Whipple's Penstemon, *Penstemon whippleanus*, has darker, wine-red to purple-black flowers borne in clusters in the axils of the upper leaves. This plant has erect stems about 2ft tall, with opposite, ovate leaves, and flowers in late summer. It grows in moist meadows and woods on the eastward side of the Rocky Mountains, from southern Montana south to Arizona and New Mexico.

Pale Beardtongue, *Penstemon pallidus*, is one of several white-flowered species, this one found in light, often sandy soils in woods and prairies from Maine to Minnesota, and south to Virginia and Arkansas. It forms a clump of hairy stems up to 3ft tall, with opposite, leathery leaves, and small racemes of white, mauve-tinged flowers in the upper leaf axils.

Azure Penstemon, *Penstemon azureus*, forms a clump of stems up to 2ft tall, woody at the base, with waxy, blue-green, opposite leaves clasping the stems. At the tops of the stems are loose, terminal racemes of deep blue-purple flowers. The plant grows on dry slopes in chaparral and pine woods from California to southern Oregon. The Foothill Penstemon, *P. heterophyllus*, is very similar and grows in similar places, but has yellow buds, while *P. azureus* has blue ones.

Many penstemons, like those already described, have large flowers, often over an inch long. But some have smaller flowers only half this size. **Pincushion Penstemon**, *Penstemon procerus*, is one such. This plant forms a rosette of firm, ovate leaves, with slender stems up to 1ft tall bearing whorls of deep blue-purple, white-throated flowers in late summer. It grows on rocky slopes and meadows near and above the timberline in the Sierra Nevada from California to Oregon and Nevada.

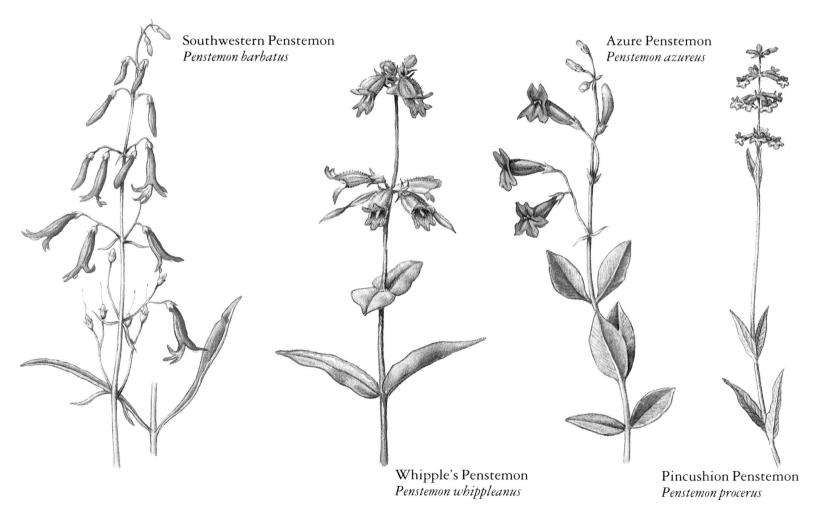

Southwestern Penstemon
Penstemon barbatus

Azure Penstemon
Penstemon azureus

Whipple's Penstemon
Penstemon whippleanus

Pincushion Penstemon
Penstemon procerus

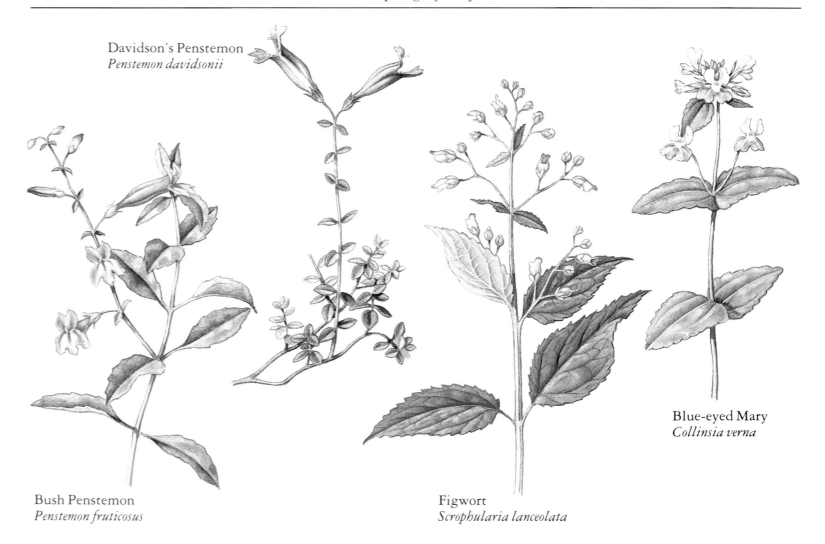

Davidson's Penstemon
Penstemon davidsonii

Bush Penstemon
Penstemon fruticosus

Figwort
Scrophularia lanceolata

Blue-eyed Mary
Collinsia verna

Some penstemons are low, bushy or mat-forming plants, with a woody base and many branching leafy stems. Plants of this type are often grown in rock gardens. **Bush Penstemon**, *Penstemon fruticosus*, is a low-growing, shrubby plant, only 15in tall at most, and forming dense patches of woody stems, with opposite, lance-shaped leaves and showy lavender flowers. It is found on damp, rocky slopes from British Columbia to Montana, and south to Oregon and Wyoming. **Davidson's Penstemon**, *P. davidsonii*, forms creeping mats, with woody stems and thick, rounded or elliptical leaves. The purple-violet flowers grow in small clusters on erect stems only 4in tall. The plant grows in rocky places above the timberline in the high Sierra Nevada, in forests and in sage brush, from California to Washington and Nevada.

Figwort, *Scrophularia lanceolata*, is a hairless plant with an erect, leafy stem up to 6ft tall, opposite, long-stalked leaves, and many small flowers. The flowers are two-lipped, shiny brown outside and green inside, each with five stamens. The fifth stamen is sterile, yellow-green in color, and lies just beneath the top lip. Figwort grows in open woods, on woodland edges, and on roadsides from Quebec and Minnesota south to Georgia and Louisiana. It flowers from May to July. A similar species, Maryland Figwort, *S. marilandica*, grows in open woods from Quebec to Louisiana; it has greenish-brown flowers and a brownish-purple sterile stamen.

Blue-eyed Mary, *Collinsia verna*, is a winter annual plant which flowers in spring. It has weak stems, often lying on the ground near the base, then turning upward to grow 6-18in tall. The leaves are opposite, triangular-ovate in shape, the lower ones with stalks but the upper ones sessile. From nodding buds grow whorls of flowers on long, slender stalks in the axils of the uppermost leaves. The flowers are two-lipped with long lobes. Each has two white upper petal-lobes, three blue lower ones; the middle lobe of the three lower petal-lobes is folded longitudinally into a pouch enclosing the stamens. Blue-eyed Mary grows in rich, moist woods from New York to Wisconsin, and south to West Virginia and Arkansas.

Many of the **Speedwells**, *Veronica* species, found in North America are weeds, invaders from Europe that have established themselves on roadsides, in waste places, in lawns, meadows, and woods throughout much of the continent. They are mostly small, spreading, often prostrate annual or perennial plants, with opposite leaves and blue or white flowers. Speedwell flowers are distinctive, with a very short tube, and four lobes looking like four petals in the form of a broad, upright cross. The upper lobe is larger than any of the others. The flowers have only two long stamens and these project beyond the petals toward the sides of the flower.

Thyme-leaved Speedwell, *Veronica serpyllifolia* (p. 172), is typical of many of these little plants. It is perennial, with

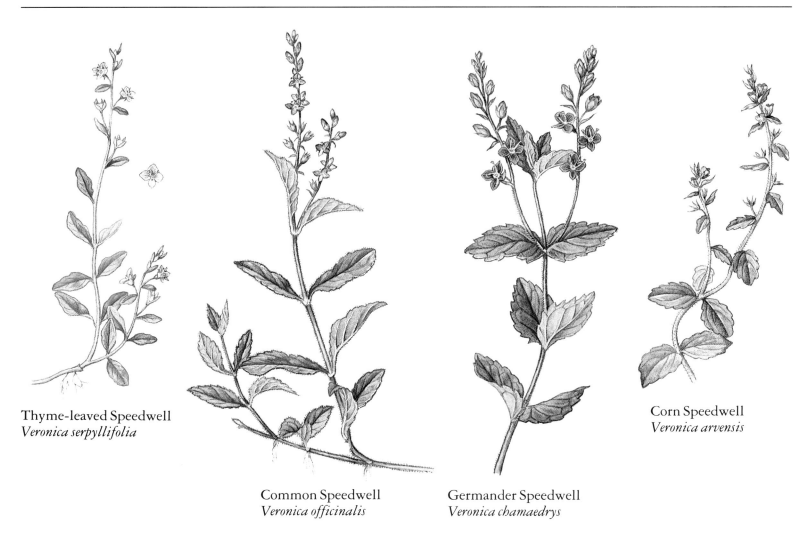

Thyme-leaved Speedwell
Veronica serpyllifolia

Corn Speedwell
Veronica arvensis

Common Speedwell
Veronica officinalis

Germander Speedwell
Veronica chamaedrys

creeping, rather hairy, somewhat sticky stems and ovate leaves, the stems turning upward to bear small flowers in the upper leaf axils. The flowers are white with dark blue lines. This is a cosmopolitan weed found in open woods and meadows, lawns and fields in North America. **Common Speedwell**, *V. officinalis*, is similar, with hairy, creeping stems and pale lilac-blue flowers. It is a European plant found in dry fields and woods in the east.

Germander Speedwell, *Veronica chamaedrys*, has some of the brightest, bluest flowers in the whole plant kingdom, a constant source of surprise on a plant that qualifies as a weed (it always grows in the wrong place). This is another creeping plant, with upturning stems, hairy, serrated leaves, and flowers on long stalks in the upper leaf axils. It comes from Europe, growing in lawns and disturbed places in northeastern areas of the U.S. **Corn Speedwell**, *V. arvensis*, also has bright blue flowers, but they are tiny, borne in leafy spikes at the tops of the stems. This is a little, annual plant, with sprawling stems only 10in tall at most, and often much smaller. It grows as an inconspicuous weed in lawns and yards over much of North America.

American Brooklime, *Veronica americana* (p. 173), is a rather different plant, a native species that grows in wet places, in marshes, and along streams in much of North America, except the extreme south. It is a fleshy, hairless plant with creeping, sprawling stems, and opposite, lance-shaped leaves. Its blue flowers grow in loose racemes on long stalks in the upper leaf axils. The young shoots of this plant can be eaten in salads like watercress, but they are bitter and need to be mixed with other salad plants.

Snow Queen, *Synthyris reniformis* (p. 173), grows in moist coniferous woods on the lower slopes of the Cascades and Coast Ranges in California and into Oregon. It forms rosettes of scallop-edged, rounded leaves growing on long stalks. This is a spring-flowering plant, its pale blue-lavender, bell-shaped flowers borne in terminal racemes on sprawling, leafless stalks. Mountain Kittentails, *S. missurica*, is a showier plant, with dense spikes of blue-purple flowers overtopping its rosettes of rounded leaves. It grows in grassy places quite high in the mountains from California to Washington and Idaho.

There are several **Toadflaxes**, *Linaria* species, in North America. The name "Toadflax" comes from the supposed resemblance between the open flower and a toad's mouth, and from the way the leaves resemble those of Flax. **Butter-and-eggs**, *L. vulgaris* (p. 173), is a European species naturalized in waste places and along roadsides and railroads throughout temperate North America. It is a perennial plant, forming colonies of erect stems 1–3ft tall, with linear leaves, and bright yellow and orange flowers. The flowers open in summer, forming long spikes terminating the erect stems; each one is

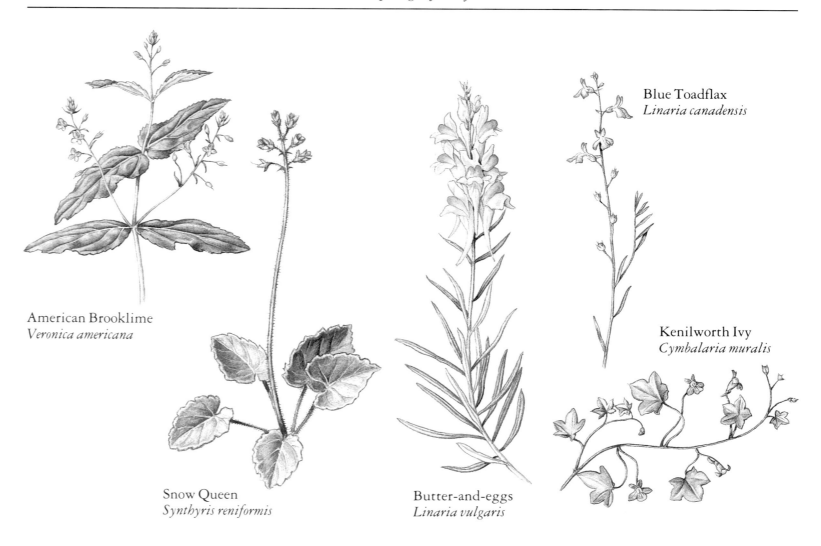

American Brooklime
Veronica americana

Blue Toadflax
Linaria canadensis

Kenilworth Ivy
Cymbalaria muralis

Snow Queen
Synthyris reniformis

Butter-and-eggs
Linaria vulgaris

two-lipped with a straight spur and an orange palate. The plant has a long history of use in herb medicine and was recommended for treating jaundice and dropsy. Steeped in milk, it makes a good fly poison.

Blue Toadflax, *Linaria canadensis*, is a slender annual with a rosette of short, more or less prostrate, leafy stems, and erect, leafy flowering stems 5-20in tall. The flowers grow along the erect stems in summer, and are light blue, two-lipped and spurred, with two white spots on the palate. Blue Toadflax grows in sandy soil throughout much of the U.S. and in parts of southern Canada, but it is more common in the east than elsewhere in the continent.

Kenilworth Ivy, *Cymbalaria muralis*, is often found growing along roadsides and on walls in eastern Canada, the northeastern U.S., and in California, where it escapes from cultivation; it comes originally from Eurasia. It is a small, hairless, perennial plant with trailing stems and long-stalked, palmate, rather thick leaves. Solitary flowers grow on long stems in the leaf axils in summer; they are blue-mauve with yellow palates and long spurs.

Several different **Snapdragons**, *Antirrhinum* species, grow in the chapparal and mountains in the southwest. They are mostly annual plants with erect or sprawling stems and two-lipped, sac-like flowers. Yellow Twining Snapdragon, *A. filipes*, is a small, twining plant that may be found in springtime growing in sandy places in Creosote Bush scrub in the deserts from California to Utah and Nevada. Its bright green stems twine through shrubs and bear yellow snapdragon flowers in the leaf axils. **Common Snapdragon**, *A. majus* (p. 174), is an introduced species grown in gardens; it may sometimes be found growing wild in waste places.

Foxglove, *Digitalis purpurea* (p. 174), is another European plant now found in North America, this one naturalized in the Pacific areas of the U.S. and Canada from British Columbia to California, and also, although much less commonly, in the northeastern states and eastern Canada. It grows in open places and along roadsides. Foxglove is a biennial plant, with a rosette of softly hairy, large, lance-shaped leaves in the first year, and an erect, leafy flowering stem 3–6ft tall in the second. The large, tubular flowers are mauve-pink in color, lighter on the inside, with dark pink spots. They hang on one side of the tall flowering spike in summer. Foxgloves are grown commercially in North America for the glycoside digitoxin which is present in their leaves. This poisonous substance is used in medicine to regulate heart function.

Many of the members of this family are semi-parasites. They have well-developed green stems and leaves, but their root systems are poorly developed and they attach themselves to the roots of other plants, especially to grasses, and obtain water and mineral salts from their host plants. Some species cannot

Common Snapdragon
Antirrhinum majus

Foxglove
Digitalis purpurea

Purple Gerardia
Agalinis purpurea

Downy False Foxglove
Aureolaria virginica

survive without a host, while others do grow and survive, but are stunted and do not do well. Sometimes the area of host plants affected can be seen, for a patch of short grass, which appears to have been trampled, will surround the parasite. All the following plants in the family are semi-parasites.

Purple Gerardia or False Foxglove, *Agalinis* (or *Gerardia*) *purpurea*, is one of several similar species found in the east, parasites on grasses and other herbaceous plants. Some grow in dry, sandy soil and prairies, others in moist places, on shores, and salt marshes. They are mostly wiry plants, with opposite, linear leaves, bearing pink or purple, bell-shaped flowers in late summer. Each flower lasts for only a day. Purple Gerardia is one of the most common, a branched plant 1–4ft tall found on shores and in bogs from Nova Scotia to Mexico.

Downy False Foxglove, *Aureolaria virginica*, is parasitic on the roots of Oak trees, like all *Aureolaria* species. It is a downy, perennial plant, with an erect, unbranched stem 3–4ft tall, pinnately lobed lower leaves, and lance-shaped upper leaves. The flowers are borne in summer in a terminal, leafy raceme at the top of the stem; they are yellow and tubular, each one with five spreading petal-lobes. Plants grow in dry, open woodland beneath trees of the White Oak group, from Ontario to Michigan, south to Florida and Alabama.

There are over 30 different **Louseworts**, *Pedicularis* species, in North America, many found in the west and north. They are

perennial plants, with opposite, divided leaves and spikes of two-lipped flowers. The name "Lousewort" is supposed to come from an old belief that cattle picked up lice from the plants; various explanations have been given to account for this erroneous belief, none of which seem convincing. **Elephant Heads**, *P. groenlandica* (p. 175), is a western species growing in wet places, especially in meadows, throughout the Rocky Mountains. It has narrow, pinnate leaves and dense spikes of pink flowers which resemble elephants' heads. The upper lip forms the trunk, and the side lobes of the lower lip form the ears. **Wood Betony**, *P. canadensis* (p. 175), grows in woods and prairies from Quebec to Manitoba, and south to Florida and Texas. It has dense clusters of red or yellow flowers at the tops of stems, with opposite, finely cut leaves.

Yellow Rattle, *Rhinanthus crista-galli* (p. 175), grows in moist places around the North Pole, south in North America to Oregon and Colorado in the west, and to New York in the east. It has unbranched stems with opposite, triangular leaves, and yellow flowers in the upper leaf axils. The flowers have characteristic calyces, inflated with reticulate veins and four lobes; each calyx becomes more inflated than ever in fruit, enclosing the flattened capsule with its winged seeds. The plant is called "Rattle" or rattlebox because as the capsules mature, their tissues dry and shrink inside, freeing the seeds which then rattle every time the plant blows in the wind.

Eyebright, *Euphrasia americana*, was given the name because it was used in herb medicine to treat sore and tired eyes—it brightened the eyes! It is originally native to Europe but is now widely naturalized in North America on roadsides and in grassy places from Newfoundland to Quebec, and south to New York. It is also found occasionally in the northwest. This is a small plant, with branched stems only about 1ft tall; its opposite leaves are ovate in shape with 3–5 teeth on the margin. The flowers grow in the axils of the upper leaves; each flower is two-lipped, the white lower lip with three notched lobes and purple veins, the bluish upper lip hooded. There are several other similar species in the east.

Indian Paintbrushes get their name from an Indian legend about a brave who was trying to paint a prairie sunset. When he could not catch the colors the Great Spirit helped him, and the flowers grow where he threw down his brushes. They come in reds, oranges, and yellows—all the colors of the prairie sunsets. They belong to the genus *Castilleja* and there are over 200 species in the New World, many in the prairies and mountains of the west. It is easy to recognize one of them as an Indian Paintbrush, but more difficult to identify them to species, since many are alike and they intergrade with one another. They are annual or perennial plants, with alternate, lance-shaped or narrowly segmented leaves, and distinctive flower clusters with colored, often three-lobed bracts at the tops of the stems. The actual flowers are very small, and it is the bracts and calyces which form the colored parts of the "paintbrushes." The Wyoming Paintbrush, *C. linariaefolia* is the state flower of Wyoming.

Desert Paintbrush, *Castilleja chromosa* (p. 176), is a common perennial plant of sagebrush and other dry places in the Rocky Mountain area from Idaho across to Oregon, and south to California and New Mexico. It forms clumps of erect, unbranched stems up to 15in tall, with leaves divided into three or five lobes, and bright orange or scarlet three-lobed bracts and calyces in the flower clusters.

Giant Red Paintbrush, *Castilleja miniata* (p. 176), is another western plant, but found in wet places, beside streams in mountain meadows and forest clearings from British Columbia to California. It is a larger perennial, with erect, unbranched stems up to 3ft tall, and bright scarlet bracts and calyces, the calyces deeply cleft and giving a ragged appearance to the flower clusters.

Sulfur Paintbrush, *Castilleja sulphurea* (p. 176), forms a clump of unbranched stems with broadly lance-shaped leaves. The bracts in the flower spike are also broad, and similar to the leaves in form but pale yellow in color, almost hiding the greenish flowers. The plant grows in meadows and on lower mountain slopes from Alberta to New Mexico, east to South Dakota. This is one of several species with yellow bracts.

Wood Betony
Pedicularis canadensis

Elephant Heads
Pedicularis groenlandica

Yellow Rattle
Rhinanthus crista-galli

Eyebright
Euphrasia americana

The only paintbrush in the east, and known there consequently just as Indian Paintbrush or **Painted Cup**, is *Castilleja coccinea*. It grows in woods, meadows, and prairies from Ontario to Manitoba, south to South Carolina and Oklahoma. This paintbrush is an annual plant, with an unbranched stem and three-lobed, scarlet-tipped bracts.

There are about 25 species of **Owl's-clovers** in the genus *Orthocarpus*, most found in western North America. They resemble Indian Paintbrushes, but their flowers are more conspicuous and the bracts proportionately less significant. Each flower has an arched upper lip, and a three-lobed, pouched lower lip. The flowers and bracts vary from yellow to pink, often with contrasting blotches on the pouch.

Common Owl's-clover, *Orthocarpus purpurascens* (p. 177), has bracts which are greenish at the base, purple-green in the middle, and velvety, rose-pink at the tips. The calyces have the same color pattern, and the corollas are purplish, each with a yellow-tipped, purple-dotted pouch! This is an annual plant, like all owl's-clovers, with erect, often branched stems up to 15in tall, and pinnately divided leaves with threadlike segments. It blooms in spring, often in profusion in a wet season, in grassy places, open woods, and coastal sage scrub in southern California, inland to Arizona and into Mexico.

Yellow Owl's-clover, *Orthocarpus luteus* (p. 177), is a much more widely distributed plant, the most widespread of the owl's-clovers. It grows in sandy plains and prairies, and in sagebrush scrub from British Columbia to Manitoba, south to Arizona and New Mexico. It has unbranched stems up to 15in tall, narrow leaves, and long spikes of plain yellow flowers.

There are about 35 species of **Bird's-beaks** in the genus *Cordylanthus*, all from western North America. They are branched, annual plants, their leaves entire or divided into narrow segments. Their yellow or purple flowers are borne in spikes or clusters terminating the stems. Beneath each flower are two bracts, the inner one resembling a calyx-lobe and borne opposite the one true calyx-lobe; the two together look like a bird's beak with the flower inside. The corolla is two-lipped, the upper lip hooded and the lower one often pouched. **Wright's Bird's-beak**, *C. wrightii* (p. 177), grows in sandy soils, in pine woods, and on the plains from Arizona to Texas. Many species are found in California in a variety of habitats, from coastal salt marshes and alkaline places, to dry hills, slopes, and coniferous woods. Most bloom in late summer.

Broomrape family
Orobanchaceae

A small family of strange, parasitic plants with about 10 genera and 170 species, mainly found in the warm temperate

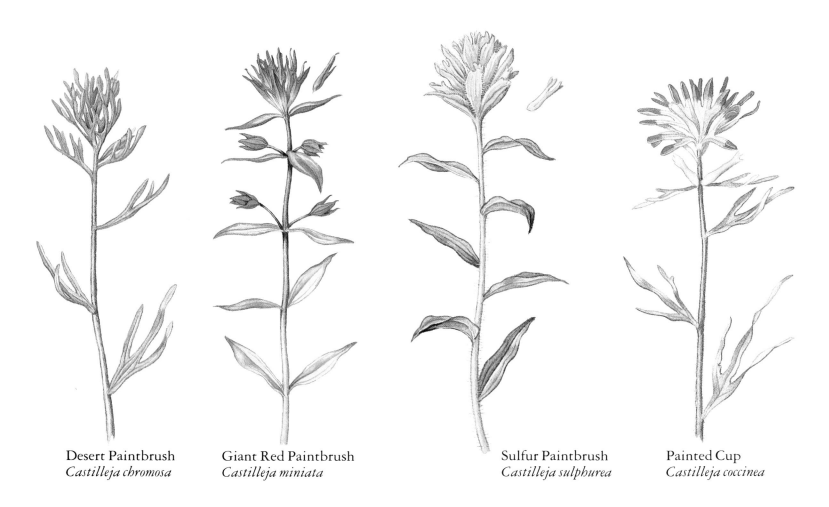

Desert Paintbrush
Castilleja chromosa

Giant Red Paintbrush
Castilleja miniata

Sulfur Paintbrush
Castilleja sulphurea

Painted Cup
Castilleja coccinea

regions of the Old World. They are mostly perennial herbs, lacking chlorophyll, and completely parasitic on the roots of other flowering plants and trees.

Family features The flowers are hermaphrodite and bilaterally symmetrical, with a toothed or lobed calyx, and a five-lobed corolla which is often curved or two-lipped. There are four stamens (two long and two short) alternating with the corolla-lobes. If a fifth stamen is present, it is sterile. The ovary is superior with one cell. The fruit is a capsule with very many tiny seeds. These plants have erect stems, with colorless, alternately arranged scale leaves at the base, and dense, terminal spikes of flowers.

There are only a few representatives of this family in North America, the majority being about 12 species of **Broomrapes** belonging to the genus *Orobanche*. They are parasitic on a wide variety of plants, especially on members of the daisy family like artemisias and sunflowers, but also on crop plants like clovers and tobacco.

Cancer-root, *Orobanche uniflora* (p. 178), has underground stems from which grow a few erect, slender stems, 8in tall at most, each with one white or violet, fragrant flower in early summer. This delicate plant grows in moist woods and thickets, in grassy areas and along stream banks from Nova Scotia to the Yukon, south to northern Florida and California.

Spike Broomrape, *Orobanche multiflora* (p. 178), is much more substantial than the ethereal Cancer-root. It has thick stems up to 20in tall; they look like cones and are brownish in color, with scale-like bracts, and purplish, two-lipped flowers in the axils of the bracts. The plant is parasitic on members of the daisy family, including artemisias, and is found in the west, in prairies and deserts, from Washington south to Mexico, and east to Texas.

Squawroot, *Conopholis americana* (p. 178), is parasitic on trees, mostly oaks and beech, and is found beneath its host trees in rich woods from Nova Scotia to Michigan, and south to Florida and Alabama. In early summer it produces fleshy, erect stalks covered with brownish scales and resembling 6-in long pine cones. These bear numerous hooded, yellowish flowers emerging from the scales. The stalks remain after flowering is over, becoming dry and brown, blending in with the fallen leaves of the woodland floor.

Beechdrops, *Epifagus virginiana* (p. 178), is parasitic on the roots of beech trees. It forms erect stems up to 20in tall, with small, scattered leaf scales and two kinds of flowers. The upper flowers are tubular, light brown with fine magenta lines; they open to reveal stamens and style but are sterile. The lower flowers are only a fraction of an inch long, never open, and soon fall off, displaced by the enlarging ovaries that develop into capsules full of seeds. A strange system this— upper flowers that look attractive to insects but are sterile, and

Common Owl's-clover
Orthocarpus purpurascens

Yellow Owl's-clover
Orthocarpus luteus

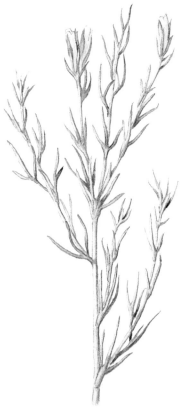

Wright's Bird's-beak
Cordylanthus wrightii

lower flowers that can never be pollinated but produce the seeds! Beechdrops grows beneath beech trees from Nova Scotia to Quebec and Wisconsin, south to Florida and Louisiana.

Acanthus family

Acanthaceae

This is a mainly tropical family that has a few representatives in warmer temperate regions. There are about 250 genera and 2500 species of herbs and shrubs in the family. Some, including gloxinias and the Shrimp Plant, *Beloperone guttata*, from Mexico, are grown as houseplants or in greenhouses. Bear's Breeches, *Acanthus* species, are grown in flower gardens, and their leaves inspired the decorative carvings on the Corinthian columns in ancient Greece.

Family features The flowers are hermaphrodite and bilaterally symmetrical, often with conspicuous colored bracts. The calyx of each flower has 4–5 lobes, and the corolla is tubular, usually two-lipped. Each flower has two or four stamens alternating with corolla-lobes. The ovary is superior, with two cells. The fruits are capsules. The leaves are opposite and stipules are absent.

Ruellia, *Ruellia caroliniensis* (p. 179), is a perennial plant with erect stems up to 3ft tall, opposite, ovate leaves, and clusters of flowers in the upper leaf axils. The flowers are large and showy, each with a tubular throat and five spreading corolla-lobes, light mauve in color. This plant grows in open woods from New Jersey to Indiana, and south to Louisiana and Texas. Several similar species grow in the woods and prairies of the east and midwest.

Water-willow, *Justicia americana* (p. 179), is an aquatic marginal plant, growing in shallow water, beside ponds and streams from Quebec to Wisconsin, south to Georgia and Texas. It has creeping rhizomes from which grow colonies of erect stems, and has opposite, narrow leaves, like those of Black Willow. Dense spikes of flowers grow on long stalks from the axils of the upper leaves; the flowers are white, spotted with purple, and two-lipped, with a hooded upper lip arching over the three-lobed lower lip.

Moschatel family

Adoxaceae

Moschatel, *Adoxa moschatellina* (p. 179), is quite unlike any other plant in its appearance and is the only species in its family. It is a small, perennial plant, only about 1ft tall at most, with creeping rhizomes, and clumps of light green, more or less three-lobed leaves growing on long stems. In early

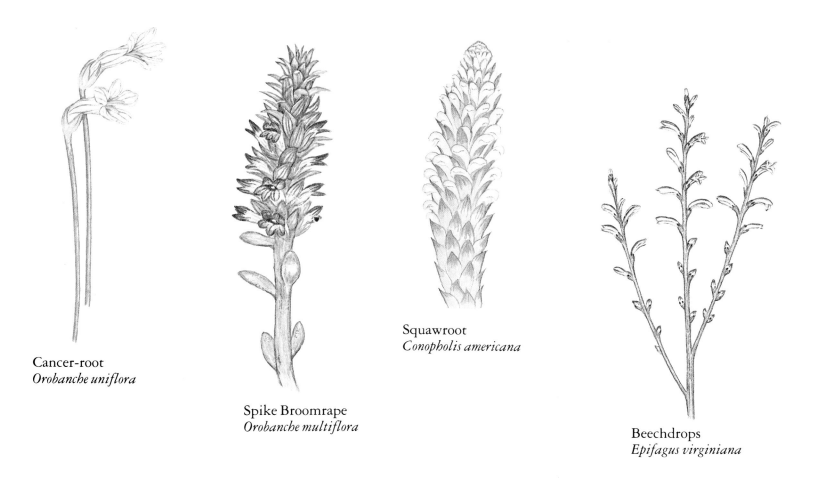

Cancer-root
Orobanche uniflora

Spike Broomrape
Orobanche multiflora

Squawroot
Conopholis americana

Beechdrops
Epifagus virginiana

Ruellia
Ruellia caroliniensis

Water-willow
Justicia americana

Moschatel
Adoxa moschatellina

summer it bears its extraordinary flowers growing in terminal clusters on stems that have a single leaf about halfway up. It is the form of the flower cluster that makes this plant so unique, for each cluster has five flowers in it, four of them forming the sides of a square and the fifth on top, facing the sky. The side flowers have three sepals and five petals, the top flower two sepals and four petals; all are yellow-green in color. If fruits are formed, they are drupes, produced in the same formation as the flowers, and heavy enough to make the stems droop; however, the flowers often fail to set seed and the plant spreads mostly by its creeping rhizomes.

The strange appearance of this plant has earned it the names of Townhall Clock and Five-faced Bishop in Europe, while the name of Moschatel or Musk-root comes from its musky scent. It grows in woods and forests, among mosses and rocks, around the North Pole. In North America it is found from northern Canada as far south as Colorado, Iowa, and Delaware.

Plantain family

Plantaginaceae

A small family found throughout the world, but mainly in the northern temperate regions, with 3 genera and about 270 species of herbs.

The **Plantains** themselves, inconspicuous plants belonging to the genus *Plantago*, account for 260 of these. Some of them are weeds of gardens and roadsides, others grow in dry places, some in marshes, and some are associated with the coast. Plantains are annual or perennial plants, mostly with a rosette of basal leaves, and leafless, unbranched flower stalks. The flowers are small and inconspicuous, each with four green sepals and four membranous petals. The stamens, however, are colored and noticeable, often protruding from the flowers to display their anthers, and the flowers are pollinated by wind. The spikes remain long after flowering, with the withered petals around the fruiting capsules, until they finally break up.

Several plantains are cosmopolitan weeds, like **Common Plantain**, *Plantago major* (p. 180). This plant was probably originally native to Europe, Asia and parts of North America, but is now found throughout the U.S. and southern Canada in fields and lawns, on roadsides, and waste land, especially on paths or in places where the ground is well trodden. It is a perennial plant, forming rosettes of long-stalked, broadly ovate, almost hairless leaves. In summer it bears narrow spikes of green flowers with purple anthers, the spikes reaching nearly 2ft in height if conditions are right. If it is growing on a path, it may be tiny.

English Plantain, *Plantago lanceolata* (p. 180), is another weed from Europe and Asia, now thoroughly naturalized in

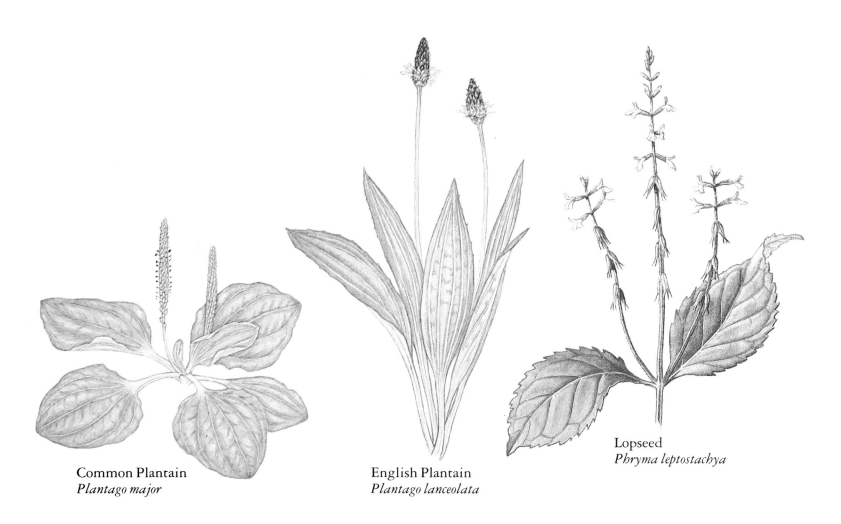

Common Plantain
Plantago major

English Plantain
Plantago lanceolata

Lopseed
Phryma leptostachya

North America and many other parts of the world. Its leaves are lance-shaped, held more or less upright, and gradually narrowing into very short stalks at the base. The leafless flowering stalks that appear in summer have five furrows running along their lengths and short terminal spikes of green flowers with whitish stamens. The stems and leaves have long silky hairs.

Lopseed family

Phrymaceae

There is only one species in this family, the **Lopseed**, *Phryma leptostachya*, a plant which occurs in North America and Asia. It is a perennial found in moist woods and thickets from Quebec to Manitoba, south to Florida and Oklahoma. It has an erect, branched stem up to 3ft tall, with opposite, serrated, quite large leaves. Narrow spikes of white or lavender flowers terminate the stems and grow from the upper leaf axils. Each flower has a two-lipped calyx, with three teeth in the upper lip and two in the lower lip, and a two-lipped corolla, with a short upper lip and a longer, spreading, three-lobed lower lip. The flowers grow in opposite pairs in the flower spike, and when they are over the calyx remains, characteristically drooping against the stem and enclosing the seed-like fruits.

Honeysuckle family

Caprifoliaceae

A small family of shrubs and herbs, with 13 genera and about 490 species, found mainly in north temperate regions and in mountains in the tropics. Several beautiful garden shrubs belong to this family, including honeysuckles, weigelas, and viburnums. Elder, *Sambucus nigra*, is famous in folk lore; its flowers and berries can be made into wine and preserves, its bark and leaves used in herb medicine.

Family features The flowers are hermaphrodite, bilaterally symmetrical or regular, usually borne in cymes. The calyx has five teeth and is usually joined to the ovary; the corolla is tubular, sometimes two-lipped, formed of four or five fused petals. There are four or five stamens inserted on the corolla and alternating with the corolla-lobes. The ovary is inferior, with 2–5 cells. The fruit is a fleshy berry. The leaves are opposite, simple or divided, and stipules are absent.

The **Honeysuckles**, *Lonicera* species, form the largest genus in the family, with about 200 species spread across the northern hemisphere in both temperate and tropical climes. The majority are shrubs, many with ornamental flowers, but some are climbers. Their flowers have long tubes and are rich in nectar, attracting insects to pollinate the flowers, but only

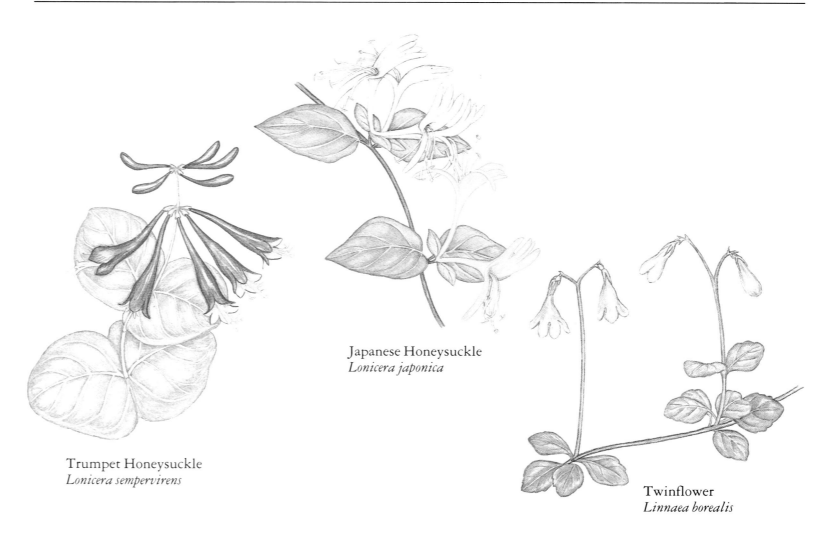

Japanese Honeysuckle
Lonicera japonica

Trumpet Honeysuckle
Lonicera sempervirens

Twinflower
Linnaea borealis

those with the longest probosces can reach the sweet riches. Many are scented, with a fragrance that is strongest in the evening, and these attract moths. The flowers are irregular at the tip of the tube, with four petal-lobes forming the top, and a single petal-lobe below.

The **Trumpet Honeysuckle**, *Lonicera sempervirens*, is a woody, climbing plant with stems that twine into shrubs and trees. It has opposite, broadly ovate leaves, the pair just below the flowers joined across the stem to form a disk, and whorls of brilliant, trumpet-shaped flowers on side stems. The flowers are red outside, yellow inside. This plant is native to woods from Connecticut to Florida, and west to Oklahoma, but also grows wild in other areas in the east, where it has escaped from cultivation as an ornamental plant.

Japanese Honeysuckle, *Lonicera japonica*, is native to eastern Asia, but now grows wild in much of the eastern and midwestern U.S., where it has escaped from cultivation. This is another climbing plant unwelcome in the wild, for it has strangling ways, trailing over and smothering native trees and shrubs. It has opposite, lance-shaped leaves and trumpet-shaped, fragrant flowers in whorls, white at first but turning yellow with age.

Twinflower, *Linnaea borealis*, by contrast, is a delicate, creeping plant found in the northern woods and bogs. It has trailing stems which run along the ground sending up leafy shoots only 4in tall. Each shoot has small, opposite, broadly ovate leaves, and ends in a pair of nodding, bell-shaped, pink or white flowers borne in summer. Twinflower grows all around the North Pole, across Canada, and south in North America to West Virginia and Indiana, to California through the Rocky Mountains in the west.

Valerian family

Valerianaceae

This is a small family with about 13 genera and 400 species of herbs found throughout the world, except in Australia. Valerian root comes from *Valeriana officinalis*, and is used in herb medicine as a nerve tonic and sedative. It is used as a perfume in the east, like the related Spikenard, which also comes from this family.

Family features The flowers are usually bilaterally symmetrical and hermaphrodite, borne in cymes or head-like inflorescences, sometimes with an involucre of bracts. The calyx is formed of 1–3 minute or inrolled sepals, and the corolla usually has five lobes; it is often two-lipped, and is often spurred or swollen at one side of the base. There are usually three or four stamens alternating with, but fewer than, the corolla-lobes. The ovary is inferior, with 1–3 cells, only

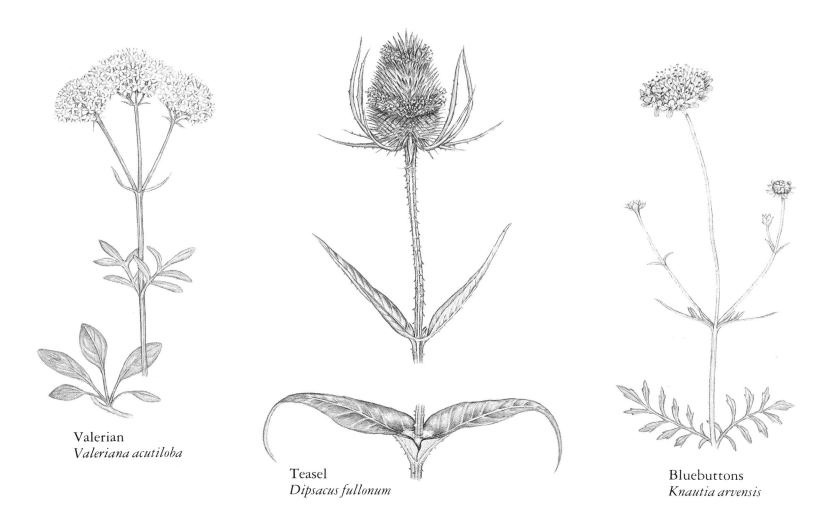

Valerian
Valeriana acutiloba

Teasel
Dipsacus fullonum

Bluebuttons
Knautia arvensis

one of which is fertile. The fruit is dry and indehiscent. The leaves are alternate, opposite or forming a rosette. Stipules are absent. Plants often have strongly scented rhizomes.

Valerians, *Valeriana* species, are perennial plants with thick, often scented roots or rhizomes, and several erect, leafy stems. Often the whole plant is scented, with a distinctive, peculiar smell. Their leaves may be entire or pinnately divided and their pink or white flowers are borne in compound inflorescences, often resembling heads or umbels. There are about 175 valerian species in the world, most found in the temperate areas of the northern hemisphere. *Valeriana acutiloba* grows in northwestern areas of North America on rocky banks high in the Rocky Mountains, often near water. It has mostly basal leaves, and white flowers growing on 2-ft tall stalks in summer.

Teasel family

Dipsacaceae

A small family of 9 genera and about 155 species, mostly herbs, the majority in the Mediterranean region and western Asia. Several family members have the common name of Scabious, a name given to them because they were believed to be useful remedies for skin diseases, like scabies.

Family features The flowers are small, often borne in dense heads with an involucre; they are hermaphrodite and bilaterally symmetrical. The calyx is small, cup-like, deeply divided into sections or into numerous hairs. The corolla is 4–5 lobed and often two-lipped. There are two or four stamens alternating with the corolla-lobes, their filaments free or joined in pairs. The ovary is inferior with one cell. The fruits are indehiscent, each with a single seed. The leaves are opposite or in whorls. Stipules are absent.

Teasel, *Dipsacus fullonum*, is a European plant which has become naturalized in many parts of North America, growing in wet places on roadsides and waste ground. Many books make a distinction between Wild Teasel, which they call *D. sylvestris*, and Fuller's Teasel, *D. fullonum*, but they are both subspecies of the same plant. Fuller's Teasel has cylindrical rather than conical heads, and stouter, more recurved prickles on the head, features which were useful when the heads were used by fullers. (A fuller was a person who finished cloth by brushing it with teasel heads to bring up the nap.) Teasel heads are still used to brush some fabrics, particularly the green baize of pool tables, and can be used for brushing clothes and for carding wool. Teasel is a biennial plant, with an erect, prickly, flowering stem 5–6ft tall in the second year, and prickly leaves, the lower ones joined across the stem, making a cup in which water collects and insects drown. The pale purple flowers grow with prickly bracts in heads at the tops of the stems. They open in the latter half of summer, forming a band which gradually "travels" from the bottom to the top of the head. Dead, dried plants and stems persist into winter.

Bluebuttons, *Knautia arvensis* (p. 182), is another European plant naturalized in North America, this one in grassy places, especially on limy soils, in the northeastern U.S. and eastern Canada. It is a small. perennial plant, with rosettes of lance-shaped, somewhat toothed leaves in spring, and erect stems with smaller but more divided leaves and terminal flower heads in late summer. The flowers are borne in flat heads where the outer flowers have very unequal petals, the largest petals forming a ring around the outside of the head. They are lilac-blue.

Bellflower family
Campanulaceae

Also called the Bluebell family or Harebell family. There are about 60 genera and 2000 species in this family, mostly herbs, found throughout much of the world. It contains many garden plants, including the *Campanula* and *Lobelia* species.

Family features The flowers are often showy, regular or bilaterally symmetrical, and hermaphrodite. The calyx is usually five-lobed and joined to the ovary. The corolla is tubular, bell-shaped, or one or two-lipped, and there are as many stamens as corolla-lobes alternating with the lobes. The ovary is inferior, with two or more cells. The fruit is a capsule. The leaves are alternate and simple, and stipules are absent. Plants usually contain milky juice.

There are about 250 species of Bellflowers, *Campanula* species, the majority found in the Old World. Many are perennials, with erect, leafy stems and blue, bell-like flowers in the axils of the upper leaves. Throatwort, *C. trachelium*, is one such plant, a bristly European species now found in waste places and on roadsides in the northeastern U.S. and eastern Canada. Creeping Bellflower, *C. ranunculoides*, is a much more invasive alien found in similar places, with creeping roots from which grow erect, leafy stems ending in racemes of blue flowers in the latter half of summer.

Tall Bellflower, *Campanula americana*, is a native annual, with stems up to 6ft tall, and clusters of light blue flowers in the latter half of summer. The flowers have widely spreading corolla-lobes, giving the blooms a starry appearance. The plant grows in moist woods from Ontario to Minnesota, south to Florida and Oklahoma.

Harebell, *Campanula rotundifolia*, is a very different kind of plant. It is a small perennial forming a clump of long-stalked leaves with rounded blades, and slender stems with narrow

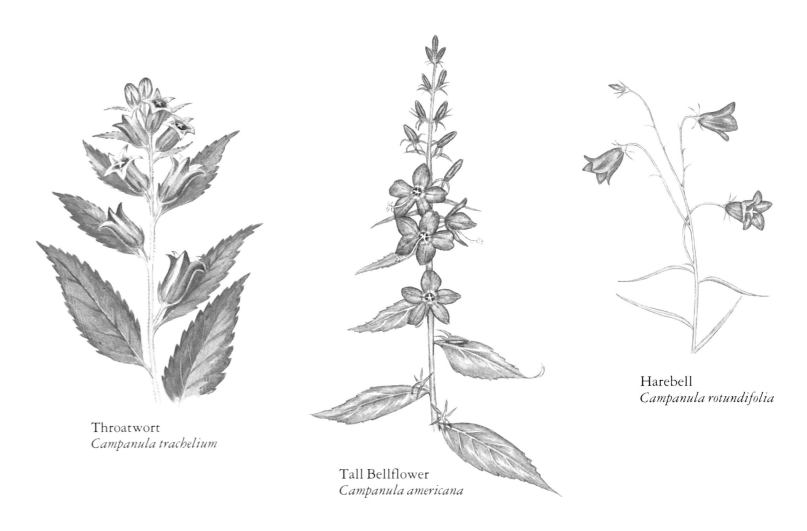

Throatwort
Campanula trachelium

Tall Bellflower
Campanula americana

Harebell
Campanula rotundifolia

leaves and nodding blue, bell-like flowers in the latter half of summer. The whole plant does not exceed 15in in height. It grows all around the North Pole, in dry grassland, on cliffs and dunes, often on poor, shallow soils. In North America it grows across Canada and south in the U.S. to New Jersey, Indiana, and Oregon. Harebell is not the only name that this plant possesses. It is called Bluebell in Scotland, and Scotch Bluebell in other parts of the world. It is also called Fairy Bells and Lady's Thimbles, with variations on these apt themes, referring to its delicate flowers. It earns the name of Sheep Bells from its tendency to grow in the kind of pastures favored by sheep.

California Harebell, *Campanula prenanthoides*, has slender stems with lance-shaped leaves, and loose spikes of starry, bright blue flowers at the tops of the stems. The flowers have narrow, reflexed petal-lobes and a protruding style, enlarged at the end like a baseball bat. This plant grows in dry coniferous woods in the Cascades and Coast Ranges from California to southern Oregon.

Venus' Looking-glass, *Triodanis perfoliata*, is an annual plant, with a simple, erect, leafy stem, usually about 18in tall. Its leaves are toothed and distinctively cupped around the stem. The flowers grow in clusters in the leaf axils, the lower ones unopening and self-pollinated, the upper ones pale lavender to deep purple, with five spreading petal-lobes. This plant often grows in disturbed habitats, in waste places, on roadsides and in gardens, fields and woods across the continent, north as far as Maine and British Columbia. Similar related species vary in details like leaf shape, presence of unopening flowers, and distribution.

There are about 6 species in the genus *Githopsis*, all from western North America. **Common Bluecup**, *G. specularioides*, is the most widely distributed, found in open places on the lower slopes of the Cascades from California to Washington, especially after a fire. It is a small, annual plant, with stiff stems up to 6in tall, and narrow, toothed leaves. The tiny, bright blue flowers appear irregularly scattered on the stems, and grow cupped in their relatively long calyx-lobes.

Members of the Bellflower family that have bilaterally symmetrical flowers, like the *Lobelia* species, are sometimes placed in a separate family, the Lobeliaceae. However, they share so many other features with the bellflowers that they are often all included in one family together, as here. There are about 250 **Lobelias** in the genus *Lobelia*, found in many warm and temperate regions of the world, with about 30 in North America. Most grow in the east and have blue flowers.

Cardinal Flower, *Lobelia cardinalis*, is exceptional in having brilliant red flowers. Most other lobelias have blue or white ones. Cardinal Flowers grow in wet places from New Brunswick to Minnesota, south to Florida and Texas, their

California Harebell
Campanula prenanthoides

Venus' Looking-glass
Triodanis perfoliata

Common Bluecup
Githopsis specularioides

Cardinal Flower
Lobelia cardinalis

flowers glowing from some distance away. This is a perennial plant forming erect stems up to 4 or 5ft tall, with narrow, toothed leaves, and a spike of flowers terminating the stem. Each flower is two-lipped, with an erect upper lip and a spreading, drooping, three-lobed lower lip. Insects find it difficult to land on these flowers, and pollination is usually effected by hummingbirds, which hover in front of the spike.

Great Lobelia, *Lobelia siphilitica*, is the largest species. It is a stout, perennial plant, with erect stems up to 5ft tall, with thin, lance-shaped to elliptical leaves, and terminal spikes of showy, blue flowers. The flowers are striped blue and white on the tube. Plants grow in wet places from Maine to Manitoba, south to North Carolina, Texas, and Colorado.

Indian Tobacco, *Lobelia inflata*, is the commonest lobelia in the east. It is a hairy, annual plant, with branched stems up to 3ft tall, ovate, toothed leaves, and small blue or white flowers in the axils of the upper leaves. The base of each flower is swollen and becomes inflated in fruit, surrounding the capsules which open at the top. The plant grows in open woods from eastern Canada to Minnesota, south to Georgia and Missouri. Indian Tobacco has been used in herb medicine to treat asthma and other chest problems. The leaves are dried and made into a tobacco that can be smoked. However, the herb is poisonous, like other lobelias, and its use has largely been discontinued as too risky.

About 12 species of *Downingia* are found in the Pacific west, usually associated with muddy flats and vernal pools. They are rather succulent, annual plants, no more than 10-15in tall, with soft stems, entire leaves, and two-lipped flowers. The flowers are generally blue, with two lobes on the small upper lip, and three fused lobes on the lower lip, which is often yellow and white. The flowers "perch" on the tips of elongated ovaries that look like long stalks growing from the axils of bracts. **Toothed Downingia**, *D. cuspidata*, is typical; it has light blue or lavender flowers blotched with yellow and white on the lower lip, and is found on wet and drying, muddy clay soils in California.

Threadstem, *Nemacladus rubescens*, is one of about 10 *Nemacladus* species found only in dry places in the southwestern U.S. These are small, annual plants, with compact rosettes of basal leaves and much-branched stems on which the leaves are reduced to awl-shaped bracts. The flowers are minute, borne in loose racemes from most of the leaf axils. Examined closely, they can be seen to have the bilaterally symmetrical corolla typical of the Lobeliaceae, with a two-lobed upper lip and a three-lobed lower lip. Threadstem grows in dry, sandy, and rocky places, among scrub and in deserts from California to Nevada and Arizona. It grows only a few inches tall, has a few elliptical, basal leaves, and yellow flowers with brown-purple markings.

Great Lobelia
Lobelia siphilitica

Indian Tobacco
Lobelia inflata

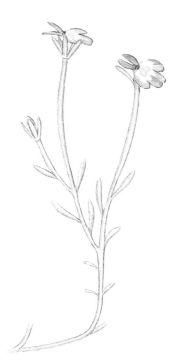

Toothed Downingia
Downingia cuspidata

Sunflower family

Compositae

Also known as the **Daisy family** and the **Asteraceae**. This is the largest family of flowering plants, with over 900 genera and 14,000 species found throughout the world. Most are herbaceous plants, although a few are woody shrubs or climbers. They grow in all kinds of habitats, from deserts to marshes, from the mountains to the woods and grasslands of the bottomlands, from the tropics to the Arctic.

There are many decorative plants in the family, grown in flower borders and greenhouses, and used as cut flowers. Chrysanthemums are probably the most popular of cut flowers, available throughout the year and easy to arrange. Dahlias are grown in many gardens, along with perennial plants like heleniums, gaillardias, goldenrods, asters, and a host of others. Annuals used in summer bedding schemes include zinnias, ageratums, and marigolds. Greenhouse and house plants include cinerarias and mutisias.

Some important vegetable and salad plants come from this family, including lettuce and chicory, artichokes, salsify, and endive. Sunflower seeds are an increasingly important source of polyunsaturated oils. Several species are used in herb medicine; for instance, Coltsfoot is a component of many cough medicines, camomile leaves make a soothing tea, and arnica is a traditional remedy for sprains.

Not all composite plants are welcome in gardens—indeed many are unwelcome weeds, like dandelions, groundsel, thistles, lettuces, and hawkweeds. Ragweed pollen causes problems for thousands of hay fever sufferers every year.

Family features The flower structure in this family is unique and is presumed to account for its success. Individual flowers are small but they are gathered into flower heads surrounded by green bracts. The heads are often conspicuous and are highly attractive to insects; because of the design of the flowers within each head, a high proportion are pollinated and many seeds produced. Many species also have effective seed dispersal mechanisms.

Individual flowers are called florets and have a corolla which may be tubular in form (disk florets) or strap-shaped (ray florets). A flower may be made wholly of disk florets or of ray florets, but in many species disk florets form the center of each flower head, with ray florets around the margins. Each floret has a calyx which may be a membranous ring, or formed of hairs, bristles or teeth. Flowers may be male, with five stamens, or female with an inferior ovary, or have both male and female parts. The fruits are hard, nut-like achenes containing a single seed, and crowned by the pappus, the remains of the calyx.

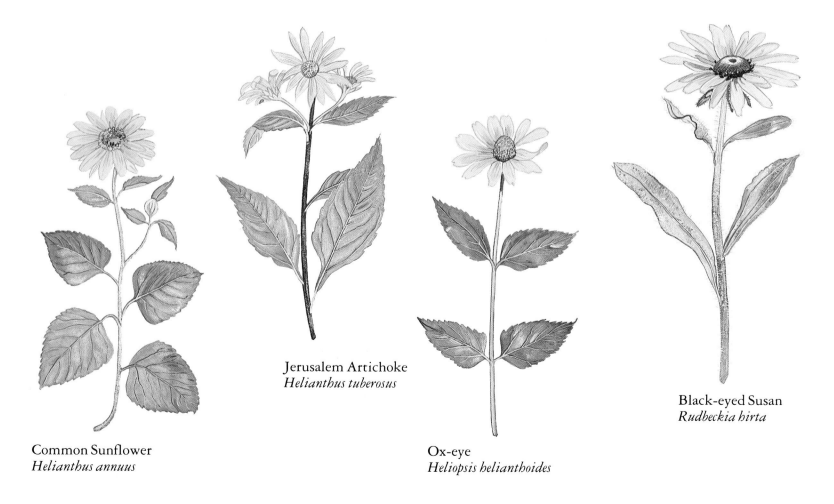

Common Sunflower
Helianthus annuus

Jerusalem Artichoke
Helianthus tuberosus

Ox-eye
Heliopsis helianthoides

Black-eyed Susan
Rudbeckia hirta

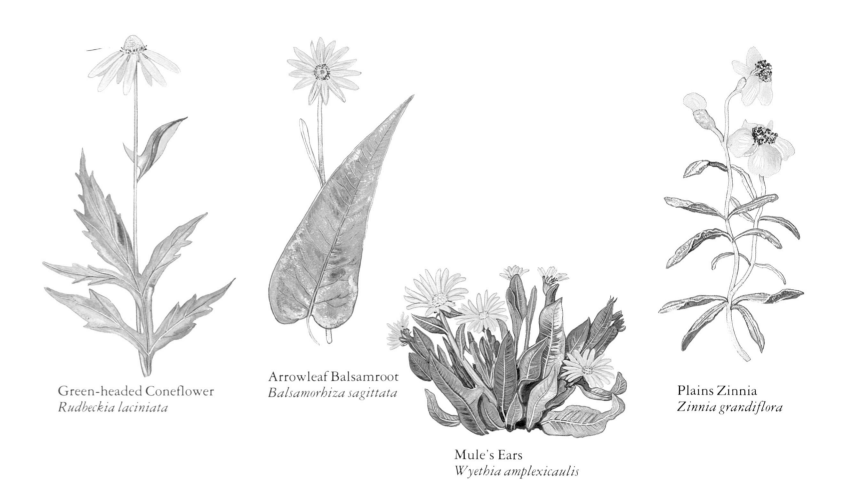

Green-headed Coneflower
Rudbeckia laciniata

Arrowleaf Balsamroot
Balsamorhiza sagittata

Mule's Ears
Wyethia amplexicaulis

Plains Zinnia
Zinnia grandiflora

Sunflowers are among the most familiar of the composites. The wild sunflower is *Helianthus annuus* (p. 186), known as the **Common Sunflower**, and one of over 40 species of the genus in North America. It is an annual plant with an erect, branching stem growing up to 10ft tall when conditions suit it. It has alternate, large, toothed leaves up to 1ft long, ovate or heart-shaped in outline, and rough in texture. The wild sunflower has several flower heads, each up to 6in across, with brownish-purple disk florets and bright yellow ray florets. Sunflower fruits are formed only by the disk florets, and the seeds may be eaten like those of cultivated plants. Sunflowers may be found in dry places and prairies, also on roadsides, from Minnesota to Washington state, and southward to Missouri and California.

Other sunflowers have edible seeds, but differ from Common Sunflower in having all yellow flowers, and many are perennials. **Jerusalem Artichoke**, *Helianthus tuberosus* (p. 186), is a midwestern species with roots that swell to form the edible tubers eaten as a vegetable.

Ox-eye, *Heliopsis helianthoides* (p. 186), may be mistaken for a sunflower, for it has similar, yellow-rayed flower heads. However, its flowers have conical disks. This short-lived perennial plant grows in dry woods, prairies, and waste places across southern Canada, more commonly in the east than in the west, south in the U.S. to Georgia and New Mexico. It has erect stems up to 5ft tall, with opposite, ovate, serrated leaves, and terminal, usually solitary flower heads in summer.

The showy flowers of **Black-eyed Susan**, *Rudbeckia hirta* (p. 186), decorate a variety of habitats, from hillsides to prairies and open woods, roadsides and fields. The plant is found from Newfoundland to British Columbia, south to Florida and Mexico. It is a biennial, with a rosette of leaves in the first year and flowering stems in the second, with variably toothed, lance-shaped, or elliptical leaves, all rough textured, with coarse hairs. Its flower heads are 2–3 in across, with up to 20 golden yellow ray florets, and a purple or brown domed disk. **Green-headed Coneflower**, *R. laciniata*, has a similar distribution but grows in moist places. Each flower has a domed, green central disk and its leaves are deeply cut into three or five sections.

Arrowleaf Balsamroot, *Balsamorhiza sagittata*, is one of about 12 *Balsamorhiza* species found in western North America. It produces a clump of leaf rosettes, formed of foot-long leaves, with long stalks and silver-velvety hairs, especially on the undersides of the leaves. The plants flower in early summer, producing solitary, bright yellow flower heads subtended by woolly bracts on erect, almost leafless stalks. Each flower has a yellow disk and 8–25 ray florets. This plant grows in sandy soils, on the plains, in openings among sagebrush and pine woods, and on the lower slopes of the

Stemless Goldflower
Hymenoxis acaulis

Sunray
Enceliopsis nudicaulis

Golden Crownbeard
Verbesina encelioides

Nodding Bur-marigold
Bidens cernua

mountains from California to British Columbia, east to Colorado and South Dakota.

Like the Balsamroots, **Mule's Ears**, *Wyethia amplexicaulis* (p. 187), is considered a weed when growing on rangeland, and in some areas both have been eradicated. They are similar plants, but Mule's Ears has leafy stems, while those of Balsamroots are leafless. Mule's Ears is a perennial, with a multiple rosette of shiny, elliptical leaves, each one up to 15in long. In the early part of summer the plant produces erect, leafy flowering stems bearing solitary, bright yellow flower heads. Plants grow in grassland and foothills from Washington to Montana, south to Nevada and Colorado. There are about 12 other *Wyethia* species in the west, all with yellow flowers. White Mule's Ears, *W. helianthoides*, has white ray florets. It grows in valleys and wet meadows in the Rockies.

The **Plains Zinnia**, *Zinnia grandiflora* (p. 187), grows in dry areas of the plains and in the deserts from Kansas to Colorado and south into Mexico. This is another species with bright golden-yellow flowers, this time with reddish disk florets and only 3–6 almost round ray florets to each head. In late summer its low-growing clumps are transformed by the numerous flower heads. This is a perennial plant with branched stems clothed with opposite, linear leaves. The Zinnia that is grown in gardens is a cultivated version of *Z. elegans*, a species that comes from Mexico.

Stemless Goldflower, *Hymenoxis acaulis*, is aptly named for it consists of a tuft of basal leaves with yellow flowers. This perennial plant grows in dry, open places, on hillsides and plains, mainly in the midwest and west, from Idaho to California, and eastward to Ontario and Ohio. Its leaves are lance-shaped, hairy when young but losing the hairs as they mature. The flowers are solitary, borne on leafless stalks in early summer. There are 5–35 broad, three-toothed ray florets on each flower head.

Sunray, *Enceliopsis nudicaulis*, is another western plant, one which grows in arid soils, in sagebrush and desert scrub from California to Arizona, and north to Idaho. It forms a clump of basal leaves, with long stalks and rounded blades, all covered with woolly hairs to cut down water loss. The flowers are borne in early summer, growing singly on leafless stalks, often only 1ft tall; they are very bright and attractive, with showy yellow ray florets and a central yellow disk. Two other similar species also grow in the arid southwest.

Golden Crownbeard, *Verbesina encelioides*, is a southern and western plant, ranging from Florida to California, north to Kansas and Montana, and south into Mexico. It grows in a variety of habitats, in rangeland and pastures, as a common weed along roadsides and field edges, in washes and waste places. It is an annual, with much branched, minutely hairy stems and gray-green, triangular leaves. The many flower

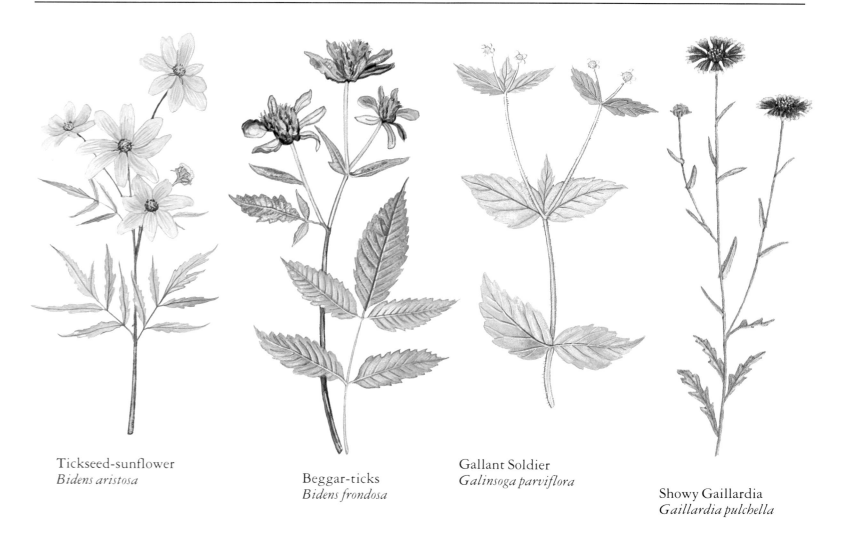

Tickseed-sunflower
Bidens aristosa

Beggar-ticks
Bidens frondosa

Gallant Soldier
Galinsoga parviflora

Showy Gaillardia
Gaillardia pulchella

heads grow on long stalks; they have broad, bright yellow, toothed ray florets and a yellow disk. Related plants from the east are the Wingstems, like *V. occidentalis*, a perennial plant with a single winged stem and flower heads with only 2–5 uneven yellow ray florets.

There are about 120 species in the genus *Bidens*, found mostly in the New World, the majority of North American species in the east. Most grow in wet places, beside streams, in marshes and coastal estuaries, or in wet waste places. They are annual or perennial, often more or less hairless plants with erect stems and opposite leaves. Some have showy flowers with large, yellow ray florets, while the flowers of others are rather dingy and lack ray florets. Their achenes bear barbed spines which stick to animal hair or clothing and so the plants are dispersed. They are variously called Beggar-ticks, Bur-marigolds, and Tickseed-sunflowers, references to their spined "seeds" and showy flowers.

Nodding Bur-marigold, *Bidens cernua* (p.188), grows in marshes, ditches, and other wet places, scattered across much of North America, Europe, and Asia. It is an annual, with branched stems up to 2ft tall, lance-shaped, toothed leaves borne in opposite pairs, and flower heads on long stalks, nodding as they age. Each flower head has a large, central, yellow disk and broad, yellow ray florets; behind the head green leafy bracts project beyond the rays. In some plants the

ray florets are small or even absent. Each spiky fruit has four barbed spines that catch on clothes.

Tickseed-sunflower, *Bidens aristosa*, is a very common plant of wet meadows, ditches, and marshes, forming spectacular patches when its yellow flowers are in full bloom. It is found from Maine to Minnesota, south to Virginia and Texas. It may be annual or biennial, has erect stems up to 5ft tall, and compound, pinnate or twice-pinnate leaves with toothed, lance-shaped leaflets. Its flattened, winged fruits have two barbed spines each. Two other similar species grow in the east and midwest.

Beggar-ticks or Sticktight, *Bidens frondosa*, is one of several *Bidens* species called Beggar-ticks. It has flat, bristly achenes, each with two barbed spines. This is an annual plant, with erect stems up to 4ft tall, compound leaves, each with 3–5 toothed leaflets, and dull yellow flower heads. The heads are solitary, lack ray florets, and are cupped in long green bracts. Plants grow in wet waste places and damp fields from Nova Scotia to Washington state, and across much of the U.S. Spanish Needles, *B. bipinnata*, is one of the few *Bidens* species to grow in drier ground; it is found in gardens, fields, roadsides, and waste places in the east and midwest. Its name comes from its needle-like clusters of achenes.

Considering its status as a cosmopolitan weed, *Galinsoga parviflora* seems unusual in its lack of a common name. It must

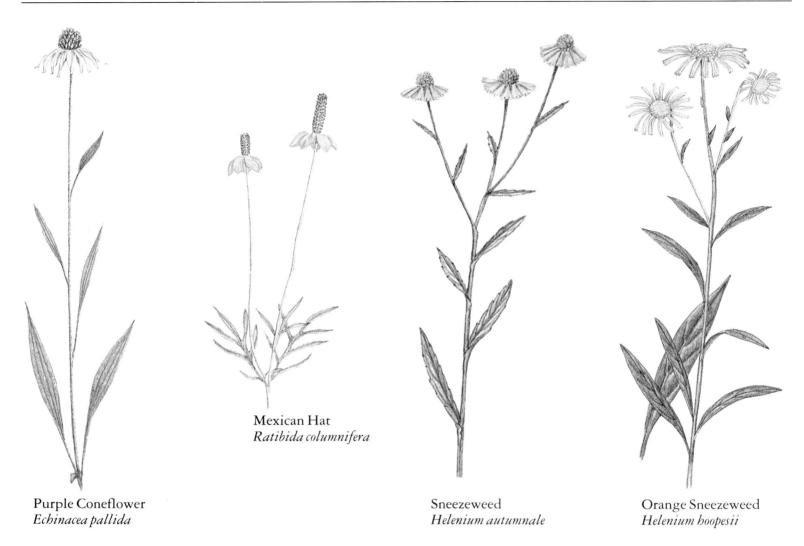

Mexican Hat
Ratibida columnifera

Purple Coneflower
Echinacea pallida

Sneezeweed
Helenium autumnale

Orange Sneezeweed
Helenium hoopesii

be because it is so inconspicuous that it goes unnoticed, yet it survives in cities from London, England, to the eastern U.S., in waste places and disturbed ground. In England it is known as **Gallant Soldier**, a corruption of the Latin *Galinsoga*. It is a little, annual plant, no more than 2ft tall, with many branching stems, ovate, toothed leaves, and flowers only a quarter of an inch across, usually with five white ray florets and a yellow disk. Its tiny fruits are flattened and bristly; they cling to clothing and are also transported by wind, two factors which make it a successful weed. It comes originally from Mexico and South America.

Gaillardias are colorful garden plants which make brilliant splashes of red and yellow in late summer gardens. There are several wild species, known as Blanket Flowers; their flowers have broad ray florets, each one deeply cleft with three teeth. **Showy Gaillardia** or Indian Blanket, *G. pulchella* (p. 189), is one of the most most widely distributed, growing in dry, sandy places, on plains and prairies, in fields and on roadsides from Missouri to Colorado, north to Minnesota, and south into northern Mexico; it also extends east along the coast from Texas, through Florida, and on to Virginia. This is an annual plant, 12–18in tall, with many branched stems, bristly leaves, and many flower heads. The plant is sometimes called Firewheel, an apt name for the colors of the ray florets, which are red with yellow tips. *Gaillardia aristata*, another prairies

Blanket Flower, is a perennial plant with yellow, purple-centered rays and a purplish disk.

Several species of **Purple Coneflower**, plants belonging to the genus *Echinacea*, grow in the east and midwest. One of them, *E. purpurea*, is grown in flower borders; its flowers bring a touch of rich purple when planted among the more common yellows and oranges of late summer composites. *Echinacea pallida* is a similar plant found only in the wild. It has a strong, woody taproot with a clump of long-stalked, more or less lance-shaped leaves, and erect stems 3–4ft tall. The stems bear smaller leaves and end in solitary flower heads; these are quite distinctive, with drooping, purple ray florets, becoming paler and more reflexed with age, and a central, domed, spiky disk. Plants grow in prairies, open woods, and other dry places from Michigan to Minnesota, south to Georgia and Texas. Both species are used as painkillers in Indian medicine, to soothe bee stings, headaches, toothaches, and burns.

If the Purple Coneflowers are distinctive with their domed flower heads, then **Mexican Hat**, *Ratibida columnifera* is remarkable. The flower heads have a "brim" of drooping, yellow ray florets, and a "crown" formed of the dark, column-like disk. The plant is a perennial, with a clump of branched stems up to 4ft tall, and pinnately cleft leaves, mostly on the lower parts of the stems. The flowers appear in late summer. Mexican Hats grow across the plains and prairies, on roadsides and in waste ground from Minnesota to the eastern edge of the Rockies, south into Mexico.

Yellows, browns, and oranges are colors seen in many gardens in late summer and fall, colors which come especially from the **Heleniums**. *Helenium autumnale* is the most important garden species, together with *H. bigelovii* and *H. hoopesii*; from these have come a multitude of hybrids, with colors ranging from deep mahogany brown to yellow. All three are native North American wild flowers.

In the wild *Helenium autumnale* (p. 190) is known as **Sneezeweed**, as some people are allergic to it; it is the most common of about 20 *Helenium* species in North America. This is a perennial plant with a clump of erect, leafy stems about 5ft tall, and lance-shaped leaves which appear to run down the stems as wings. In late summer and fall it bears many flower heads, each with 10–20 reflexed, yellow ray florets, and an almost globular, greenish-yellow disk. The effect is of a button with streamers attached. It grows in wet meadows, marshes, and ditches from Quebec to British Columbia, south to Florida and Arizona.

Orange Sneezeweed, *Helenium hoopesii* (p. 190), is a western species found in wet mountain meadows and beside streams in the Rocky Mountains. It has several stout stems 2–4ft tall, lance-shaped leaves near the bases of the stems, and loose, terminal clusters of flower heads. Each head has a broad, central yellow disk and spreading, narrow, orange-yellow rays. The plant is poisonous to sheep and spreads on over grazed land.

Several species of *Coreopsis*, or **Tickseeds**, are grown in gardens, most of them short-lived perennials with showy yellow flowers. **Garden Coreopsis** or Plains Tickseed, *C. tinctoria*, is an annual plant grown in bedding schemes and for cut flowers. It is also a North American native plant, along with about 30 other species in the same genus. It grows in low-lying ground and waste places from Manitoba to Alberta, south to Texas and Arizona, and may escape from gardens elsewhere. It is a much branched plant, 2–4ft tall, with leaves pinnately divided into long linear segments, and many flower heads in summer. The flower heads have about eight broad, yellow ray florets, each one purple-blotched at the base and with three teeth at the tip. The central disk is purple. Perennial native species also grown in gardens are *C. grandiflora* and *C. lanceolata*; both are prairie species and, like many tickseeds, they have yellow flowers with broad, notched ray florets.

Woolly Sunflower, *Eriophyllum lanatum*, is an eye-catching western plant that grows in dry places from southern California to British Columbia, and east through the Rocky Mountains. It has leaves made gray-white by a covering of woolly hairs, and numerous, solitary yellow flowers. It makes

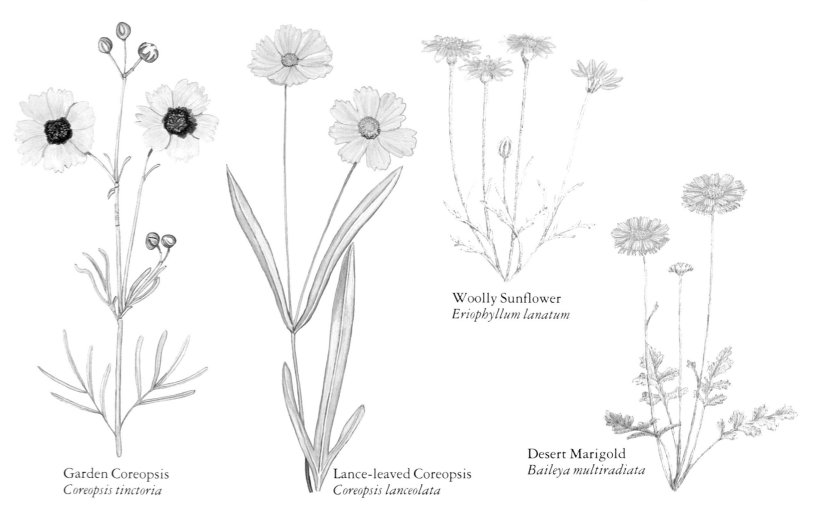

Woolly Sunflower
Eriophyllum lanatum

Garden Coreopsis
Coreopsis tinctoria

Lance-leaved Coreopsis
Coreopsis lanceolata

Desert Marigold
Baileya multiradiata

an excellent mound-forming plant for a very dry, sunny garden. The hairs help the plant to retain water and it has deep wandering roots. This is a perennial plant with a woody base and branched stems bearing narrowly divided lower leaves and linear upper leaves. The flower heads are borne on erect, woolly stems; each has 8–13 broad, yellow ray florets and a yellow disk. About 12 *Eriophyllum* species are found in the west, all perennial plants or shrubs, all more or less woolly, with yellow or white flowers.

Desert Marigold, *Baileya multiradiata* (p. 191), is another woolly desert plant with a rosette of broad, pinnately lobed leaves and branched, erect stems, only 20in tall at most and leafy near the base. The stems end in yellow flower heads, each with a yellow disk and several layers of ray florets. These are perennial plants which flower from early summer onward; they make a brilliant display in dry gardens. In the wild they grow along desert roadsides, in sandy plains, and desert scrub from Texas to California, north into Utah and south into Mexico.

Chinchweed, *Pectis papposa*, is an annual desert plant appearing after summer rains. It is found in flats and on roadsides, in arid plains and deserts, and among Creosote Bush scrub from the Mojave and Colorado deserts to New Mexico, south into Mexico and north to Utah. It has slender, forked stems up to 8in high, with opposite, linear leaves and a heavy scent of lemon on hot afternoons; the scent is produced by oil glands on the leaves. Clusters of yellow flower heads grow at the ends of the stems.

Dusty Maiden, *Chaenactis douglasii*, is one of about 25 *Chaenactis* species, all from the west and known as pincushion flowers. This little plant is usually biennial, with rosettes of cottony-glandular, lacy leaves, flowering in midsummer. The flowering stalks grow up to 16in tall, branching near the top to bear pink or white, top-shaped flower heads. They are formed solely of disk florets. Dusty Maiden grows in dry places, on gravelly slopes and sandy plains, in chaparral and pine woods from California to British Columbia, east to Arizona and Montana.

Marsh Elder, *Iva frutescens*, is a rather fleshy, shrubby plant, with branched stems about 6ft tall and lance-shaped or elliptical, toothed leaves. The many flower heads are borne singly in the axils of the upper leaves; each is greenish-white and formed only of disk flowers. Plants grow in wet places along the seashore, in marshes, and drainage ditches from Nova Scotia to Texas. Poverty Weed, *I. axillaris*, is one of several annual weedy *Iva* species. It has sprawling stems, and solitary flower heads drooping in the axils of the lance-shaped leaves. This small plant grows in alkaline soils and along the borders of salt marshes, in fields and eroded slopes from Manitoba to British Columbia, south to Oklahoma and California. Other species grow in waste places and fields.

Chinchweed
Pectis papposa

Dusty Maiden
Chaenactis douglasii

Marsh Elder
Iva frutescens

Common Ragweed
Ambrosia artemisifolia

Everyone who has suffered from hay fever knows about the **Ragweeds**. Because they are wind pollinated they release huge amounts of pollen into the air, making the pollen count climb in dry summer weather. There are several species, but the ones everyone knows in the east are **Common Ragweed**, *Ambrosia artemisifolia* (p. 192), and **Great Ragweed**, *A. trifida*. Both are annual weeds that grow in waste places, in fields, and on roadsides, Common Ragweed throughout the U.S. and southern Canada, Great Ragweed mainly in the U.S. east of the Rockies. They are coarse plants, with male and female flowers in separate heads, the numerous yellow-green male heads in elongated inflorescences at the top of the plant, and green female heads in the axils of leaves lower down the stems. Common Ragweed grows 3–5ft tall and has dissected, light green leaves; Great Ragweed is a bigger plant, 6–8ft tall, even bigger if conditions suit it, with palmate, pointed three-lobed leaves.

Cocklebur, *Xanthium strumarium*, is a strange plant that grows in waste places and fields, also on beaches on the coast and beside lakes, in the U.S. and north into southern Canada. It is probably native to South America, but it now grows as a weed in most warm temperate and subtropical regions of the world. This is an annual plant with rough, branched stems and broad, rounded-triangular leaves. Its male and female flowers are borne separately in rounded heads in the axils of the leaves, the male heads on the upper part of the plant, the females below. The female heads are prickly and enlarge in fruit to form inch-long, ovoid burs which catch on fur or clothes. The plant has probably been carried around the world with the wool trade and in animal skins.

Spiny Cocklebur, *Xanthium spinosum*, is a related plant, an annual with tripartite yellow spines at the base of each leafstalk, and with narrow, tapering leaves. The leaves have pointed lobes, are dark green on the upper surface and white-felted beneath. The flowers and burs are borne in small clusters or singly. This is another weed from tropical America, now scattered in fields and waste places through the warmer parts of North America.

The 15 *Layia* species are all found in California, usually in grassland and often near the coast; when growing in numbers, they are among the showiest wild flowers of the state. They are all spring annuals; some have flowers with white ray florets, others with yellow ones, or yellow with white tips, and they all have yellow disks. Many are much-branched plants; they have narrow, entire, toothed or divided leaves, and the flowers are borne terminating the stems. Tidy-tips, *L. platyglossa*, has white-tipped, yellow rays on its flowers. It grows in grassy flats near the coast of central California. **White Tidy-tips**, *L. glandulosa*, (p. 193) has white ray florets, which fade to purple as they age. The plant is covered with sticky hairs. It grows in

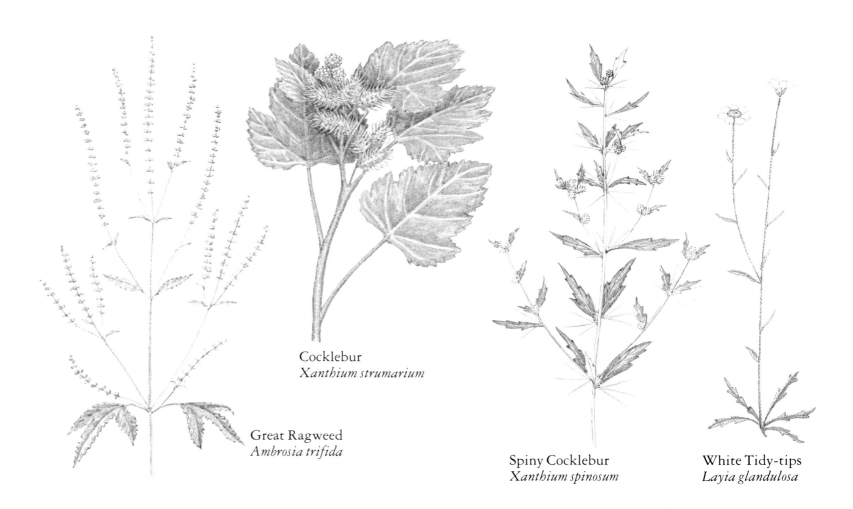

Cocklebur
Xanthium strumarium

Great Ragweed
Ambrosia trifida

Spiny Cocklebur
Xanthium spinosum

White Tidy-tips
Layia glandulosa

sandy places and deserts, through the Great Basin from California to Washington, and east to Idaho and New Mexico.

There are several different genera of composite plants called **Tarweeds** in the west, the name being given to the *Madia* species because of their glandular nature and heavy scent. **Common Madia**, *M. elegans*, is a plant found in many habitats—foothills and valleys, dry, open slopes and grass-land, along roadsides—often in large numbers in the Western Cascades and Sierra Nevada of Oregon and California. It is a branched, erect plant up to 4ft tall, with linear leaves, densely glandular and hairy. The many flower heads are borne in loose, compound clusters. They open in the day, closing again at night; they are colorful when open, each with 8–16 yellow ray florets, often blotched with maroon at the base, and yellow or maroon disk florets. There are several varieties of this plant, varying mainly in the color of the flowers and in the time of year at which they flower. One variety flowers in spring, another through the summer, and a third in fall.

The *Hemizonia* species are a group of about 30, all found in California. Many are known as tarweeds, others spikeweeds. They are glandular and aromatic plants, with entire or lobed basal leaves, and most flower in the fall, producing yellow or white flowers. **Common Spikeweed**, *H. pungens*, is the most widely distributed, growing not only in California but also in Oregon, and occasionally in Washington. It grows in dry

places, fields, and grassland in the interior valleys and foothills. It has stiffly rigid, branched stems growing up to 4ft tall, with many yellow-green, spine-tipped leaves. The lower leaves are lobed like those of dandelions, but each lobe bears a spine; the upper leaves are reduced and entire, but still bear their spines, and have clusters of yellow flower heads in their axils. The plant has a pungent scent.

About 40 *Dyssodia* species are found in the southwestern areas of the U.S. and in Mexico. They are herbaceous or subshrubby plants, strongly scented, with numerous oil glands on their foliage. Their flower heads are borne terminally on the stems, and have a ring of ray florets around a central disk. **Common Dogweed**, *D. pentachaeta*, is like a low mound, no more than 8in tall. Its wiry stems bear opposite leaves at the base and a single flower head at the top, well above the foliage. The leaves are pinnately divided with prickly lobes and the flower heads are deep yellow. The plant grows in arid, rocky areas and deserts, among pinyon and juniper, and in scrub from Utah to Arizona, across to Texas and into Mexico.

The **Rosinweeds**, *Silphium* species, are coarse perennial plants, with erect stems, often 5–7ft tall, most of them with leafy stems. They are found in the east and midwest in woods and prairies. **Cup Plant**, *S. perfoliatum* (p. 194), is well named, for its upper leaves are joined across the stem to form a cup. This large, coarse plant may reach 8ft in height; it has

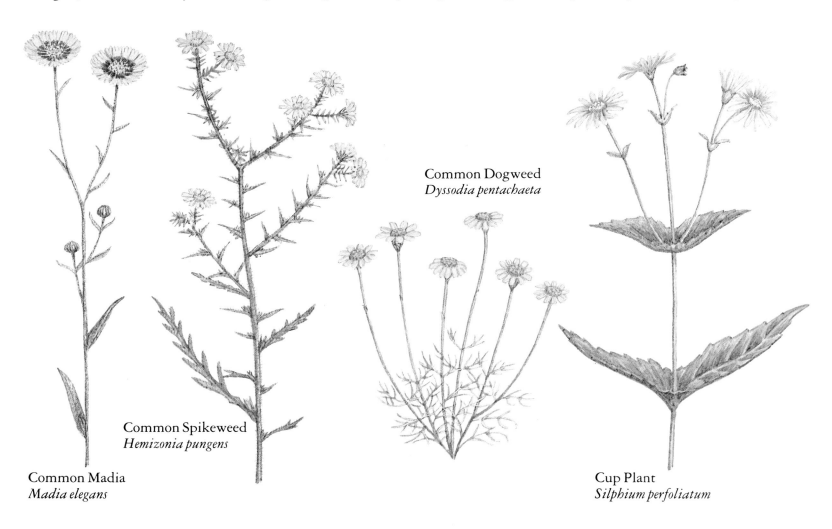

Common Dogweed
Dyssodia pentachaeta

Common Spikeweed
Hemizonia pungens

Common Madia
Madia elegans

Cup Plant
Silphium perfoliatum

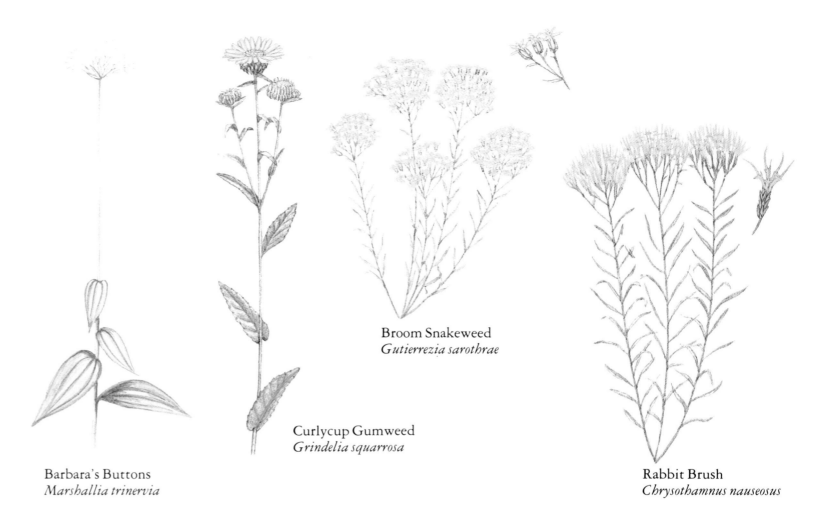

Broom Snakeweed
Gutierrezia sarothrae

Curlycup Gumweed
Grindelia squarrosa

Barbara's Buttons
Marshallia trinervia

Rabbit Brush
Chrysothamnus nauseosus

square stems and its rough leaves are opposite, although the lower ones are not joined together. The flower heads grow in loose, terminal clusters on long stalks which appear to be growing from the cupped upper leaves. Each head has 20–30 narrow ray florets and a central yellow disk. Rosinweeds are named for the resinous sap which oozes from their cut stems, hardening into gum when exposed to air. The Indians have used the sap of several species, including Cup Plant, as chewing gum to sweeten the breath and in their herbal medicine. It is said to provide a useful remedy for dry coughs and asthma. The Compass Plant, *S. laciniatum*, has deeply-cleft, very large leaves, the lowest up to 2ft long.

Barbara's Buttons, the *Marshallia* species, are generally rare plants found in wet places in the southeast—in pine barrens and damp deciduous woods, beside streams, in marshes and bogs. They are perennials, with alternate leaves and white or pinkish flower heads terminating long flower stalks. The heads are formed of disk florets only. *Marshallia trinervia*, grows on cliffs and on the rocky banks of streams in damp woods from Virginia to South Carolina, and west to Tennessee and Mississippi.

Gumplant is one of several names given to *Grindelia* species; others include Gumweed, Tarweed, and Rosinweed. All are references to the sticky flower heads and leaves typical of these western plants. **Curlycup Gumweed**, *G. squarrosa*,

grows in dry, open and waste places, invading rangeland that has been overgrazed, and may become a serious weed. Native to the Great Plains, it is now found from British Columbia to Quebec, south to California and Texas. It is a biennial or perennial plant, with branched stems up to 3ft tall, and many stalkless, toothed leaves covered in translucent dots and often sticky. In the latter half of summer it bears many yellow flower heads. Each head has 25–40 ray florets and is cupped in several layers of sticky bracts which curl backward at their tips. Gumweed has been used by Indians as a remedy for asthma and coughs; they infused the flower heads or leaves to make a tea, or smoked the dried leaves. There were problems with these remedies if the plants used had been growing in soil high in selenium, a toxic element which can be found in high concentrations in some soils in the west. Gumplants can absorb large amounts of selenium and are then poisonous.

Another plant of overgrazed rangeland, also used by the Indians in their herb medicine, is **Broom Snakeweed**, *Gutierrezia sarothrae*. Like Gumweed, it has a variety of names indicating its sticky nature (Turpentine Weed), its use as an Indian snakebite remedy (Snakeweed), and the way in which its stems can be tied together and used as a broom (Broom-weed). It is a perennial, with a woody base and many slender, brittle stems clothed with narrow leaves. In late summer it bears many yellow flower heads in flat-topped inflorescences,

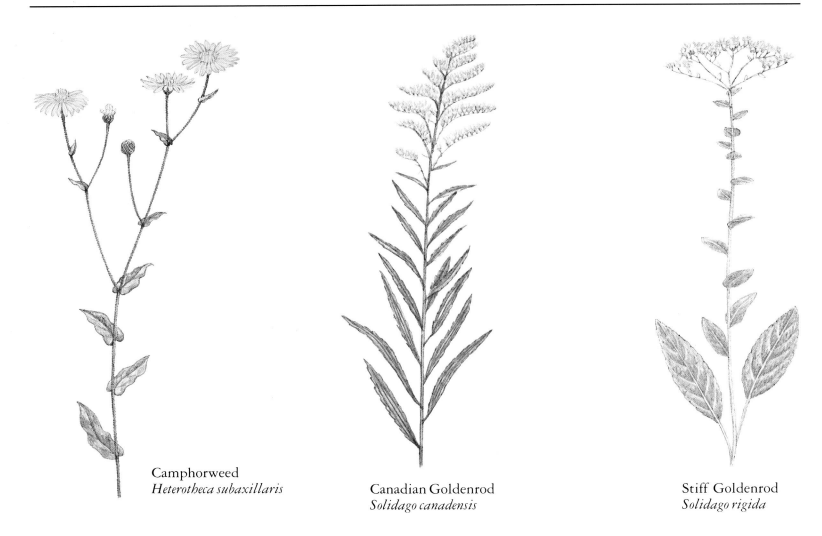

Camphorweed
Heterotheca subaxillaris

Canadian Goldenrod
Solidago canadensis

Stiff Goldenrod
Solidago rigida

like those of some goldenrods. Individual flower heads are tiny, with only 3–8 ray florets and the same number of disk florets in each. Plants grow in dry plains and foothills from Saskatchewan to Oregon, and south to California and Mexico, most commonly in the southwest where the shrubby plants may cover large areas.

Rabbit Brush, *Chrysothamnus nauseosus* (p. 195), is also found on overgrazed or eroded land. It grows on dry, open mountains, hills, and plains in the west, from British Columbia to Saskatchewan, south to Texas and California, and into Mexico. The much-branched, gray-white shrubs may cover large areas and prefer poor, especially alkaline soils. The plants are 2–3ft tall, with stems thickly covered in gray or white hairs, many linear leaves, and an aromatic, rather unpleasant scent. The late summer flowers resemble those of goldenrods; the yellow flower heads are narrow, formed only of disk florets, and borne in dense, terminal clusters. The fruits which follow have many dull white hairs. Rabbit Brush is one of about 12 *Chrysothamnus* species, a genus found only in western North America.

Camphorweed, *Heterotheca subaxillaris*, is another plant that grows on overgrazed rangeland, but this is an annual or biennial plant from the east and midwest. It has tall, leafy stems branching at the tips to bear a few yellow flower heads. It grows in dry, sandy soils, in prairies, on roadsides, and in waste places from Florida and Texas north to Delaware and Illinois, extending its range northward in recent years.

Goldenrods have plumes or spikes or flat-topped clusters of yellow flowers that glow in the woods and roadsides of late summer and fall, their freshness a surprise against the dusty, dull green or brown-tinged foliage of other plants fading toward winter. They are members of the genus *Solidago*, a large group difficult to separate and identify, with many hybrids to further confuse the issue. Estimates of the number of species in North America vary from about 70 to around 120, depending on the author. The majority are found in the east.

Goldenrods grow in a variety of habitats from mountain crevices to swamps and prairies, from pine barrens or dunes to moist, shady woods. They are perennial herbaceous plants with erect, leafy stems, varying in height from a few inches to 4ft tall. Their leaves are alternate and simple, often toothed in some way. The individual flower heads are small, with several layers of bracts forming a cup for the yellow ray florets and central yellow disk. The impact of the plant comes from the way in which these small flower heads are borne in large, striking inflorescences.

Although Goldenrods are difficult to identify, the form of the inflorescence, together with the shape and arrangement of the leaves, are features which can be used to sort them into groups. Many have plume-like inflorescences, with branches

Lance-leaved Goldenrod
Solidago graminifolia

Showy Goldenrod
Solidago speciosa

Slim Goldenrod
Solidago stricta

Wreath Goldenrod
Solidago caesia

Silver-rod
Solidago bicolor

arched or straight. The branches may be relatively short and densely packed with flower heads, or long and narrow with more loosely packed flower heads; the flower heads may be relatively large or small but are usually all on the upper side of the stem. Other species have narrow, erect, spike-like inflorescences, or the inflorescence, although erect, may be broad and more club-like; the flowers are often arranged all around each branch. A third kind of inflorescence is the flat-topped cluster, where the flower stalks growing from lower down the stem are longer than those higher up the stem. A few species have a zigzag arrangement where the flower heads are borne in clusters in leaf axils; since the leaves are alternate this gives the plant a zigzag appearance.

Canadian Goldenrod, *Solidago canadensis* (p. 196), has stems up to 5ft high, and lance-shaped, toothed leaves. It has large, plume-like inflorescences with arching branches, and each flower head has 10–17 ray florets. This is one of the most widespread species, growing in woodland clearings and open places across most of the U.S. and Canada, only missing from the southern states like Texas. Sweet Goldenrod, *S. odora*, is a similar species, with smooth, toothless leaves, and 3–5 rays on each flower head. This plant can be identified by the aniseed scent of its crushed leaves, which can be used to make a fragrant tea – a pleasant drink and a remedy for intestinal gas. The plant grows in dry, open woods in the eastern U.S.

Stiff Goldenrod, *Solidago rigida* (p. 196), gets its name from the hard, rigid, oval leaves which clasp the upper part of the stem. It grows about 5ft tall, making clumps of hairy, erect stems with large, long-stalked lower leaves, small upper leaves, and flat-topped clusters of flower heads. The heads are relatively large, each with 7–10 ray florets, and are arranged all along the upper side of each stem. Stiff Goldenrod is found in dry, open places, woods, and prairies from Connecticut to Alberta, south to Georgia and New Mexico, more commonly in the west. **Lance-leaved Goldenrod**, *S. graminifolia*, another common species with flat-topped inflorescences, has rough, willow-like leaves. It grows in damp, open places and beside streams.

Showy Goldenrod, *Solidago speciosa*, has a dense, pyramidal inflorescence made up of many ascending branches crowded with flower heads on all sides. Each flower head has 6–8 ray florets. This is one of the last goldenrods to flower, coming into bloom between August and October. It is a tall plant, with a thick, erect, rather reddish stem, and smooth, elliptical leaves. The leaves may have wavy margins but lack teeth. Showy Goldenrod grows in prairies and plains, fields, woods, and thickets from New Hampshire to Wyoming, and south to Georgia and Texas.

Slim Goldenrod, *Solidago stricta*, is a species with a tall, slender inflorescence terminating an erect stem about 6ft tall.

Stemless Goldenweed
Haplopappus acaulis

Tansy Aster
Machaeranthera tanacetifolia

Golden Aster
Chrysopsis villosa

New England Aster
Aster novae-angliae

The leaves are firm, long, and elliptical at the base of the stems, progressively reduced higher up, until they become like small bracts pressed against the stems just below the flower spike. Plants grow in moist places, in pine barrens and sandy places in the coastal plain from New Jersey to Florida and Texas. **Wreath Goldenrod**, *S. caesia* (p. 197), has clusters of flowers in the axils of narrow leaves; grows in woods from Nova Scotia to Wisconsin, south to Florida and Texas.

Silver-rod, *Solidago bicolor* (p. 197), is unusual among members of this genus, for the flower heads have white ray florets; the heads are borne in slim spikes terminating erect, grayish, leafy stems about 3ft tall. Plants grow in dry, open woods and on open, rocky slopes from Nova Scotia to Wisconsin, south to North Carolina and Missouri.

There are about 150 *Haplopappus* species, all found in the west, in North and South America. They are a variable group of herbs and shrubs, often with thick, glandular leaves. Their flowers are usually yellow, and may or may not have ray florets. Many are perennials with erect or sprawling stems, and difficult to distinguish from each other, but **Stemless Goldenweed**, *H. acaulis*, is rather different and easier to recognize. It has a taproot which branches at the top to produce numerous stems, each one with a dense group of leaves at the base and a solitary flower head at the top. The effect is of a tufted, leafy mat which may measure 2–3ft across, studded

in early summer with yellow flower heads. The leaves are narrow, linear or spoon-shaped, rigid and held erect, roughly hairy to the touch. Each flower head has 6–10 ray florets. This plant grows on dry, rocky ridges and slopes, from foothills to mountains, in sagebrush scrub and pine forests from California to Oregon, east to Colorado and Montana, then in dry, eroded hills into Saskatchewan.

Tansy Aster, *Machaeranthera tanacetifolia*, is another western plant growing in dry, open places in the plains and deserts from Alberta to South Dakota, and south to Mexico. Its name comes from its finely divided leaves, which resemble those of Tansy. It is an annual plant, with numerous flower heads, each one with many narrow, bright blue-purple ray florets around a yellow disk. This is one of about 20 western species of *Machaeranthera*, many of them rather similar, with spiny-edged leaves and blue or purple flowers; they are known as spine asters.

Golden Aster, *Chrysopsis villosa*, forms mounds of branched, leafy stems, at most 20in high, growing from a woody base. The gray color of the plant comes from the dense covering of hairs on the small, lance-shaped leaves, but in summer it turns yellow with numerous flower heads. The heads grow in small clusters on the ends of the branches; each has 10–16 ray florets which roll under as the flowers age. This plant grows in abundance in dry, open places, on roadsides, plains, and hills from Minnesota to British Columbia, south through the Great Plains and Rocky Mountains to Mexico. There are several other species of *Chrysopsis* in North America with similar golden flowers, some with grass-like leaves, others hairy like *C. villosa*. The name Golden Aster indicates the resemblance that some of them have to the true asters, but asters have pink, white or blue rather than yellow flowers.

Michaelmas Daisies or Asters, *Aster* species, are familiar garden plants which flower in late summer or fall. They are associated with harvest and thanksgiving, their purple, blue or white flowers contrasting with the yellows and bronzes of the season. Their popularity has grown during the course of this century, mainly with the development of the Ballard hybrids; today they come with flowers in many shades, in single and double forms, from tall, back-of-the-border plants to tight mounds for the front. The two wild species which have contributed most to their development are two North American species: the New York Aster, *Aster novae-belgii*, and the New England Aster, *A. novae-angliae*.

There are over 100 species of **Wild Asters** in North America. They are mostly perennial plants, with erect stems and simple, alternate leaves, bearing many small flower heads in late summer and fall. Their flowers are blue, white or purple, with narrow ray florets, and red, purple or yellow disk florets. The majority are found in the east and midwest.

The **New England Aster**, *Aster novae-angliae* (p. 198), grows in the wild in wet meadows and swamps from Quebec to Saskatchewan, and south to Alabama and New Mexico. It forms a clump of hairy stems up to 7ft tall, with many lance-shaped leaves, their bases clasping the stem. The flower heads are borne on long, sticky stalks growing in the upper leaf axils; they have many reddish-purple ray florets, 45–100 on each flower, and a central yellowish disk.

Smooth Aster, *Aster laevis*, is only 3ft tall, with smooth stems and leaves, often with a grayish bloom. Its leaves are small with clasping bases, and it has a terminal, open cluster of blue or purple flowers. Each flower has 15–25 ray florets and a yellow disk. This plant grows in dry, open places across southern Canada, and south to Georgia and New Mexico.

There are many *Aster* species with small white flowers, often distinguishable from each other only by technical characters; to complicate the issue, they hybridize as well. **Small White Aster**, *A. vimineus*, is typical of many. It forms clumps of erect stems 2–5ft tall, with many linear leaves, the lower ones toothed and the upper ones becoming progressively smaller. The flower heads are borne on many branches on the upper part of the stem. Each has 15–30 white rays and a yellow disk. Plants grow in moist, open places and wet meadows from Ontario to Maine and along the coastal plain, up the Mississippi River valley to Missouri and Ohio.

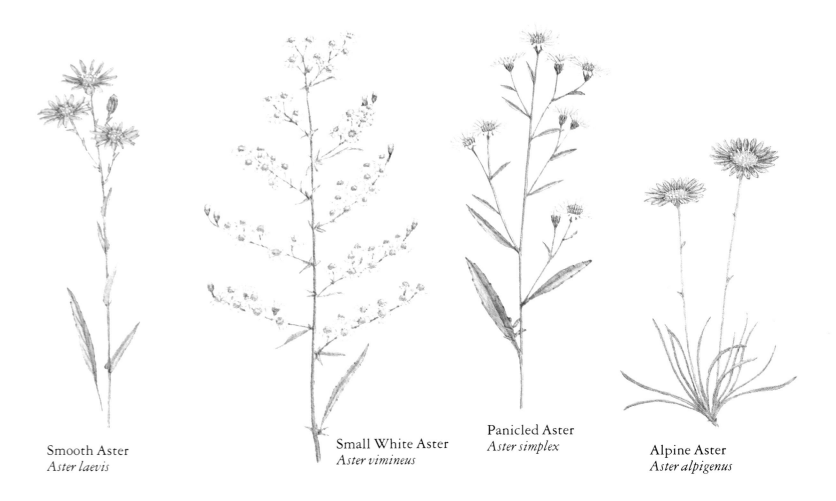

Smooth Aster
Aster laevis

Small White Aster
Aster vimineus

Panicled Aster
Aster simplex

Alpine Aster
Aster alpigenus

A species with larger white flowers is **Panicled Aster**, *Aster simplex* (p. 199). It is a smooth, colonial plant, with erect stems up to 5ft tall, stalkless, lance-shaped or linear leaves, and flower heads in long, leafy inflorescences. It grows in moist, low-lying places from Nova Scotia to North Dakota, south to Virginia and Texas.

Alpine Aster, *Aster alpigenus* (p. 199), is a rather different plant from the Pacific west. It forms tufts of grass-like leaves in moist mountain meadows, and in summer bears solitary pink or purple flower heads on leafless stalks.

The **Fleabanes**, *Erigeron* species, are another large group, with over 100 in North America. Several species are grown in gardens and there are many hybrids, with flowers in shades of pink and purple. One of their most attractive features is the large number of narrow ray florets in each flower, 100–200 being not uncommon; the rays are usually arranged in two rows. Fleabanes are not unlike asters and may be mistaken for them, except that fleabanes generally flower in spring and early summer, whereas asters flower in late summer and fall.

Common Fleabane, *Erigeron philadelphicus*, is typical, a biennial or perennial plant, with rosettes of narrowly ovate leaves, and erect, leafy stems up to 30in tall, ending in branched clusters of pink flower heads. Each head has 150 or more ray florets around a wide, yellow disk. This plant grows in fields and woods across southern Canada and much of the U.S. **Robin's Plantain**, *E. pulchellus*, is similar, but has soft, hairy leaves and shorter flowering stems with fewer, larger, usually blue flowers. It grows in woods from Maine to Minnesota, north into Ontario, south to Georgia and Texas.

Daisy Fleabane, *Erigeron annuus*, is a hairy, annual plant with a leafy stem and a terminal cluster of white, or sometimes pink, flower heads. Each head has 80–120 ray florets. This plant is a weed in northern and eastern U.S. and southern Canada, found in waste places, fields, and roadsides.

The **Seaside Daisy**, *Erigeron glaucus*, is a perennial fleabane, like many others. It has a fleshy base, with prostrate branches and many rosettes of spoon-shaped leaves. From these arise the leafy flowering stems, lying flat at the base and then turning upward to reach a height of about 15in, each one bearing a solitary, terminal flower head. Each head has about 100 lavender ray florets and a yellow disk. This is a Pacific coast plant, growing on sandhills and beaches, on bluffs and in coastal scrub, from Oregon to southern California. The slight succulence of the plant is a feature shared by many coastal plants.

Other perennial fleabanes are similar in their form, with a branched base and leaf rosettes, but most have a woody base. **Cut-leaved Daisy**, *E. compositus* (p. 200) is a dwarf species with crowded rosettes of glandular-hairy, fan-like leaves and solitary, rose-pink or whitish flowers. Each flower head has 25–50 ray florets. This is a mountain plant, growing on rocky

Common Fleabane
Erigeron philadelphicus

Robin's Plantain
Erigeron pulchellus

Daisy Fleabane
Erigeron annuus

Seaside Daisy
Erigeron glaucus

ridges and slopes in the Rocky Mountains from California and Arizona to Alaska, and in alpine fell-fields to Greenland.

Horseweed, *Conyza canadensis*, is one of those plants associated with disturbed ground, waste places, roadsides, and open fields. It cannot survive much competition with other plants. It grows across the U.S. and southern Canada, and because of its use in herb medicine, is now also found in Europe and other parts of the world. It is used as a remedy for diarrhea and to stop bleeding, and it also has insecticidal properties. It was known to the Indians long before its uses became more widely accepted. This is a coarse, bristly, annual plant, with a rosette of basal leaves at first, then a stem up to 5ft tall, very leafy with many lance-shaped, more or less toothed leaves. From the axils of the upper leaves grow clusters of tiny flowers, each one with minute, white ray florets and a yellow disk. The flowers are followed by tiny achenes, each capped by a tuft of white hairs.

Easter Daisy, *Townsendia exscapa*, is a dwarf, tufted plant, not unlike some of the fleabanes. It has dense clusters of narrow leaves, with pink or white flower heads nestled among them in early spring. This plant may be found in dry plains and open juniper and pinyon woods from the prairie states of southern Canada, south to Arizona and Texas. This is one of about 20 *Townsendia* species, all low-growing tufted plants, most from the Rocky Mountain region.

English Daisy, *Bellis perennis*, is an alien, an invader from Europe that may be found in grassy waste places and lawns throughout the U.S. It is a spreading plant, forming many small rosettes of spoon-shaped leaves, no more than 6in tall. In summer the rosettes produce numerous, solitary flower heads on slender, leafless stalks. The ray florets may be white or tinged with pink.

Wormwood, *Artemisia absinthium* (p. 202), is only one of several European members of this genus used as medicinal or kitchen herbs. Wormwood is definitely medicinal, being bitter and used to remedy digestive problems. All the species are aromatic, with an odor distinctive to each. There are many species of *Artemisia* in North America, some naturalized European species like Wormwood, which now grows wild in fields and waste places across southern Canada and the northern U.S. Others are native, especially to the west. They are herbs or shrubs with alternate leaves and small flower heads made up entirely of disk florets. The heads are gathered into large, complex inflorescences.

Big Sagebrush, the gray-green plant which covers so many of the valley floors in the Rocky Mountain area, is *Artemisia tridentata* (p. 202). Like many of the western species, it is an evergreen shrub, but is one of the biggest (up to 10ft tall). Its silver-gray leaves are wedge-shaped, with three teeth on the end, and have a characteristic, quite pleasant scent. Typically,

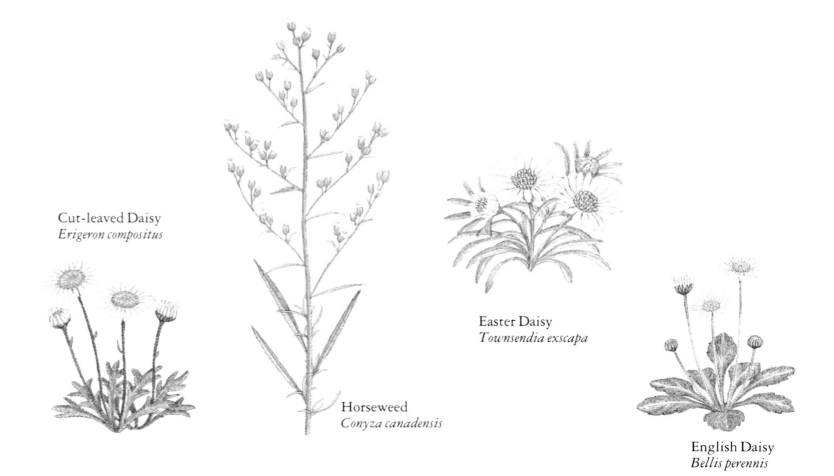

Cut-leaved Daisy
Erigeron compositus

Horseweed
Conyza canadensis

Easter Daisy
Townsendia exscapa

English Daisy
Bellis perennis

this shrub has a short, single trunk, then several sprawling branches which end in a mass of leafy stems. In late summer and fall tiny, yellow-white flower heads open in many dense, elongated clusters near the ends of the stems; their pollen is a common cause of hay fever. This plant has a long history of use in Indian medicine, mainly to treat stomach disorders and indigestion. It makes a good insect repellent.

Mugwort, *Artemisia vulgaris*, is a perennial European plant, now a weed of roadsides, waste places, and fields throughout most of the eastern U.S. and Canada. It has strong, erect stems with many clasping, deeply cleft leaves. These leaves are smooth and very dark green above, white with cottony hairs below. The plant produces many flower heads, growing from every leaf axil on long, branched, leafy stems; each head is reddish-brown, and inconspicuous. The plant is dull but also obvious with its dark and light leaves.

Yarrow, *Achillea millefolium*, is a plant that grows all around the northern hemisphere. It is aromatic, like the wormwoods, and is also used in herb medicine, yarrow tea being a good remedy for colds. Traditionally it was used as a wound herb. The Greek hero Achilles is supposed to have recommended it as an effective treatment for wounds made with iron weapons. It is very variable—tall in shady positions but flat to the ground in exposed sites, in a wide variety of habitats but most often in disturbed places like roadsides and

fields. It has many underground stems and creeps into large colonies if left alone, with soft, ferny, dark green leaves. The erect stems bear more or less flattened, terminal clusters of white flower heads. Each flower head is small, with roughly five broad ray florets and 10–20 disk florets.

Tansy, *Tanacetum vulgare*, is another European species, a medicinal plant brought to New England and naturalized in waste places, in fields, and on roadsides through much of the U.S. and southern Canada. Its name comes from the Greek word for immortal, and it was strewn over corpses to keep worms and flies away. Certainly it does repel insects; they seem not to like its bitter scent. It plays little part in modern herb medicine because an overdose can be fatal, but may be used as a wash for sprains and bruises. It is a perennial, with creeping underground stems and many erect, robust stems with soft, ferny leaves. When they are about 3–4ft tall, the stems bear terminal clusters of yellowish flower heads; the heads contain only disk florets, many packed densely together.

Mayweeds and **Chamomiles** are a confusing group, not least because they keep changing their botanical names. For instance, the old name for Chamomile, the plant used in Chamomile tea, is *Anthemis nobilis*, and it can still be found under this name in many herbal books. But it has been known more accurately for many years as *Chamaemelum nobilis*, and in botanical books is given this name.

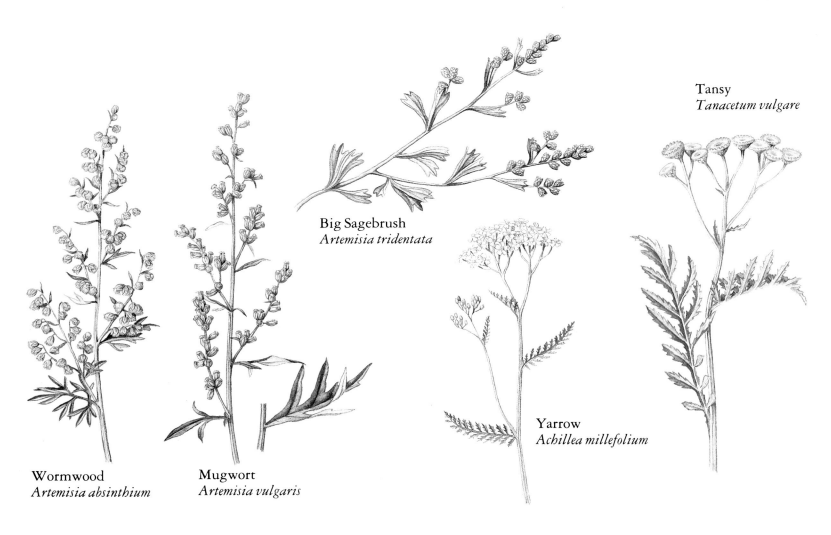

Big Sagebrush
Artemisia tridentata

Tansy
Tanacetum vulgare

Yarrow
Achillea millefolium

Wormwood
Artemisia absinthium

Mugwort
Artemisia vulgaris

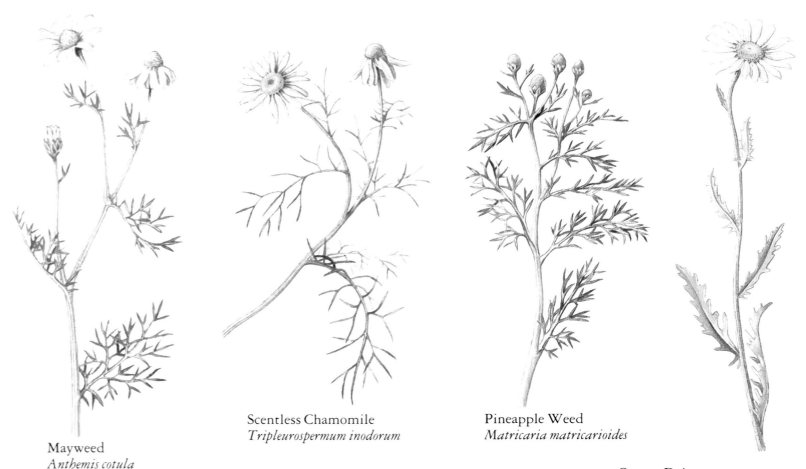

Mayweed
Anthemis cotula

Scentless Chamomile
Tripleurospermum inodorum

Pineapple Weed
Matricaria matricarioides

Ox-eye Daisy
Chrysanthemum leucanthemum

Mayweed or Stinking Chamomile, *Anthemis cotula*, is a common weed of fields, waste places, and roadsides in many parts of the world, including North America, although it originated in Europe. It has an unpleasant odor that comes from glands on its leaves (hence the name Stinking Chamomile), and their acrid secretion can cause blisters. This is an annual plant, with a branched, erect stem up to 2ft tall, and soft, finely dissected, quite smooth leaves. It bears white, daisy-like flowers in summer, with 10–20 sterile, white ray florets, and a dome-shaped, yellow disk.

Scentless Chamomile, *Tripleurospermum inodorum*, is one of those with several name changes in its past. It was thought to be an inland subspecies of *Matricaria maritima*, subsp. *inodora*, at one time, then was transferred into the genus *Tripleurospermum* as *T. maritima*, subsp. *inodorum*, and has recently been made into a full species as *T. inodorum*. These name changes may seem unimportant, and in a sense they are, for the plant remains the same even if the name alters. But the problem that arises when a plant has a history like this is tracking it down, for it may be found under any of these names in different books, and then it may appear that the books are describing different plants when, in fact, they are the same one with different names. Scentless Chamomile is an annual, almost scentless, hairless plant, with a branched, sprawling stem up to 2ft tall, and leaves so divided that their segments are linear.

In the latter part of summer it bears many daisy-like flowers, each with 12–25 white ray florets which droop as the flower ages, and a dome-shaped, yellow disk. It is native to Europe, but has become naturalized in roadsides and waste places in much of the northern U.S. and Canada.

Pineapple Weed, *Matricaria matricarioides*, can sometimes be found under the name *Chamomilla suaveolens*, making yet another contribution to the superabundance of names in this group. It is another weed, but a native one this time, at least in the west, introduced into the east and now found almost throughout the continent, except the extreme south. It grows in waste places and on roadsides. It is a scented, hairless, annual plant, with a branched, often sprawling stem only about 2ft tall, and pinnate leaves divided into linear segments. Its crushed foliage smells of pineapples. It bears many distinctive flower heads, each with a hollow, highly domed, greenish-yellow disk, and no ray florets. The disk is cupped by green bracts with papery edges.

The **Ox-eye Daisy**, *Chrysanthemum leucanthemum*, is not a weed or medicinal plant but a perennial grown in flower borders in many yards. It was originally found in Europe and Asia, but is now naturalized throughout much of the northern hemisphere, growing in fields, in waste places, and on roadsides, as well as in gardens. It forms spreading colonies of leaf rosettes from which grow erect stems up to 3ft tall, with

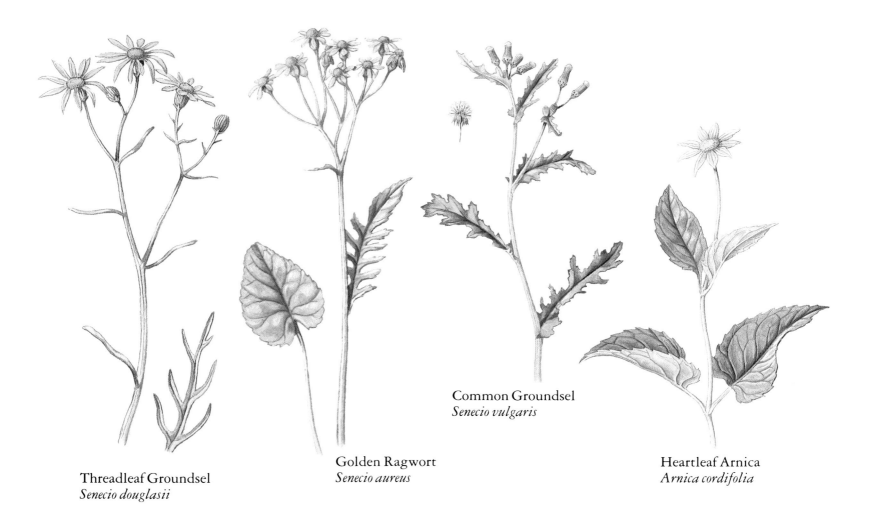

Threadleaf Groundsel
Senecio douglasii

Golden Ragwort
Senecio aureus

Common Groundsel
Senecio vulgaris

Heartleaf Arnica
Arnica cordifolia

dark green, pinnately divided leaves, the upper ones clasping the stem. Each stem bears a solitary, large, daisy-like flower, with 15–30 white ray florets and a flat, yellow disk. This plant is another with many names, common ones including Moon Daisy and Marguerite, and one large-flowered garden form is known as the Shasta Daisy. It has another Latin name too, *Leucanthemum vulgare*.

Groundsels, Ragworts, and **Butterweeds** all belong to the same genus, *Senecio*, united by botanical details of the flowers. This is a very large genus, with about 1000 species worldwide, including not only herbaceous plants, but also shrubs and climbers. There are nearly 100 species of *Senecio* in North America, the majority with bright yellow ray-floretted flowers. They often grow in wet places, swamps, streambanks, and wet woods, in bottomlands, prairies, and mountains, but some western ones are desert and scrub species.

Threadleaf Groundsel, *S. douglasii*, multiplies on rangeland because the cattle avoid it, and since it is toxic, its presence is unwelcome. It also grows on dry, rocky plains and deserts from Arizona and Colorado to Texas, south into Mexico. It is quite an attractive plant, with bushy clumps of branched stems 1–3ft tall and clothed with narrowly divided leaves, bluish-green in color, with woolly hairs when young. In summer it bears numerous yellow flower heads, each with a narrow disk and 10–13 ray florets.

Golden Ragwort, *Senecio aureus*, is a perennial, forming clumps of heart-shaped basal leaves. From the clumps grow erect stems up to 3ft tall, with irregularly toothed leaves and terminal, branched clusters of yellow flower heads. Each head is cupped in green, purple-tipped bracts, and has 8–12 ray florets and a yellow disk. The plant is found in swamps, wet meadows, and woods from Labrador to Minnesota, south to Georgia and Arkansas.

Some *Senecio* species are cosmopolitan weeds found throughout the world. **Common Groundsel**, *S. vulgaris*, is a familiar weed of back yards, waste places, and roadsides—disturbed environments everywhere. It is a small, annual plant, no more than 1ft tall, with a branched stem and irregularly toothed leaves. It bears many small flower heads, each one with a cup of green bracts and many yellow disk florets, so that the head resembles a shaving brush. After flowering, each head becomes a dome of white-haired fruits. This plant has several generations a year, and is so successful at colonizing that it may take over whole areas of waste ground or complete vegetable gardens if left to seed.

About 30 species of *Arnica* grow around the North Pole, many of them in Canada and in the western mountains in the U.S. The original Arnica of herbal medicine came from a plant in this genus, *Arnica montana* from Europe. It is still used as an effective treatment for bruises and strains. Some North

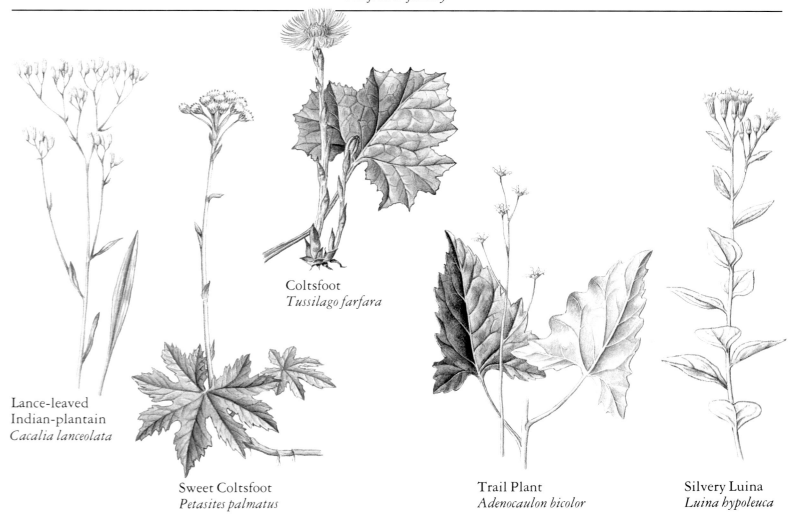

Lance-leaved
Indian-plantain
Cacalia lanceolata

Coltsfoot
Tussilago farfara

Sweet Coltsfoot
Petasites palmatus

Trail Plant
Adenocaulon bicolor

Silvery Luina
Luina hypoleuca

American arnica species have similar medicinal uses, including **Heartleaf Arnica**, *A. cordifolia* (p. 204), a widespread western species. It grows in open woods in the foothills and mountains from Alaska to California, east to Michigan and New Mexico. Like other western arnicas, this plant has opposite leaves, but is the only one with heart-shaped leaves; it grows in spreading colonies, forming stems up to 2ft tall, and bearing 1–3 terminal, yellow flower heads in early summer.

Lance-leaved Indian-plantain, *Cacalia lanceolata*, is one of several Indian-plantains, *Cacalia* species, found in the east, all perennial plants with erect stems, alternate leaves, and white flowers formed only of disk florets. Its stems grow up to 6ft tall; they bear large, lance-shaped leaves near the base and end in branched inflorescences of many flower heads in late summer. The plant grows in low-lying, wet pine barrens and savannahs, in the coastal plain from Florida to North Carolina.

Sweet Coltsfoot, *Petasites palmatus*, is a plant to be noticed, both in spring when it produces erect flowering stems, and later in summer when its large basal leaves emerge. It grows in wet, lowland meadows and damp woods, often in deep shade, all around the North Pole, across Canada, south to Massachusetts and Minnesota, and in the Coast Ranges to California. In spring its creeping rhizomes send up thick flowering shoots up to 2ft tall, covered with linear, parallel-veined bracts, and bearing terminal clusters of white or

pinkish flowers formed of disk florets and small ray florets. The leaves grow on long stalks and have broad, palmately lobed blades with dense white hairs on the underside; they grow up to 15in across.

Like Sweet Coltsfoot, **Coltsfoot**, *Tussilago farfara*, produces flowers on bare stems in early spring, and large leaves later in summer. The flower heads are yellow, formed only of ray florets, and borne singly on reddish, scaly stems only about 6in tall; they often appear in large clumps, for this plant spreads into wide colonies. The flowers are followed by clock-like fruits, and finally the leaves emerge, white-felted all over at first, remaining white-felted beneath as they unfurl. They are large and rounded, shallowly lobed, and deep green above once mature. This is a European plant, naturalized in waste ground and disturbed places in eastern Canada and the northeast U.S. It is rich in mucilage, and used both in herb medicine and in commercially produced cough medicines, for it is an effective remedy for coughs.

Trail Plant, *Adenocaulon bicolor*, is a western plant, growing in moist, shady woods in the Coast Ranges and Sierra Nevada from California to British Columbia, and across the continent to Michigan. It forms perennial colonies of erect stems up to 3ft tall, leafy near the base, with large, thin, triangular leaves, green above and white-woolly beneath. In the latter half of summer clusters of tubular white flowers appear on the

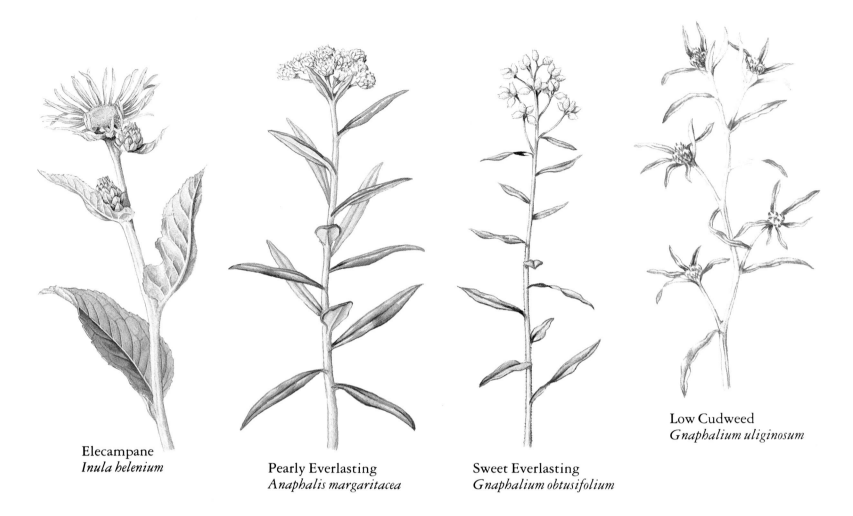

Elecampane
Inula helenium

Pearly Everlasting
Anaphalis margaritacea

Sweet Everlasting
Gnaphalium obtusifolium

Low Cudweed
Gnaphalium uliginosum

branched upper parts of the stems, to be followed by sticky clinging achenes.

Silvery Luina, *Luina hypoleuca* (p. 205), has white-woolly stems and white wool on the undersides of the leaves. The upper surface of the leaves is greenish but still woolly. This is a perennial plant, with erect stems up to 15in tall, many elliptical leaves, and dull yellow flower heads growing in branched clusters at the tops of the stems. It is found in dry, rocky places on the slopes of the Cascades and westward, from California to British Columbia but it is not a common plant.

Elecampane, *Inula helenium*, is an ancient herbal plant, known to the Greeks and Romans, and used since then in the treatment of bronchitis, asthma, and other chest complaints. In its native Europe it is also used in the preparation of absinthe. In North America it now grows wild from Quebec to Minnesota, south to North Carolina and Missouri. It favors damp places on roadsides, fields, and waste places, especially on rough ground, not a common plant but a widely scattered one. It is a stout perennial, with a basal rosette of pointed-ovate leaves, each up to 18in long, and thick stems up to 6ft tall bearing smaller leaves, their bases clasping the stem. The stems and the undersides of the leaves are softly hairy. The stems branch near the top to bear clusters of bright yellow flower heads that resemble small sunflowers; each head has a yellow disk and narrow ray florets.

Some members of the daisy family have flowers with a curious texture, like paper. They are often known as **Everlasting Flowers**, for their naturally dry blooms last long beyond the normal time span of most flowers. Some are used in dried arrangements, like **Pearly Everlasting**, *Anaphalis margaritacea*, which is grown in gardens as well as being a native plant. In the wild it grows in dry, open places across Canada and the northern U.S., south to North Carolina, Kansas, and California. It forms patches of erect stems, only 2–3ft tall at most, both stems and linear leaves covered with white woolly hairs that give it a pale green appearance. The flower heads grow in branched clusters at the tops of the stems, male and female flowers on separate plants. Each head is globe-shaped, with a central group of yellow disk florets surrounded by white, papery bracts. It is these which give the flowers their texture and which last so long.

The **Cudweeds**, *Gnaphalium* species, are a whole group of plants with everlasting flowers, approximately 100 species altogether, about 25 in North America. They are found throughout the continent and are woolly-haired plants, with alternate, entire leaves and complex branched clusters of whitish or yellowish flower heads, all formed of disk florets. The bracts which surround the flower heads may be completely papery or may have only papery tips. **Sweet Everlasting**, *G. obtusifolium*, has fragrant flowers, as might be expected from its name. It is an annual plant, similar to Pearly Everlasting but less showy, with whitish hairs on its stems, and linear leaves, yellow-white flower heads, and papery bracts beneath the heads. This is an eastern and midwestern species found in dry, open places from Nova Scotia to Manitoba, south to Florida and Texas.

Low Cudweed, *Gnaphalium uliginosum* (p. 206), is found not only across North America, but in Europe as well. It favors streambanks, damp waste places, roadsides, and ditches, especially on acid soils. It grows across Canada and into the U.S., south as far as Indiana and Virginia in the east. It is a small, inconspicuous plant, almost a weed, an annual with gray woolly stems and leaves. Its stem is branched, with many overlapping linear leaves, the whole plant no more than 8in tall. In late summer curious, little, brownish-white flower heads are borne in small clusters in the axils of the leaves and terminating the stems.

Pussytoes, *Antennaria* species, also have flowers which answer to the description of "everlasting." They are a group of about 30 species, many found in North America. These are small, perennial, woolly-stemmed plants, mostly with basal rosettes of simple leaves and erect flowering stems. The stem leaves are few and may be reduced to little more than scales, and the flower heads are borne in dense, terminal clusters. **Plantain-leaved Pussytoes**, *A. plantaginifolia*, is found in open woods and dry places from Quebec to Minnesota, south to Florida and Texas. It makes spreading mats of leaf rosettes, green on the upper surface, white silky-haired beneath. Its flower-bearing stems grow up to 15in tall, and in summer have terminal clusters of white flower heads spotted with crimson styles and often with pinkish bracts.

Some of the *Antennaria* species are grown in rock gardens, especially varieties of the mat-forming **Rosy Everlasting**, *A. rosea*, which have deep pink bracts around the flower heads and gray-felted leaves. This is quite a common plant in the wild, growing in a variety of more or less wooded places in the mountains from California to Alaska, and across Canada to Ontario. Most of the plants are female.

Marsh Fleabane, *Pluchea purpurascens*, may be annual or perennial. It has erect, leafy stems up to 3ft tall, with glandular-hairy, lance-shaped or ovate leaves, and terminal, flat-topped clusters of pinkish-purple flowers in late summer. The flowers are formed only of disk florets and, like everlasting flowers, can be used in dried arrangements. This plant grows in salt marshes in the coastal states from Massachusetts to Florida, and in California. It may also be found occasionally in freshwater marshes and inland in Michigan and Kansas. It has a slight scent of camphor, but nothing like as strong as the similar Camphorweed, *P. camphorata*. This foul-scented plant grows in moist woods and ditches in the southeast.

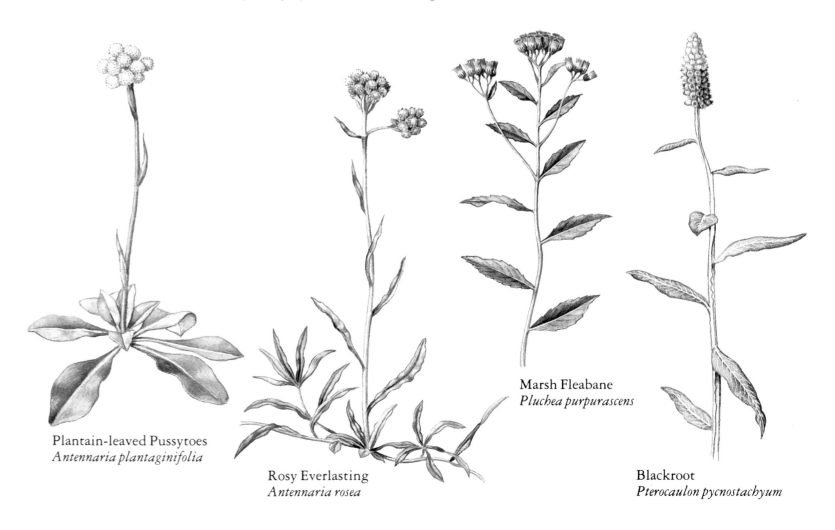

Plantain-leaved Pussytoes
Antennaria plantaginifolia

Rosy Everlasting
Antennaria rosea

Marsh Fleabane
Pluchea purpurascens

Blackroot
Pterocaulon pycnostachyum

Blackroot, *Pterocaulon pycnostachyum* (p. 207), gets its name from its large, tuberous, black roots. It is a perennial plant, with erect stems 2–3ft tall, and alternate, lance-shaped leaves densely covered with fine hairs. The flower heads are very small and gathered into cylindrical spikes terminating the stems. Plants may be found in pine barrens and open, sandy places in the coastal plain from North Carolina to Florida.

There are about 20 species of **Thoroughworts**, white-flowered members of the genus *Eupatorium*, in eastern North America. They are perennial plants flowering in late summer and fall, their fuzzy flowering heads borne in complex, branched clusters at the tops of erect, leafy stems. The leaves are entire and grow in opposite pairs. Their flower heads contain only disk florets. They are best identified by leaf shape, but since they hybridize, this is not always easy. Leaves vary in shape from linear to round, and may clasp the stem, lack stalks, or have distinct stalks.

White Snakeroot, *Eupatorium rugosum*, has pointed-ovate, serrated leaves on slender stalks, and flat-topped clusters of flower heads at the tops of the stems. It grows in rich woods and thickets from Nova Scotia to Saskatchewan, south to Georgia and Texas. This plant is poisonous and may be lethal to grazing animals. The poison can be transmitted to people or young animals in milk and butter, and retains its lethal potential in the process.

Boneset, *Eupatorium perfoliatum*, is a plant well known to American Indians and to later settlers for its usefulness in reducing fever and as a tonic; it was used by the Indians as a treatment for malaria before modern drugs became available, and can still be effective in reducing the symptoms of colds and flu. Boneset forms clumps of hairy, leafy stems up to 5ft tall, its opposite leaves distinctive for the way their bases join so that the stem seems to grow through them. The leaves are large and wrinkled, lance-shaped with serrated margins. At the tops of the stems the flower clusters branch to form flat, spreading masses of white flower heads. This plant grows in moist places, in low ground, in prairies and wet, low-lying woods, in marshes, on shores, and along estuaries from Nova Scotia to Manitoba, and south to Florida and Louisiana.

The **Joe-pye Weeds** are also *Eupatorium* species, but have pink or purple flowers. There are several species growing in moist places in the east, like *Eupatorium maculatum*. This can be quite a large plant, with stout stems 6ft tall, streaked and spotted with purple, and whorls of 3–5 lance-shaped leaves. Its fuzzy purple flowers open in the latter half of summer in dense, flat-topped clusters terminating the stems. It grows in damp meadows and woods, especially in calcareous soils, from Newfoundland to British Columbia, south through the northern U.S., to Maryland in the east, to Illinois, and to New Mexico in the west.

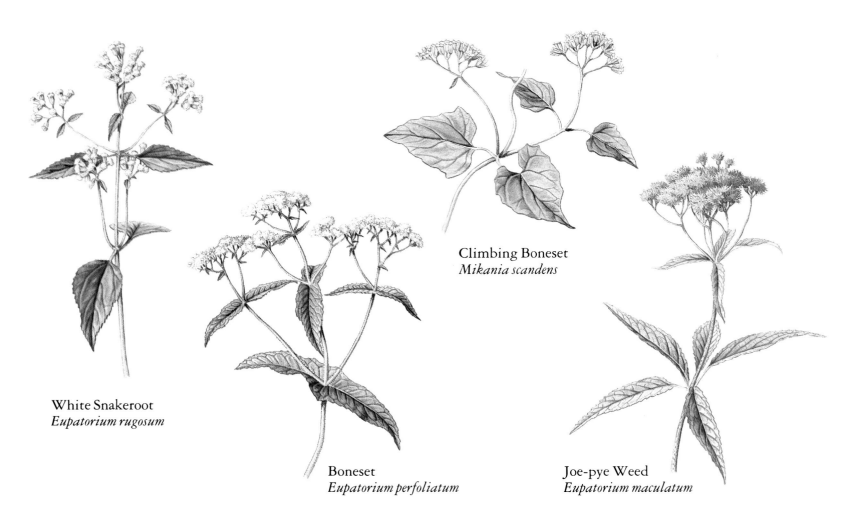

White Snakeroot
Eupatorium rugosum

Boneset
Eupatorium perfoliatum

Climbing Boneset
Mikania scandens

Joe-pye Weed
Eupatorium maculatum

Climbing Boneset or Climbing Hempweed, *Mikania scandens* (p. 208), is a twining, perennial vine which forms extensive aerial "carpets" over other plants with its intertwining, tangled stems and opposite, pointed heart-shaped leaves. All through the summer it produces flat-topped clusters of white or pinkish flowers growing in the leaf axils and resembling those of Boneset. It may be found in moist woods and along streams, usually near the coast, from Maine to Florida and Texas, on into tropical America.

Blazing Stars, *Liatris* species, are also known as Gayfeathers, both good names for plants with bright purple, fluffy flowers. They are perennials, mostly found in dry, open places, in open woods, barrens, and prairies in the east and midwest. Each plant has a clump of simple basal leaves and leafy stems bearing long spikes of purple flower heads. They tend to flower in late summer and fall. **Rough Blazing Star**, *L. aspera*, is one of the most widespread species, found from Ontario to North Dakota, south to the Carolinas and Texas.

Several *Liatris* species are used in herb medicine. **Dense Blazing Star**, *L. spicata*, is used as a gargle for sore throats. It has narrow, dense flower spikes and linear leaves; it grows in moist meadows from New York to Michigan, and south to Florida and Louisiana. Scaly Blazing Star, *L. squarrosa*, is said to be helpful in treating rattlesnake bites. Some of the showiest species are grown in flower gardens, including the **Prairie**

Blazing Star, *L. pycnostachya*, and Dense Blazing Star, *L. spicata*. They always attract comment for the unusual way the flowers open within the spike, from the top downward.

There are almost 100 *Brickellia* species, sometimes called **Brickellbushes**, in western North and South America, occurring mostly in the warmer regions. They are a variable group; many are much-branched shrubs, others are perennials or annual herbs. **Large-flowered Brickellbush**, *B. grandiflora*, is one of the most widespread and one of the few to penetrate into Canada. It is a perennial herbaceous plant, with erect stems up to 2ft tall, and pointed heart-shaped leaves growing on long stalks. In the latter half of summer the flower heads appear in little nodding clusters on side branches in the leaf axils and terminating the stems; they are pale yellow or greenish and contain only disk florets cupped in bracts striped green and yellow. This plant grows in rocky places, on slopes and cliffs in many parts of the Rocky Mountains from California just into British Columbia. Farther east it occurs in canyons and on hillsides as far as Nebraska and New Mexico.

The **Ironweeds** are a group of about 15 species belonging to the genus *Vernonia*, found in woods and prairies of the east and midwest. At one time certain species were used in herb medicine, and still may be found in herbals, recommended for stimulating appetite and aiding digestion. In appearance they resemble Joe-pye Weeds, but have alternate leaves and more

Rough Blazing Star
Liatris aspera

Dense Blazing Star
Liatris spicata

Prairie Blazing Star
Liatris pycnostachya

Large-flowered Brickellbush
Brickellia grandiflora

open flower clusters. They are perennials, with erect stems growing 3–6ft tall, simple leaves, and complex clusters of purple flower heads in late summer and fall. The heads contain only disk florets. **New York Ironweed**, *V. noveboracensis*, grows by streams, in marshes, and wet woods from Massachusetts along the coastal plain to Florida and Mississippi.

Elephant's Foot, *Elephantopus tomentosus*, is a southeastern species, a distinctive perennial with a flat leaf rosette. The leaves are large, up to 1ft long and 6in wide, softly hairy beneath. In late summer an erect stem grows from the center of this rosette, branching to bear small clusters of pink flower heads cupped in conspicuous bracts. The heads have disk flowers only. The plant grows in dry woods from Florida to Texas, north to Virginia, Kentucky, and Oklahoma.

There are over 60 **Thistles** belonging to the genus *Cirsium* in North America. They are spiny plants, with alternate, toothed or divided leaves, usually with prickles on their margins. Their flower heads are formed only of disk florets cupped in a series of bracts forming a structure known as an involucre; in many species at least some of the bracts are tipped with spines. The achenes bear several rows of feathery hairs.

Bull Thistle, *Cirsium vulgare*, and Canada Thistle, *C. arvense*, are not native American plants, despite the common name of the latter species. They come from Europe, where they are minor weeds found on roadside verges and waste land, but not presenting major problems or invading crops in large numbers. By contrast, in North America they have spread rapidly throughout the continent, invading and taking over large areas to the detriment of crop plants. They illustrate a well-known principle—that in their native lands plants are controlled by the insects that feed on them, but in a strange land where these insects are absent, the plants lack natural controls and can become pests. In Europe many insects feed on these thistles, weakening the plants, curtailing their seed production, and slowing their spread.

Canada Thistle, *Cirsium arvense*, forms spreading colonies with many erect stems in fields and waste places. The plants grow up to 5ft tall, have many wavy, lobed, spiny-edged leaves, and bear flower heads, either singly or in small clusters, in the axils of the upper leaves. The heads are pale purple, each cupped in an involucre of spine-tipped bracts. The flowers are followed by many achenes with dull brownish hairs; these are borne away by the wind to form fresh colonies.

Bull Thistle, *Cirsium vulgare*, is a biennial plant, with a rosette of deeply divided, wavy, spine-tipped leaves in the first year, and a flowering stem in the second. This grows to 5ft tall and has wings running along its length adorned with long spines; its many leaves are large, deeply lobed, and spine-tipped, with shorter spines on the upper surface. The flower heads are solitary or borne in small clusters on long stalks in

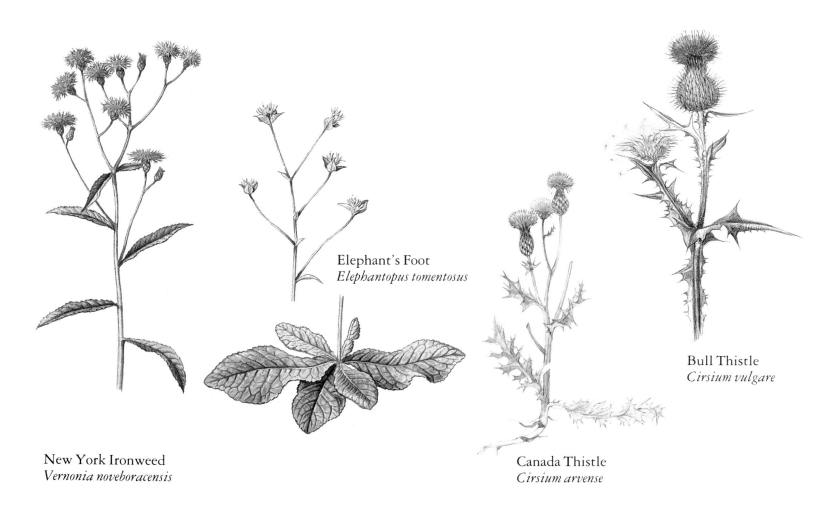

Elephant's Foot
Elephantopus tomentosus

Bull Thistle
Cirsium vulgare

New York Ironweed
Vernonia noveboracensis

Canada Thistle
Cirsium arvense

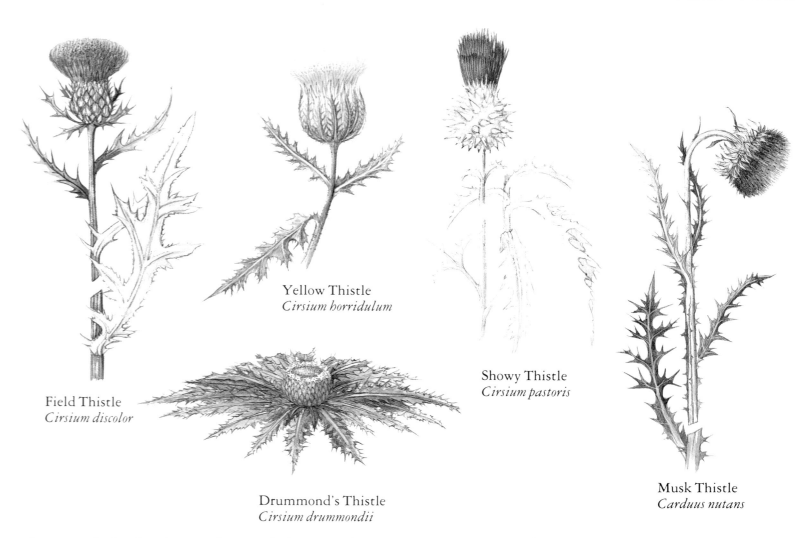

Field Thistle
Cirsium discolor

Yellow Thistle
Cirsium horridulum

Showy Thistle
Cirsium pastoris

Musk Thistle
Carduus nutans

Drummond's Thistle
Cirsium drummondii

the upper leaf axils; they are large and showy, with spiny involucres and red-purple florets.

Field Thistle, *Cirsium discolor*, is a native species similar in appearance to Bull Thistle in that it has solitary purple flower heads at the tops of erect stems; these may grow up to 9ft tall. There are spiny bracts beneath the involucre of each flower head. The leaves are large with spiny margins, and are white-woolly beneath. The plant grows in open woods and river bottoms, in waste places and fields from New Brunswick to Manitoba, south to Kansas and Virginia.

Yellow Thistle, *Cirsium horridulum*, is another native species, this one usually with yellow flowers. It grows on roadsides and in fields, also along shores and on the edges of salt marshes, mostly in the coastal plain from Maine to Florida and Texas. It is often found in overgrazed pastures. This is probably a biennial plant, with a large rosette of divided, spiny leaves, and an erect stem reaching 4ft in height. The stem is covered with short white hairs, has similar leaves to those in the rosette, and also has several large flower heads, each one surrounded by smaller, narrow, spiny leaves held erect. Although usually yellow, the flowers may be purple, especially on plants growing in the south or further inland.

Showy Thistle, *Cirsium pastoris*, is a western species. It is a showy plant, as its name implies, with an erect stem up to 4ft tall, bright white and woolly in color and texture, with many white-woolly, prickly leaves. The flower heads are crimson and borne in spiky, white involucres. This plant grows on dry slopes, in grassland, among brush, or in open woods from California to Oregon and Nevada.

Drummond's Thistle, *Cirsium drummondii*, is another western species, but quite distinctive for it is virtually stemless, forming flat rosettes of spiny leaves, each with a white or pale pink-purple flower head in the center in late summer. This thistle grows in meadows and other damp places in woods in the Rocky Mountains and Sierra Nevada from California to British Columbia.

Not all thistles belong to the genus *Cirsium*. Some belong to another genus, *Carduus*, the difference being in several botanical details. One of the easiest to see is that the hairs on the achenes of *Carduus* species are simple and unbranched instead of feathery as in *Cirsium* species, but even so, a hand lens is required to see this clearly.

Musk Thistle or Nodding Thistle, *Carduus nutans*, is another introduction from Europe, growing on roadsides and in waste places in many parts of the U.S. and southern Canada. This is a biennial thistle, with a rosette of wavy, spiny leaves in the first year, and an erect flowering stem up to 3ft tall in the second. Its stem is winged, but the wings end some distance below the flower heads. The stem leaves are deeply dissected, with spiny tips; and the flower heads are nodding, formed of

Scotch Thistle
Onopordon acanthium

Milk Thistle
Silybum marianum

Blessed Thistle
Cnicus benedictus

purple disk florets, and surrounded by large, reflexed, spine-tipped bracts. The name of Musk Thistle refers to the scent of the plant when warmed by the sun.

Scotch Thistle, *Onopordon acanthium*, is similar to some of the *Cirsium* species, with erect stems up to 5ft tall, large, prickly-margined leaves near the base of the stem, and solitary flower heads terminating the many branches at the top of the stem. The heads are purple and cupped in a rounded involucre of spiny bracts. The plant comes originally from Europe, but may be found scattered on roadsides and in waste places over much of the U.S.

The **Milk Thistle**, *Silybum marianum*, grows as a weed in waste places scattered through much of the U.S. and southern Canada, but is only really common in California. It is native to the Mediterranean area of Europe and is happiest in the south. It is an annual or biennial plant, with a rosette of shining, white-mottled, lobed leaves with spiny margins. The erect stem grows up to 4ft tall, has smaller, clasping leaves, and in early summer it produces large, solitary, nodding flower heads, with red-purple florets. The plant is used in herb medicine and homeopathy for the treatment of liver complaints. It was at one time thought to increase the flow of milk in nursing mothers, hence Milk Thistle.

Blessed Thistle, *Cnicus benedictus*, is a distinctive plant, its flower heads quite unlike those of other thistles. It forms a branched, erect, brown stem about 2ft tall, with many lobed, spiny-margined, white-veined leaves. A single yellow flower head is produced at the top of each stem branch; the head is cupped in several rows of bracts, green and white-veined with spreading spines at their tips. This is a southern European plant, found occasionally in waste places throughout the U.S. and southern Canada. It was probably introduced for its medicinal properties, as it was thought to be a cure for all ills. It still has a use in the treatment of headaches and infections, and as a tonic for the digestive system.

There are over 20 *Centaurea* species in North America, known commonly as **Knapweeds** or Star-thistles, many of them European aliens which have escaped and become naturalized. Some of the most attractive species are grown in gardens; in the showiest of these the outermost florets are enlarged and may be dissected into linear segments. Knapweeds may be annual or perennial plants, with alternate or basal leaves; often they have relatively few flower heads terminating the erect stems. Their flower heads are distinctive, formed entirely of conspicuous, pink or purple, tubular florets, with several series of dark bracts forming the involucre beneath the head; the bracts may have papery edges or may be spine-tipped.

Spotted Knapweed, *Centaurea maculosa* (p. 212), is a European plant that now grows in fields, pastures, and

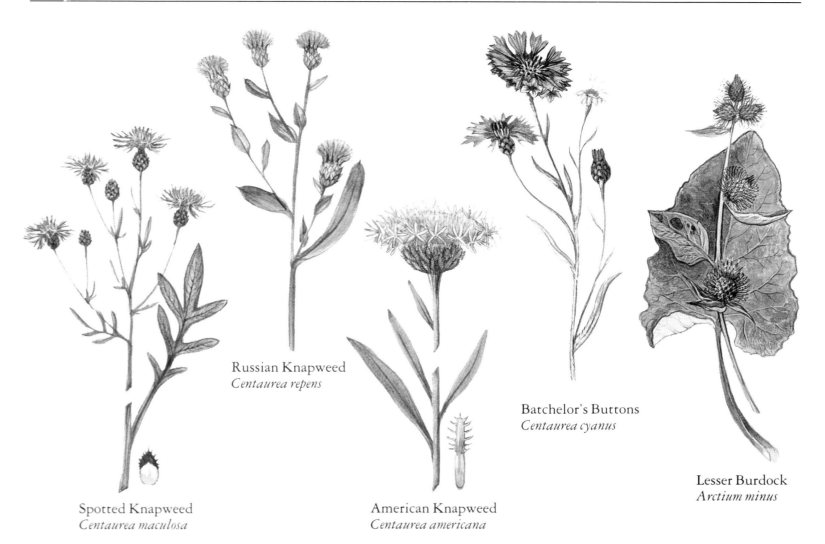

Russian Knapweed
Centaurea repens

Batchelor's Buttons
Centaurea cyanus

Lesser Burdock
Arctium minus

Spotted Knapweed
Centaurea maculosa

American Knapweed
Centaurea americana

roadsides in eastern areas of the U.S. and Canada, usually on basic or neutral soils. It is a biennial plant up to 4ft tall, with many wiry, much-branched stems. Its dissected, linear leaves are largest at the base of the plant and become simpler near the tops of the stems. Its many flower heads have involucres formed of black-tipped bracts, and the florets are pink-purple, tubular in form, with the outer ones enlarged and divided. **Russian Knapweed**, *C. repens*, came originally from Asia, but is now established in the west from the Pacific coast east to Michigan and Missouri. It has slender, branched stems, narrow leaves, and many small purple flower heads. The florets in the heads are all the same.

American Knapweed, *Centaurea americana*, is a large native species with very large flower heads. It grows up to 4ft tall, has narrow leaves, bristle-tipped bracts in the involucre, and solitary flower heads 2–3in across terminating the stems. The heads have tubular pink florets in the center, and larger, paler pink florets around the margins. This plant grows in prairies and plains from Missouri to Kansas, south to Louisiana and Arizona.

Batchelor's Buttons, *Centaurea cyanus*, is a plant with a long history as an agricultural weed, especially in its native Europe, but it is now far less common in the wild than it was before the advent of modern farming methods. However, since it is also a favorite garden plant, it is unlikely to become

extinct. Batchelor's Buttons is an annual, with an erect, wiry, grooved stem up to 3ft tall, many slender branches, and a cottony texture, especially when young. It has linear leaves and many flower heads with tubular florets, mostly blue but also pink and white, especially in garden varieties. The marginal florets are much enlarged and conspicuous. The plant grows in fields, waste places, and on roadsides across southern Canada and in much of the U.S.

Lesser Burdock, *Arctium minus*, and Greater Burdock, *A. lappa*, are weeds in many parts of North America, as well as in their native Europe, growing in waste places and on roadsides. Lesser Burdock grows to about 5ft tall (whereas Greater Burdock may grow twice as tall), and forms a bushy plant with reddish, often cottony stems, and large, long-stalked, pointed-ovate and rather heart-shaped lower leaves; the leaves become smaller and less heart-shaped higher up the plant. The flower heads have red-purple, tubular florets and hooked bracts making up the involucre. The fruits are hooked "burs," which cling to animal fur and to clothing, providing great entertainment for the younger members of the family! Their purpose is to ensure dispersal of the plant. In Lesser Burdock the flower heads are generally less than 1in across and borne in tight clusters on short stalks in the leaf axils; in Greater Burdock the heads are generally more than 1¼ in across. Burdocks are used in herb medicine to purify the blood, and in

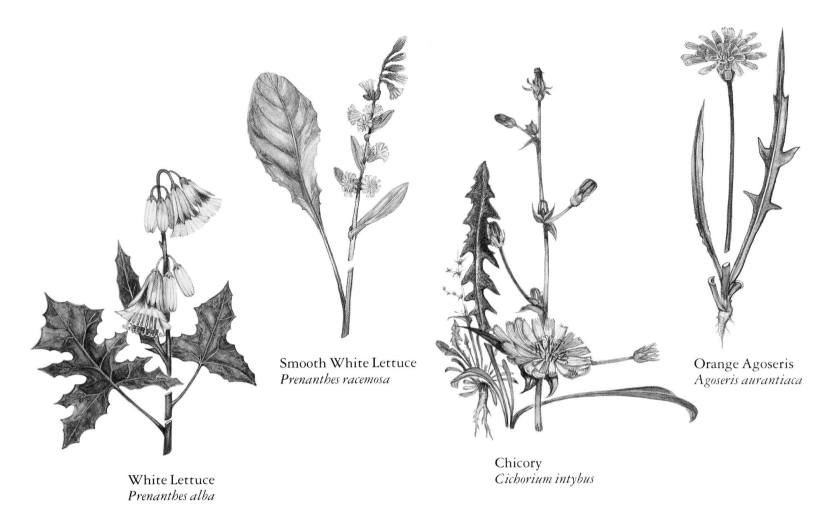

Smooth White Lettuce
Prenanthes racemosa

Orange Agoseris
Agoseris aurantiaca

Chicory
Cichorium intybus

White Lettuce
Prenanthes alba

poultices to relieve inflammation. They are high in Vitamin C, and young leaves and roots can be eaten as vegetables.

White Lettuce, *Prenanthes alba*, is one of about 15 *Prenanthes* species found in North America, mainly in the east, but also in the midwest and southern Canada. They are perennial plants filled with milky juice; they have erect, leafy stems and characteristic, nodding, bell-like flower heads formed only of ray florets. Their leaves are alternate and large, often deeply lobed or toothed. White Lettuce is also called Rattlesnake-root, since at one time it was believed to be of use in treating snake bites; the leaves are still used to alleviate insect bites. The plant grows in woods from Quebec to Manitoba, south to Virginia and Missouri. It has an erect, purplish, white-bloomed stem up to 5ft tall, with triangular, often lobed lower leaves, and lance-shaped upper ones. Its nodding flower heads are usually yellow-white, but may be pinkish; they hang in clusters near the top of the stem.

Smooth White Lettuce, *Prenanthes racemosa*, is a hairless plant with purplish flower heads in narrow spikes. It grows beside streams and in moist prairies from Quebec to Alberta, south to New Jersey and Colorado.

Chicory, *Cichorium intybus*, is one of those cosmopolitan weeds originally from Eurasia, now spread throughout much of the temperate world in waste places, fields, and on roadsides. It is a striking plant, with its bright blue flowers

catching the eye even from a moving automobile. In Europe the plant is grown commercially. Its young shoots are eaten in salads and make a good vegetable; the roots are ground and roasted, and added to coffee or used alone as a coffee substitute. This is also a medicinal plant, stimulating liver action and aiding digestion. It is a perennial, with a branched stem up to 4ft tall, alternate, wavy-toothed leaves forming a basal rosette, and similar, alternate clasping ones on the stem, and with many flower heads composed entirely of strap-shaped florets growing in clusters in the upper leaf axils.

There are about 10 *Agoseris* species in the Rocky Mountain area of western North America, where they are known as **Mountain Dandelions**. They are very similar to the true Dandelion, with a basal rosette of linear leaves, toothed in some species, and flower heads borne singly on leafless stalks; they also exude milky juice like a dandelion, but are less succulent in texture. Their flower heads are formed solely of ray florets, and most of the species have yellow flowers. However, **Orange Agoseris**, *A. aurantiaca*, has striking, burnt orange ones which turn purple or deep pink as they age. This plant grows in moist, grassy places within coniferous forests in the Sierra Nevada and the Rocky Mountains from British Columbia to California.

Desert Dandelion, *Malacothrix glabrata* (p. 215), is one of about 15 *Malacothrix* species in western North America, many

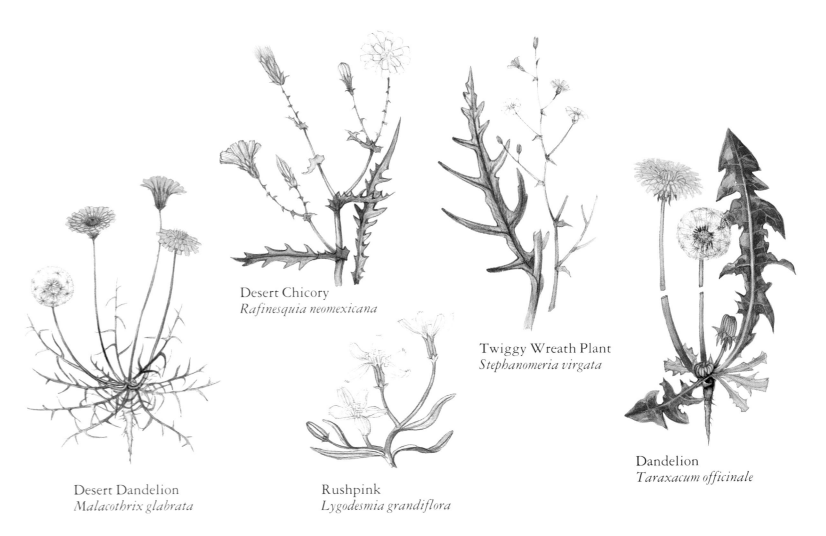

Desert Chicory
Rafinesquia neomexicana

Twiggy Wreath Plant
Stephanomeria virgata

Dandelion
Taraxacum officinale

Desert Dandelion
Malacothrix glabrata

Rushpink
Lygodesmia grandiflora

of them from dry, sandy places, deserts and coastal sage scrub, dry, grassy plains and washes. They have rosettes of toothed or divided basal leaves; their usually leafless flowering stems may bear a loose cluster of flower heads or only one; and their flower buds commonly nod before they open. Most have yellow flowers, but a few species have white ones. Desert Dandelion has narrow leaves deeply divided into narrow, linear segments; its flowering stems have few branches, each one with two or more flower heads, opening one after the other. It grows in dry, sandy plains and washes, among scrub, in the deserts and interior valleys from Oregon to Idaho, south to California and Mexico. It flowers in spring, and in wet years may form carpets of yellow flowers in the deserts.

Desert Chicory, *Rafinesquia neomexicana*, is another western desert plant, found in canyons or shaded by scrub in deserts from California to Texas, and north to Utah. It is an annual, with a few sparse branches to its weak stems, pinnately divided leaves at the base of the stems, and a few smaller ones higher up. The flower heads are fragrant, borne singly at the tops of the branched stems; each one is large, over an inch across, and formed of white ray florets.

Twiggy Wreath Plant, *Stephanomeria virgata*, is one of about 12 *Stephanomeria* species, all found in western North America. It is a stiff, annual plant with straight branched stems; the lower stems bear spoon-shaped leaves that wither

before flowering. Farther up the stems the leaves are small and linear, and the uppermost branches lack leaves but bear pinkish flower heads in late summer. The flowers are followed by achenes which bear long white hairs. This plant grows in disturbed places and fields, on the coastal strand, in sage scrub and in many other similar places from California to Oregon and Nevada.

Rushpink, *Lygodesmia grandiflora*, has branched stems only 20in tall at most, with linear leaves and pink flower heads at the tops of the stems. The heads are formed of 5–10 ray florets only, and somewhat resemble the flowers of the pink family. This plant grows in dry, open places in the foothills of the Rocky Mountains. It is one of about six *Lygodesmia* species, all found in North America.

Dandelion, *Taraxacum officinale*, is a garden weed found throughout the temperate regions of the world. Individual plants are quite small, but they seed themselves near and far, rapidly taking over an area if unchecked. The plants form rosettes of wavy-lobed leaves; in early summer they bear several yellow flower heads, each one on the end of a hollow, slightly succulent stalk. Both stalk and leaves exude milky juice if broken. The flower heads are followed by "blowballs"—round balls of parachuted seeds which drift in the wind, transporting the potential plants to new invasion sites. Dandelions are edible; their leaves, although bitter, make a useful addition to salads; their roots can be roasted and ground to make a caffeine-free coffee substitute; and their flowers can be made into wine.

Nipplewort, *Lapsana communis*, is an annual plant with milky juice. It has leafy stems up to 5ft tall, the upper half branched to form a complex inflorescence. The lower leaves of the plant are thin and lobed, with a large, terminal lobe and several small lobes or a wing near the base; the upper leaves are lance-shaped. The flower heads are small and numerous, formed of ray florets, lemon yellow in color, and borne in many clusters. This plant, has been introduced from Europe and now grows as a weed in waste places, woods, and fields in much of the U.S. and southern Canada. Its young leaves can be eaten raw in salads or cooked like spinach.

Sow-thistles look a bit like a cross between a thistle and a dandelion, but belong to the genus *Sonchus*. The species found in North America are cosmopolitan weeds, originally from Europe. They are annual or perennial plants which exude milky juice if broken; they have characteristic alternate leaves with clasping bases, and more or less prickly margins, and they have several to very many yellow flower heads in branched clusters terminating the stems.

Prickly Sow-thistle, *Sonchus asper*, and Smooth Sow-thistle, *S. oleraceus*, are both annual plants, common weeds of waste places and gardens. Prickly Sow-thistle has lower leaves with bases which curl around the stems, very prickly leaves, and few to several flower heads. Smooth Sow-thistle has lower leaves which clasp but do not curl around the stem, weakly spiny leaves, and many flower heads. At the beginning of the flowering season its flower clusters are a tight mass of buds, but gradually the clusters open out to form a large, branching inflorescence by the end of the season. The young leaves of both plants are edible in salads or cooked as a potherb, provided the spines are removed.

Field Sow-thistle, *Sonchus arvensis*, is a similar but perennial plant, another invader from Europe found in waste places and on roadsides. It forms spreading colonies of erect stems up to 4ft tall, with spiny-margined leaves, the lowermost lobed but the upper ones simple. It has open clusters of yellow flower heads, the stalks and involucres all covered with black, glandular hairs.

Lettuces are *Lactuca* species. Garden Lettuces are varieties of *L. sativa*, a plant which probably originated in Asia, but which has been cultivated for so long that its origins are obscure. There are about 10 native American lettuces, annual or perennial plants with milky juice, alternate leaves, and usually with many flower heads in large, compound inflorescences. **Wild Lettuce**, *L. canadensis*, grows in open woods, waste places, and fields from Quebec to Saskatchewan, south to Florida and Texas. It is a tall, leafy, annual plant, up to 10ft

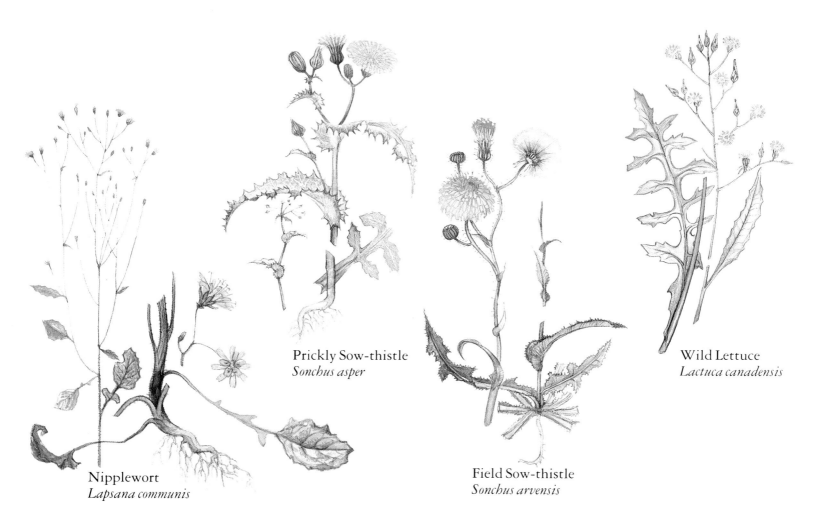

Prickly Sow-thistle
Sonchus asper

Wild Lettuce
Lactuca canadensis

Nipplewort
Lapsana communis

Field Sow-thistle
Sonchus arvensis

in height, with dandelion-like leaves and a large, branched inflorescence of small, pale yellow flower heads in late summer. These are followed by parachuted seeds. Young leaves of this plant can be eaten in salads but they are more bitter than those of cultivated lettuces. Prickly Lettuce, *L. scariola*, has prickly stems and leaves.

Florida Lettuce, *Lactuca floridana*, is one of several North American lettuce species with blue flowers, known as **Blue Lettuces**. It grows in woods and thickets, and in moist, open places from New York to Kansas, and south to Florida and Texas. This is an annual or biennial plant, with toothed, dandelion-like leaves, and a complex, much branched inflorescence of pale blue flower heads. The heads are followed by clusters of white-haired seeds, which are blown by the wind to new sites. Similar species are found in the west and north—west to the prairies and Pacific states, north to southern Canada and Alaska.

Yellow Salsify, *Tragopogon dubius*, is one of three European *Tragopogon* species naturalized in much of the U.S. and southern Canada. They grow in waste ground and on roadsides, this one in dry, open places. Yellow Salsify is usually biennial, with elongated leaves, mostly in a basal rosette, but a few smaller leaves grow with sheathing bases on the erect, hollow stem. The plant oozes milky juice if broken. The stem has only a few branches, each one bearing a single flower head at the top. The

heads are large and quite showy, formed of pale yellow, strap-shaped florets, with a series of slender bracts beneath the head, longer than the florets and projecting beyond them. All three species have spectacular fruiting heads—large balls of achenes with feathery parachutes.

Cat's-ear, *Hypochoeris radicata*, may be mistaken by the unwary for a dandelion, but is a hairy plant and each of its tough, solid flower stems branches to bear several flower heads. There are small, dark bracts on each stem, and each yellow flower head is cupped in an involucre formed of a series of small, bristly, overlapping bracts. This is another common weed in North America, found on grassy roadsides, in waste ground, fields, and pastures.

Fall Dandelion, *Leontodon autumnalis*, resembles Cat's-ear. It has a rosette of pinnately lobed leaves, the lobes deep and narrow; several solid stems, branching near the top to bear yellow flower heads; small bracts on the flower stems; and an involucre of overlapping bracts beneath each flower head. This Eurasian plant is a common weed in the northeast from New Jersey northward, but is also found scattered much more rarely in the northwest. It grows in grassy places, on roadsides and in pastures, and in waste ground.

Hawkweeds, *Hieracium* species, are a huge group, with somewhere between 10,000 and 20,000 species, mainly found in the temperate and Arctic regions of the northern hemi-

Florida Lettuce
Lactuca floridana

Yellow Salsify
Tragopogon dubius

Cat's-ear
Hypochoeris radicata

Fall Dandelion
Leontodon autumnalis

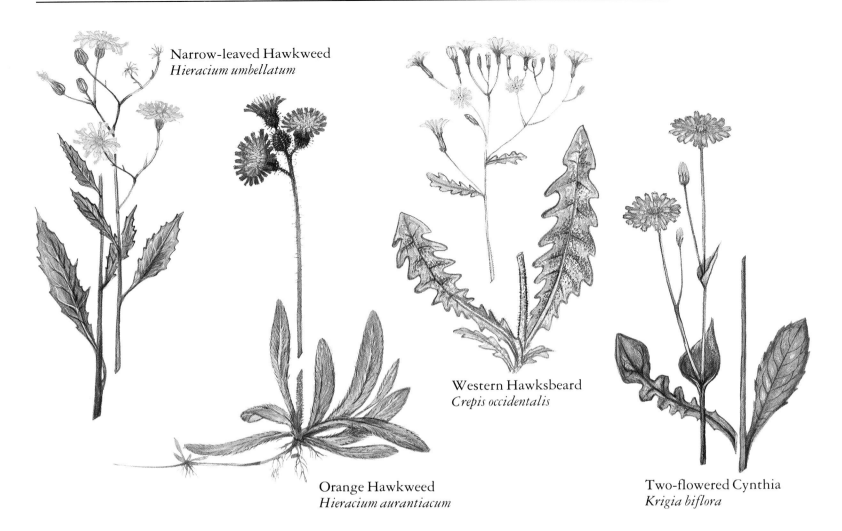

Narrow-leaved Hawkweed
Hieracium umbellatum

Western Hawksbeard
Crepis occidentalis

Orange Hawkweed
Hieracium aurantiacum

Two-flowered Cynthia
Krigia biflora

sphere. It is impossible to be precise about the exact number of species in this group because many of them produce seeds without pollination. This results in the formation of closed populations of plants, all descended from one individual. Since such a group is separated from all others by this process, it could be said to be a species. Hawkweeds are perennial plants, either with most of their leaves in a basal rosette or with leafy, erect stems. Their flowers are borne in flower heads composed of ray florets like those of dandelions, but each erect stem is branched and carries several to many heads; most species have yellow flowers. Beneath each head the involucre is formed of bracts in overlapping rows.

Narrow-leaved Hawkweed, *Hieracium umbellatum*, grows around the North Pole, across Canada and the northern U.S. in North America. It has leafy stems up to 3ft tall, with narrow, linear, slightly toothed leaves, and a branched cluster of yellow flower heads terminating the stem. It grows in open woods and thickets, in damp meadows, and on shores.

Orange Hawkweed or King-devil, *Hieracium aurantiacum*, is an introduced species, a weed that grows in fields and on roadsides from Newfoundland to Minnesota, south to North Carolina and Iowa, and also in the Pacific states. It forms rosettes of elliptical, hairy leaves and produces glowing orange flower heads on leafless stalks in summer. It spreads into mats with short underground stems, and can be a weed.

Hawksbeards, *Crepis* species, are similar to the hawkweeds, but there are not so many of them — only about 200 species, mainly from Europe and Asia. About 20 native and introduced species grow in North America. **Western Hawksbeard**, *C. occidentalis*, grows in dry, rocky places, often quite high up in the mountains from California to Washington and Wyoming, and east to New Mexico. It is typical of many *Crepis* species, with sinuately lobed leaves, the largest in a basal rosette, the stem leaves smaller and simpler. From each rosette grow one or more stems, each one about 10in tall, and branching to form erect inflorescences of many yellow flower heads. Stems and leaves are all covered in gray, felt-like hairs. The achenes that follow the flowers bear parachutes formed of many rows of white hairs.

Two-flowered Cynthia, *Krigia biflora*, is one of several *Krigia* species native to North America. It is a perennial plant with milky juice. It has a basal rosette of lance-shaped, often toothed leaves, and several flowering stems; each of these has a few clasping stem leaves, the uppermost two almost opposite, and with several forked, flower-bearing stalks in their axil. The solitary flower heads terminate the forked stalks; they are orange-yellow and formed completely from ray florets. This plant is found in woods and meadows, on roadsides, and in fields from Massachusetts to Manitoba, west to Colorado, south to Georgia and Arizona.

Atlantic coast of Maine in late summer, with New England Aster (*Aster novae-angliae*) in the foreground.

Water Plantain family

Alismataceae

A small family with 13 genera and about 90 species, mainly from temperate and tropical regions of the northern hemisphere. They are herbaceous plants, fully aquatic or found in marshes and other wet places. They bear an extraordinary resemblance to the buttercups in their flower structure and in their habitats; some experts consider the two families to be related, even though buttercups are dicotyledons and water plantains are monocotyledons.

Family features The flowers are hermaphrodite and regular, often borne in whorls or racemes. Each flower has six perianth segments arranged in two whorls; the outer three are green and sepal-like, overlapping and persistent; the inner three are petal-like and overlapping, and soon fall. There are usually six stamens and many free carpels forming a superior ovary. The fruit is a cluster of achenes. The leaves are basal, long-stalked with open, sheathing bases, and linear to ovate, often arrow-shaped blades. The leaves have prominent veins.

There are 10 **Water Plantains**, *Alisma* species, in the world, from northern temperate regions and Australia. Four grow in North America, including *A. plantago-aquatica*, a plant which grows all around the North Pole, across Canada, and south in the U.S. to California, Wisconsin, and New York. It grows in marshes and ponds, slow-moving streams and ditches, its leaves and flowering stems emerging from the water to grow 3ft tall at most. It forms a clump of long-stalked leaves with elliptical or ovate blades, and in the early part of summer its much-branched flowering stalk bears numerous small, white or pale pink flowers in many umbel-like clusters. The flowers open in the afternoon. They are followed by flattened, disk-like fruits borne in rings.

Fringed Water Plantain, *Machaerocarpus californicus*, forms a clump of long-stalked leaves with ovate blades, and produces a leafless flowering stalk in summer. Its pink or white flowers grow in whorls and have unevenly fringed petals. This plant grows in mud or shallow water from northern California to Oregon and Idaho.

Arrowhead, *Sagittaria latifolia*, grows on the shores of ponds, slow-moving streams and ditches, in marshes and wet meadows, from Nova Scotia to British Columbia, and south to South America. It gets its other name of Duck Potato from the tubers produced by its rhizomes as they grow beneath the mud. These tubers were once a valuable source of food for many Indian tribes; they can be collected from late summer to spring, although they may be difficult to harvest in winter from plants in frozen ponds! Arrowhead is a perennial with a clump of long-stalked leaves, the stalks emerging from the

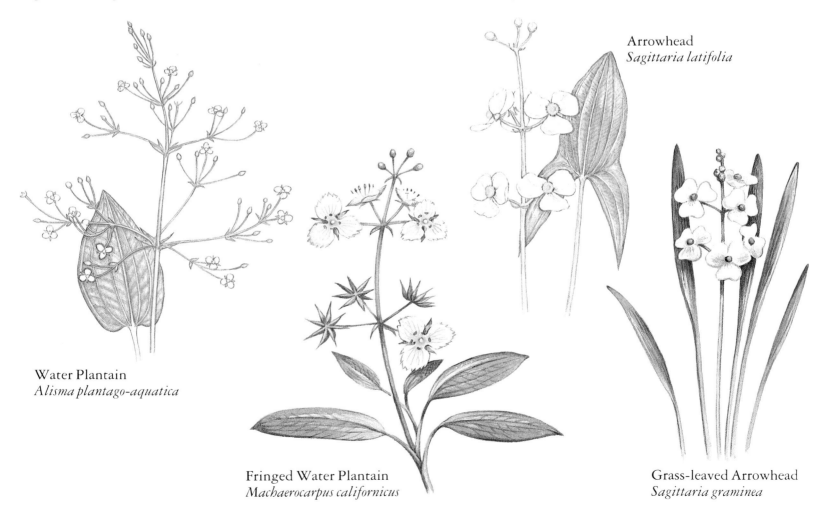

Arrowhead
Sagittaria latifolia

Water Plantain
Alisma plantago-aquatica

Fringed Water Plantain
Machaerocarpus californicus

Grass-leaved Arrowhead
Sagittaria graminea

water to bear narrow, arrow-shaped blades. In summer its unbranched flowering stalks grow up to 4ft tall and bear whorls of white flowers, male flowers near the top of the stem and female flowers lower down. The female flowers are followed by rounded heads of winged, flattened achenes.

This Arrowhead is only one of about 15 *Sagittaria* species in North America, differing mostly in distribution and leaf shape. **Grass-leaved Arrowhead**, *S. graminea*, has linear, grass-like leaves and grows in wet mud or shallow water from Newfoundland to Minnesota, and south to Florida and Texas. Sessile-fruited Arrowhead, *S. rigida*, is an eastern and midwestern species with ovate leaf blades. Both these plants produce edible tubers.

Agave family

Agavaceae

A family of about 19 genera and 500 species, found in sub-tropical and tropical regions of the world, many adapted to life in dry areas and deserts. Some of the *Agave* species are important economically as a source of fibers; sisal and Bombay hemp, for example, are used to make rope and string. Others are used in herb medicine, as a source of food, and to make liquor. Mescal and tequila are both made by fermenting *Agave*

species (the liquors have the same relationship to each other as moonshine and whiskey). Some members of this family are decorative garden plants, not only the recently fashionable phormiums, but also dracaenas and yuccas.

Family features The flowers are regular or somewhat irregular, hermaphrodite, borne in racemes or compound inflorescences. The perianth segments are petaloid, often fleshy and united into a partial tube. Each flower has six stamens inserted on the tube. The ovary may be superior or inferior, and has three cells. The fruit is a berry or capsule. The leaves are crowded into a basal clump, or on the base of the stem; they are narrow, often prickly-margined, often fleshy, often fibrous. These are mostly xerophytic plants, with well-developed rhizomes.

There are about 40 *Yucca* species, often known as **Spanish Bayonets**, distributed through the dry regions of western and southern North America and the West Indies. Some are grown in gardens. The leaves of all of them are fibrous, and the fibers can be used for cloth and string; some have edible fruits, others edible seeds. Many are shrubs with a dense clump of sword-like leaves.

The **Blue Yucca**, *Yucca baccata*, forms a clump of spine-tipped leaves about 3ft high. The leaves have a few whitish fibers on their edges. The plant flowers in summer, forming a thick flowering stalk up to 20ft tall, fleshy in the upper part

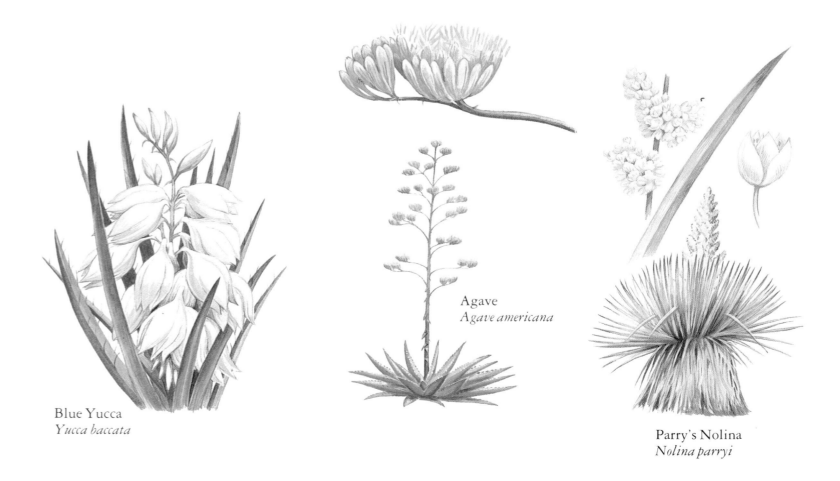

Blue Yucca
Yucca baccata

Agave
Agave americana

Parry's Nolina
Nolina parryi

where the flower branches grow, and often tinged red-purple. It has about 15 branches and bears many waxy, bell-like flowers, often red-brown on the outside, creamy white on the inside. The flowers are followed by fleshy pods. Blue Yucca grows in grassland, dry slopes, and deserts, in Joshua Tree scrub and open woods from California to Colorado and Texas, south into Mexico. The fruits of this plant are eaten by Indians; when baked they taste like sweet potatoes.

There are about 300 **Agaves**, *Agave* species, plants from the warm, dry areas of the western hemisphere, with about 130 in North America. They are rosette-forming perennials, with thick crowns and rosettes of persistent, fleshy, spine-edged, spine-tipped leaves. *Agave americana* (p. 221) is typical of a whole group of agaves. It is a medium to large species, forming rosettes 3–6ft tall, and producing many suckers, so that it is commonly seen as clumps of rosettes. Its usually light green or gray-green leaves are variable; they may be flattened on top, or form a trough, or be bent backward. An individual rosette may grow for many years before it flowers; it then produces seeds and dies. The inflorescence grows up to 25ft tall, with a straight, slender stem, small, triangular bracts, and umbel-like branches with many yellow flowers, followed by oblong capsules with shiny black seeds.

Parry's Nolina, *Nolina parryi* (p. 221), resembles a yucca, forming a dense clump of linear leaves. Its stout stem grows about 5ft tall and bears a dense, terminal inflorescence of many tiny, whitish flowers. The leaves are concave on the top surface and have greatly expanded, rigid bases. This is one of about 25 *Nolina* species all found in the southwest. It grows on dry slopes in deserts, in sage scrub, chaparral and pinyon woods in southern California.

Lily family
Liliaceae

A large family of about 240 genera and 3000 species, found throughout the world. Most are herbs; a few are climbers. There are many beautiful garden plants in this family, including lilies, day lilies, tulips, hyacinths, hostas, red hot pokers, and Lily-of-the-valley. Many have showy flowers, others have attractive leaves. It would be difficult to imagine cooking without onions and garlic, both of which come from the genus *Allium*.

Many members of the family contain chemicals which are active medicinally, either of beneficial use in medicine, or poisonous. Lily-of-the-valley contains convallaramin, which can be used as a less powerful heart tonic than digitalin, the active ingredient in Foxglove. Colchicine is obtained from Autumn Crocuses, *Colchicum* species; in small quantities, and

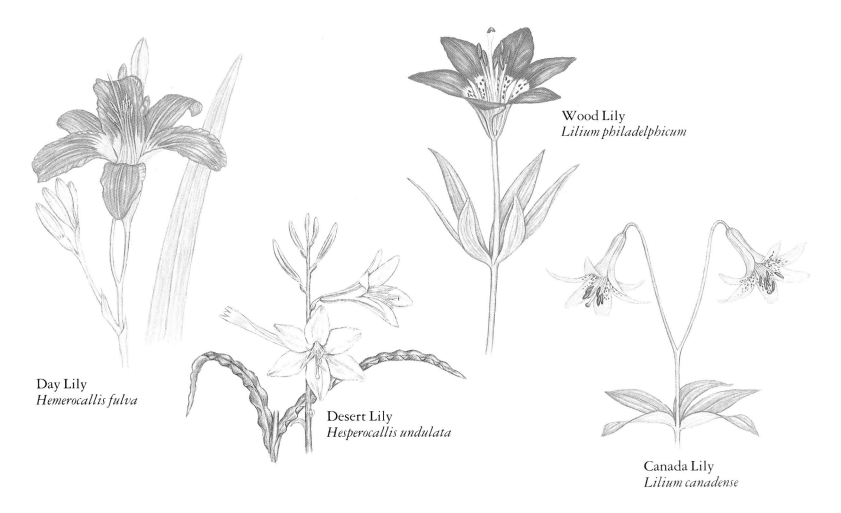

Day Lily
Hemerocallis fulva

Desert Lily
Hesperocallis undulata

Wood Lily
Lilium philadelphicum

Canada Lily
Lilium canadense

Columbia Lily
Lilium columbianum

Sego Lily
Calochortus nuttallii

Club-haired Mariposa Tulip
Calochortus clavatus

Sagebrush Mariposa Tulip
Calochortus macrocarpus

with medical supervision, the drug is used to treat rheumatism, but the plants contain sufficient quantities to be poisonous. Several species of *Aloe* are used as a source of the drug aloes, used as a laxative and in skin creams.

Family features The flowers are regular or slightly irregular, usually hermaphrodite. There are usually six petal-like perianth segments in each flower; these may be free or partly fused into a tube and are mostly borne in two distinct but similar whorls. Flowers usually have six stamens opposite the perianth segments and a superior ovary; this generally has three cells and many seeds. The fruit is a capsule or fleshy berry. The leaves are basal, or may be alternate, or whorled on erect stems. The plants in this family may have rhizomes, corms or bulbs.

Among the oldest groups of garden plants in this family are the **Day Lilies**, species and varieties of *Hemerocallis*, grown for several centuries in gardens. *Hemerocallis fulva* (p. 222) is originally from Japan, but is grown in the eastern U.S. and has escaped from many gardens over the years to grow on roadsides. It forms clumps of arching, broadly grass-like leaves up to 3ft tall. In summer large and well-established clumps send up leafless stems with terminal clusters of tawny orange, funnel-shaped flowers.

A related native plant, the **Desert Lily**, *Hesperocallis undulata* (p. 222), grows in the southwestern deserts of the

U.S. and in Mexico. It forms clumps of immediately recognizable leaves, sword-like with wavy-crinkled margins, and in summer produces an erect stem with a raceme of white, funnel-shaped, typically lily-like flowers.

The true **Lilies**, *Lilium* species, are a large group of about 90 species, with about 25 found in North America. Lilies are temperate region plants, many of them prized ornamentals for gardens, associated most often with woodland gardens, where the light shade and well-drained soils approximate most closely to their native habitats. Lilies form bulbs, underground overwintering organs which store food. A bulb always has the same structure; it is actually an extremely shortened stem, with fleshy, food-storing leaves folded around it, and a growing tip from which the new plant will form.

The **Wood Lily**, *Lilium philadelphicum* (p. 222), is typical of many native species. It grows in dry, open woods and prairies across southern Canada, south to North Carolina in the east, Kentucky and Arizona in the west. It forms an erect stem 2–3ft tall, with whorls of lance-shaped leaves and 1–5 flowers at the top. These are funnel-shaped, opening toward the sky, orange-red or yellow, with purple spots on the narrow bases of the petals.

The **Canada Lily**, *Lilium canadense* (p. 222), grows in wet meadows and along woodland edges from Nova Scotia to Ontario, south to South Carolina in the mountains, and to

White Dogtooth Violet
Erythronium albidum

Yellow Fawn Lily
Erythronium grandiflorum

Checker Lily
Fritillaria lanceolata

Yellow Bell
Fritillaria pudica

Alabama. This plant has slender stems growing up to 5ft tall, with whorls of 4–12 lance-shaped leaves and a terminal cluster of nodding flowers. The flowers are like funnels, with backward-arching petals, yellow or yellow-orange in color, and marked with purple spots. The plant has several names, including Wild Yellow Lily and Meadow Lily.

Turk's-cap Lily, *Lilium superbum*, is another eastern species of wet meadows and woods; it has striking, orange-red flowers, with petals curled so far backward that they form circles. This is a popular garden species, like the Tiger Lily, *L. tigrinum*, an eastern Asian species which has escaped from gardens to grow wild on roadsides in the east.

The **Columbia Lily** or Oregon Lily, *Lilium columbianum* (p. 223), is a western species, often also called the Tiger Lily, and now becoming uncommon because so many plants have been taken to grow in gardens. It has large orange, purple-spotted flowers nodding at the tops of 4-ft tall stems. In the wild it grows in brush and woodland through the Rocky Mountain area, along with several other *Lilium* species which are found in the west.

Mariposa Lilies are a western North American group of about 60 species in the genus *Calochortus*. They are known by a variety of names—Mariposa Tulips, Butterfly Tulips, and Star Tulips—but are more closely related to the true lilies than to tulips, even if they do have tulip-shaped flowers. Some, with pointed and very furry-looking petals, are called Cats' Ears. Each plant forms a single, often large, basal leaf, and one or more erect stems grow from the axil of this leaf to carry the flowers. These stems may be leafless or may bear small leaves. The flowers of many species are showy, and these are coveted garden plants; the flowers grow on long stalks in clusters, and may be erect or nodding, white, yellow, red, purple or blue, often with complex markings in contrasting colors inside, frequently bearded inside, and with a gland at the base of each petal. The plants produce bulbs which are protected by membranous or fibrous scale leaves on the outside. In the past the bulbs from many *Calochortus* species were an important food source for the Indians. In addition, many species produce little bulbs or bulbils in the axils of the lower leaves, and spread by this means, as well as, or instead of, by seed.

The **Sego Lily**, *Calochortus nuttallii* (p. 223), is the state flower of Utah. It grows in dry places, on the plains, and in coniferous woods, in sagebrush scrub and in pinyon scrub from Montana to North Dakota, and south to Arizona and Nebraska. This little plant has erect, unbranched stems, 18in tall at most, with long, narrow leaves which often have inrolled margins. The flowers are borne in an umbel-like cluster at the top of the stem; they are white, bearded inside, with complex markings, yellow around the gland, and a with reddish crescent above the gland.

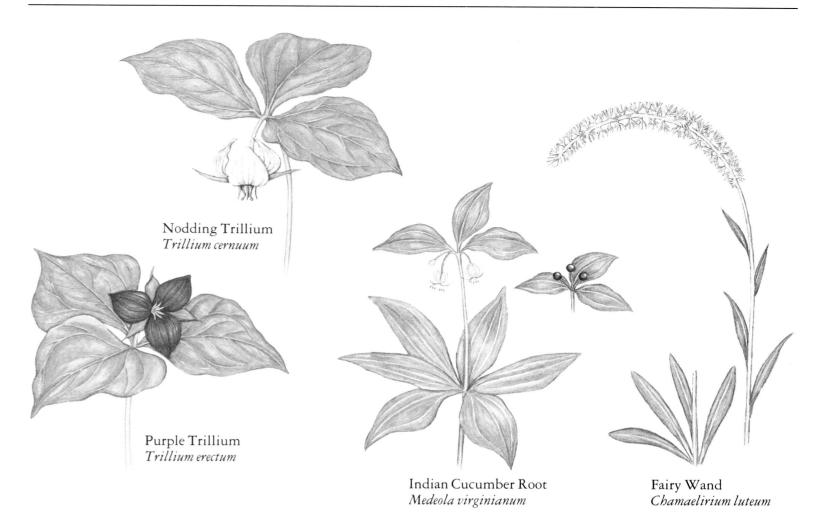

Nodding Trillium
Trillium cernuum

Purple Trillium
Trillium erectum

Indian Cucumber Root
Medeola virginianum

Fairy Wand
Chamaelirium luteum

The **Sagebrush Mariposa Tulip**, *Calochortus macrocarpus* (p. 223), grows in similar habitats to the Sego Lily—through the Rocky Mountain area from British Columbia to Montana, south to California. Its lilac flowers have three broad petals, and three narrow sepals slightly longer than the petals. The petals are marked with yellow hairs at the base and a crescent of dark red above the hairs.

Club-haired Mariposa Tulip, *Calochortus clavatus* (p. 223), is confined to California, growing on dry, often rocky slopes in chaparral and the Coast Ranges. It has yellow flowers with club-shaped hairs above the glands on the petals, and a transverse red-brown line above the hairs.

Adder's-tongues or Fawn Lilies, *Erythronium* species, are found throughout much of the U.S. and in southern Canada. There are about 18 species of these beautiful plants in North America, out of a world total of around 25. Some are grown in flower borders; they are superb planted beneath hostas, for they bloom and die down before the hosta leaves emerge.

Adder's-tongues are perennial plants, surviving and over-wintering by corms that develop on short, deep-seated rhizomes. Corms are extremely shortened stems swollen with food, and with a growing tip at the apex. In the spring the corms develop a pair of basal leaves, and the larger ones also develop flowers. Adder's-tongues tend to be woodland plants; they may have white or yellow flowers, some have funnel-shaped flowers, others have blooms with recurved petals; some have plain green leaves, others have leaves mottled with brown; several are found in the rich woods of the east but more grow in the western mountains.

Yellow Fawn Lily, *Erythronium grandiflorum* (p. 224), is found in open, coniferous woods and on grassy slopes from British Columbia across the mountains to Alberta, and south to California. It forms colonies of many plants, coming into bloom in the spring as the snow melts. Each plant has two elliptical, basal leaves, plain green in color, and a leafless flowering stalk with 1–5 nodding, yellow flowers. The flowers have six, quite separate perianth segments, green-streaked on the outside, and recurving as the flowers get older until they are bent backward.

White Dogtooth Violet, *Erythronium albidum* (p. 224), has a single white flower dangling at the top of a stout, 8-in tall stem growing from between two narrow leaves. The leaves are frequently mottled. The flowers are often tinged with yellow at the center, and with blue or green on the outside. Plants form colonies in moist woods from Ontario to Minnesota and south to Kentucky and Texas.

Fritillaries belong to the genus *Fritillaria*. They are beautiful, often delicate plants, some grown in gardens. They have bulbs formed of a single fleshy scale-leaf, and many species also form tiny, "rice-grain" bulblets. These produce

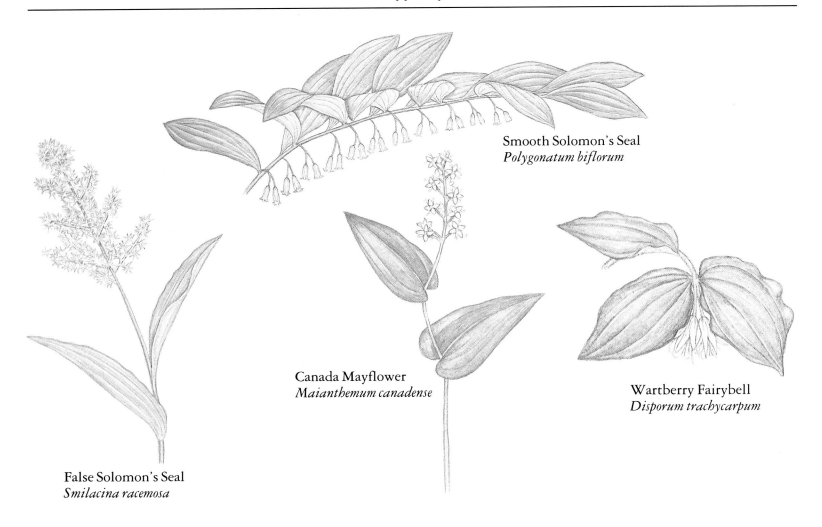

Smooth Solomon's Seal
Polygonatum biflorum

Canada Mayflower
Maianthemum canadense

Wartberry Fairybell
Disporum trachycarpum

False Solomon's Seal
Smilacina racemosa

only single small leaves in their first seasons, but they gradually grow into mature bulbs which will produce flowering stems. There are about 18 *Fritillaria* species in North America, all from the west.

Checker Lily is one name given to *Fritillaria lanceolata* (p. 224), because of the checkered appearance of its flowers. It is also called Mission Bells. This is a widespread western plant, growing from British Columbia to Idaho, and south to California in woodland and scrub on the lower slopes of the mountains. It forms many bulblets, the largest sending up slender stems up to 2ft tall, with several whorls of 3–5 lance-shaped leaves. They flower in spring, with nodding, bowl-shaped flowers hanging from the leaf axils; the flowers vary from purple-brown mottled with a little yellow to lemon yellow slightly mottled with brownish-purple, and come in all shades between. There are several similar species with brownish or greenish flowers, although the flowers tend not to be mottled.

Yellow Bell, *Fritillaria pudica* (p. 224), is a small plant, with a single stem only 1ft tall at most, several grass-like leaves, and a solitary yellow bell hanging from the top of the stem. It grows in grassland and coniferous woods in much of the Rocky Mountain area. The Adobe Lily, *F. pluriflora*, grows in adobe soils in the interior valleys of California and Oregon; it has a single stem and several pinkish nodding flowers.

Trilliums or Wake-robins are a group of unusual and beautiful plants in the genus *Trillium*, with about 23 species in North America and the rest in Asia. They are perennial woodland plants with short rhizomes; these send up erect stems in spring or early summer, each stem bearing a terminal whorl of three leaves and a single flower in the center of the leaf whorl. The flower has three green sepals and three white, pink or purplish petals. Some eastern species are called Birthroots from their use as an astringent in Indian herb medicine; they are useful in stopping bleeding, so a medicine made from the plants was given to mothers after childbirth.

Purple Trillium, *Trillium erectum* (p. 225), is one of those also called Birthroot. It grows in moist, shady woods in the eastern half of North America from Quebec to Ontario, south to Georgia and Tennessee. It has brownish-purple, more or less erect flowers, with an unpleasant scent of decaying flesh; the scent attracts flies, which pollinate the flowers. Toadshade or Red Trillium, *T. sessile*, is one of several species with erect flowers, which lack stalks and which remain more or less closed; it grows in rich, moist woods in the east and midwest.

Nodding Trillium, *Trillium cernuum* (p. 225), is another plant found in wet woods in the east, from Newfoundland to Saskatchewan and south to Georgia and Alabama, in the mountains in the south of its range. Its single white flower nods on a long stalk below the leaves. Several other white-flowered species grow in the east, but their flowers do not hang below the leaves like this. The Giant Trillium of the west, *T. chloropetalum*, grows in shady woods on the western slopes of the Cascades and Sierra Nevada. It has purple-mottled leaves and greenish-yellow flowers.

Indian Cucumber Root, *Medeola virginianum* (p. 225), is a rare plant with a rhizome that smells and tastes like cucumber; it was eaten by Indians at one time. The rhizome is woolly when young, and woolly hairs remain around the bases of the stems. The plant produces slender stems with two whorls of oblong leaves, the lower whorl with 5–11 leaves, the upper one with three. In the axil of the upper leaves hang the flowers, yellow-green with reflexed petals, followed by dark purple berries. This plant grows in rich woods from Nova Scotia to Minnesota, south to Georgia and Alabama, in mountains in the south of its range.

Fairy Wand or Devil's Bit, *Chamaelirium luteum* (p. 225), forms a clump of large, spoon-shaped leaves and an erect, leafy stem about 4ft tall, which ends in a dense drooping spike of white flowers. The flowers open in early summer, male and female flowers on separate plants, the male ones tinged with yellow from the stamens. The plant grows in moist woods, wet meadows, and bogs from Massachusetts to southern Ontario, south to Florida and Arkansas. It is sometimes grown in wet places in gardens.

There are several species of **Solomon's Seal** in the genus *Polygonatum*. They are woodland plants found in the rich woods of the east, often growing secretly in shade. **Smooth Solomon's Seal**, *P. biflorum* (p. 226), is the commonest, found in rich woods from southern Ontario to Minnesota, south to Texas and Florida. It is a perennial plant, with a knotty rhizome and arching stems in summer growing to 3ft tall, and with many opposite pairs of broadly elliptical, parallel-veined leaves. In the axil of each leaf there hang greenish-white, bell-shaped flowers, usually in ones or twos, followed by blue-black berries.

False Solomon's Seal, *Smilacina racemosa* (p. 226), has erect stems up to 3ft tall, with broad, elliptical leaves forming a kind of zigzag pattern up the stem. The flowers form creamy white, fluffy clusters at the tops of the stems in early summer, and are followed by reddish berries. This is another perennial plant with long, twisted rhizomes. It grows in rich woods across southern Canada, south in the U.S. to Georgia and Arizona. This plant is sometimes grown in gardens. *Smilacina stellata* is similar, and as widely distributed in moist, sandy woods and prairies, but has a smaller, rather insignificant cluster of fluffy flowers.

The **Canada Mayflower**, *Maianthemum canadense* (p. 226), is a much smaller plant, sometimes called Wild Lily-of-the-valley, and resembling that garden plant in its clasping leaves.

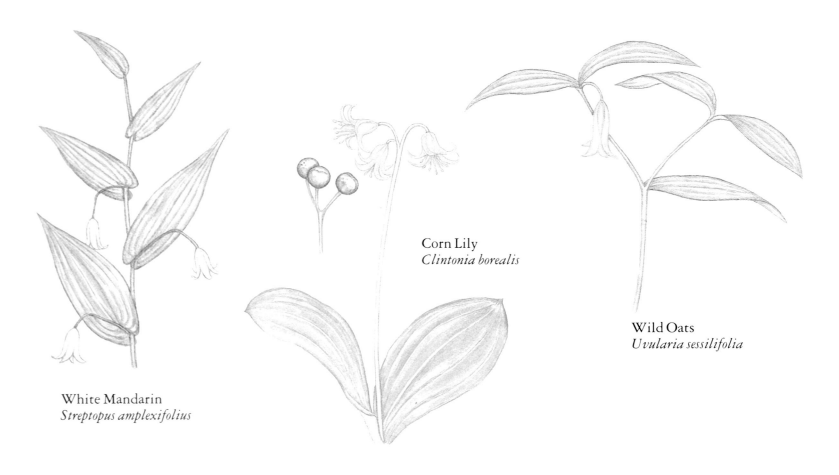

Corn Lily
Clintonia borealis

Wild Oats
Uvularia sessilifolia

White Mandarin
Streptopus amplexifolius

It has an erect, zigzag stem, only 8in tall at most, with two or three broad leaves clasping the stem, and a terminal raceme of small white flowers in summer. It spreads through moist woods with slender creeping rhizomes, and is found from Newfoundland to Mackenzie, south to Georgia in the mountains, and to Iowa in the midwest.

The **Fairybells** are a group of about 15 species in the genus *Disporum* found in North America and Asia. They are perennial plants with branched stems, alternate leaves, and drooping, terminal flowers, either greenish or white in color, borne singly or in small umbels. **Wartberry Fairybell**, *D. trachycarpum* (p. 226), grows on wooded slopes, often near streams, from British Columbia to North Dakota, south to Oregon, and in the Rocky Mountains to New Mexico. Its creamy white, narrow bells hang singly or in pairs, concealed by the leaves, and are followed by red berries.

The **Twisted-stalks**, *Streptopus* species, get their name from the bent or twisted flower stalks which occur in some species. They also have zigzag stems, the effect emphasized by the alternate leaves which originate at each turn. **White Mandarin**, *S. amplexifolius* (p. 227), grows in rich woods all around the North Pole, across Canada, and south in the U.S. mountains to North Carolina and Arizona. It has creeping rhizomes and stems 2–3ft tall, with broadly ovate, clasping leaves. Solitary, greenish-white, bell-like flowers on abruptly

twisted stalks hang in the axils of the leaves. Rose Mandarin, *S. roseus*, is similar but its leaves lack clasping bases. Its pink flowers hang on dangling stalks in the leaf axils, singly or in pairs. It grows in rich woods from Newfoundland to Minnesota, south in the mountains to North Carolina, and is also found in the northern Rockies.

The **Corn Lily**, *Clintonia borealis* (p. 227), is found in moist woods and woodland bogs, on acid soils from Newfoundland to Manitoba, south to New Jersey and Indiana, and on in the mountains to North Carolina and Tennessee. It has a knotty rhizome which produces a clump of 2–5 glossy, pointed-elliptical leaves in early summer. The leaves have sheathing bases which curl around an erect flowering stalk; the stalk grows 15in tall and bears a cluster of 3–8 drooping flowers at the tip. Each flower is greenish-yellow and bell-like; the flowers are followed by bluish berries. Wood Lily, *C. umbellulata*, from the eastern U.S., has greenish-white flowers spotted with purple-brown, and black berries.

There are five **Bellworts**, *Uvularia* species, in the east and midwest. **Wild Oats**, *U. sessilifolia* (p. 227), grows in woods and thickets from Quebec to Minnesota, south to the Carolinas, Alabama, and Arkansas, in the mountains in the southern parts of its range. It is a perennial plant, with a slender rhizome and erect stems up to 1ft tall. The stem is unbranched near the ground, then forks; the upper part of the

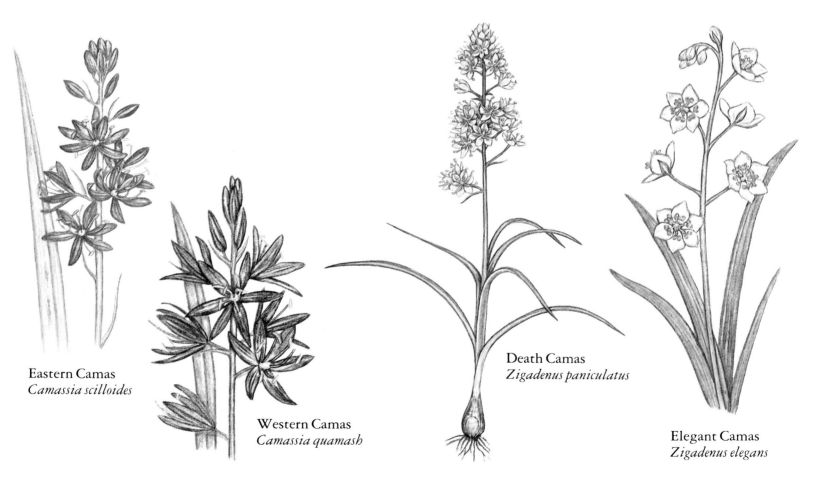

Eastern Camas
Camassia scilloides

Western Camas
Camassia quamash

Death Camas
Zigadenus paniculatus

Elegant Camas
Zigadenus elegans

stem bears stalkless leaves and drooping, creamy yellow, bell-like flowers on long stalks. The flowers appear to be in the axils of the leaves, but develop at the tips of the stem; the stems grow on so that the flowers appear axillary.

There are five **Camas Lilies**, *Camassia species*, altogether, all found in North America. The Indians have known their food value for many centuries, collecting the bulbs and baking them for several days to make them dark and sugary. They can also be used as a substitute for potatoes. The problem with Camas bulbs is that they can be mistaken for Death Camas, *Zigadenus* bulbs, when the plants are out of flower. And a mistake could well be fatal, for the *Zigadenus* species are extremely poisonous. The plants can be distinguished easily when they are in flower, as Camas plants have blue flowers, whereas Death Camas have white, green or bronze flowers.

Eastern Camas or Wild Hyacinth, *Camassia scilloides* (p. 228), is the only species that extends into the east, growing in wet meadows and prairies, and in open, wet woods from Wisconsin to Pennsylvania, and south to Texas and Georgia. It has a globe-shaped bulb, which produces several basal, linear leaves and an erect flowering stalk up to 2ft tall. The violet or white flowers grow together with bracts in a loose, elongated raceme. **Western Camas**, *C. quamash* (p. 228), grows in mountain woods and interior valleys of the northwestern U.S., and into southern British Columbia.

There are 12 *Zigadenus* species in North America, all very poisonous and growing in similar places to the Camas species; when the bulbs are intermixed in the ground, then collection of the edible ones becomes very dangerous. Two species are particularly poisonous: *Z. venenosus* and *Z. paniculatus* (p. 228). Both are commonly known as **Death Camas**, and these are most often responsible for poisoning in livestock. *Zigadenus venenosus* is found in prairies, grassy slopes, and in sagebrush scrub from British Columbia to Saskatchewan, south to Baja California and Colorado. It has grassy leaves with bases sheathing the erect, unbranched flowering stalk; this grows up to 2ft tall and bears a terminal, pyramidal raceme of whitish flowers. *Zigadenus paniculatus* is also called Sand-corn. It grows in pine woods and sagebrush scrub from Washington to Montana, south to California and New Mexico. It has grassy leaves and an erect flowering stalk up to 2ft tall, with many little side stalks, each bearing clusters of yellow-white flowers.

Elegant Camas, *Zigadenus elegans* (p. 228), has grassy leaves and far fewer flowers, which are borne in racemes on erect stems in the latter half of summer. Each flower is bowl-shaped, the shape of the bowl created by the way the petals are attached to the sides of the ovary rather than its base; the flowers are creamy or greenish-white, with a green, two-pronged gland at the base of each petal. Elegant is a good word for the flowers of this plant. It grows in meadows and rocky slopes from Alaska

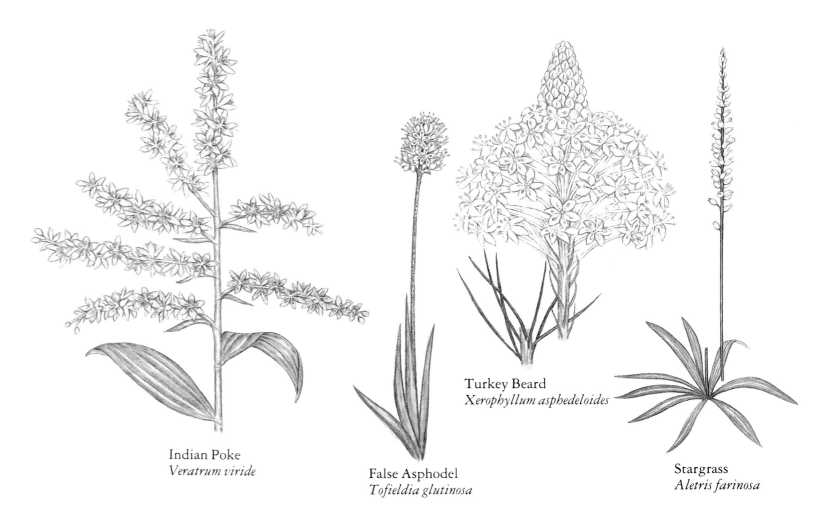

Indian Poke
Veratrum viride

False Asphodel
Tofieldia glutinosa

Turkey Beard
Xerophyllum asphedeloides

Stargrass
Aletris farinosa

south through the mountains to Oregon and Mexico, east in grassland and open woods to Alberta and Texas.

The **False Hellebores** are a group of about 12 northern hemisphere species in the genus *Veratrum*, some half of which grow in North America. They are poisonous plants, causing symptoms similar to those of a heart attack. They are stout perennials, with tall, leafy stems and large, terminal inflorescences of greenish-white to purple flowers. Many grow in wet meadows, swamps or woods, like **Indian Poke**, *V. viride* (p. 229), one of the most widespread species. It is scattered from New Brunswick to Alaska and across the U.S., south to North Carolina in the east and California in the west. It has an erect stem up to 7ft tall, with ribbed, yellow-green leaves and greenish, star-shaped flowers. It flowers in early summer and withers by midsummer, surviving by thick rhizomes till the following year. The Indians use it to slow the heartbeat.

False Asphodel or Sticky Tofieldia, *Tofieldia glutinosa* (p. 229), has a clump of linear leaves and a single, erect, leafless stem up to 3ft tall, which ends in a dense cluster of tiny white flowers. It grows in wet meadows and bogs across Canada, south in mountains in the east to North Carolina, and in the Rocky Mountain area to California and Wyoming. Its name comes from the sticky, reddish hairs on the stem.

Turkey Beard, *Xerophyllum asphedeloides* (p. 229), also has a clump of linear leaves and a stem with similar but progressive-ly smaller leaves, as well as a terminal cluster of white flowers. The flower cluster is dense and compact at first, elongating as the flowers open. The plant grows in pine barrens and mountain woods in acid soils from New Jersey to Tennessee and Georgia. Bear Grass, *X. tenax*, is a western species which grows on dry slopes and in open woods in the Rocky Mountain region. Its long, narrow, basal leaves grow over 2ft long and are used by the Indians to weave baskets; it is sometimes called Indian Basket Grass.

Stargrass or Colicroot, *Aletris farinosa* (p. 229), forms a basal clump of lance-shaped, yellow-green leaves with an erect stem, formed around midsummer and bearing an elongated spike of tiny, white, urn-shaped flowers. It grows in sandy, acid soils in woods and barrens, usually in moist places, from Maine to Ontario and south to Florida and Texas. The dried rhizome of this plant is still used in modern herb medicine as an effective remedy for intestinal colic and menstrual cramps.

The **Onions** are a large group of about 700 species in the genus *Allium*, distributed throughout the northern hemisphere and Africa. They include onions, garlic, chives, and leeks, as well as ornamental alliums grown in gardens. There are about 80 in North America, some introduced species which now grow wild, but most native plants. Many of the wild species are edible, with flavors approximating to onion or garlic, although some have a curious scent and taste which is

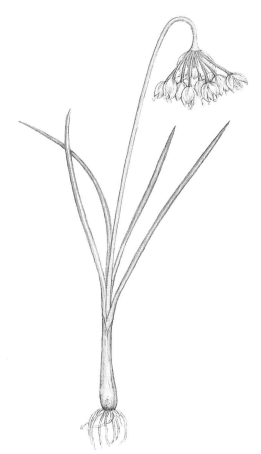

Nodding Onion
Allium cernuum

Autumn Wild Onion
Allium stellatum

Wild Garlic
Allium canadense

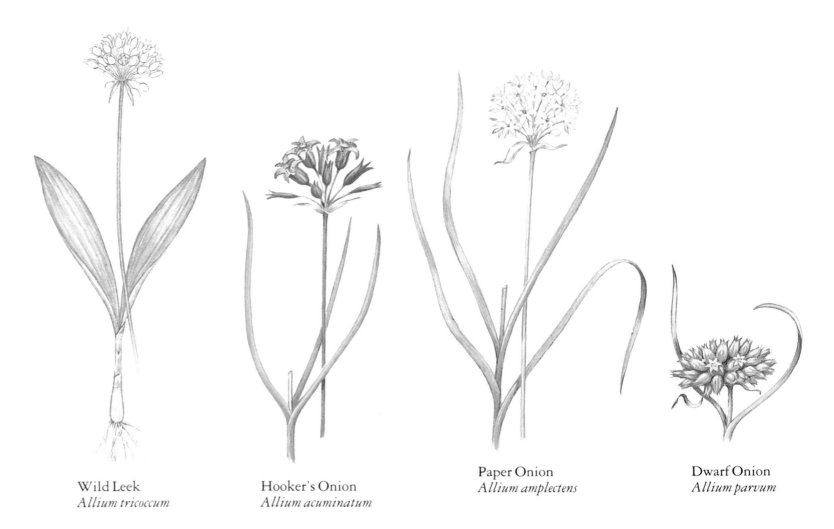

Wild Leek
Allium tricoccum

Hooker's Onion
Allium acuminatum

Paper Onion
Allium amplectens

Dwarf Onion
Allium parvum

similar but different from either. Wild plants are often stronger than cultivated forms. Their bulbs may be mistaken for the poisonous ones of Death Camas, *Zigadenus* species, but the bulbs of the latter plants lack scent. All *Allium* species are more or less scented.

Alliums are bulbous plants, with a bulb formed of fleshy scale leaves surrounded and protected by one or two membranous leaves. From this bulb grows a clump of linear, often grass-like leaves; mature bulbs also produce flowering stems with terminal umbels of flowers, the umbel at first enclosed in a leaf-like structure called a spathe. Some *Allium* species produce bulbils as well as flowers in their flower clusters; in some species the bulbils may be so numerous that they almost replace the flowers.

Nodding Onion, *Allium cernuum* (p. 230), is one of the most widespread species, found across Canada and into the U.S., to Oregon in the Pacific west, but further south to the east of the Rockies, to Mexico and to Georgia in the east. It grows in dry woods and prairies, especially in rocky places. This is one of the best wild species for eating, since it does not have too strong a flavor; its bulbs can be used like cultivated onions and the young green tops are good in salads. It sends up several soft leaves in early summer before the flowering stems appear. These latter grow to 2ft tall and bear nodding umbels of pink flowers.

Autumn Wild Onion, *Allium stellatum* (p. 230), is a related species also found in open woods, prairies, and rocky slopes across Saskatchewan to Ontario, and south through the midwestern states to Texas. It has pink flowers borne in a dome-like umbel in late summer. **Wild Garlic**, *A. canadense* (p. 230), grows in woods and meadows from New Brunswick to Ontario, south to Florida and Texas. In spite of its name, it tastes and smells like an onion. It has grass-like leaves and umbels of white or pink flowers.

Wild Leek or Ramp, *Allium tricoccum*, has strap-like, deep green leaves which form spreading colonies in rich woods of the east and midwest, frequently under maples. It is found from New Brunswick to southern Quebec, south to Georgia in the mountains, and to Iowa in the west. The leaves appear in early spring, reach their luxuriant peak in early summer, then die down, disappearing before midsummer; as the leaves die back, the plants flower, with 20-in tall flowering stems carrying domed clusters of creamy white flowers. Bulbs and leaves are edible, with an onion-like flavor, excellent in soups and casseroles.

Many wild onions grow in the west. **Hooker's Onion**, *A. acuminatum*, has narrow leaves and an umbel of pink flowers in early summer. It grows on rocky, brush-covered or wooded slopes from British Columbia to Wyoming, south to California and Arizona. **Paper Onion**, *A. amplectens*, is a white-

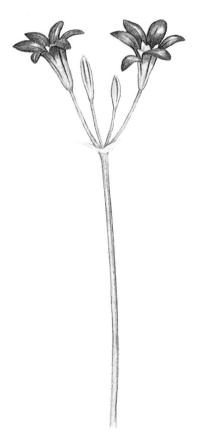

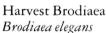

Harvest Brodiaea
Brodiaea elegans

White Hyacinth
Triteleia hyacinthina

Firecracker Flower
Dichelostemma ida-maia

flowered species found in hot, dry places west of the Sierra Nevada in California. Its leaves are often dry and withered by the time it comes into flower in early summer. **Dwarf Onion**, *A. parvum* (p. 232), grows in stony flats in the Great Basin. Its umbel of urn-like flowers grows on an extremely short stalk and its leaves are flattened.

Brodiaeas and **Triteleias**, *Brodiaea* and *Triteleia* species, are all very similar plants, closely related to the alliums. They have corms covered in a scale leaf, grass-like leaves, and erect, leafless flowering stems with umbels of flowers, each umbel subtended by a membranous bract. Brodiaeas have rounded leaves and six stamens—three fertile ones with erect anthers and three sterile ones; Triteleias have flattened leaves, and all six stamens in each flower are fertile, with versatile anthers. There are about 40 altogether, western plants, the great majority from California and the west coast into Oregon. Some, like Ithuriel's Spear, *B. laxa*, which has deep purple flowers, are grown in rock gardens.

Harvest Brodiaea, *Brodiaea elegans*, is a typical species, with a few narrow, grassy leaves that have already withered before the plant flowers in early summer. It has umbels of violet to deep purple, funnel-shaped flowers on leafless flower stems up to 15in tall. This plant grows in grassland and open woods, in the foothills of the mountains and on the plain from California to Oregon.

White Hyacinth, *Triteleia hyacinthina*, has white flowers, in contrast to the usual blue. It favors low-lying, wet places, like wet meadows, vernal pools, and streamsides, and is found from British Columbia to Idaho, and south to California. It has grassy leaves and umbels of white, bowl-shaped flowers on 2ft tall stalks in summer.

Firecracker Flower, *Dichelostemma ida-maia*, has bright red flowers, like a bunch of firecrackers, hanging in an umbel from the top of its stem in early summer. It also has three long, strap-like leaves growing in a clump around the base of the stem. This plant may be found on grassy slopes within coniferous woods in Oregon and California.

The **Greenbriars**, about 15 species belonging to the genus *Smilax*, may be included in the Lily family or placed in a family of their own, the Smilacaceae. They are twining vines, the majority with woody stems, and male and female flowers on separate plants. **Carrion Flower**, *S. herbacea* (p. 232), is a herbaceous species, with branched green stems that twine through and cling to other plants with stipules transformed into tendrils. It has alternate, pointed heart-shaped leaves, and dense, rounded clusters of yellow-green, foul-scented flowers in the leaf axils. On female plants the flowers are followed by clusters of lustrous, blue-black berries. It grows in woods in the east and midwest. The young shoots and leaves of this and several other *Smilax* species can be eaten like asparagus.

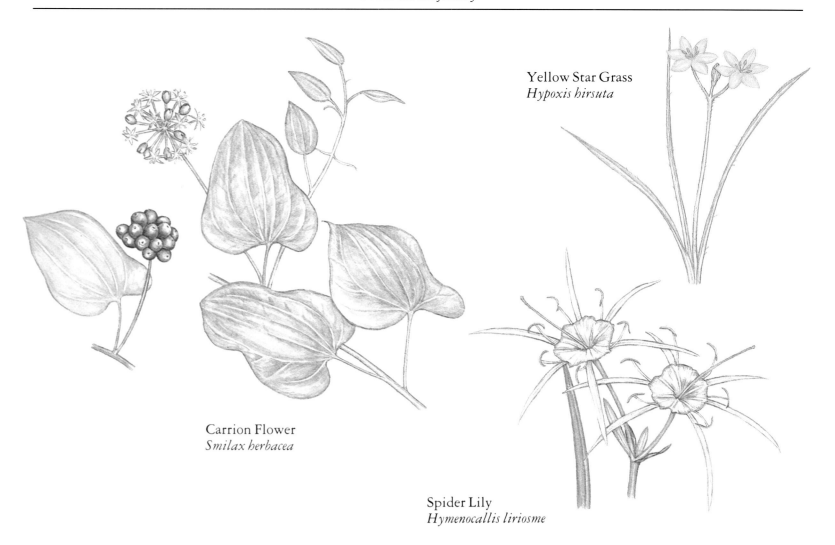

Yellow Star Grass
Hypoxis hirsuta

Carrion Flower
Smilax herbacea

Spider Lily
Hymenocallis liriosme

Amaryllis family

Amaryllidaceae

There are about 85 genera and 1100 species in this family, all bulbous herbaceous plants, the majority from the warm temperate regions of the world. Many beautiful ornamental plants come from this family, including daffodils and snow-drops, which are grown in cool northern gardens, and hippeastrums, crinums, and nerines, species which can only survive the winter in almost frost-free areas and so are most often grown in the house and greenhouse.

Family features The flowers are solitary or borne in umbels, usually regular and hermaphrodite. Each flower has six perianth segments in two separate whorls, sometimes with a corona. There are six stamens in two whorls opposite the perianth segments. The ovary is inferior with three cells and many seeds. The fruits are usually capsules. These are bulbous plants, with basal linear leaves.

Yellow Star Grass, *Hypoxis hirsuta*, is a plant of dry, open woods in the east and midwest, found from Maine to Manitoba, south to Georgia and Texas. It forms a little clump of linear, hairy leaves no more than 6in tall, and quite likely to be mistaken for a grass unless it is in flower. However, no grass ever had star-like, yellow flowers like this plant; they grow in a small umbel of 2–6 flowers at the top of a slender stalk in the early part of summer.

The **Spider Lilies**, about 12 species in the genus *Hymeno-callis*, have striking flowers with narrow perianth segments extending outward beyond a membranous, saucer-shaped corona. The stamens appear to grow from the edge of this corona. These are bulbous plants with linear, basal leaves, sheathing at their bases, and leafless flowering stems bearing terminal umbels composed of several flowers. They are southern plants on the whole. *Hymenocallis liriosme* grows in marshes and ditches from Louisiana to Texas. Its striking white flowers may measure as much as 7in across.

Pickerelweed family

Pontederiaceae

A small family, with about 7 genera and 30 species of aquatic, herbaceous plants from temperate and tropical areas of America, Africa, and Asia.

Family features These are aquatic, erect or floating plants with sheathing leaves, and their flowers are borne in spikes or singly. Each flower is regular or bilaterally symmetrical, hermaphrodite, with six perianth segments, three or six stamens, and a superior ovary.

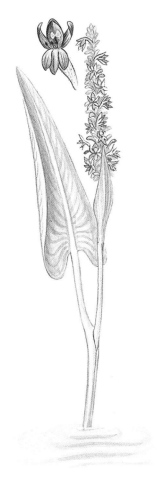

Water Hyacinth
Eichhornia crassipes

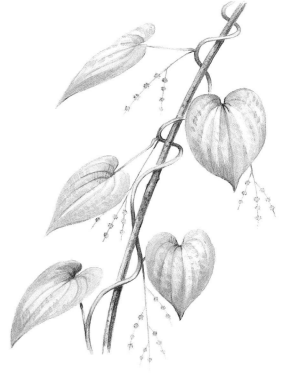

Wild Yam
Dioscorea villosa

Pickerelweed
Pontederia cordata

Pickerelweed, *Pontederia cordata*, is found in shallow water in marshes and along the edges of streams and ponds from Nova Scotia to Ontario and Minnesota, south to Florida and Texas, much less commonly inland. It has creeping rhizomes and long-stalked, basal leaves with arrow-shaped blades which emerge from the water to grow up to 1ft tall. In summer the flowers are borne in terminal spikes on stems which reach 2ft tall, and which bear two bracts, the lower one resembling a leaf and the upper one in the form of a sheath. The flowers are blue-violet, funnel-shaped, and two-lipped, the upper lip marked with two yellow spots. The fruits resemble achenes and develop in the persistent tube of the flower; each contains an edible seed which can be eaten like a nut or ground into flour. Young leaf stalks are also edible.

Water Hyacinth, *Eichhornia crassipes*, has been introduced into the southeast U.S., where it grows in canals, drainage ditches, ponds, and lakes, often spreading rapidly. It is a tropical plant and consequently its exuberance diminishes in the more northern areas of its range, since it has little tolerance for frost. It forms free-floating rosettes of rounded leaves; the leaves have distinctive inflated leaf stalks beneath the water, which act as flotation devices, but may not be visible if the plants are crowded. The flowers form showy, terminal, lavender-blue clusters on separate stalks; each bloom is tubular, with six large lobes.

Yam family

Dioscoreaceae

A family of twining vines, with 8–9 genera and about 750 species found in tropical and warm temperate regions.

Family features The flowers are small, regular, and unisexual, borne in spikes or racemes in the leaf axils. Each has six perianth segments arranged in two rows of three, joined at the base into a tube. There are three or six stamens in the male flowers, an inferior ovary with three cells in the female ones. The female flowers often have three sterile stamens. The fruits are capsules or berries, often with winged seeds. These twining plants have thick, tuberous or woody rhizomes, herbaceous or woody stems, and alternate or whorled leaves. The leaves are usually heart-shaped, with palmate main veins.

Yams are members of the genus *Dioscorea*, a genus with about 600 species, some of which are cultivated in the tropics for their huge tubers. Several species are found in eastern North America. **Wild Yam**, *D. villosa*, is typical, with twining green stems and alternate heart-shaped leaves. In summer it bears tiny, greenish-white flowers in the leaf axils, male and female on separate plants; the male flowers are produced in simple spikes, the female ones in compound spikes. Plants twine through trees and shrubs in damp woods and thickets, on roadsides and in other disturbed areas from Florida and Texas north to Ontario, although they become rare in the north. Wild Yam tubers are not edible but contain steroids, and are used in folk medicine to alleviate rheumatism. The steroids are also used in the birth control industry.

Spiderwort family
Commelinaceae

A family of perennial herbaceous plants, with about 38 genera and 500 species, mainly from tropical and subtropical regions of the world. There are some beautiful garden and house plants in this family. The Dayflowers and Spiderworts are grown in flower borders, while Wandering Jews are house plants.

Family features The flowers are usually regular, hermaphrodite, solitary, or borne in cymes in the axils of leaf-like spathes. Each flower has six perianth segments in two whorls; the outer whorl of three resemble free, overlapping sepals; the inner whorl of three resemble free, overlapping petals. There are usually six stamens in two whorls of three, but they may be reduced to three. The ovary is superior, usually with three cells. The fruits are capsules. The leaves have tubular, sheathing bases which are membranous in texture. The plants are often succulent.

There are several **Spiderworts**, *Tradescantia* species, in North America, mainly in the southern U.S. **Virginia Spiderwort**, *T. virginiana*, is one of those which has contributed to the garden varieties, bringing its hardy constitution to them; in its native form it is found farther north than many. It grows in moist woods and prairies from Georgia to Missouri, and north to Maine and Minnesota. This perennial, somewhat succulent plant forms a clump of erect stems up to 3ft tall, with alternate, linear leaves. From a distance the effect is one of interlocking leaves, rather than of stems, an effect created by the long, sheathing leaves which hide much of the stems, and also by the long bracts in which the flower clusters grow. These bracts are even longer and wider than the leaves and are held out at acute angles to the stems, cutting across each other and creating a considerable tangle. The flowers have blue or purple petals and open a few at a time in each cluster. The young shoots and leaves of this plant can be eaten raw in salads or cooked as a vegetable, as can those of the Dayflowers.

Asiatic Dayflower, *Commelina communis*, is an introduced species, which grows in disturbed habitats in the east, in moist and shady places, on roadsides, in woods, and as a weed in gardens. It is an annual plant, with stems which branch and sprawl, spreading and rooting at the nodes. The stems bear alternate, lance-shaped leaves with sheathing bases, and

Virginia Spiderwort
Tradescantia virginiana

Asiatic Dayflower
Commelina communis

Yellow-eyed Grass
Xyris iridifolia

terminal clusters of flowers growing in the axils of heart-shaped, folded spathes. Each flower has three petals—two large, upper, blue ones and a third lower, much smaller, whitish petal. Several similar native species grow in the eastern and midwestern U.S.

Yellow-eyed Grass family
Xyridaceae

A very small family, with only 2 genera and about 40 species, found in the tropical and subtropical regions of the world.

About 18 **Yellow-eyed Grasses**, *Xyris* species (p. 235), are found in the southeastern U.S., especially in Florida, the majority beside ponds and ditches, in marshes and wet pine barrens. They are annual or perennial plants, with a clump of straight leaves, either linear or rounded in cross-section, growing around the leafless flower stalks. The flowers grow in distinctive terminal spikes, on flower stalks at most 3ft tall; each flower spike consists of a cone-like arrangement of woody bracts which conceal the buds and fruit, and from which the yellow flowers protrude.

Each flower has three sepals—an outer one which is hooded, curved around the corolla in the bud, and soon shed as the bud opens, and two lateral ones which are boat-shaped or winged,

and which persist after the flower opens; a three-lobed yellow corolla formed of three fused petals three stamens opposite the petal-lobes and alternating with three sterile stamens in some species; and a superior ovary, with one cell.

Iris family
Iridaceae

A large family, with about 60 genera and 800 species of perennial herbaceous plants, distributed throughout the world. The family contains many ornamental plants. These include many species and varieties of irises, as well as crocuses and montbretias. Freesias make superb cut flowers.

Family features The flowers are hermaphrodite, regular, or bilaterally symmetrical, usually with one or two bracts forming a spathe around their base. Each flower has six perianth segments joined at the base into a tube, and arranged in two whorls of three (the perianth segments may be alike in both whorls or dissimilar). There are three stamens opposite the outer perianth segments. The ovary is inferior with three cells. The fruits are capsules. These plants have rhizomes, bulbs, or corms and form clumps of flattened leaves, folded and overlapping at the base, and sheathing the bases of the separate flowering stems.

Blue Flag
Iris versicolor

Rocky Mountain Iris
Iris missouriensis

Yellow Flag
Iris pseudacorus

Red Iris
Iris fulva

The **Irises** form one of the largest groups in the family, with about 300 species in the genus *Iris*, found throughout temperate regions of the northern hemisphere. About 25–30 species grow wild in North America. They are perennial plants, some with fleshy rhizomes, others forming bulbs. They have clumps of sword-shaped leaves, their bases folded over each other so that they form two opposite, overlapping rows. The flowers grow in terminal clusters on stems which originate between the leaves.

Iris flowers are showy, with three clawed, outer perianth segments (known as "falls") usually flexed downward and larger than the inner segments; three clawed inner segments (known as "standards"), which are usually erect, and bearded in some species; and a three-cleft style (known as the "crest"), with three petal-like sections, each one arching over a stamen.

The **Blue Flag**, *Iris versicolor* (p. 236), is one of several blue-flowered irises found in the east. It grows in marshes, wet meadows, and on shores from Newfoundland to Manitoba, south to Virginia and Minnesota. It forms large clumps of sword-shaped leaves up to 3ft tall; among these in midsummer grow the flowering stalks, each one with a terminal cluster of violet or blue-violet flowers. The falls are reticulated with darker blue, and variegated with yellow or white at the base. The rhizomes of this iris are poisonous (like those of many others), causing inflammation of the stomach and intestines.

The **Rocky Mountain Iris** or Western Blue Flag, *Iris missouriensis* (p. 236), is one of several blue-flowered western irises. It forms clumps of sword-like leaves, and grows in wet meadows and beside streams in the Rocky Mountains, east of the Sierra Nevada, east to South Dakota and New Mexico.

The rhizomes of **Yellow Flag**, *Iris pseudacorus* (p. 236), may be mistaken for those of the edible Cattails, like those of Blue Flag, and are also poisonous. This is an introduced species from Europe, now naturalized on the sides of ponds and streams, in marshes and ditches from Newfoundland to Minnesota, and southward. It forms clumps of stiff, erect leaves growing from tangled rhizomes, and erect flowering stems about the same height as the leaves. The flowers are yellow, with three broad, hanging falls, three upright standards, and three arching styles, ragged at their tips.

Red Iris, *Iris fulva* (p. 236), is also known as Copper Iris, both names coming from the color of the flowers. This is another wetland plant, growing in swamps and wet woods from Pennsylvania to Illinois, south to Georgia and Missouri. It forms a clump of sword-shaped leaves about 3ft tall, with flowering stems in late spring. The flowers are relatively flat, with three broad, reflexed falls, three narrower but also reflexed standards, and three arching styles.

Not all irises grow in wet places. Many grow in dry or grassy situations, like the **Ground Iris**, *Iris macrosiphon*. This is a

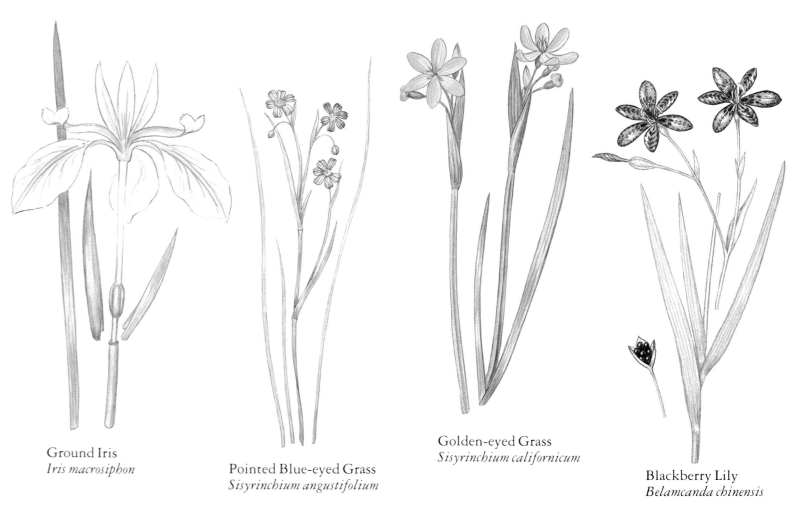

Ground Iris
Iris macrosiphon

Pointed Blue-eyed Grass
Sisyrinchium angustifolium

Golden-eyed Grass
Sisyrinchium californicum

Blackberry Lily
Belamcanda chinensis

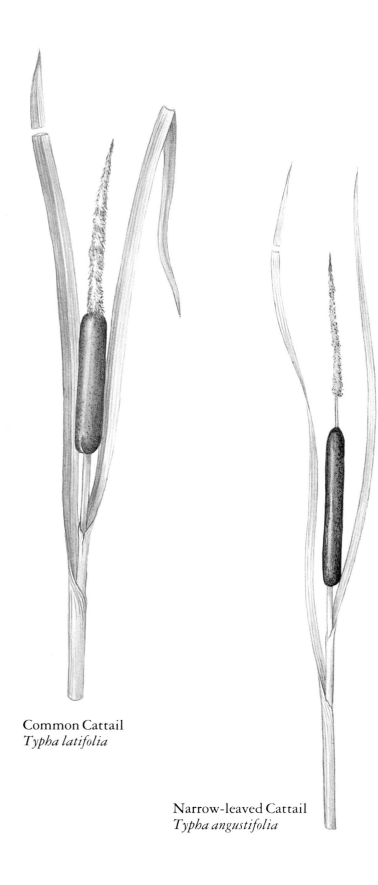

Common Cattail
Typha latifolia

Narrow-leaved Cattail
Typha angustifolia

Californian species found on open slopes in the foothills of the Sierra Nevada and inner Coast Ranges. It is a small plant with a tuft of sword-like leaves only 8in tall, and stems bearing a few flowers in spring. The flowers may be golden or creamy yellow, pale lavender, or deep blue-purple.

The **Blue-eyed Grasses**, *Sisyrinchium* species, form a group of about 100 found only in the New World, except for one species in Ireland. **Pointed Blue-eyed Grass**, *S. angustifolium* (p. 237), is typical, its blue or violet flowers having the yellow center which gives the group common name. It forms tufts of grass-like leaves, 20in tall at most, and through much of the summer produces flowering stems that open a succession of flowers from terminal umbels. The perianth segments are all alike and look like six petals. The plant grows in meadows and open woods, in fields and shores throughout much of the U.S. and southern Canada, in mountains in the southern parts of its range. It is grown in rock gardens.

Golden-eyed Grass, *Sisyrinchium californicum* (p. 237), is a Pacific coast species found in moist places and marshes west of the Cascades from California to Oregon. It forms tufts of grass-like leaves, usually no more than 15in tall, and has separate flowering stems, with umbels of yellow flowers growing from spathes in early summer. The petals of the flowers are veined with brown.

Blackberry Lily, *Belamcanda chinensis* (p. 237), is an introduced species, originally from Asia but now found wild on roadsides and hillsides, in open woods and around old homesites from Connecticut to Nebraska, and south to Georgia and Texas. Its leaves are much like those of an iris, but its red-spotted, orange flowers are more like those of a lily. The capsules which follow the flowers burst open to expose clusters of black seeds like blackberries.

Pipewort family
Eriocaulaceae

A mostly tropical family, with 9 genera and 360 species of aquatic plants, a few found in warm temperate regions.

The **Pipeworts**, *Eriocaulon* species, grow in shallow water and bogs, wet pine barrens and on muddy shores in the east and midwest. They are perennial plants with clumps of linear leaves, but it is when they are in flower that they stand out from their surroundings, for their white flowers grow in dense "buttons" on tall, angular, leafless stems. Individually the flowers are small, with males and females separate, in some species on separate plants. *Eriocaulon decangulare* (p. 239) grows on the coastal plain from New Jersey to Florida and Texas. Other species grow farther north, in eastern Canada and around the Great Lakes. Pipewort is not the only name given to these plants; they are also called Hatpins and Buttonrods, obvious references to the flowers on their erect stems.

Cattail family
Typhaceae

A very small family, with only one genus, *Typha*, and 10 species, but found throughout the world. They are known by a variety of names, including cattails and bulrushes. All 10 species grow in shallow water, in marshes and swamps, along the edges of ponds, slow-moving rivers, and ditches.

They are tall, perennial plants with creeping rhizomes and may form extensive colonies. Their erect stems grow up to 9ft tall in the largest species, with thick, sword-like leaves growing from the bases of the stems in overlapping rows. The stems are stiff and unbranched, and bear the flowers in terminal, cylindrical heads, the greenish female flowers below, and the male flowers above, yellow with pollen when in full bloom. The male flowers are shed after their pollen has blown away to pollinate the female flowers, leaving a bare stalk, but the female flowers form a brown fruiting head. This lasts for months, persisting into winter until it breaks up.

Common Cattail, *Typha latifolia* (p. 238), is the largest, growing up to 9ft tall with leaves up to ¾ in across. Its male and female flowers form one continuous, cylindrical flower spike. The **Narrow-leaved Cattail**, *T. angustifolia* (p. 238), is not more than 6ft tall, with leaves only ¼in wide. Its male and female flowers are separated by a section of stem up to 3in long. Both species grow in many parts of the world.

Their wide colonies form hiding and nesting places for many aquatic birds, and for mammals like muskrats. Many of their parts are edible. The spring shoots can be eaten like asparagus, the young flower spikes like corn on the cob; the pollen can be mixed with flour to make muffins or pancakes; white flour can be made from the winter rhizomes.

Bur-reed family
Sparganiaceae

A small family of aquatic plants, with only one genus and about 20 species, found in many parts of the world.

The **Bur-reeds**, *Sparganium* species, are perennial aquatic plants which spread by means of creeping rhizomes in marshes or along the edges of ponds and slow-moving rivers. Some have erect stems and two-ranked, grass-like leaves, the bases of the leaves sheathing the stems. Others are floating plants. Their flowers are borne in several small, green balls, male flowers near the tip of the stem, female ones below. *Sparganium americanum* is one of about 12 species found throughout North America; it is an erect plant with a stout stem up to 3ft tall found in swamps and ponds from Newfoundland to Minnesota, and south to Florida and Louisiana.

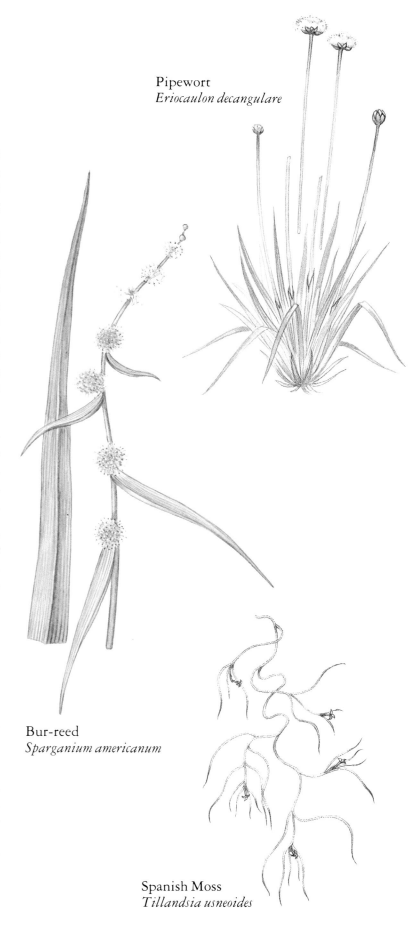

Pipewort
Eriocaulon decangulare

Bur-reed
Sparganium americanum

Spanish Moss
Tillandsia usneoides

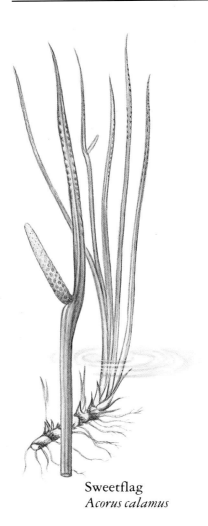

Sweetflag
Acorus calamus

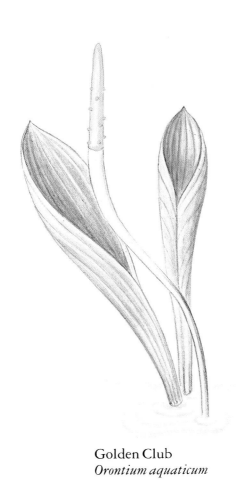

Golden Club
Orontium aquaticum

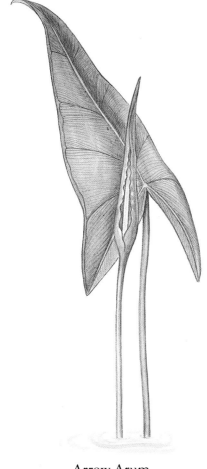

Arrow Arum
Peltandra virginica

Pineapple family

Bromeliaceae

A mostly tropical family from warmer areas of America, with about 59 genera and 1300 species. The majority are epiphytic plants: they grow attached to other plants but are not parasitic, and get their nutrients from air and rain. Pineapples are members of this family. A variety of bromeliads are popular as house plants.

Many plants in this family form rosettes of stiff, strap-shaped leaves resembling vases, which collect water in the center. Often the leaves have spiny edges and are brightly colored at the base. The plants known as Wild Pines, various species of *Tillandsia* which grow in the Florida swamps and hammocks, are of this form. However, **Spanish Moss**, *T. usneoides* (p. 239), is atypical of the family as a whole, both in its form and in its more northern distribution. This is the plant that hangs from Live Oaks and telegraph wires in the south, found on the coastal plain from Florida and Texas north as far as Maryland. It looks like moss but consists of wiry, branching stems and tiny, thread-like leaves all covered with silver scales that trap water and dust, and so the plant obtains its water and nutrient needs. It bears tiny, yellow-green flowers on short side branches in early summer.

Arum family

Araceae

A family of herbaceous plants, with about 115 genera and 2000 species, found mainly in tropical jungles. Temperate species are most commonly found in wet places. Several popular house plants come from this family, mostly grown for their impressive leaves. They include philodendrons, dieffenbachias, and monsteras. Many plants in the family contain poisonous juice, including those found in North America. They rarely cause serious poisoning because the juice is so acrid that it burns the mouth and is not swallowed.

Family features The flowers are very small, often with an offensive scent, and borne in a dense spike (a spadix), usually subtended by a leafy bract (a spathe). The flowers may be hermaphrodite or unisexual; if unisexual, then the male flowers are borne on the upper part of the spadix, the females below. Hermaphrodite flowers usually have a perianth, with 4–6 lobes or forming a cup, but this is absent in unisexual flowers. There are 2–8 stamens opposite the perianth segments. The ovary is superior or embedded in the spadix, and has 1–3 cells. The fruit is usually a berry, but may be leathery and split open. The leaves often have sheathing bases; they generally form a basal clump growing from the rhizome.

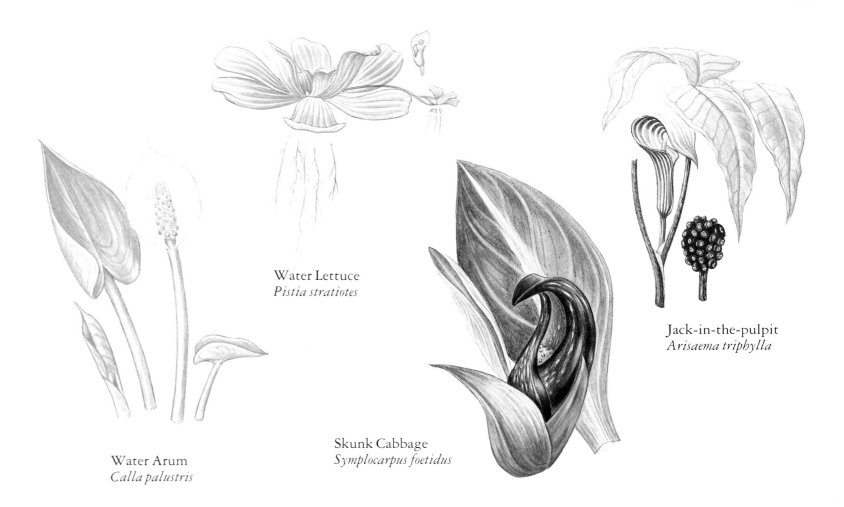

Water Lettuce
Pistia stratiotes

Jack-in-the-pulpit
Arisaema triphylla

Skunk Cabbage
Symplocarpus foetidus

Water Arum
Calla palustris

Sweetflag, *Acorus calamus* (p. 240), is found in swamps and beside ponds and rivers from Nova Scotia to Alberta, south to Florida and Colorado. Its rhizomes creep in the mud and form colonies of sword-like, wavy-edged leaves up to 5ft tall. The leaves have a scent of tangerines and cinnamon when bruised. Stems that look like three-angled leaves also grow from the rhizomes to bear flower spikes about halfway up, growing at an angle of about 45 degrees. The spikes bear densely packed, yellowish, hermaphrodite flowers with an unpleasant scent. Sweetflag rhizomes yield a volatile oil known as Calamus Oil, used in perfumery; the rhizomes are also used in herb medicine and in the production of the tonic medicine known as Stockton Bitters. The leaves were strewn as rushes on the floors of churches, castles, and manor houses in medieval times.

Golden Club, *Orontium aquaticum* (p. 240), grows in swamps, marshes, and ponds from New York to Florida and Louisiana, inland to Mississippi and Kentucky. It is a perennial, with thick rhizomes and clumps of large, elliptical, long-stalked leaves. Golden yellow flowers are borne in dense spadices terminating the leafless flower stalks; a narrow, sheathing spathe grows at the base of each stalk. The rhizomes and fruits are eaten by the Indians; raw they burn the mouth, but dried and cooked they become edible.

Arrow Arum, *Peltandra virginica* (p. 240), grows along shallow rivers and pond edges, in marshes and swamps, often forming large colonies in such places. It is found from Maine to Michigan, south to Florida and Texas, north into Canada. It has fleshy leaves with long stalks and broadly triangular blades. In early summer the flower spathe develops, curved closely around the spadix, covering the lower female flowers, opening to expose the upper male ones. The flowers are followed by black-brown berries.

Water Arum, *Calla palustris*, is a northern plant, also preferring wet places, growing in swamps and bogs, along the edges of ponds and lakes from Nova Scotia to Quebec, south to Pennsylvania and Minnesota. From its elongated rhizomes grow many long-stalked leaves with ovate blades, 1ft tall at most; solitary white spathes, also growing on long stalks, open to reveal the spadices of yellow flowers. They develop in early summer and are followed by red berries. The whole plant is so acrid that it causes skin irritation.

Water Lettuce, *Pistia stratiotes*, is a floating plant with velvety leaves growing in rosettes, and small, white spadices hidden in small spathes among the leaves. This is an aggressive, introduced plant that is invading ponds, ditches, and swamps from Florida to Texas.

Skunk Cabbage, *Symplocarpus foetidus*, is found in wet meadows and marshy woods, muddy ground and swamps. It grows across much of southern Canada, south in the east and midwest to North Carolina and Iowa. This is a perennial plant

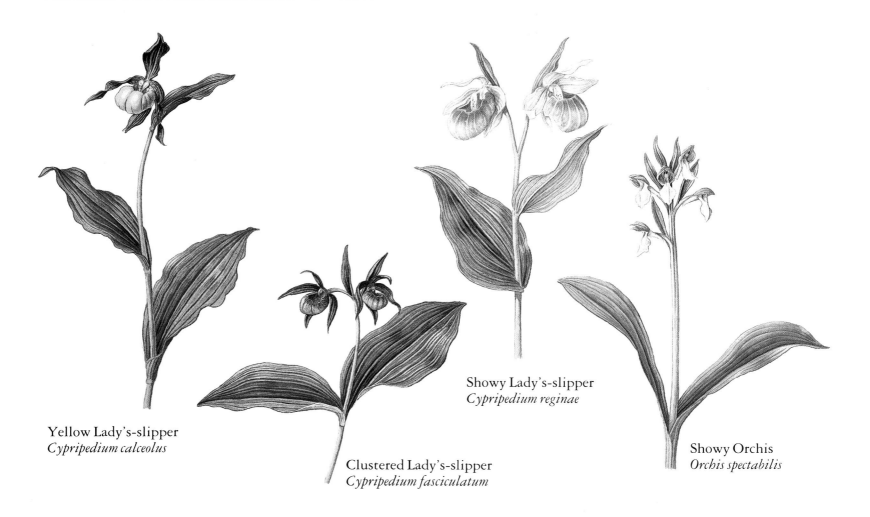

Yellow Lady's-slipper
Cypripedium calceolus

Clustered Lady's-slipper
Cypripedium fasciculatum

Showy Lady's-slipper
Cypripedium reginae

Showy Orchis
Orchis spectabilis

with a thick rhizome. In early spring its purple-brown, green-mottled spathe erupts from the ground, melting the snow around. It protects the knob-like spadix, which emits a scent of decay to attract flies to pollinate its flowers. The leaves emerge later in tight rolls, unfurling to grow up to 2ft across, like those of giant cabbages.

Jack-in-the-pulpit or Indian Turnip, *Arisaema triphylla* (p. 241), grows in moist woods, often in boggy places, from Nova Scotia to Minnesota, south to Florida and Louisiana. It is a perennial plant, with a large acrid corm, said to be edible if dried or cooked, although opinions vary. The plant produces two large leaves on long stalks up to 5ft tall, with each blade divided into 3–5 leaflets. The "jack-in-the-pulpit" is the spadix in the spathe; the latter has a long stalk, a tube around the yellow spadix, and an arching, hood-like tip, which varies in color from green to maroon, and is often streaked with purple. The flowers are followed by scarlet berries.

Orchid family

Orchidaceae

This is one of the largest plant families, with about 735 genera and 17,000 species known to date; the figures increase every year as more are discovered and named. Many are found in temperate regions of the world, but far more grow in tropical jungles, and it is these jungle species which contribute most new species each year.

Family features Orchid flowers may be solitary, or borne in a spike, raceme, or compound raceme. They are hermaphrodite and bilaterally symmetrical. Each flower has six perianth segments in two whorls; sometimes the two whorls are similar, but often they are unlike, the outer ones resembling sepals and the inner ones petals. Often there is one central sepal, which becomes the uppermost part of the flower, and two lateral sepals; and frequently there are two lateral petals, and a central one, which becomes twisted to hang downward, forming the lip or labellum. This latter structure is often highly complex and also spurred, with nectar in the spur. The lateral sepals and petals often resemble each other. There may be one or two stamens, their anthers borne with the stigmas on a special structure known as the "column." The pollen grains often adhere to each other to form small packets known as "pollinia." The ovary is inferior, usually with one cell. The fruit is generally a capsule containing numerous minute seeds (millions in some species). Orchid leaves are entire, and usually arranged in two overlapping rows at the base of the stem or alternately. They are often fleshy, with a sheathing base that circles the stem, but may be reduced to scales.

For many years horticulturists failed to get orchid seeds to germinate. Finally it was realized that most orchids grow in a mycorrhizal association with a fungus. The fungus grows through and around the roots, and the orchid gets much of its water and nutrients from the fungus, not directly from the soil. Germinating orchid seeds contain no food reserves and die if they do not connect with the right fungus quickly.

There are about 10 **Lady's-slipper Orchids** in North America, all in the genus *Cypripedium*, most of them growing in damp or wet woods and swamps. They are spectacular orchids, but not common; many have been overcollected and are now rare. Their name comes from the pouched lip of the flower, which is said to resemble a slipper; sometimes they are called Moccasin Flowers for the same reason. These plants all have rhizomes, an erect stem, and two or more leaves, either sheathing the base of the stem or higher up. They often have only one flower, and bear four at most.

The **Yellow Lady's-slipper**, *Cypripedium calceolus* (p. 242), grows in wet woods and bogs around the North Pole, across Canada, and into the U.S., south to the Carolinas, Louisiana, and through the Rocky Mountains to New Mexico. It is common nowhere. In early summer it forms an erect stem up to 2ft tall; this stem bears 3–5 large, elliptical leaves and one or two flowers at the tip, in the axil of a leafy bract. The flowers have yellow to purple, often wavy sepals, one erect at the top

and the two lateral ones joined and pointing downward; two spirally twisted, linear petals, similar in color to the sepals; and a creamy to bright yellow pouched lip, spotted with magenta inside.

The **Showy Lady's-slipper**, *Cypripedium reginae* (p. 242), is a rare species which has been a target for collection for many years; consequently its numbers are now very depleted in the wild. It grows in mossy woods, bogs, and swamps, especially in areas where the underlying rock is limestone, from Newfoundland to North Dakota, and south to Georgia and Missouri, in mountains in the southern parts of its range. It forms an erect stem up to 3ft tall, with several elliptical, strongly ribbed leaves. Both stem and leaves are covered with glandular hairs. One to three flowers are borne at the top of the stem; they have white sepals and lateral petals, and a striking pouch, white, pink or purple with pink or purple veins, and deeply furrowed.

Some of the Lady's-slippers have duller flowers, like **Clustered Lady's-slipper**, *Cypripedium fasciculatum* (p. 242). This plant has greenish sepals and petals veined with brown, and a yellow-green pouch. It grows in open, rocky woods in the mountains from California to Washington.

The **Showy Orchis**, *Orchis spectabilis* (p. 242), produces a stout flowering stem up to 1ft tall, growing from a pair of large, glossy, elliptical leaves which sheath its base. It

Snake-mouth
Pogonia ophioglossoides

Whorled Pogonia
Isotria verticillata

Small Round-leaved Orchis
Orchis rotundifolia

Giant Helleborine
Epipactis gigantea

produces several showy flowers at the top of the stem; each flower has a hood formed by the fusion of the sepals and lateral petals, and a long, tongue-shaped, hanging lip which has a backwardly directed spur. The flowers vary in color from white to pink, sometimes with a pink hood and a white lip. They grow in the axils of long, leaf-like bracts. This orchid is not very common; it grows in rich woods from New Brunswick to Nebraska, south to Georgia and Arkansas. **Small Round-leaved Orchis**, *O. rotundifolia* (p. 243), has a much wider distribution—through Canada, around the Great Lakes, and south to New York in the east. It grows in wet woods and on the edges of swamps. It is a smaller plant, with rounded leaves and white or mauve flowers.

The **Snake-mouth** or Rose Pogonia, *Pogonia ophioglossoides* (p. 243), is quite rare, growing in open bogs and seepage slopes from Newfoundland to Minnesota, south to Florida and Texas. It produces a slender stem up to 2ft tall, with a single, lance-shaped or elliptical leaf part way up, and a terminal, solitary, fragrant pink flower in the axil of a leaf-like bract. The flower has three similar sepals forming a triangle, two similar lateral petals arching over the lip, and a spatula-shaped lip, fringed and bearded with short yellow bristles.

Whorled Pogonia or Five-leaves, *Isotria verticillata* (p. 243), has a slender stem ending in a whorl of five or six oblong leaves, and a solitary flower in the center of the whorl. The flower has three long, narrow, brownish-purple sepals projecting forward over the flower, two yellow-green petals joined over the lip, and a lobed, purple-streaked lip. The plant grows in woods in acid soils from Maine to Wisconsin, south to Florida and Texas. Little Five-leaves, *I. medeoloides* is one of the rarest orchids in North America, apparently extinct in many places, although it may remain dormant for years.

The **Giant Helleborine**, *Epipactis gigantea* (p. 243), is also known as the Stream Orchid, since it grows on stream banks, or beside lakes and springs. It is found in the west from British Columbia to South Dakota, south to California and Texas. It is a perennial plant with colonies of erect, leafy stems up to 3ft tall. The leaves are large, lance-shaped to broadly ovate, those at the base of the stem the largest. The flowers grow in a few-flowered raceme, each one in the axil of a leaf-like bract. They have greenish-brown, concave sepals, shorter, purplish, lateral petals, and a deeply spoon-shaped, purple lip with a salmon-pink tongue. All parts of the flower are purple-veined.

The genus *Habenaria* is a large one, with about 500 species, mainly found in the warmer parts of the world. However, the approximately 30 species in North America are northern orchids, many growing in acid bogs and wet places, some as far north as Alaska and Greenland. They are known as Bog Orchids and Rein Orchids, and some, with fringed petals, are known as Fringed Orchids.

White Bog Orchid
Habenaria dilatata

Bracted Orchid
Habenaria viridis

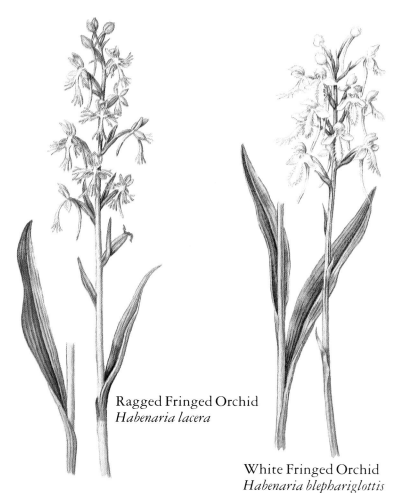
Ragged Fringed Orchid
Habenaria lacera

White Fringed Orchid
Habenaria blephariglottis

The **White Bog Orchid** or Bog Candles, *Habenaria dilatata* (p. 244), is typical of many North American species in this genus. It is a perennial plant, with an erect leafy stem 2–3ft tall, with many sheathing leaves growing smaller higher up the stem, and merging with the bracts of the inflorescence. The waxy, white, spurred flowers grow in an elongated raceme terminating the stem, opening over a long period of time during the summer. This orchid grows in wet woods and bogs, along streams and in wet meadows from Greenland to Alaska, throughout Canada, south into the U.S. to Massachusetts, Indiana, and to California in the west.

The **Bracted Orchid** or Frog Orchid, *Habenaria viridis* (p. 244), grows in moist woods all around the North Pole, south in North America to northern areas of the U.S., through the Appalachians to North Carolina, and in the Rocky Mountains to Colorado. It has many broadly lance-shaped leaves merging into linear bracts in the inflorescence, and greenish flowers, often tinged with purple, inconspicuous in the axils of the bracts.

The **Fringed Orchids** are distinguished by the distinctive fringed edges of the lip in their flowers and are often put into a separate genus of their own. **Ragged Fringed Orchid**, *Habenaria lacera* (p. 244), grows in open swamps and bogs from Newfoundland to Manitoba, south to South Carolina, Alabama, and Arkansas. It has an erect stem 2–3ft tall, with lance-shaped leaves on the lower part of the stem, and creamy yellow or greenish-yellow flowers; the lip is divided into three lobes, each one deeply cut to form the fringe.

Fringed Orchids come in a variety of colors. **White Fringed Orchid**, *Habenaria blephariglottis* (p. 244), has white, fringed flowers. It grows in wet meadows and marshes from eastern Canada south to Florida and Mississippi. **Purple Fringed Orchid**, *H. psycodes*, decorates wet woods and meadows with rose-purple flowers. It is found from Newfoundland to Manitoba, south to North Carolina and Tennessee, in mountains in the south of its range.

The **Grass-pink**, *Calopogon pulchellus*, has a rounded corm, which produces a single, grass-like leaf and flowering stalk in early summer. It has unusual flowers in which the lip forms the top part of the flower above the other petals and sepals which are all similar. The flowers vary from pink to rose-purple and each has a yellow beard on the lip. This orchid is found in wet meadows and bogs from Newfoundland to Ontario and around the Great Lakes, south through New England to Florida, and then to Texas.

Three-birds Orchid, *Triphora trianthophora*, is a delicate plant with a slender stem, curved at first but straightening as it grows to its final height of about 1ft. It has small, clasping leaves scattered along the stem and a few ephemeral pink and white flowers growing in the axils of the uppermost leaves.

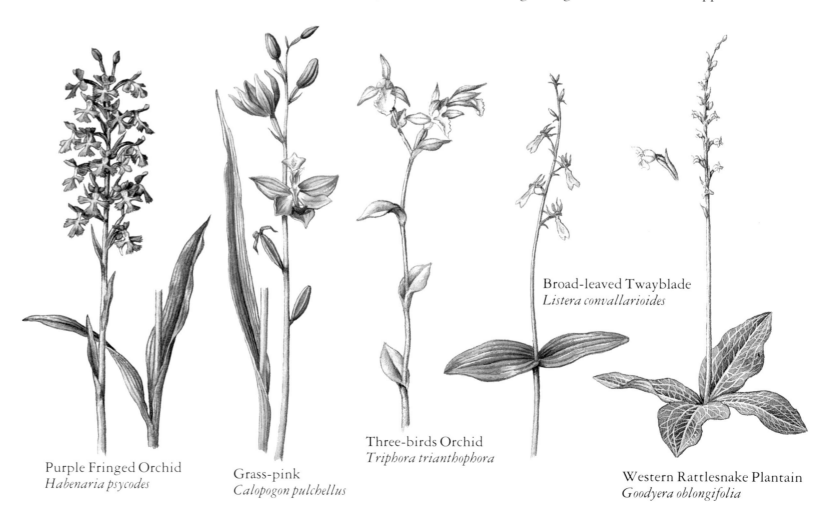

Broad-leaved Twayblade
Listera convallarioides

Three-birds Orchid
Triphora trianthophora

Purple Fringed Orchid
Habenaria psycodes

Grass-pink
Calopogon pulchellus

Western Rattlesnake Plantain
Goodyera oblongifolia

Bog Twayblade
Liparis loeselii

Fairy Slipper
Calypso bulbosa

Dragon's Mouth
Arethusa bulbosa

Nodding Ladies Tresses
Spiranthes cernua

The lips of the flowers are marked with green veins. This plant appears sporadically in rich woods, often growing on rotting logs, from Maine to Wisconsin, south to Florida and Texas.

The **Twayblades**, *Listera* species, are a group of about 30 northern orchids. They have fibrous roots and slender, erect stems with a pair of broad, opposite leaves near the middle. The small flowers lack spurs, are dull, greenish or purplish, and borne in a slender raceme. **Broad-leaved Twayblade**, *L. convallarioides* (p. 245), is found in wet woods from Newfoundland to Alaska, south in the U.S. to Massachasetts, Minnesota, and California in the west. It has broadly ovate leaves and up to 20 translucent, yellow-green flowers.

Rattlesnake Plantains belong to the genus *Goodyera*. There are four species in North America. The feature that makes them immediately recognizable is their leaves, borne in a basal rosette, and reticulately veined with white so that they resemble snakeskin. **Western Rattlesnake Plantain**, *G. oblongifolia* (p. 245), grows in woods and forests from British Columbia to Quebec and around the Great Lakes, south through the Rocky Mountains to California. It is the largest of the four, with a stout, erect stem reaching 18in tall and carrying a terminal spike of whitish, glandular-hairy flowers. Each flower has a hood-like upper lip formed of the dorsal sepal and attached lateral petals, separate lateral sepals, and a spurless, pouched labellum.

Bog Twayblade, *Liparis loeselii*, has two shiny basal leaves and an erect stem with several yellow-green flowers. The flowers have thread-like petals and a broad hanging lip. Plants grow in bogs and wet woods from Nova Scotia to Manitoba, south to New Jersey, Alabama, and Nebraska. The related Large Twayblade, *L. liliifolia*, has brownish flowers, each with an expanded, translucent lip. This orchid grows in rich woods in the east and midwest.

The **Fairy Slipper**, *Calypso bulbosa*, produces a single leaf in fall, which survives through the winter and the flowering season of the following year, only withering and dying once flowering is over. The bulb from which it grows persists beneath the ground, sending up another leaf as fall comes again. In the spring it produces a single stem with a solitary, terminal flower; the three sepals and two lateral petals are all linear and pink-purple, arching at the top of the pouched lip. The lip hangs downward and is shaped like a shoe, white in color with pink blotches, and bearded with yellow hairs; it has two tiny horns at the toe.

The **Dragon's Mouth** or Bog-rose, *Arethusa bulbosa*, grows in *Sphagnum* bogs, wet woods, and meadows from Newfoundland to Minnesota, south to New Jersey, and in the mountains to South Carolina. However, its wide distribution is deceptive, for this is a rare orchid. It flowers in summer, producing a single stalk with 1–3 scale-like bracts and a solitary, scented

Spotted Coralroot
Corallorhiza maculata

Cranefly Orchid
Tipularia discolor

Striped Coralroot
Corallorhiza striata

Hooded Ladies Tresses
Spiranthes romanzoffia

flower at the tip. This is bright pink, with three erect sepals, two lateral petals arching over the lip, and a showy lip spotted with deeper pink and with many yellow hairs. As the flower fades and the fruiting capsule develops, the single grass-like leaf appears, maturing with the capsule.

The **Ladies Tresses** are a group of about 200 species belonging to the genus *Spiranthes*, with over 20 species in North America. They are small orchids, with leafy, erect stems and characteristic, spirally twisted racemes of flowers. **Nodding Ladies Tresses**, *S. cernua* (p. 246), is typical. It grows in open woods and meadows, in fields and bogs, usually on acid soils, from Newfoundland to Minnesota, south to Florida and Texas. It has grass-like leaves, mostly concentrated in a basal rosette, and an erect flowering stem which grows to about 3ft tall. Its flowers are white and arch downward (hence Nodding Ladies Tresses), and are borne in an elongated raceme. **Hooded Ladies Tresses**, *S. romanzoffia*, has a denser inflorescence and the flowers are not nodding.

Cranefly Orchid, *Tipularia discolor*, forms a series of bulbs beneath the ground, linked by short rhizomes. The youngest of these produces a leaf in fall, which remains green through the winter, withering in the spring before the slender, leafless flowering stem appears in summer. The flowers have long spurs and pale greenish-purple sepals and petals veined with purple. The lip is pale purple. This plant is quite common in

rich woods from New York to Indiana, south to Florida and eastern Texas.

Coral-roots, members of the genus *Corallorhiza*, are saprophytic orchids. They are yellowish or brownish plants with no roots; instead they have much-branched, fleshy, rounded rhizomes which resemble a piece of coral, hence the name. These orchids depend entirely on their associated mycorrhizal fungi for their water and nutrients. They are woodland plants, growing where there is ample organic matter in the soil for them to feed on. There are about 15 species altogether, from northern and mountain regions of the northern hemisphere, with several in North America.

Spotted Coralroot, *Corallorhiza maculata*, grows in damp, upland woods from Newfoundland to British Columbia, south to North Carolina in the Appalachians, and in the Rocky Mountains to Mexico. Its coral-like rhizomes produce yellowish or purplish flowering stalks, 10–20in tall, in late summer. Each stalk has a few tubular sheaths near the base, the remnants of the leaves, and a raceme of flowers. The sepals and lateral petals are similar in color to the stalks, but the lip is whitish and spotted with purple. This is the largest of the coral-roots. **Striped Coralroot**, *C. striata*, has striped, red-purple flowers. It grows in rich woods across much of Canada, around the Great Lakes, and south in the U.S. mountains in the east and west.

Glossary

Achene A small dry indehiscent fruit with a single seed. Its thin wall distinguishes it from a nutlet.

Alien An introduced plant which has become naturalized.

Alternate An arrangement of leaves on a stem, such that each node bears one leaf on alternate sides of the stem (see Fig. 2).

Annual A plant completing its life cycle within a single year: germinating from seed, flowering, and setting seed itself, then dying.

Anther The portion of a stamen in which the pollen is formed (see Fig. 5).

Axil The place between a lateral branch of a stem, twig or leaf, and the main stem.

Bearded With bristly hairs.

Berry A fleshy fruit, usually containing several seeds. Often used as a more general term for any fleshy fruit.

Biennial A plant which completes its life cycle in two years, developing a root and leaves in its first year, overwintering by means of food stored in the root, then flowering and setting seed in the second year, and dying.

Blade The expanded, flat portion of a leaf, in contrast to the stalk.

Bract A specialized leaf with a flower growing in its axil. Bracts may closely resemble leaves, or may differ in size, color or texture, cf. Spathe (see Fig. 1).

Fig. 2 Leaf Arrangements

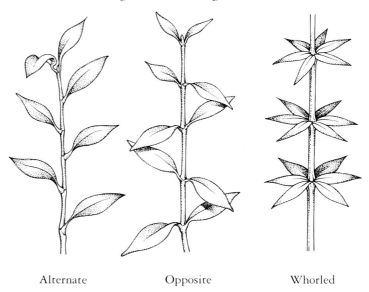

Alternate   Opposite   Whorled

Fig. 1 Parts of a Plant

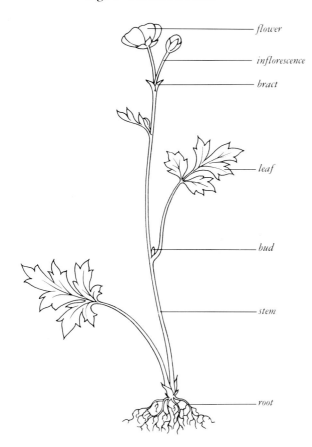

- *flower*
- *inflorescence*
- *bract*
- *leaf*
- *bud*
- *stem*
- *root*

Bud An undeveloped flower or shoot protected by sepals (flower bud) or bud scales (shoot).

Bulb An extremely shortened underground stem with many swollen, fleshy leaves or leaf bases in which food is stored. Bulbs may or may not be enclosed in a protective tunic. They are common overwintering and food storage organs in some monocotyledonous plants.

Bulbil A small bulb produced by some plants in the axils of leaves or in the inflorescence.

Calyx The sepals of a flower form the calyx. They are usually green and leaflike, and enclose and protect the flower in bud. They may be joined or free, colored or absent. In many families the calyx persists to enclose the fruit. In a calyx where the sepals are joined, the basal tubular portion is the calyx-tube, and the upper free parts are the calyx-lobes (see Fig. 5).

Capsule A dry fruit formed of several cells, which splits open to release the seeds.

Carpel One of the segments or cells which make up the ovary.

Chaparral A habitat composed of thickets of evergreen, often stiff or spiny shrubs.

Claw The narrow basal section of some petals and sepals.

Compound inflorescence A branched inflorescence composed of several racemes or cymes.

Compound leaf A leaf formed of several leaflets (see Fig. 3).

Corm A short, erect, underground stem, swollen with food and frequently acting as an overwintering organ. It is often protected by a scaly tunic. The following year's corm develops on top of the spent one of the previous year.

Corolla The petals of a flower form the corolla. They are often colored and conspicuous, and may bear nectaries, all features designed to attract insects. In some plants they are small, insignificant, or absent (see Fig. 5).

Fig. 3 Leaf Types

Simple Leaves

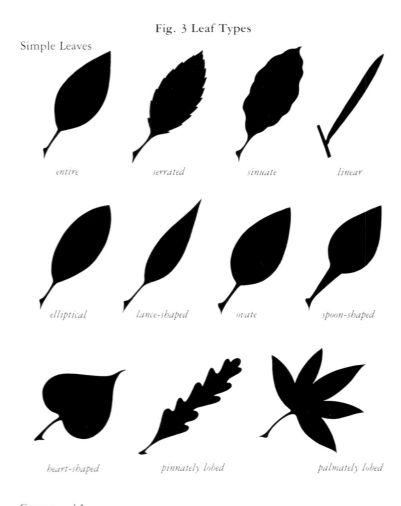

entire   *serrated*   *sinuate*   *linear*

elliptical   *lance-shaped*   *ovate*   *spoon-shaped*

heart-shaped   *pinnately lobed*   *palmately lobed*

Compound Leaves

pinnate   *dissected*   *palmate*

Corona In some plants the flowers have an additional structure between the petals and the stamens (as in the milkweeds). This is called the corona.

Creeping With stems growing along the ground, rooting at the nodes.

Cyme A flat-topped or conical inflorescence in which the branches develop equally from the center, the central flower opening first in each branch. Each flower is the terminal one when it is formed (see Fig. 4).

Dehiscent Splitting open to release the seeds.

Disk The central portion of the flower head in a member of the Sunflower family. It contains only tubular florets.

Dissected Of a leaf, one cut deeply into segments, and where the segments are themselves deeply cut (see Fig. 3).

Divided Of a leaf, cut into segments, the divisions extending as far as the midrib or the base, cf. Lobed (see Fig. 3).

Drupe A fleshy fruit, usually with a single seed surrounded by a hard or stony layer.

Elliptical Of a leaf (see Fig. 3).

Entire Of a leaf, with an unbroken margin, not toothed (see Fig. 3).

Evergreen A plant that does not lose its leaves in winter.

Family A unit of biological classification, consisting of a collection of genera sharing particular features, cf. Genus.

Fertile Capable of reproduction; of a stamen, one which produces pollen; of a flower, one which produces viable seed.

Filament The stalk of a stamen (see Fig. 5).

Floret A single flower in the flower head of a member of the Sunflower family. Disk florets are tubular, ray florets are strap-shaped. Flower heads may be composed wholly of disk florets or of ray florets, or may have disk florets forming the central disk and ray florets around the margin.

Follicle A dry, dehiscent fruit, opening along one side only.

Free Not joined to other organs.

Fruit A ripened ovary which contains matured seeds, ready for dispersal.

Fused At least partially joined together, united.

Genus (plural genera) A unit of biological classification consisting of a group of species considered to be related through common descent, and indicated by sharing the same first name, cf. Species.

Gland An area on a plant which secretes a liquid, usually an oil or resin. When a plant has many glands, it is described as glandular; when the glands are situated on hairs, it is described as glandular-hairy.

Glochid A barbed hair.

Hair A small, usually slender outgrowth from a plant.

Head A dense flower cluster consisting of many stalkless flowers (see Fig. 5).

Herb A non-woody annual, biennial, or perennial plant. If perennial, then dying back to ground level at the end of the season.

Herbaceous Having the texture of a herb; dying back to the ground each year.

Hermaphrodite Containing both male and female organs (stamens and carpels).

Hybrid A plant originating from the cross between two species.

Indehiscent Not opening at maturity to release the seed(s).

Inferior Of an ovary, located beneath the other flower parts (see Fig. 5).

Inflorescence The flower cluster of a plant, including the branches, bracts, and flowers (see Fig. 4).

Inserted The point of attachment, e.g. of stamens to the corolla.

Intergrade When the features of one species pass by imperceptible degrees into those of another, the two species may be said to intergrade into each other.

Introduced Not native; having been brought to the country by man within historic times.

Involucre A set of bracts forming a structure like a calyx beneath an inflorescence. Often used specifically for the structure beneath the condensed, head-like inflorescence of the members of the Sunflower family.

Irregular Bilaterally symmetrical.

Lance-shaped Of a leaf (see Fig. 3).

Latex Milky juice or sap.

Legume A dry, dehiscent fruit characteristic of the Pea family. It opens along both sides to release the seeds.

Linear Of a leaf (see Fig. 3).

Lobed Of leaves, divided but with the divisions cutting less than halfway to the midrib. The leaves are therefore not divided into leaflets (see Fig. 3).

Membranous Thin and flexible, but usually not green.

Midrib The central vein of a leaf.

Mycorrhiza An association between the roots of certain plants and soil fungi. Orchids cannot survive without their mycorrhizal partners.

Native Endemic; not introduced by man.

Naturalized Well established and growing wild in an area, but coming from another region or part of the world.

Nectary A gland which secretes nectar, usually found on the receptacle or the petals of the corolla.

Node A point on a stem where leaves or roots, or both, arise.

Nodule A small swelling.

Nutlet A small, dry, indehiscent fruit with a relatively thick wall and only one seed.

Fig. 4 Inflorescence Types

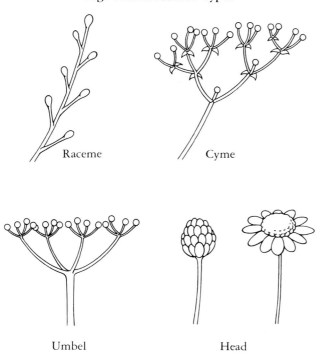

Raceme   Cyme

Umbel   Head

Fig. 5 Parts of a Flower

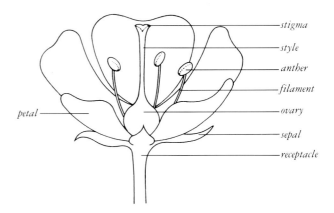

stigma
style
anther
filament
petal
ovary
sepal
receptacle

Opposite Two organs, such as leaves, growing opposite each other at a node (see Fig. 2).

Ovary The part of a flower which contains the ovules (see Fig. 5).

Ovate Of a leaf (see Fig. 3).

Ovule The structure which contains the egg. It develops into a seed after fertilization.

Palmate Of leaves, divided into three or more lobes or leaflets, all arising from the same point on the leaf stalk (see Fig. 3).

Pappus The crown of hairs, bristles, or scales on the achene of a member of the Sunflower family.

Parasite A plant which obtains its water and nutrients from another plant to which it becomes attached.

Perennial A plant which lives for several years, usually flowering each year, and (of herbaceous perennials) dying back at the end of the growing season.

Perianth The petals and sepals together.

Perianth segments The separate "segments" which make up the perianth—they may be like petals or like sepals. This term is often used when all the parts of the perianth are similar, and there is no clear division into sepals and petals.

Persistent Remaining attached to the fruit, especially of sepals or petals.

Petal One segment of the corolla. The petals are often brightly colored and may have nectaries at the base (see Fig. 5).

Pinnate A compound leaf composed of more than three leaflets, arranged in two rows on either side of the central axis or midrib (see Fig. 3).

Pod A dry, dehiscent fruit which opens along both sides. Usually used specifically to describe the fruits of the Pea family.

Pollen grains The structures which develop inside the anthers, and which contain the male cells. They are carried to the stigma and there develop a pollen tube which grows down the style, carrying the male nucleus with it. When the pollen tube reaches the ovary, the male nucleus fuses with the ovule, and the fertilized ovules develop into seeds.

Pollination The carrying of pollen from the anthers to the stigma. It is usually transferred by wind or by insects.

Prickle A sharp outgrowth from a stem or leaf, but irregularly arranged, cf. Spine.

Prostrate Lying flat on the ground.

Raceme An inflorescence with an elongated, unbranched central axis, and flowers growing on stalks on each side. The lowermost flowers open first. In theory a raceme can go on elongating indefinitely as the youngest flowers are at the growing tip (see Fig. 4).

Receptacle The flat end of a flower stalk on which the flower parts arise (see Fig. 5).

Regular Radially symmetrical.

Rhizome A perennial, underground stem, growing horizontally. Rhizomes may act as an overwintering device, as a food storage organ, or as a method of spreading the plant.

Rosette A basal clump of leaves appearing to radiate outward from a single spot.

Saprophyte A plant which lacks green coloring and which feeds on dead organic material, often with the help of mycorrhizal fungi.

Scale A thin, membranous bract or leaf.

Seed A ripened ovule.

Sepal One segment of the calyx. The sepals are usually green and leaflike, and together they enclose and protect the flower bud (see Fig. 5).

Serrated Of a leaf, with a toothed margin where the teeth are pointed.

Simple With a single, undivided blade.

Sinuate Of a leaf, with a wavy margin (see Fig. 3).

Species A group of similar-looking individual plants which can interbreed and produced similar-looking offspring true to type.

Spike Strictly, a raceme in which the flowers lack stalks. In a more general use, any spike-like inflorescence.

Spine A stiff, sharp-pointed projection from a plant, often a modified leaf or stipule, cf. Prickle.

Spur A hollow, often slender projection from the base of a sepal or petal, usually containing nectar.

Stamen One of the male reproductive organs of a flower (see Fig. 5).

Sterile Incapable of producing viable pollen (of stamens), or seed (of plants).

Fig. 6 Flower Types

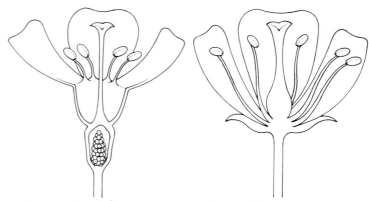

Flower with an inferior ovary   Flower with a superior ovary

Stigma The receptive tip of the style on which pollen grains must land and adhere for pollination to occur (see Fig. 5).

Stipule An often leaflike appendage found at the base of the leaf stalk where the stalk is attached to the stem. They usually occur in pairs, one on each side of the stalk.

Style The structure at the top of the ovary, connecting it to the stigma where the pollen grains land (see Fig. 5).

Superior Of an ovary, located above the other floral parts and free from them (see Fig. 5).

Tendril A climbing organ formed from part of a stem or leaf. In the Pea family, where tendrils are common, they are formed from the terminal leaflet of a compound leaf.

Tuber A thickened portion of a root or rhizome acting as a food storage organ.

Tubercle A rounded swelling.

Tunic The dry, often brown and papery covering around a bulb or corm.

Umbel An umbrella-like inflorescence in which all the flower stalks arise from the same point on the stem (see Fig. 4).

Versatile A term used to describe an anther, which is attached to the filament only at its middle so that it is free to swing.

Weed A plant growing where it is not wanted.

Whorl A circle of three or more leaves or flowers growing from a node (see Fig. 2).

Xerophyte A plant adapted to life in a dry or desert environment.

Index

Bibliography

The following books are regional floras, which have technical details of the plants in their areas. Some are illustrated with line drawings.

Henry A. Gleason & Arthur Cronquist, *Manual of Vascular Plants of Northeastern United States and Adjacent Canada* (D. Van Nostrand Co. Inc., Princeton, 1963)
C. Leo Hitchcock & Arthur Cronquist, *A Flora of the Pacific Northwest* (University of Washington Press, Seattle, 1973)
E.H. Moss, *Flora of Alberta* (University of Toronto Press, 1959)
Philip A. Munz, *A California Flora* (University of California Press, Berkeley and Los Angeles, 1959)
Philip A. Munz, *A Flora of Southern California* (University of California Press, Berkeley and Los Angeles, 1974)
Albert E. Radford, Harry E. Ahles & C. Ritchie Bell, *Manual of the Vascular Flora of the Carolinas* (University of North Carolina Press, Chapel Hill, 1964)
Per Axel Rydberg, *Flora of the Prairies and Plains of Central North America* (Dover Publications Inc., New York, 1971)

The following are books that contain more general information and color illustrations or photographs.

John J. Craighead, Frank C. Craighead, Jr. & Ray J. Davis, *A Field Guide to Rocky Mountain Wildflowers* (Peterson Field Guide Series, Houghton Mifflin, Boston, 1963)
Wilbur H. Duncan & Leonard E. Foote, *Wildflowers of the Southeastern United States* (University of Georgia Press, Athens, 1975)
Lady Bird Johnson & Carlton B. Lees, *Wildflowers Across America* (Abbeville Press, 1988)
Theodore F. Niehaus, *A Field Guide to Southwestern and Texas Wildflowers* (Peterson Field Guide Series, Houghton Mifflin, Boston, 1984)
Theodore F. Niehaus & Charles E. Ripper, *A Field Guide to Pacific States Wildflowers* (Peterson Field Guide Series, Houghton Mifflin, Boston, 1976)
William A. Niering, *The Audubon Society Field Guide to North American Wildflowers: Eastern Region* (Alfred A. Knopf Inc., New York, 1979)
Roger Tory Peterson & Margaret McKenny, *A Field Guide to Wildflowers of Northeastern and North-central North America* (Peterson Field Guide Series, Houghton Mifflin, Boston, 1968)
Sylvan T. Runkel & Dean M. Roosa, *Wildflowers of the Tallgrass Prairie: The Upper Midwest* (Iowa State University Press, Ames, 1989)
Richard Spellenberg, *The Audubon Society Field Guide to North American Wildflowers: Western Region* (Alfred A. Knopf Inc., New York, 1979)
Zile Zichmanis & James Hodgkins, *Flowers of the Wild: Ontario and the Great Lakes Region* (Oxford University Press, Toronto, 1982)

The following are books with information on particular aspects of wildflowers.

Thomas S. Elias & Peter A. Dykeman, *A Field Guide to North American Edible Wild Plants* (Outdoor Life Books, New York, 1982)
M. Grieve, *A Modern Herbal* (Penguin Books, Harmondsworth and New York, 1976)
J. Hutchinson, *The Families of Flowering Plants*, Volumes I & II (Oxford University Press, London, England, 1959)
Reader's Digest, *Magic and Medicine of Plants* (Reader's Digest, New York, 1986)

Acknowledgments

The author and publisher would like to thank the libraries of the British Museum (Natural History), the Royal Horticultural Society, and the Linnean Society for their help.